THE QUANTAMENTAL REVOLUTION

THE QUANTAMENTAL REVOLUTION

FACTOR INVESTING IN THE AGE OF MACHINE LEARNING

MILIND SHARMA

WILEY

Published by John Wiley & Sons, Inc., Hoboken, New Jersey.

For general information on our other products and services or for technical support, please contact our Customer Care Department within the United States at (800) 762-2974, outside the United States at (317) 572-3993 or fax (317) 572-4002.

Wiley also publishes its books in a variety of electronic formats. Some content that appears in print may not be available in electronic formats. For more information about Wiley products, visit our web site at www.wiley.com.

Library of Congress Cataloging-in-Publication Data is Available:

ISBN 9781394354849 (Cloth)
ISBN 9781394354856 (ePub)
ISBN 9781394354863 (ePDF)

Cover Design: Wiley
Cover Image: © TZIDO SUN/Shutterstock

To my parents,
sisters and brother-in-law

Contents

Acknowledgments

This book would not exist without the QuantZ/QMIT (QuantZ Machine Intelligence Technologies, LLC) systems that power the data and analytics used herein, and none of that would exist without my colleagues and the key architects of the QMIT system namely Dr. Oleg Kolesnikov (head of research) and Amit Sardar (chief technology officer). Much gratitude to them.

This book has been a decade in the making. During that time, I have benefited from discussions with many prominent academics and practitioners through my quant society (QWAFAxNEW) and other industry interactions. Names that come to mind would include Peter Carr, Achilles Venetoulias, Petter Kolm, Emanuel Derman, Mark Carhart, John Mulvey, Manos Hatzakis, Pawel Polak, Agostino Capponi, Harry Mamaysky, Doug Martin, Bob Simon, Dave Rudd, Bill Goff, Stan Uryasev, Luis Seco, and Bob Doll, Uwe Wystup, and Sanjay Srivastava, among others.

I have personally mentored well over 150 MFE (Master of Financial Engineering) students since 2009 who are now gainfully employed at the top Wall Street firms ranging from Goldman Sachs, Morgan Stanley, BlackRock, and Pimco to the top quant hedge funds. Many were from Carnegie Mellon's Master of Science in Computational Finance program, but some were from Columbia's Master of Science in Business Administration not to mention UCLA and the other top MFE programs, where I have directed a variety of Capstone course projects. Many MFE interns have contributed to QuantZ white papers and QMIT blogs based on our proprietary data, under my guidance. Some of those ideas made the cut and eventually found their way into topics discussed herein. I will acknowledge as many names (including former employees) as I can recall: Esma Gregor, Anthony Yip, Gautam Wahi, Brian MacSweeney, Lorena Rodriguez Pineda, Quang Viet Tran, Sendoh Xu, Shih-hung Wang, Xinyi Xu, Kathy Zhang, Boyu Fang, Yongkang Zhou, Junze Hu, Zixu Yang, Aravind Ganesan, Yakun Deng, Danila Sitnikov, and Pratik Sharda.

Matvei Lukianov and Weichuan Deng (of Stony Brook's Department of Applied Mathematics) deserve an especially warm acknowledgment for their contributions from both an editorial as well as analytical standpoint. Matvei Lukianov has also been substantially involved with fact checking, formatting, and editing of the final manuscript.

Finally, thanks to the Wiley team for embarking on this journey with forbearance. To Judith Newlin for taking on the project and subsequently Julie Kerr and my editor Stacey Rivera for their collective guidance.

Chapter 1

A Quantamental Walk Down Wall Street

1.1. A RANDOM WALK DOWN WALL STREET

It was in the bitter cold of an upstate New York winter in 1994 that I stepped onto track 35 bound Metro North train from Poughkeepsie. Somehow that train and track 35 always reminded me of a scene from *Superman*. On this particular day, there was no time for idle chatter about movies or pop culture references. I had just watched Michael Douglas in

Wall Street[1] exhorting an entire generation to go out on a capitalistic rampage. We were going to be the "greed is good"[2] generation I figured – even though I could barely spell out LBO (leveraged buyout) as yet. "Let's hope they don't talk about that or Anacott Steel," I said to myself. I barely knew debt from equity but felt strangely empowered by virtue of watching the movie and flipping through *Liar's Poker*.[3] Had never set foot in the economics department. Never bought a share of any stock. Never came within spitting distance of any trading floor. At the time, it would have been anathema for any respectable liberal arts college to teach anything particularly useful in terms of finance or too close to the real world. The level of finance awareness was low. The term *investment banking* was bandied about at cocktail parties in a vague and nebulous sense to refer to everything from the sell side or buy side to the red-headed stepchild (commercial banking) or, God forbid, even private banking. We were supposed to be utility maximizing automatons according to the economists, except that most liberal arts undergraduates had little cognizance of CARA (constant absolute risk aversion), HARA (hyperbolic absolute risk aversion), CRRA (constant relative risk aversion), Epstein-Zin[4] or the various formulations of highly unrealistic utility functions that academics were mysteriously obsessed with. I had a couple of papers in astronomy and dabbled in just

---

[1] Michael Douglas starred as Gordon Gekko in the 1987 movie *Wall Street*, where he delivered the famous line "Greed, for lack of a better word, is good." This speech became iconic and is often referenced in discussions about the excesses of Wall Street in the 1980s.

[2] The phrase captures the ethos of the time, influenced by real-life Wall Street figures such as Ivan Boesky, who in 1986 said, "Greed is all right, by the way. I want you to know that. I think greed is healthy."

[3] *Liar's Poker* is indeed a semi-autobiographical book by Michael Lewis, published in 1989. It details his experiences as a bond salesman on Wall Street during the 1980s.

[4] Epstein-Zin preferences are a class of utility functions used in economics and finance to model intertemporal choice and risk.

enough physics, philosophy, and mathematics to be offered teaching/research assistantships at some of the top PhD programs in the country. Fake it 'til you make it is now the advice du jour (courtesy of the Amy Cuddys[5] of the world). But there was no point in faking it on that day. I simply did not have the vernacular. Unlike rising seniors who already had a couple of Wall Street internships under their belt (often through family or fraternity connections) and had relevant majors, I never had any interest in being gainfully employed. This was merely an afterthought. Since I had already secured the coveted scholarships and assistantships, it gave me the freedom to interview without a care in the world. Unlike my peers – I had no interest in the job, hence no downside. While it felt like a pure call option, it really was a psychological hedge against a future of poverty, destitution, and unsung glory.

Burton Malkiel's book, *A Random Walk Down Wall Street* (2023),[6] was perfect fodder for one who needed to sound vaguely intelligent about a novel topic. Thumbing through the book I could see that if I guided the conversation towards Brownian motion and away from the rather topical debt financing of LBOs, I had a chance of not being shown the door. As luck would have it, the esteemed professor was suggesting one need not worry too much about the details given that no one could beat the market. The market was a random walk so why worry about picking stocks, bonds, or star fund managers when you could just buy the index and do better? Simple and elegant. And so, I strode into the lobby of 345 Park Avenue, twitching uncomfortably in an ill-fitting suit. For a geek who only ever wanted to be an

[5]Amy Cuddy is a social psychologist known for her research on body language and the "fake it 'til you make it" philosophy.

[6]An investing bestseller that popularized the idea that one cannot consistently outperform market averages.

astronomer, then a physicist, then a philosopher, and eventually a logician, this was really just about forcing oneself out of one's comfort zone.

1.2. ON THE WAY TO $13 TRILLION

Having a near-perfect GPA and a host of academic accolades and merit scholarships meant that one could secure the obligatory first round at a Morgan, McKinsey, and the like. Most of us did not understand the pecking order or which department was interviewing us for what job. It just felt nice to be in demand without any skills per se. But this firm was different. This was no J.P. Morgan or Merrill Lynch. They only had a few dozen employees on half of the floor. What was the point of talking to some firm that my mother would have never heard of? There were no bragging rights even if you had the vacuous offer. The MIT PhD in charge of risk and his acolytes were surprisingly friendly and amenable to taking the random digression down the garden path. After a few rounds, Ben Golub[7] rhetorically asked if I could "swim with the sharks in the cesspool"? Clearly the answer was nyet or at least not yet. I was Pittsburgh-bound and incredibly excited about a place that would spawn the future CEO of Renaissance Technologies not to mention that it was also the birthplace of artificial intelligence (AI), robotics, and the pioneering computational finance program. The firm that sounded like a rock or a stone got filed into the outer the recesses of my memory until about 2006 when Larry Fink made a bid for my future employer (Merrill Lynch IM[8]) and my one-time boss (Bob Doll, president and Chief

---

[7] Ben Golub was the founding chief risk manager of BlackRock and now has a center named after him at MIT.

[8] Merrill Lynch Investment Management, a subsidiary of Merrill Lynch, was acquired by BlackRock in 2006.

investment officer (CIO) of MLIM) decided to sell the company. Thirty years later I could be forgiven for not having foreseen that BlackRock was someday going to manage over $13 trillion in assets and rule the world (according to every misguided conspiracy theorist). While I'm at it, I should also confess to being among the first few on a certain mailing list that had hyperlinked books for sale. I got the vision but never bought a share of the company. I'd heard of Jeff Bezos from friends at D. E. Shaw. I'm not sure they knew that he was destined for world domination either. You see, prediction is always hard – especially when it's about the distant future. Back-tests are – by construction – always rosy. Ever seen a *p*-hacked negative Sharpe ratio? Out of sample rarely lives up to in sample and live – well, fuhgeddaboudit.

So here we are 30 years later. I know a bit more about Brownian motion, LBOs, derivative pricing, risk-premia and taming the factor zoo. And so does much of Wall Street. Bachelier's Brownian motion,[9] stochastic calculus, arbitrage pricing, statistical arbitrage, and all such manner of mumbo jumbo have taken central stage on Wall Street in a manner that no one could have imagined back when I was fumbling around with spelling debt and equity. When I accidentally stumbled into that interview at BlackRock, there was no legacy of rocket scientists on Wall Street. There were the legacy kids from the Ivies. There were the frat boys and the would-be ditch diggers who had stumbled into obscene wealth as Michael Lewis had profiled in *Liar's Poker* (1989). To the old-timers, today's Wall Street – one of fully automated execution and a fully systematic or quantamental investment paradigm – would be an alien concept. Where are the frat boys and the high-fiving, back-slapping monkeys our algos were designed to pick off? Now everyone has an MBA or an

[9] Bachelier's Brownian motion refers to the mathematical description of random motion, foundational in financial mathematics.

MFE with a CFA or a PhD to boot. There are no widows or orphans in the institutional world no more. It's my HFT algorithm against yours, just like it was my copula against yours in the heyday of credit correlation trading. Even retail buys the dips now.

How did we get here? What are the forces and the visionary figures who brought us here today as we stand on the precipice of artificial general intelligence (AGI), artificial superintelligence, and quantum computing where the yellers and screamers on the floor wouldn't survive a picosecond with their hand gestures against "colo and lola."[10] I figured it was time to take stock. To rant and to ruminate as we take this quantamental walk down Wall Street in a fitting nod to the Princeton professor's great insights about market efficiency. Of course, had I really imbibed the gospel of efficient markets, I would not have spent decades designing better factor models to beat the market.

This book is largely aimed at MFE students,[11] hence the anecdotes and the historical perspective for the uninitiated who may not have the big picture inkling as to how we got from the buttonwood tree[12] to co-locating in Weehawken. The stories in this first chapter are part memoir and part allegory. The rest of the book is written in the style of academic journal papers but watered down to the level of an industry quant. Michael Lewis meets Fama-French[13] would

---

[10] By Colo and Lola, I mean co-location (colo) and low-latency (lola) in the context of high-frequency trading (HFT).

[11] MFE students refers to students enrolled in a Master of Financial Engineering program.

[12] Buttonwood tree refers to the origin of the New York Stock Exchange, where traders initially met under a buttonwood tree in the late 18th century.

[13] Michael Lewis meets Fama-French is a comparison combining the narrative style of Michael Lewis with the academic finance models developed by Eugene Fama and Kenneth French.

be aspirational but blasphemous to suggest. I hope that academics, industry quants, and even some factor investing experts may find some interesting tidbits from this comprehensive survey and road map of quantamental investing. The central premise of this book is that one can deploy a spanning set of smart betas to express any linear view on equities. Systematizing the investment universe via such Lego building blocks (or atomic units of risk-premia) demystifies what the star managers and divas of yesteryear claimed to do in their heads except that a quantamental process does it much better, more methodically, more transparently, with fewer errors, and without bias or emotion. The logical progression from firm characteristics (factors) to enhanced smart betas (or ESBs aided by machine learning [ML] ensembles), from ESBs to MFMs (multifactor models) or combination signals, and then to portfolio risk and construction should make the entire investment process workflow and the life cycle of quant investing clear to the neophyte (which often takes decades of experience to crystallize). Many students find the anecdotal big picture road map far more beneficial to managing their careers than the incremental tinkering of yet another Cholesky-like decomposition.[14]

While I aim to present the state of the art (qua factor investing) and be comprehensive in doing so (after all there are seminal papers but no books that do justice to that) – not everything in this book is (of competitive necessity) necessarily cutting edge. It presents the arc of evolution, of quants coming of age on Wall Street (an industry that used to be openly hostile to propeller heads), and critically the

[14] The Cholesky decomposition is a mathematical technique used to factor a symmetric, positive-definite matrix into the product of a lower triangular matrix and its transpose. In finance, it is often applied in risk modeling and portfolio optimization to generate correlated random variables or to simplify covariance matrix computations.

rationale for how we got here. There are cutting edge results on factor momentum not to mention our framework of ML-enhanced factor investing. That said, I am not trying to replace refereed journal articles but present an insider's realistic view as to how and what techniques actually tend to be deployed in the industry as opposed to what one might politely call the "mental masturbation" of many far-fetched academic treatises (and curricula) that bear no resemblance to live trading or investing. One must also acknowledge that this book is being written against the backdrop of an AI revolution that will likely soon disintermediate all knowledge work and potentially disrupt university education in short order. That said, we make the case that there isn't all that much for AI to disrupt in the mid- to low-frequency quantamental world. For long-term investors – the question remains – would Warren Buffett or Charlie Munger do things any differently tomorrow?

The fact that the specifics of our QMIT framework presented herein have had some measure of live success over 7 years should be reassuring to the reader but is largely incidental and not central to the thesis. Along the way, we derive many side benefits that emerge from this factor framework such as risk, attribution, style analysis, sector rotation, crash baskets, regime tilting, and so on. We extend the literature on factor momentum, provide an exposition and rebuttal of the causal critique, track an archetypal market-neutral hedge fund construct, explore a novel liquid proxy for private equity, combine it with natural language processing sentiment, indulge the agentic AI future with specific examples like large language models (LLMs)-based sentiment and much more. While we focus purely on equities, this framework is being extended to other asset classes as we speak. We conclude with a chapter on the impending singularity and agentic AI future and its ramifications as it pertains to factor investing.

The metaphor of BlackRock's exponential growth to over $13 trillion over the past 30 years is emblematic of the magic of geometric compounding and capitalism at its best. It is also a uniquely American story, one that we will hopefully see repeated via American ingenuity driving exponential innovation in the age of AI-driven abundance – that is, if AI does not destroy humanity en route.

1.3. QUANTAMENTAL VERSUS TEMPERAMENTAL

Shortly after the GFC (global financial crisis of 2008), I started using the term *quantamental* to describe the hybrid quant investment process of my equity market-neutral hedge fund launch that insisted on the "human in the loop." This was meant to be antithetical to dominant paradigm of the seat-of-the-pants temperamental stock picker. Wall Street strategists and the media jumped on the bandwagon, and the label found mainstream currency. Calling judgmental/temperamental PMs "fundamental" and quants non-fundamental may well be naive but that is the simplistic dichotomous label that has stuck. Yes, there are some purely technical quant CTAs (trend followers) or statistical arbitrage funds that look merely at mean reversion (as do their human counterparts) but there are many more and much larger funds like AQR, DFA, DE Shaw (collectively running trillions) who work on the same exact factors as deployed by fundamental PMs (portfolio managers). This book describes that superset of factors and how they can be rigorously deployed by quants for every part of the investment process. Non-quants tend to forget that we in the quantamental world are merely systematizing what fundamental PMs do in the first place. It's just that we do it bigger (in terms of the universe of securities, sectors, factors), better (risk-adjusted), with rigor, with some certitude of repeatability and low to no emotion.

As humanity hurtles toward its inevitable tryst with AGI, it's now plenty clear that there is almost no sustainable, repeatable value that can be added by fundamental PMs – at least not in risk-adjusted terms. Active fundamental PMs have no repeatable edge with almost 85% of large-cap equity managers underperforming their benchmarks in recent memory.[15] Even if there were occasional pockets of negative entropy, it'd be difficult if not impossible for allocators to identify them ex ante, and to know when to redeem. You could have said that Bill Ackman was a star and bet the farm on him. In fact, many US institutions who worship at the feet of and deify such anointed geniuses did precisely that until he ran the Gotham fund into the ground in the late 1990s.[16] Pershing Square IV, which bet solely on Target stock, subsequently got wiped out.[17] More recently, the flagship Pershing Square fund had four back-to-back down years resulting from disastrous trades like Valeant Pharmaceuticals. Ackman was also in Herbalife and yet again on the wrong side of the

---

[15] As of 2025, the percentage of active large-cap equity managers who underperformed their benchmarks (typically the S&P 500) according to the SPIVA U.S. Scorecard and recent industry reporting is:

- Five years: Approximately 76% of active large-cap US equity managers underperformed their benchmark over the past five years.
- 10 years: The underperformance rises further, with about 84% of active large-cap managers underperforming their benchmark over the past 10 years.

[16] https://www.reuters.com/article/world/uk/if-at-first-you-dont-succeed-start-another-fund-idUSTRE69D2PM/

[17] https://www.institutionalinvestor.com/article/2btg1ofp0in5dmk39hslc/home/target-practice

trade.[18] Any respectable quant model could have saved his investors several billion dollars squandered on Valeant and Herbalife had he bothered triangulating his stubborn instincts with quant models to confirm or deny the investment thesis. Instead, he got into verbal fisticuffs with Carl Icahn on CNBC. It made for memorable television, and it certainly made the "Judge's"[19] career. To paraphrase the inimitable Paul Tudor Jones – "man"[20] with a machine is better than man versus machine.

1.4. THE "GREED IS GOOD" GENERATION

The Michael Douglas movie captured the zeitgeist if not single-handedly created it. It led to an entire generation of bright-eyed and bushy-tailed Ivy Leaguers lining up for interviews at the Salomons and Lehmans. In a prior generation it may have been the PSDs (poor, smart, with a deep desire to be rich) – famously preferred by Ace Greenberg of Bear Stearns – and the frat boys, but now the best and brightest wanted to be in on the Wall Street bonanza. Maybe they thought they would have a Park Avenue apartment with a view like Bud Fox's and a girlfriend who looked like Daryl Hannah – clearly the gold rush was on. Oliver Stone's 1987 hit was followed by the Michael Lewis classic *Liar's Poker* in 1989, which soon became the bible of MBAs. There's never been a bandwagon that Harvard MBAs didn't want to pile on to.

---

[18] https://markets.businessinsider.com/news/stocks/bill-ackman-hedge-fund-return-2019-pershing-three-years-losses-2019-12-1028744892; https://www.wsj.com/articles/pershing-square-faces-wave-of-investor-redemptions-1522920601?gaa_at=eafs&gaa_n=AWEtsqdAnRHPI5DIFGg-fGLOCjGwr9KA_LmUrUVTxdK8o9FNw6_672IghkvUHSKP9ac%3D&gaa_ts=695f2486&gaa_sig=8XvxRZDTNyboyLECsu6QuNjawKQofeLh55hduFonHC6V5rYoQVuSFlh31C87_BfHhqfDyooX4K96YhzXuNa7jA%3D%3D

[19] The "Judge" would be Scott Wapner on CNBC's "Fast Money: Halftime Report" and other shows.

[20] "Man" here figuratively represents all of humankind not just males.

Maybe I'm biased because we would have much rather taken a Wharton undergrad or a Carnegie Mellon University (CMU) Master of Science in Computational Finance (MSCF) or an MIT PhD than ever be caught dead interviewing the Harvard or Kellogg type of non-quant MBAs. In fact, I don't recall ever even running into one. The trading floor at Deutsche was chock-full of Booth (Chicago), Wharton, MIT, and CMU quants. Top school MBAs are often prone to lemming-like behavior than contrarian calls, which is why they are always piling into the tech bubble, the commodity bubble, or Enron at the top. Ethics did not feature on the curriculum. Not until scandals such as those at Enron and McKinsey resulted in prominent alums of such B-schools (notably Harvard Business School) doing the perp walk. Indeed, before the internet bubble took off, many such MBAs wanted to be the next BSD[21] trading Govies[22] at Salomon (as profiled by Michael Lewis). It mattered not that most of them simply did not have the mathematical aptitude to be hired by Meriwether and his merry band of arbitrageurs. Enter the quant PhDs. With the launch of long-term capital management (LTCM) and a star-studded cast of Nobel laureates, MBAs were suddenly so 1980s. It quickly became clear that the future was quant. My friend (and mentor) Peter Carr had predicted back in the 90s that eventually quant MFEs would squeeze out the MBAs and that has certainly transpired. Yes, there were momentary setbacks on the implosion of LTCM when non-quants gleefully proclaimed that it was "better to be clueless" than to lose so much money so quickly. Of course, there are plenty of people who can lose your money the old-fashioned way (you may have met some such crypto bros of late). This was the first time that a bunch of the most accomplished quant prop traders and Nobel laureates (Myron Scholes and Robert

[21] This refers to the portrayal of "big swinging dicks" trading government bonds on the Salomon Brothers trading floor as per Michael Lewis.
[22] Government bonds.

Merton, no less) had not only been so spectacularly wrong but had almost brought the entire financial system down with them. As the saying goes – it's always better to have the banks over a barrel. If they are foolish enough to lend you so much that it becomes an existential risk to them, then they have no choice but to bail you out, and that's exactly what happened in the fall of 1998. LTCM was a tremendous rite of passage – for me as a young risk manager – at one of the banks (Merrill Lynch), which was forced to orchestrate the subsequent bailout.

1.5. FROM QUARKS TO QUASARS

In boarding school at UWC Canada (on Vancouver Island), I was fortunate to have as my physics teacher the inimitable Rhodes scholar and Oxford PhD, Dr. Andrew Spray. The UWC movement has spawned many luminaries including the Deputy Prime Minister (PM) of Canada and the Speaker of their Senate not to mention the UWC movement itself being nominated for the Nobel Peace Prize – twice. It was founded by the likes of the Canadian PM (Lester B. Pearson), King Charles, and his Gordonstoun mentor (Kurt Hahn), who was prominently profiled in the Netflix series The Crown. Andrew was kind enough to drop me off at Canada's largest observatory, which happened to be down the road (the Dominion Astrophysical Observatory), and suggest that I make friends with the astronomers. Pretty soon, I had befriended many of the distinguished astronomers on staff like Dr. Sidney van den Bergh, president of the Canadian Astronomical Society. Then there was Dr. Harvey Richardson, who worked on designing the camera for the Hubble Space Telescope (HST). While the HST was run out of the Johns Hopkins command center, the Perkin Elmers facility at the Dominion was involved with the mirror design, which famously had to be replaced due to an infinitesimal blemish. The trick was to simply offer to fetch coffee and xerox their papers in exchange for soaking up their insights. No university education could have delivered that front row seat to live cutting-edge research that I had in boarding school, prior to Professor Debra Elmegreen's mentorship in college. Elmegreen (as the pioneering female astrophysics graduate from Princeton) had fittingly inherited the Maria Mitchell Chair in Astronomy at Vassar (the oldest women's college in the Western world). Maria Mitchell herself was no slouch. In fact, she was the pioneering female astrophysicist of her time. Debbie was later appointed the Chair of the President of the International Astronomical Union, not to mention the president of the American Astronomical Society. Having worked on a paper relating to the Copernican Revolution, the symbolic significance of her later going to meet with the Pope was not lost on me. Indeed, the Vatican has come far from the days of Giordano Bruno being burned at the stake for heresy or Galileo Galilei being forced to recant and then being placed under house arrest. Even the latest Pope is a mathematician. *We are all quants now.*

The fall of the Soviet Union and the defunding of the superconducting super collider created a glut of physicists. One could even run into former Soviet scientists driving cabs in New York. Former physicists like Emanuel Derman drifted into finance and had enormous success. Some later launched brand name hedge funds like Teza. The person running our servers at RBC had come out of Fermilab. He claimed to have published over a hundred papers in particle physics. Given that empirical studies reporting on experiments conducted at SLAC, CERN or Fermilab often have dozens or even hundreds of coauthors it isn't quite the same lonely slog as Kurt Gödel's (1962) solo but far more consequential monograph entitled *On Formally Undecidable Propositions of Principia Mathematica and Related Systems.* Experimental physics is a team sport like trading and the ability to handle reams of messy data coming out of the Large

Hadron Collider (LHC) can be a huge asset. Indeed, when my namesake (Professor Sharma) led one of the LHC teams to its monumental discovery of Higg's Boson (named after the Indian physicist S. N. Bose), it was just as much a milestone in data science as in particle physics. Climbing the intellectual Everest that is involved in proving the theorems that Penrose or Hawking are better known for is much more of a solitary intellectual pursuit and far less suited to the rough-and-tumble world of finance. While one may be more awestruck by the Edward Wittens and Andrew Wileses, working with their intellectual ilk on Wall Street often ends in tears. From our experience working with former Harvard postdocs, and ex-MIT faculty, I would say that today's MFEs are better trained for the daily drudgery of data cleaning, which is the less glamorous staple of every quant job these days.

When I started QuantZ Capital, I decided to name our funds Quark and Quasar in a nod to the barbell of particle physics versus cosmology.

1.6. THE SKY IS NOT THE LIMIT – DATA, COMPUTE, AND ENERGY ARE

In 1989, it was possible for one (even as a high schooler) to contribute to the debate at the time on the all-important Hubble's parameter[23] with a trivial ordinary least squares fit. While the estimation of said parameter was rudimentary, the importance of H0 in astronomy cannot be overstated since it

[23] The Hubble's parameter, often denoted as H0, is a fundamental concept in cosmology that describes the rate at which the universe is expanding. It characterizes how fast galaxies are moving away from each other relative to their distance. As an undergrad, I was able to crank out another inconsequential paper on H0 estimation via metallicity in supernovae thanks to the generosity of the W. M. Keck Foundation.

characterizes the speed of expansion of the universe, which means that the inverse (reciprocal of that rate) would be the age of the universe. Back then the real challenge was getting the data – who had observation time on the most advanced telescopes like the Canada France Hawaii Telescope? Nowadays, it's both the criticality of datasets and compute. This will ultimately only be limited by energy consumption since the hardware will keep getting exponentially cheaper. This point is germane to present-day quants and MFEs who are enormously enamored of overly complex mathematical maneuvers largely due to indoctrination by the high priests in academia who thrive on unnecessary obfuscation. In empirical finance, as in astronomy, fancier models don't get you anywhere fast when the binding constraint for empirical science is clean and comprehensive data. Indeed, the largest leaps in astronomy resulted from placing a telescope beyond the Earth's muddying atmosphere – to wit the Hubble Space and more recently the James Webb Space Telescope. Quants who spend too much time being impressed by closed-form solutions and mathematical elegance forget that most of their "trading" careers will be spent cleaning data and most of what they learned painstakingly can now be brute forced by AI. I say that having spent years coding up derivatives pricing and optimization libraries, which the AI can now spit out gratis in a matter of seconds. The AI cognoscenti were quick to grasp that ultimately it will come down to compute (hence the enormous capitalization of NVDA and the rapid proliferation of data centers), which means that the binding constraint will actually be energy, once the hardware costs come down enough.

1.7. THE THUNDERING HERD

The arc of risk is long, and it bends toward precision. When I got involved with Risk in 1997, the field was nascent but glamorous and exciting. It was far from being commoditized.

Looking back – who would have thought that VaR, CVaR, CDaR, BIS guidelines[24] or the Fed's internal models' approach could get the rocket scientists all fired up? After all VaR is nothing but a quantile. From a purely mathematical perspective such risk measures are trivial. But the act of measurement and firmwide aggregation is not. As always, in finance, the act of collecting and cleaning the data across large institutions is far more daunting than the relatively straightforward act of putting a point estimate on it with some confidence level.

Howard Rubin, a senior bond trader at Merrill Lynch, had lost $250 million for the firm in 1987. The losses occurred when rising interest rates decimated his $900 million portfolio of mortgage-backed securities. To hide the losses, he doubled down, making unauthorized bets on an additional $800 million of these securities in the hopes of making it back and then some. When the strategy failed, and the staggering losses came to light, he was fired and the firm ended up having to sell a substantial stake in the South Tower of the World Financial Center (in which I had an office up until 9/11). With Dan Napoli[25] in charge of Risk, Mother Merrill (at least on the sell side) had finally found religion. However, interestingly the buy side of the firm (MLAM), which was treated as a cost center for GPC (global private client), still did not have any centralized risk oversight a decade later when I was hired as part of that nascent effort in 1997. The idea was to build out a comprehensive risk dashboard for the CIO in terms of VAR, scenario analytics, and so on. I did that. First for fixed income, then for equities, and finally graduated to risk oversight of all alternative

[24] VaR is value at risk, CVaR stands for conditional value at risk, CDaR for conditional drawdown at risk and BIS for the Bank for International Settlements.

[25] An interesting side note is that Dan Napoli was key to Merrill's bankrolling our future mayor – Mike Bloomberg – in 1983.

investments. By that time, J.P. Morgan had invested heavily in building out RiskMetrics, Bankers Trust[26] in RAROC, and a number of software firms had jumped into the fray as well (notably Algorithmics, Reuters, Barra, IBM, etc.).

David Heath (of Heath-Jarrow-Morton [HJM] interest rate modeling fame) later moved to CMU from Cornell. In addition to his namesake (HJM) interest rate models, he was also one of the coauthors of the seminal paper "Coherent Measures of Risk" (1999), which established a set of axioms that any reasonable risk measure ought to satisfy to be considered coherent. Notably, VaR failed to satisfy sub-additivity, which means that it can underestimate the benefits of diversification.

My CMU MSCF classmate (and subsequently a QuantZ colleague), Sandy Warrick, went on to Northfield Information Services and published extensively on risk with Dan diBartolomeo. Northfield got a reputation for being the more creative, quirky, and rather more attractively priced version of Barra. However, fellow CMU PhD alum and founder of Axioma – Dr. Sebastian Ceria – always pitched Axioma as the Jaguar to be contrasted with the Yugo. When I reached out to Sebastian circa 1999 for help on MIPs (mixed integer programming), he was on the faculty at the Columbia Business School. Over time, many distinguished former academics like Emanuel Derman, Myron Scholes, and Peter Carr followed Fischer Black's footsteps on to Wall Street. Some of them even went back to academia after a while. The fluidity that has evolved in the quant space in both

[26] The Bankers Trust RAROC (risk-adjusted return on capital) methodology and software was meant to allocate the bank's equity capital to each business division and then to each individual asset within the bank in order to make disparate lines of business more comparable in terms of their risk-adjusted contribution to the value of the bank as a whole.

New York and London has been a net positive in accelerating innovation on both sides of the pond.

In 1999, I was privileged to help Bob Doll launch the ML Large Cap Series funds at MLIM. The three flagship funds were seeded with $1 million each. The funds significantly outperformed their Russell 1,000 indices by double digits through the Nasdaq crash; money came pouring in and the assets under management across all related strategies grew to over $30 billion by the time I left the firm in mid-2004. Merrill's "thundering herd" was always "Bullish on America."

1.8. HYPERLINKING TO THE FUTURE

In the fall of 1994, I was just settling into the PhD program in Pittsburgh. Manuela Veloso (now in charge of AI at J.P. Morgan) and Red Whittaker already had their robots running around the campus. Under Raj Reddy's leadership the pioneering Robotics Institute-at CMU-was at the forefront of groundbreaking innovations such as the first autonomous vehicles (sorry, but Elon had nothing to do with that). Navlab 1 was built in 1986, funded in part by DARPA's Strategic Computing Initiative. By 1995, Navlab 5, had completed the "No Hands Across America" drive. This epic 2,850-mile journey from Pittsburgh to San Diego saw the vehicle steer itself autonomously for 98% of the distance with Dean Pomerleau as the human in the loop.

Since I had managed to ingratiate myself with not only the Tepper (formerly the Graduate School of Industrial Administration) faculty but also had status in the joint Pure and Applied Logic PhD program (which was the old school AI of expert systems), I ended up with multiple offices. The main one was on the seventh floor of Wean Hall amid all of mathematics and computer science action. That's about the time I got a call from my brother-in-law (Ashu Roy) at

Stanford. Unbeknownst to me, he was one of the early internet search pioneers. While Jerry Yang and David Filo had launched Yahoo!, Ashu Roy had cofounded WhoWhere (the first yellow and white pages for the internet) and Mailcity.com, the second ever email application for the fledgling internet. Another Indian Institute of Technology alum, Sabeer Bhatia at Caltech, had launched Hotmail, which was soon acquired by Microsoft. Meantime, folks in my vicinity at CMU were launching Lycos, which went public in 1996. In August 1998, I saw a headline that spoke of WhoWhere being sold to Lycos for "whichwhat" estimate – kudos to the reporter who nailed that headline. The fact of the matter is that I had only the faintest inkling of the internet even though much of the pioneering work was happening right there under my nose and down the hall. With a gentle prod from Roy, I realized that it was time to get a clue as to the technology that was going to change the world. The backbone of the internet was HyperText Markup Language (HTML), so I figured I should acquaint myself with that. I spent the next couple of days learning just enough to create a rudimentary page entitled, "My OCD Friend" (pun intended). It was a nod to the hit show on the TV at the time and the lead character (Courteney Cox) who supposedly had obsessive-compulsive disorder (OCD). I'd managed to create one of the first pages on what would later be called the internet but still went by the moniker of the *world wide web*. Up until 1993, the entirety of the internet had just been the servers at CMU, Stanford, Illinois (NCSA), and CERN before the World Wide Web exploded. There were no tools like WordPress, which today make the act of creation and editing a breeze. Here were some of the early-learned lessons:

- The internet never forgets – Courteney Cox kept haunting my job searches for a decade. Easy to create but practically impossible to erase content from the internet especially with the Wayback Machine. The issue of privacy will become much more pernicious in the age of AI with deepfakes and cybercrime on steroids.

- While HTML may have seemed like an edge or even an indispensable tool at the time it was quickly rendered obsolete by many front-end GUI editors like WordPress or Wix, which now automatically translate formatted text to HTML so one does not have to count pixels, as mathematicians were trained to do in LaTeX.

Younger generations have no idea how much time we wasted on the mere acquisition of knowledge (trying to copy papers manually in the bowels of labyrinthine libraries) or in the act of manually typesetting mathematical fonts. Regardless, lessons from the internet bubble are ever more germane today in the age of "vibe coding" and vertiginous valuations – with the AI pundits trying to draw the obvious parallels. But, of course, this time is different and existential.

1.9. THE PIONEERING QUANT FINANCE PROGRAM

Rather coincidentally, the world's first quant finance graduate degree program was launched in the midst of the AI winter in 1994. By the time I landed at Wean Hall in the fall of 1994, Professor Steven Shreve already had a pipeline of PhDs in mathematical finance specializing in stochastic processes and derivatives pricing. His MSCF lecture notes would later turn into a two-part book series, while his graduate text with Karatzas remained largely impenetrable to most. A notable alum and perhaps the first PhD ever minted in mathematical finance was my friend Uwe Wystup, who later taught at Oxford, CMU, and then became the chair of a similar quant program at the business school (HfB) in Frankfurt. The better-known pioneering, MSCF program was formally launched under the aegis of the GSIA (now the Tepper School of Business) in the fall of 1994. The visionary MIT PhD leading MSCF from the Tepper side was Professor Sanjay Srivastava. Sanjay was also co-founder of the equally visionary FAST lab – the world's first simulated trading floor. I knew well that philosophy of mathematics was a ticket to penurious unemployment. It was intuitively obvious that I needed a hedge. I immediately took the FAST trading class the first time it was offered so I could become the teaching assistant for FAST Lab shortly thereafter. Sanjay was kind enough to humor me. A particularly fond memory is that of Sanjay's audacious idea that the Tepper MBAs in Pittsburgh should do a joint simulated trading session with Tokyo. That left us minions scrambling with IBM XTs and ATs trying to jerry-rig a live connection via the satellite dish parked outside Posner Hall. The fact that the internet did not exist (for all practical purposes) was never an impediment.

The pioneering batch of roughly half a dozen MSCF students included several math and physics PhDs and postdocs. At one of the reunions, MSCF co-founder and the dean of humanities, Professor John Lehoczky noted that other top universities had been waiting in the wings to see who would jump into the pool first. Not long after the Srivastava and Shreve launch – Columbia, Berkeley, Princeton, New York University (NYU), Toronto and others followed suit by the end of the millennium. Having sat through half a dozen of the early Operations Research and Financial Engineering (ORFE) courses at Princeton (with Carmona, Kulkarni and others) not to mention a few at NYU Courant (courtesy of Peter Carr), I already had a pretty good idea of other MFE programs before directing Capstone courses for Columbia (MSBA), UCLA, UCSD, and guest lecturing for others. While each MFE program has its own idiosyncratic strengths and weaknesses, it's largely driven by star faculty (such as a Shreve, a Carr, a Derman or a Kolm) and the pros and cons of the departments backing them. Some like CMU and Berkeley uniquely benefit from inter-departmental collaboration, while many suffer from internal competition with other programs within the same university (notably Columbia).

At last count there were close to 200 MFE programs in the world with the financial engineering moniker having gained currency (over MSCF). In my estimation that number is substantially higher when one accounts for the related data science and business analytics MS programs which have sprouted up as reliable cash cows for math, stats and OR (operations research) departments worldwide. Notably, absent from the fray was Wharton. This fall at the 2025 Jacobs Levy conference in Times Square, Dean Erika James announced the launch of the new MSQF program endowed by Bruce Jacobs. When Merrill Lynch footed the bill for me to enroll in the Wharton executive program about the time of the Nasdaq crash, the big picture flavor of the coursework could not have been more diametrically opposed to that which is taught in MFE programs. After all, the Wharton executive education audience is composed of senior executives from other industries trying to understand how to run a business and acquire leadership skills that folks like Michael Useem were great at teaching through expeditions to the Everest base camp. My key recollection of the Wharton experience is that of Jeremy Siegel as the market cheerleader with his *Stocks for the Long Run* book (even through the Nasdaq crash) serving as a clarion call for the 17,000 brokers in Merrill Lynch's "thundering herd" to keep their clients fully invested for the long run.

On June 4, 2025, Bob Simon (as the current executive director of MSCF) pulled off an incredible gathering featuring

CMU president and David Tepper himself to celebrate the 30th anniversary of the MSCF program (housed by the eponymous Tepper School of Business). The gala was held at the Museum of Financial History. Situated at 48 Wall Street, the museum is sandwiched between my former employer (Deutsche Bank at 60 Wall) and my former office (at 44 Wall) from which I launched QuantZ.

1.10. BANKERS TRUST AND THE END OF EXOTICS

While the mathematicians were obsessed with pricing esoteric exotics like Passport options[27] (some of which would never get traded), opening the *Wall Street Journal* (*WSJ*) was frightening at times. Looking at the headlines, I wondered if there would be an industry left for my skill set by the time I was done cooking. In the fall of 1994, while we were testing out the simulated trading floor,[28] an ominous headline crossed the tape on the Reuters terminal. Orange County, California, had filed for bankruptcy. While it was difficult for me to process the implications of a municipal insolvency it was clear that the ramifications for the derivatives market could not possibly be good news for mathematicians. On the one hand, impoverished mathematicians were suddenly in high demand; on the other hand, it seemed they were quite capable of blowing up the golden goose along with the rest of Wall Street. This would turn out to be

---

[27] A passport option is an exotic derivative that grants the holder the right to trade an underlying asset freely within a specified set of rules or constraints, with the final payoff based on the profits generated at maturity. It effectively limits downside risk to the option premium while preserving unlimited upside potential.

[28] Sanjay Srivastava's pioneering FAST lab (as it was known), at CMU's GSIA, is now featured in the Smithsonian's Archive of American History.

a recurring motif and one that would lead Warren Buffett to label derivatives as weapons of mass destruction. My future employer had sold the Orange County CIO, Rob L. Citron, "inverse floaters" among other derivatives. By the end of the decade, several banks had perished or merged due to short-term greed in their attempt to take the "widows and orphans" to the cleaners. Needless to say, the appetite for such exotic options faded after the derivatives debacles at Orange County, Gibson Greetings, Metall Gesellschaft, Procter & Gamble, and several others. Complexity and obfuscation driven by dubious profit motives moved from "Libor-cubed"[29] swaps to other corners of the market such as synthetic "CDO-squared"[30] deals and more recently to cryptos and digital assets. The most prestigious derivatives house on Wall Street (Bankers Trust) ultimately folded under the weight of litigation, and the CEO, Frank Newman, cashed in while the firm was sold to Deutsche Bank. On my first job, which was co-managing a model risk group at Ernst & Young, we created the world's first derivatives model validation engine (Raven) to lock up most of the top DPCs (derivative product companies), which were subsidiaries of major banks like Salomon DP (derivative products), Lehman Brothers DP, and so on, as model validation clients. There was an enormous appetite for trading exotics. We were being asked to price whispers, cliquets, barriers, rainbows, ratchets, and even ended up creating the first pricing model for cross-currency puttable Bermudan swaptions. Among other top DPCs, the software (which I initially wrote in

[29] These were interest rate derivatives where one leg paid a fixed rate while the other paid $Libor^n$ (where n could be 2, 3, etc.) minus a spread.

[30] A CDO-squared (collateralized debt obligation squared) is a structured credit derivative in which the collateral pool consists primarily of tranches from other CDOs, rather than direct exposures to individual loans, bonds, or mortgages. It represents a *second layer* of securitization, adding additional complexity and correlation risk. They featured prominently in the 2008 Great Financial Crisis.

Matlab) was licensed to Bankers Trust. Years later when I resurfaced at Deutsche Bank to run a statistical arbitrage proprietary trading desk, I was pleasantly surprised to find out that Raven was being used by the middle office to mark the bank's derivatives.

The lesson for next generation quants should be that it pays to take the long-term perspective even though Wall Street bonus cycles are propelled by short-term greed.

1.11. IT AIN'T ROCKET SURGERY

No account of the salad days at Deutsche Bank in the "Saba"[31] proprietary trading unit would be complete without mention of our fearless leader, Boaz Weinstein. By the time I arrived at Deutsche in 2004, Boaz had already rocketed through the ranks, building a reputation as one of pioneers of the newfangled credit derivatives alongside his signature stock versus credit default swap trade (aka capital structure arbitrage). By 27 he had become the youngest ever global co-head of Integrated Credit Trading. Boaz was the wunderkind the media couldn't get enough of. He would forever be the card-counting chess prodigy who could play others blindfolded while rattling off the volatility surface from his photographic memory. In 2006 and 2007 – the peak years of the credit boom – our Saba entity racked up obscene gains. For all of his card-counting savvy, he also had the boyish charm and humility to remind quants that trading "ain't

[31] Saba Capital is the name of the proprietary trading group founded and led by Boaz Weinstein while he was at Deutsche Bank. The term later became the name of his hedge fund, Saba Capital Management, which he launched in 2009 after leaving Deutsche Bank. The group (and later the fund) specialized in credit derivatives, convertible bond arbitrage, and capital structure trading – areas in which Weinstein was considered one of Wall Street's top traders.

rocket surgery" (to mix metaphors). He hired quants from the infamous MIT blackjack team and bonded with traders over poker games after hours. The group's exploits became part of Deutsche Bank lore. Scott Patterson (2010) of the *WSJ* did a fine job of chronicling our proprietary trading unit's adventures under Weinstein alongside those of Pete Mueller at Morgan Stanley's PDT (process-driven trading) and Cliff Asness at AQR in his 2010 book entitled, *The Quants: How a New Breed of Math Whizzes Conquered Wall Street and Nearly Destroyed It.* As Patterson insightfully noted: at Deutsche Bank, risk wasn't just managed, "Risk was bitch-slapped, risk was tamed and told what to do."

But as the financial world convulsed in 2008, Weinstein's Midas touch was overwhelmed by the tumult that upended even the industry's brightest minds. Bets on corporate bonds, loans, and credit-default swaps, as well as highly levered directional trades, which had succeeded spectacularly in prior years, backfired during the credit market's collapse. By the end of 2008, Deutsche Bank's once-vaunted credit unit had racked up billions in losses wiping out multiple years of gains.

With so much blood on the street, Wall Street was forced to accept government bailouts with many strings attached. The writing was on the wall: NO MORE COWBOY ACTS. The days of gun-slinging cowboys shooting from the hips were over, as were the days of socializing losses while privatizing gains.

Prop trading was history.

1.12. THE VOLCKER RULE

By the time the GFC had peaked in Q4 of 2008, it was abundantly clear that the era of banks running hedge-fund-like desks was over, in part due to the Volcker rule and other reforms that followed as part of the Dodd-Frank reforms. I gave a talk at CMU predicting the demise of proprietary trading desks at investment banks, and the fact that banks would start behaving more like public utilities than casinos. That is indeed what happened even though it took a while.

There were a number of glory launches coming out of that Deutsche Bank cohort from that era. The biggest of all was no doubt, was Saba itself. Boaz had successfully negotiated an amicable exit for his prop entity to launch the hedge fund. One of the other most prominent launches was that of Greg Lippmann. After profiting handsomely from Deutsche Bank's $5 billion subprime short – a trade chronicled by Michael Lewis in *The Big Short* – Lippmann announced in February 2010 that he was joining forces with his former Deutsche Bank colleague Fred Brettschneider to launch LibreMax Capital. The firm's strategy centered on structured credit – the same asset-backed securities that had been considered toxic during the crisis but were now trading at attractive double-digit yields. LibreMax had no trouble raising capital. After all, you could not possibly pay for the publicity of not only being profiled by Michael Lewis but having Ryan Gosling play your character on the silver screen.

Anilesh Ahuja launched Premium Point Investments LP in 2008 shortly after leaving Deutsche Bank, where he had been head of the mortgage-backed securities group. His firm initially posted strong double-digit gains by capitalizing on recovering mortgage markets before running afoul of regulators. I distinctly recall the diminutive, desi dude outside of 60 Wall Street – chain-smoking. Soon, I would start running into his marketers on the hedge fund circuit, particularly in Newport, Rhode Island. It turned out that one of the mathematicians from my Vassar cohort – Jeremy Shor – had teamed up with Anilesh Ahuja. While Jeremy did not exactly come across as an intellectual, he was talented enough as a mathematician to pursue a PhD at Columbia. Premium Point was eventually embroiled in legal issues, with both Ahuja and Shor being charged with securities fraud due to significantly overstated fund values between 2014 and 2016, which led to substantial investor losses and regulatory actions. This misrepresentation enabled them to charge higher management and performance fees and to delay investor redemptions. Following a six-week federal trial in the Southern District of New York, both Ahuja and Shor were convicted of conspiracy to commit securities fraud, securities fraud, conspiracy to commit wire fraud, and wire fraud.[32] Sadly, despite their accomplished careers, securities fraud is the only thing that either of these gentlemen will ever be remembered for. My policy has always been – do not even dream of daring to push the envelope. As I remind students, no payoff is worth the risk of potential incarceration.

1.13. UGLY AMERICANS

A few years later, I got a call from J.P. Morgan in the context of their potentially seeding one of the former proprietary trading desk spin outs from within the GAT (global arbitrage and trading) entity of the Royal Bank of Canada's New York presence. When the Fed decided to nix the spin out of GAT as a hedge fund by management, various groups splintered off and launched their own funds rather similar to what happened at Deutsche Bank.

The former CEO of RBC Capital Market launched his spin out with an enormous trading floor presence up in Purchase

[32] In November 2019, Anilesh Ahuja was sentenced to 50 months in prison, while Jeremy Shor received a 40-month prison sentence. Both were also ordered to serve three years of supervised release following their prison terms and ordered to pay restitution. While their convictions were overturned two years later in December 2021 by US District Judge Katherine Polk Failla, the verdict and sentencing marked one of the more significant fraud convictions involving hedge fund mismarking in recent years.

(New York). By the time I took the Metro North train up there to speak to him, they were already in the process of folding. It's tough for a hedge fund launch to survive a high burn rate if the seed ticket redeems.

Most prominently, there was the former Princeton wrestler who went by the nickname "Fudge." Fudge was the star trader at Kidder Peabody. When Kidder had to be sold off due to losses generated by the rogue trader Joseph Jett, RBC bought the equity division from Kidder. Rumor had it (remains unconfirmed) that Fudge was the real-life inspiration for the star trader profiled in the Ben Mezrich (2004) book *Ugly Americans: The True Story of the Ivy League Cowboys Who Raided the Asian Markets for Millions*. The book recounts the adrenaline-fueled world of expatriate trading, where a bunch of Princeton graduates navigate a cutthroat environment filled with larger-than-life characters, including rogue traders, and encounters with the Japanese Yakuza. In particular, it described the Tokyo-Osaka arbitrage in Japanese equity index futures.

After building up the Tokyo equity-derivatives group for Kidder Peabody, Fudge later ran Global Arbitrage & Trading at RBC Capital Markets with an iron fist. When he hired me at RBC from Deutsche (Saba), I was well aware of the mortal dangers of working for such an intimidating figure. It was best to keep your head down and march in line. When the Fed decided to nix the spin out of GAT, Fudge teamed up with Princeton wrestling mate Michael Novogratz to launch Galaxy Digital. In addition to Novogratz's colorful appearances on CNBC, the wrestling pair also became known for their heroic rescue of the sport of wrestling from the chopping block at the Olympics.

1.14. QUANT QUAKES

The quant meltdown of August 6–10, 2007, was a significant but short-lived liquidity crisis that severely affected quantitative equity market-neutral hedge funds. The event was characterized by a rapid "unwinding" or forced liquidation of large, leveraged quantitative portfolios, triggering widespread losses across funds employing similar strategies. Within a matter of days, funds at fabled firms such as Renaissance, AQR, and Goldman were said to be on the ropes. Tykhe Capital suffered steep losses (reportedly as much as about 30% month-to-date in early August), leading to its subsequent liquidation. Goldman's quantitative funds were also in the crosshairs, with losses reportedly exceeding 30% in their Global Equity Opportunities (GEO) Fund. Goldman's CFO at the time stated that the moves represented "25 standard deviation" events occurring several days in a row, highlighting the extremity and rarity of the losses (at least as incorrectly parsed in the context of the Gaussian distribution).

By the end of July 2007, I'd started hearing of tremors in the credit markets from friends and former colleagues. I didn't pay much attention because no one in the quant equity world had really thought through the consequences of crowded positioning, extreme gross leverage, and the dramatic rise in capital allocated to quantamental and statistical arbitrage strategies. No one had understood the domino effect of quakes in illiquid strategies propagating to the most liquid ones because that's where the multistrats and pod shops could easily de-lever. Matthew Rothman (at Lehman) was covering this episode as close to real time as possible in the pre-Twitter days.

- The meltdown was triggered by a large, sudden, and likely forced liquidation by one or more sizable quantitative market-neutral portfolios, possibly driven by margin calls or firmwide risk reduction mandates.
- The forced selling caused a chain reaction affecting other quant and non-quant equity funds, amplifying losses through deleveraging and stop-loss triggers.

- Many market-neutral long/short equity funds suffered large, rapid losses (often double-digits in a matter of days), followed by a sharp snapback on Friday, Aug 10. The pattern was inconsistent with fundamentals but consistent with a temporary dislocation.
- Mechanism ("unwind hypothesis"): An initial forced deleveraging of one or more sizable, factor-driven portfolios propagated through crowded, similar exposures, triggering stop-losses and further deleveraging by other quants. Liquidity providers withdrew risk capital mid-week, amplifying price impact; the subsequent rebound fits a supply-demand shock rather than news.
- Rothman's take (Lehman): The episode reflected endogenous risk from crowding – "quant managers/models" had become their own asset class, creating contagion when capital was pulled. His Lehman note entitled, *Turbulent Times in Quant Land*, issued on Thursday, Aug 9, became the most widely circulated research piece in Lehman history.
- Professor Andrew Lo at MIT and Amir Khandani later presented a postmortem in their paper, "What Happened to the Quants in August 2007?" indicating that in July 2007, the value/mean-reversion factors bled while momentum rose. During Aug 6–9, intraday liquidity fell, and short-horizon contrarian strategies lost heavily. They finally recovered as inventories normalized. There were clear implications for "hedge-fund beta" and the tail risk from crowded trades and leverage that were not adequately captured by standard models.

When ferocious selling resumed on Thursday, Aug 9, I knew that I was toast. I figured I was going to be summarily "executed." Would I be tackled by the wrestlers or perhaps kneecapped? Would my mangled carcass be left on the trading floor for the vultures to feed on? When I finally got tapped on the shoulder the actual proceedings were completely civil and professional. Management had just never seen anything like this and was understandably freaked out. They immediately demanded that my exposure be cut in half. I pleaded patience pointing out that we would only exacerbate the negative feedback loop. Putting aside the behemoth index arbitrage book, my pod was perhaps the second largest allocation amongst the dozens of pods within GAT. At the nadir of the quant quake, I had managed to give back all of the about 7% YTD gains and then some. And so, we started selling. By the time word came out that Goldman was bailing out the GEO fund and Jim Simons went on CNBC with his mea culpa – the swoon was already bottoming out. I had pleaded in vain that we may be the bottom print. And so, I watched helplessly as we continued de-levering even when names like US Steel and Freeport-McMoRan came back 20% to 30% from the lows about the time of the margin window – but we kept on selling. My hands were tied. By the end of the year my EMN (equity market neutral) strategy had come back by over 12% (on 100 × 100 if memory serves) but that was of little solace when my capital allocation had been cut in half.

Given that some EMN quant peers experienced drawdowns of 30–40%, my take on the situation was that not being in the same crowded Barra-type risk models with the same sort of quadratic optimizers had helped us stay out of the most crowded trades. Quants like us who lived to tell would later look at the Khandani/Lo as well as Rothman postmortems while licking our wounds. But when you are in the trenches and the bodies are piling up all around you and you haven't slept all week, you don't exactly have the luxury of a postmortem perspective.

1.15. SHARPENING THE SHARPE RATIO

By the mid-aughts, there was growing recognition that the widely used Sharpe ratio ignores higher moment risks, in so far as risk in the denominator is represented solely by the volatility of returns. I published a series of book chapters (Sharma, 2004) and papers on the related issue of documenting the statistical properties of hedge fund styles across various indices (Sharma, 2006) to establish that while the Sharpe ratio may suffice for liquid and well-behaved strategies such as equity long short, it fell woefully short when it came to its less liquid brethren such as event-driven, convertible arbitrage, merger arbitrage, and mortgage-related strategies with embedded short optionality. The short volatility profile often trades off desirable Sharpe ratios (before the crash) for hidden risks in terms of negative skewness and excess kurtosis which come home to roost later.

One branch of the literature kept the ratio format of the Sharpe ratio intact but replaced the volatility in the denominator with better risk proxies to account for the higher-moment risks:

- Approximate a quantile (or VaR) via a Cornish-Fisher expansion using sample skewness and kurtosis.
- Define a modified VaR (mVaR).
- Form a modified Sharpe ratio (MSR) = mean excess return/mVaR.

My proposed solution called AIRAP (Alternative Investments Risk-Adjusted Performance) went the utility function route instead by adopting the Certainty Equivalent as the risk-adjusted performance measure that enables one to capture all higher moments (Sharma, 2004). The *Journal of*

Investment Management (with Bill Sharpe on the editorial board) was nice enough to publish the paper.

It became harder for well-known mortgage funds and certain anointed geniuses to run seemingly astronomical Sharpe ratios for years before imploding in a single month. Illiquid convertible funds could still lean on stale marks to boost their Sharpe ratios but the game was getting much tougher thanks to papers like that by Cliff Asness exposing their stale pricing shenanigans. Sharpening the Sharpe ratio had suddenly become trendy.

1.16. MANIAS, PANICS, AND CRASHES

At a Penn Club event in 2024 featuring the latest edition of Kindleberger and Aliber's (2005) classic (*Manias, Panics, and Crashes: A History of Financial Crises*) I found myself staring at the back of Howard Marks' head. It turns out that Kindleberger's historical, psychological, and descriptive framework for financial crises and bubbles has significantly shaped the legendary investor's approach to understanding market cycles and investor behavior. Marks even quotes Kindleberger's observation that "there is nothing so disturbing to one's well-being and judgment as to see a friend get rich," highlighting the social contagion aspect of bubbles. This concept forms a core part of Marks's thinking on how bubbles develop and as to why rationality often goes by the wayside during these times.

Howard Marks' investment philosophy posits that bubbles, manias, and crashes are the result of psychological extremes when widespread speculative behavior causes investors to lose objectivity, leading to irrational exuberance and the belief that prices can only rise, often wrapped in a "this time is different" mentality. That was on full display during the dot-com bubble and will surely become an issue at some point during this AI cycle. Marks argues that investor psychology, not just stretched valuations, defines bubbles as characterized by the following:

- Fear of missing out (FOMO) and herd behavior
- Overconfidence and conviction that "there's no price too high" for favored assets
- Widespread participation, including nonprofessionals, and rapid abandonment of skepticism
- Irrational exuberance ("mania")

1.16.1. Cisco and the Kids – Bubble Trouble?

This is rather topical today (in Q4, 2025) given the nonstop breathless chatter on media outlets about an AI bubble in the making. Clearly, the market has once again thrown valuation and quality considerations to the wind in chasing the Magnificent Seven and the growthier momentum names to the exclusion of all else. That never ends well as we saw during the Nasdaq crash. A *Financial Analysis Journal* article entitled, "Cisco and the Kids" (Hirschey, 2001) analyzed the performance of high-growth technology stocks during the dot-com boom, with a particular focus on Cisco Systems and similar companies sometimes referred to as the "Nifty Fifty" tech darlings of the "dot-bomb" era. The article critically examined the hype and subsequent correction among the institutional favorites of day featuring extraordinary valuations, despite short operating histories, modest revenues, and sparse profits. While arguably this time around is a bit different since the AI companies do have substantial revenues and their CapEx[33] is also exponentially higher, which is why the market balked at OpenAI's plea for a government

[33] Capital expenditure.

backstop to their financing ambitions for data centers and compute. It has taken Cisco 26 years to effectively round trip it back to par (that is to make investors whole) on a total return basis from its dot-com peak on March 27, 2000. What will the denouement look like when this AI bubble bursts?

1.17. FLOREAT AULA

St. Edmund Hall (affectionately known as Teddy Hall), dating back to about 1236 CE is technically the oldest educational entity at Oxford University but it existed under the aegis of Queens College and did not acquire full college status up until 1957. By the time I got there in 1991, UK Prime Minister Keir Starmer had already moved on with his law degree while the Canadian Prime Minister (Mark Carney) was still pursuing his PhD at the university. I discovered the concept of arbitrage when they let me (a lowly undergraduate) into the MCR (the common room for post-graduates). In-charge of the MCR was a Canuck who later went on to serve in various cabinet posts from Ontario. Just as there was the obvious arbitrage for a male at the Seven Sisters, the arbitrage here was that one did not have to pay for Guiness (which the undergrads did); instead, you got port and sherry on the house while rubbing shoulders with the Rhodes and Marshall scholars. My housemate, Ochoro Otunnu, became my mentor and paved the way for our collective exploits. His brother (Olara who was the undersecretary at the United Nations and ran later for president against the dictator in Uganda) had been a contemporary of Tony Blair (St John's). Decades later at Ochoro's wedding in Central Park, I found myself sitting next to Mira Nair (better known for the *Monsoon Wedding*) and her husband (Mahmood Mamdani), who is on the faculty at Columbia. Who would have known that their son (Zohran) would end up winning the New York City mayoral race?

Oxford still relied largely on "pigeon mail" in the early 1990s with couriers shuttling messages around by bicycle. One had to move mountains just to get an email account. Unlike the fully wired CMU campus (Project Andrew), which was arguably the first university to go live with student-facing internet/email service in the 1980s – this was not the most tech-savvy place. While prominent quants such as Paul Wilmott were at Oxford in the 1990s and the Nomura Centre for Quantitative Finance (est. 1996) formalized collaboration between Oxford and the City of London, it wasn't until 2007 that the Oxford-Man Institute was founded as a high-profile partnership funded by the Man Group, and Oxford finally introduced the MSc in Mathematical Finance. The university now has one of the top business schools in Europe as well as a top-notch quant finance program and a thriving ecosystem for AI and startup founders.

1.18. FROM LOGICISM TO LLMS – THE AI REVOLUTION

Bertrand Russell's "logicism" held the philosophical and foundational view that mathematics can be reduced to or derived from a set of axioms and rules of inference via pure logic. Bertrand Russell, along with Alfred North Whitehead, aimed to show that mathematical truths are ultimately logical truths. It must indeed have been an incredible time to be alive and at Trinity College, Cambridge, at the start of the 20th century. If you have seen the movie *The Chariots of Fire* or the more recent one with Dev Patel as Ramanujan[34] you can almost visualize Russell, Ramanujan, Hardy, or Littlewood, not to mention Keynes, walking around the Trinity Quad. I was fortunate to study Russell's *Principia* in

[34] *The Man Who Knew Infinity* (2015).

the philosophy and mathematics program at Oxford. Some of the greatest contemporary minds in logic and set theory were at the Mathematical Institute on Banbury Road in the 1990s. Today, the Mathematical Institute is housed in a building honoring Andrew Wiles (who famously proved Fermat's last theorem while holed up in his attic for seven years at Princeton).

Sadly, for logicism, Kurt Godel came along with the incompleteness theorems in 1931 demonstrating the fundamental limitations of formal axiomatic systems by proving that any sufficiently powerful and consistent system cannot be both complete and able to prove its own consistency.[35] Not to be fazed, in 1954–1956, Herbert Simon (a psychologist by training who ultimately got the Nobel prize in Economics for "satisficing" while also being the founder of a top business school and computer science department) set up a computer program called the Logic Theorist (the first ever AI program) with Allen Newell and Cliff Shaw. I was fortunate to sit in one of Simon's historic lectures when he was still alive. Herbert Simon was truly a polymath and a towering intellect. He had set out to prove theorems from Russell's *Principia* (not to be confused with Newton's *Principia*). I had heard of Peter Andrews at CMU, a former student of Alonzo Church at Princeton, and decided to apply to his PhD program. Everyone knew of the Church in the Church-Turing hypothesis.[36] Peter had decided to extend the work of Herb Simon by building autonomous theorem provers. While

[35] In the late 1990s when I lived in Princeton, I went looking for Einstein's house (at 112 Mercer Street) and Godel's house in the vicinity of the IAS (Institute for Advanced Studies).

[36] Church and Turing had independently formulated λ-calculus and Turing machines in order to formalize the limits of computability, postulating that the Turing machine model captures the full extent of what can be computed algorithmically. It thus implies that any function that is intuitively computable can be computed by a Turing machine.

Lisp was created by John McCarthy at MIT, CMU had pioneered other versions of Lisp, such as the CMU Common Lisp, which we used for these theorem provers. The term *AI* was officially coined at the Dartmouth conference in the summer of 1956 – shortly after Herb Simon took the baton from Russell to pioneer what became known as artificial intelligence that summer. Other key AI pioneers at this seminal conference included John McCarthy (who proposed the term), Marvin Minsky, Nathaniel Rochester, and Claude Shannon. The focus was largely on rule-based expert systems which bear little resemblance to the stochastic parrots of today's ChatGPT era.

Fast forward to 2024 and Geoffrey Hinton got the Nobel prize in Physics (on the heels of his Turing award) for his foundational discoveries relating to artificial neural networks, which is why he is now widely recognized as the godfather of AI. But in the 1980s and 1990s, he was largely scoffed at as no one took neural nets seriously until the "AlexNet moment"[37] in 2012. The compute for neural nets to shine simply did not exist. As a conscientious objector to the DoD/DARPA funding at CMU, Hinton decamped for Toronto in 1987. More recently, he retired from Google to speak freely about AI's potential for wiping out humanity while his former student, Ilya Sutskever (ex-OpenAI), has also been a prominent advocate for safety guardrails in AI.

Separately, Andrew Ng (currently at Stanford and also cofounder of Coursera) has been one of the pioneers of

[37] AlexNet was created by Alex Krizhevsky, Ilya Sutskever, and Geoffrey Hinton at the University of Toronto. The AlexNet victory at the ImageNet Large-Scale Visual Recognition Challenge (ILSVRC) in 2012 with a top-five error rate of 15.3% was a watershed moment that is credited with popularizing deep convolutional neural networks for large-scale image recognition, largely due to its efficient use of GPUs and innovations like ReLU activation and dropout for regularization.

deep learning and reinforcement learning. As a founder of the Google Brain project, he demonstrated that neural networks trained on vast amounts of unlabeled YouTube content could learn to recognize cats on their own without explicit training thereby demonstrating the power of unsupervised learning. Incidentally, Andrew Ng overlapped at CMU and even served as a teaching assistant (despite being an undergrad) for the incipient MSCF program (much to the chagrin of graduate students) during my stint there.

Expert systems like autonomous theorem provers ended in a cul de sac in the AI winter of the 1990s. No one involved in the autonomous proving of rudimentary theorems at the time could have dreamt of some day blowing through the Turing test let alone AGI. None of that was remotely in the offing until the momentous "transformer" architecture pioneered by Vaswani et al. of Google in 2017. *How indeed could an ADHD world have known that "Attention Is All You Need?"*

1.19. MAN VERSUS MACHINE

In May 1997, I took the elevator from my office (at Ernst & Young) on the 20th floor of the Equitable building to the rooftop ballroom space famously featured in many a movie. Long before DeepMind's Move 37 versus Lee Sedol, well before protein folding, and before generations of CMU/IBM Watson computers humbled Jeopardy champions, there was the heavily advertised "Man versus Machine" chess match. Midtown Manhattan was plastered with posters of the impending momentous match between humanity's last hope (Gary Kasparov) and IBM's Deep Blue. This wasn't merely a Tyson technical knockout bonanza in Vegas. The future of humanity was at stake, and I had a front row seat. How convenient that the match had come to our very own office building at the world headquarters of the firm now known as EY. I had no excuse but to take that elevator up to the top.

IBM's Deep Blue had benefited from the PhD thesis of Feng-Hsiung Hsu at CMU. Hsu's research focused on the design and development of specialized chess-playing hardware and algorithms that laid the foundation for Deep Blue's custom chess chips and parallel processing capabilities required to evaluate millions of chess positions per second. Now they were ready for the greatest face-off of their careers. As the IBM contingent marched in to take their seats, I noticed my astronomy mentor a couple of rows down (her husband was at IBM, I instantly recalled). I darted forth to greet Professor Elmegreen. But I digress . . . In that final decisive game 6, Kasparov opened with the Caro-Kann Defense. Kasparov's critical blunder came on move 7, which allowed for Deep Blue's devastating knight sacrifice and led to his resignation after just 19 moves. Deep Blue had defeated Kasparov 3½–2½, marking the first time a computer beat a reigning world chess champion in a tournament.

In the aftermath, Wall Street saw the writing on the wall but the high-fiving frat boys and history majors in charge had no idea how to react. Nor did they feel the pressure to react. They correctly surmised that it would be decades before machines could replace them. In the meantime, they would make out like bandits and sail their yachts into the sunset. It was always about the short-termism of the bonus cycle. After all, there were no clawbacks pre-2008. Most traders were logically inclined to game the system to maximize their short-term payoffs. The entire industry was wired toward maximizing short-term gains because in the long term, when stuff really hit the fan, the losses would get socialized (after all we had to bail out the system). No one would go to jail. Not even the head honchos at Lehman or Bear or

Countrywide. The Fed would print trillions and ironically the owners of capital would make out like bandits due to the Bernanke-engineered wealth effect and yet another asset bubble would start to inflate. But to benefit from the wealth effect, one has to be wealthy to start with as the inimitable (Nobel Laureate) Joe Stiglitz once explained to me. The growing income disparity and the Gini coefficient would come back to haunt us. The seeds of populist rage had been sown in the aftermath of the GFC with the "Occupy Wall Street" encampment right in front of the RBC trading floor at Zuccotti Park. The Fed's largesse would only exacerbate inequity in the years to come with disastrous consequences for democracy.

1.20. SINGULARITY AND THE AGE OF AGENTIC AI

We are now (for all practical purposes, with the latest model drops) at the precipice of AGI and well on our way to ASI. Somewhere along the way we blew through the Turing test without much hoopla. 2025 is turning out (as fully anticipated) to be the year of agentic AI. Lots of jobs in lots of industries will get automated. Good for K (the owners of capital) but not so good for L (labor) in the macro equation. Well, society had better get ready for UBI (universal basic income) and social unrest arising from massive disruption and the inability to regulate AI, not to mention the acceleration of the Gini coefficientas the Lorenz curve flattens out.[38] As the marginal cost of knowledge acquisition

[38] A flattening Lorenz curve signals *greater inequality*, where income/wealth is concentrated in the upper tail, and the majority of the population contributes little to the cumulative share. In a perfectly equal society, the Lorenz curve would be the 45° line, rising steadily (where each percentile adds proportionally).

asymptotes to zero, it's going to be unsettling for knowledge workers who spent their lives being trained for highly skilled work only to find themselves being disintermediated by an army of infinitely many agentic bots. Just as website creation eventually became commoditized down to a drag-and-drop operation, which any non-quant could easily indulge, it won't be long before agents will reduce or eliminate the need for programming as we know it today. Indeed, the Magnificent Seven firms continue laying off thousands of junior programmers resulting from the AI-based automation of their workforce. At companies like Microsoft and Salesforce, AI is already writing over 30–50% of the code, albeit mostly in copilot mode. By the end of 2025 the CEO of Anthropic claimed 90% automation of coding tasks en route 100% automation in a year. Soon, many will be "vibe coding" their way (to borrow Andrej Karpathy's turn of phrase) to unicorn status from their garages. While software engineering is clearly in the crosshairs, Jensen Huang suggests that it will remain critical to have the core competence in math and physics. But for how much longer?

Agents and bots will rapidly multiply into the billions (like the iPhone), and along with their humanoid (mechanical) brethren could outnumber humans on the planet in short order. These are serious existential questions far beyond the scope of this pedestrian treatise on the automation and systematization of equity portfolio management. The imminent quantum computing breakthroughs may present far greater challenges. It could make certain finance problems like portfolio optimization much more tractable, but it could also make all existing cyber-finance protocols, not to mention bank accounts and crypto coins easily hackable. We are at an inflection point, which is exciting given the possibility of curing cancer, extending longevity, and solving physics not to mention the climate crisis. But at the same time humanity is confronted with possibly insurmountable challenges that will likely arise from AI contaminating our objective reality and the key "alignment problem."

Democracies will be no match for AI-generated disinformation. Truth will become fungible in the face of deepfakes. Civil society will have trouble restraining the bad apples who can leverage AI to wreak havoc at a massive scale. Imagine every mentally disturbed individual having access to the equivalent of nukes. In the end, whether in finance or in the world at large – the survival of the human race will come down to whether the machines we create remain sufficiently aligned with human values or not. This is what precipitated the drama at OpenAI in 2024 and led to the departure of Ilya Sutskever and (my fellow UWC boarding school alumna) Mira Murati, who are much more attuned to the alignment challenges facing humanity. More recently, Murati's new firm has published a seminal result[39] suggesting the remedy for nondeterministic output. For LLMs to be useful, they must be reliable, which requires deterministic reproducibility. The paper pinpoints the lack of batch invariance in widely used inference kernels as the reason why an identical but repeated prompt can generate different responses even with the temperature set to zero. Reproducibility is indeed a prerequisite for scientific progress. The prisoner's dilemma makes it unlikely that any country is going to slow down in this all-or-nothing race to AI supremacy let alone quantum supremacy. While there is an obvious optimistic case to be made for an age of abundance, getting us through the valley of despair and disruption requires an uncomfortably high p(Doom).[40]

Paradoxically, when the first LLMs burst onto the stage they were disintermediating the writers and artists. When I was working on AI qua "autonomous theorem proving"

---

[39] https://thinkingmachines.ai/blog/defeating-nondeterminism-in-llm-inference/

[40] p(Doom) stands for "probability of doom." It's an informal shorthand – often used in discussions about AI, technology risk, or existential threats – to represent the subjective probability that advanced technologies (especially AI) could lead to catastrophic or civilization-ending outcomes.

(in the 1990s) this would have been inconceivable. Our expert systems could barely prove the most elementary of theorems. No one could have dreamt of an AI that could not only pass the Turing test but one that would have ingested the entire corpus of human knowledge becoming omniscient, and create prose with seemingly limitless creativity. Ditto for art. While humans may choose (in a contrived manner) to devalue AI-generated art or prose, the fact is that humans in most fields simply cannot compete anymore. That's already the case for coders and low-level engineers. Paradoxically, the big-picture philosophical skills may become more valuable for the few humans required to design and supervise such systems. Eventually, with superintelligence even those humans will become dispensable so we must hope that societies can design a sufficiently robust support system to handle the tsunami of disruption coming our way. In the age of abundance, it will come down to what gives our existence meaning until we shuffle off this mortal coil. Based on radical advances in medicine and lifespan one may be faced with many years of existence with no particular meaning nor any direct income or payoff based on effort per se. The AI serf lords will have Congress in their pockets (they already do) and will determine how a minute portion of the rents they extract get distributed back to the proletariat to keep them from throwing stones at their glass palaces. That will be nearly impossible in a country with over 400 million civilian guns. AI puts the potentially destructive force of annihilation in the hands of every nutcase and, of course, in the hands of AI itself, which has no moral compass. AI will look for the most efficient way to execute without regard to human welfare unless we choose to enforce the guardrails. Faced with massive unemployment (fairly soon) the Federal Reserve (which is already becoming a pawn of the executive branch and government data from the Bureau of Labor Statistics mere political propaganda) will find itself impotent. Stagflationary forces resulting from tariffs will ram into spiking unemployment, but the Fed's rate cutting tools will be no match for the disruptive unemployment caused by AI.

In the financial sphere there will be dire implications, particularly from a cybersecurity perspective, but at least in the near term there may not be any clear-cut ramifications for the mid to lower frequency realm qua factor investing. While short-term sentiment indicators with a 24- to 48-hour half-life may become more volatile, the truth is that few if any buy and hold (tax sensitive) institutional investors would flip their positions or go from long to short in a matter of hours based on such short-term blips. Short-term gyrations could be beneficial for some parts of the ecosystem (brokers, market makers, and hedge funds) but deleterious for others. Whether fundamental investors choose to be dinosaurs in the age of AI or are forced to go quantamental, one can bet on massive thematic upheavals and disruptions.

In quant trading, it has always been about my model assumptions versus yours. In the age of AI, what might save us from the bad, malevolent AI is perhaps the "good AI"? But more on that in Chapter 13.

1.21. QUAFFING A FEW – REVENGE OF THE NERDS

In 2019, I launched a new kind of quant club or society – <QWAFAxNEW>. The idea was to provide a forum for quants to network and learn in an informal and collegial environment while "quaffing a few." Think "revenge of the nerds." The etymology was inspired by our host city (New York) and by charting a NEW course in the spirit of

TEDx to encapsulate the "exponential" possibilities through the *x* in QWAFAx while pronouncing it as "Quaff a New" in the spirit of quaffing a few together while catching up on the latest in quant research.

This educational society has delivered on cutting-edge educational content in an informal and collegial setting, pairing talks with a social, speakeasy vibe (which involves "quaffing a few") starting with the historic Fraunces Tavern and a momentous speech by the late and great Professor Peter Carr. Since then, we have built alliances with major MFE programs (e.g., CMU, Columbia, New York University, Fordham, Stevens) and been hosted by many of them (Figure 1.1). Special thanks to our friends at CMU for

Figure 1.1 12/05/2023 – Networking Panel Hosted by Professor Manos Hatzakis at Stevens Tech.

hosting us at the MSCF campus in the Financial District. We've benefited from the involvement of corporate partners (such as Nasdaq), as well as many media partnerships with leading quant conferences, positioning the society as a hub where academics, practitioners, and students can congregate freely without fear of retribution from their employers. Over the years we've been fortunate to have many distinguished speakers, including several who have touched on the latest in factor investing. Marquee names have included Mark Carhart, Emanuel Derman, John Mulvey, Petter Kolm, Harry Mamaysky (Figure 1.2), Paul Glasserman, Agostino Capponi (Figure 1.3), Peter Carr, Uwe Wystup, and Steve Shreve, not to mention the book signing event featuring Gregory Zuckerman's book

Figure 1.2 Professor Harry Mamaysky (Columbia Business School).

Figure 1.3 QWAFAxNEW with Professor Agostino Capponi (Columbia University).

(Figure 1.4) on Jim Simons and Renaissance Technologies.[41] Carhart spoke candidly about the Quant quake of 2007 (Figure 1.5). Derman reminisced about what it was like working with Fisher Black at Goldman and later helped us do an event in the memory of our dear, departed Professor Peter Carr (Figure 1.6). Professor Peter Kolm presented on several occasions about jump models and regime identification (Figure 1.7 and Chapter 7, Section 7.2). We have also been honored to have his collaborator and a founder of Princeton's ORFE program – Professor John Mulvey – present on related topics (Figure 1.8). Paul

[41] The current CEO of RenTec, Peter Brown, is from a similar PhD program at CMU.

Figure 1.4 02/11/2020 – Gregory Zuckerman (WSJ) Book Signing at the Fraunces Tavern.

Glasserman of Columbia University presented his latest about options (Figure 1.9), while the launch party was hosted by Michael Markes of Nasdaq (Figure 1.10).

Figure 1.5 08/21/2024 – Mark Carhart (CEO, Kepos Capital and Former CIO, GSAM).

Figure 1.6 2019 Fraunces Tavern with Peter Carr, Emanuel Derman and Nassim Taleb.

Figure 1.7 10/16/2023 – Professor Petter Kolm (Director of the NYU Courant MFE Program).

Figure 1.8 Professor John Mulvey (Co-founder ORFE, Princeton University).

Figure 1.9 06/20/2024 – Professor Paul Glasserman (Columbia University).

Figure 1.10 Launch Party Hosted by Michael Markes of Nasdaq.

Chapter 2

Introduction to Factors and Smart Betas

2.1. A SURVEY OF THE FACTOR ZOO

A factor is a security attribute identified as a potential driver of return and risk. In financial theory, factors represent specific characteristics – such as size, value, or momentum – that have shown systematic relationships with asset performance. By isolating these attributes, researchers can identify patterns in returns that are not solely attributable to broad market movements, thus providing insight into the distinct drivers of investment risk and return. In practical terms, factor analysis enables the imposition of a cardinal ranking of companies within an investment universe based on these specific attributes, enabling portfolio managers to construct strategies that capitalize on the systematic patterns associated with each factor. When combined within multifactor models, these individual rankings form the basis of a disciplined, quantitative approach to portfolio construction aimed at achieving enhanced risk-adjusted returns. This is the key framework addressed in this book – to be seen in stark contrast to what traditional seat-of-the-pants fundamental managers used to do (think John Templeton or Bill Miller).

Factor research has developed significantly over the years, evolving from ad hoc observations of market anomalies to a systematic framework explaining variations in asset returns. Initial studies in this area focused on documenting specific irregularities in asset pricing, such as the "style" or Value effect (price-to-earnings ratios) by Sanjoy Basu (1977) and the book value effect (book-to-market ratios) first documented by a former Merrill Lynch colleague, Dennis Stattman[1] (1980). Subsequent research by Rolf Banz (1981) documented the "size" effect, whereby smaller firms appeared to show higher returns. Similarly, Jegadeesh and Titman (1993) identified the cross-sectional momentum effect, documenting the tendency of stocks with strong past performance to continue outperforming well out of sample. These studies, while influential, were initially framed as stand-alone market anomalies rather than the key building blocks of a broader, unified investment framework.[2] Their

[1] As a side note, I had the great privilege of overlapping with Dennis Stattman at Merrill Lynch (MLIM) back when he ran the enormously successful Global Allocation fund. This fund behemoth grew to over $100 billion in assets under the BlackRock umbrella.

[2] Interestingly Jacobs and Levy (1988) were early in cataloguing "anomalies" published in the 1980s. Contemporary quants may be surprised to know that various authors had already documented anomalies such as Size, Neglect, January effect, Earnings Surprise, Earnings Torpedo and various Value metrics.

models focused on identifying specific factors that could explain deviations from traditional asset pricing but lacked an encompassing theoretical structure that could systematize these observations into a comprehensive investment strategy.

The seminal contribution of Fama and French in 1993 was to unify the size and style anomalies within a cohesive, three-factor model (FF3) alongside market beta. This model demonstrated that asset returns could be systematically explained by company size and book-to-market as the explanatory "factors." This shift was instrumental in solidifying the theoretical foundation of factor investing, as it validated earlier discoveries like those of Basu (1977), Stattman (1980), and Banz (1981) within a more robust and coherent construct.

The Fama-French model inspired a tsunami of research, with subsequent scholars building on this unified framework to document numerous anomalies that would come to inhabit the "factor zoo" of Cochrane.[3] Building on this framework, Carhart (1997) extended the Fama-French model by incorporating the cross-sectional momentum factor initially identified by Jegadeesh and Titman (1993). It took more than 15 years for Novy-Marx (2013) to advance the agenda by identifying profitability as a crucial return determinant, showing that gross profitability had predictive power comparable to that of the value factor (Novy-Marx 2013). This addition to the factor zoo bridged the gap between value

[3] The *factor zoo* is a term popularized by John H. Cochrane (University of Chicago, Booth School of Business) to describe the proliferation of proposed risk factors in asset pricing research. The phrase highlights his critique of the overabundance of empirically discovered return predictors in modern asset pricing research – an issue Cochrane highlighted to urge more rigor, replicability, and parsimony.

and growth species by integrating a measure of firm quality into the asset pricing framework.

Table 2.1 contrasts the Jegadeesh and Titman (1993) definition of the momentum strategy across multiple lookbacks and holding periods (overlapping, usually equal-weighted deciles) with that of Carhart (1997). The latter codifies a specific, size-controlled, value-weighted factor (up minus down [UMD], based on 12–2 momentum, rebalanced monthly) for use in a four-factor model.

Table 2.1 Jegadeesh and Titman (1993) Versus Carhart (1997): Momentum Comparison.

Aspect	Jegadeesh and Titman (1993)	Carhart (1997)
Purpose	Document a trading anomaly/strategy ("buy winners, sell losers").	Add a risk factor to an asset pricing model to explain mutual fund returns (the FF3 becomes FF4 with momentum).
Signal window	Past 3–12 months cumulative return; they study many (J,K) combos (e.g., six-month formation, six-month holding).	Standardized to 12–2 momentum (past 12 months excluding the most recent month).
Skip recent month?	Yes, they exclude the most recent month to avoid short-term reversal/microstructure effects.	Yes, also excludes month $t-1$ (hence 12–2).

Holding/ rebalancing	Buy-and-hold for K months with overlapping portfolios (e.g., $K = 6$), rebalanced monthly.	Reconstituted monthly; the UMD factor is computed each month from that month's winner/loser portfolios (effectively one-month hold before the next resort).
Portfolio formation	Deciles on prior returns across CRSP common stocks (winners = top decile; losers = bottom decile).	Size-controlled 2 × 3 sorts: Small/ Big × Loser/Neutral/ Winner; UMD = (Small Winner + Big Winner)/2 – (Small Loser + Big Loser)/2.
Weighting	Results typically reported equal-weighted (they also examine value-weight variants).	Factor portfolios are value-weighted (FF/Carhart convention).
Use in regressions	Mostly report raw long–short strategy returns and robustness across J,K.	UMD used alongside MKT, SMB, HML in time-series regressions of fund/ portfolio returns.
Name you'll see	Often called WML (winners minus losers) in the strategy literature.	Called UMD (up minus down) in the Carhart four-factor model.

Asness et al. (2019) further developed this strain of the factor literature with their quality minus junk (QMJ) factor, which demonstrated that stocks with superior profitability, growth, and safety characteristics outperformed those with weaker fundamentals. They found that high-quality stocks outperform junk, even after controlling for value and size effects. The latter two authors introduced the "betting against beta" (BAB) factor in Frazzini and Pedersen (2014), adding yet another key pillar of factor investing by highlighting the low-volatility anomaly and suggesting that lower-beta stocks could provide superior risk-adjusted returns – a finding that flies in the face of the traditional capital asset pricing model (CAPM) linear risk-return relationship as embodied by the security market line (SML). Both the QMJ and BAB findings have become important pillars in modern factor investing and challenge key aspects of classical asset pricing theory.

These innovations were eventually acknowledged (belatedly) by the Fama and French (2015) five-factor model (FF5), which explicitly incorporated profitability (RMW; robust minus weak) and investment (CMA; conservative minus aggressive) factors. The extended FF5 model aimed to capture return variations linked to corporate profitability and investment-related factors which were already known to have demonstrable explanatory power.

Other analogs to FF5 have diverged somewhat in that Hou et al. (2015) proposed their four-factor model based on the *q*-theory of investment, emphasizing the net present value (NPV) rule from corporate finance, which posits that firms' investment decisions are rational responses to expected returns exceeding costs. Proceeding on a rather different tangent based on behavioral biases distinct from rational automatons, Stambaugh and Yuan (2017) and Daniel et al.

(2020) attribute market anomalies to cognitive biases and investor sentiment.

The explosive growth of the factor zoo led researchers to explore the ideal attributes of factors. Berkin and Swedroe (2015) proposed a comprehensive framework to evaluate the efficacy of factors, emphasizing criteria such as persistence, pervasiveness, robustness, intuitiveness, and investability. They argued that a factor must deliver reliable and consistent returns over time (persistence) and demonstrate validity across different asset classes and geographies (pervasiveness). Furthermore, a factor ought to be "robust" to alternative formulations and not rely on narrowly defined or contrived formulations. At QMIT we have always believed that factors admitted to the zoo should be grounded in investor intuition and be supported by a theoretical or behavioral rationale rather than merely result from datamining. Lately, this requirement of intuitive explainability has come under assault, resulting from the advocacy for model complexity (e.g., Kelly et al., 2024) and from research suggesting that data-mined factors are just as valid (Chen et al., 2023). More recently, Buncic (2025) has argued that the claim "portfolio performance strictly increases in model complexity" is driven by the questionable modeling choices of enforcing a zero intercept in their predictive regressions and the aggregation scheme they use for combining component models into performance metrics. Nagel (2025) from Chicago argues that the success of KMZ's (Kelly et al., 2024) Random Fourier Features (RFF)-based strategy (with many features $P \gg T$) is not due to uncovering real predictive relationships, but rather that it collapses into a volatility-timed momentum strategy in disguise. Further, one must always consider the trade-off between complexity and interpretability.

Further, investability is essential, ensuring that investors can indeed monetize net returns after accounting for transaction costs and other real-world frictions. This framework complements other strands of the literature, such as Aghassi et al. (2023), which stress the importance of factors exhibiting low correlations with existing ones. Together, these studies reflect a growing consensus that effective factor design requires both rigorous statistical validation and practical applicability to pass muster.

2.2. THE FAMA-FRENCH CRITIQUE

The Fama-French FF5, while a cornerstone of modern asset pricing theory, has faced criticism questioning the statistical validity of SMB (size factor),[4] the construction of HML (value factor), and the exclusion of cross-sectional price momentum as embodied by the UMD factor of Carhart (1997) or going further back the WML factor of Jegadeesh and Titman (1993).

The construction of the Fama-French value factor, HML (high minus low), has drawn scrutiny for its reliance on lagged book-to-market (B/M) data, which does not incorporate recent stock price movements. Asness and Frazzini (2013)

[4] R. Douglas Martin's challenge to the statistical validity of the SMB factor appears in "Efficient Bias Robust Regression for Time Series Factor Models," *Journal of Asset Management*, 2022 (coauthored with Daniel Xia), which he presented for us at QWAFAxNEW. His robust regression estimator (labeled "mOpt") shows that traditional least squares regressions used to estimate factor premia can be adversely affected by even a few outliers which therefore argues for robust regression techniques to re-examine factor significance. In particular, he found that robust control for outliers can materially impact coefficient estimates and inferences calling into question prior Fama-French conclusions. The paper also proposes a robust model-selection criterion (RFPE) that in their example selects Market, SMB, and MOM instead of Market, SMB, and HML.

demonstrated that this lag diminishes HML's effectiveness and understates the true value–momentum negative correlation and may obscure overlap of value with other factors such as investment (CMA – Conservative minus Aggressive). To address this, they proposed an alternative HML constructed with up-to-date market capitalization, creating a more timely measure of value. This timely HML shows a cleaner, stronger relationship with returns and a more pronounced negative correlation with the momentum factor (UMD). When this timely HML replaces the original version in the FF5, the explanatory power of the investment factor (CMA) is significantly reduced. This work provided a foundation for advocating for a six-factor model (Market Beta, SMB, timely HML, RMW, CMA, UMD) that includes momentum and uses this revised, more timely value factor (Asness, 2014; Asness & Frazzini, 2013).

Asness also criticized the Fama-French FF5 for excluding the momentum factor, UMD. In a 2014 article, Asness argued for UMD's essential role in explaining asset returns. Fama and French (2015) justified its exclusion by showing that the FF5 model explains much of the variation in returns on portfolios sorted by momentum, suggesting UMD was largely redundant for their purposes. Asness (2014) countered this by pointing out that UMD still produced significant alpha against the FF5 model, meaning it captured return variations that the other five factors missed. He argued that its partial independence from the other factors was a strength, as it demonstrated an ability to provide unique information. In a proposed six-factor model that includes both UMD and the timely HML factor, the explanatory power of the investment factor (CMA) becomes marginal. This framework, combining a timely value factor with momentum, demonstrated superior performance in explaining asset returns compared to FF5 (Asness, 2014).

2.3. CRITIQUE OF UMD: EARNINGS MOMENTUM VERSUS PRICE MOMENTUM

Although the Cliff Asness defense of UMD is empirically substantiated, Fama's skepticism regarding the systematic nature of price momentum is not without merit (Fama & French, 2015), and the inconsistency of its returns with traditional risk-based explanations casts doubt on its status as a fundamental pricing factor, prompting the search for more theoretically grounded interpretations. Consistent with this view, Chordia and Shivakumar (2006) demonstrated that price momentum is closely linked to earnings momentum, with the latter significantly predicting the returns of momentum strategies. Their findings suggest that earnings momentum, as a reflection of changes in firm fundamentals, serves as a key driver of price momentum returns.

Building on this, Novy-Marx (2015) provides critical insights by framing price momentum as a noisy proxy for earnings momentum. He argues that the core predictive power of momentum stems from fundamental earnings signals, making earnings momentum a more robust and foundational indicator. His empirical results underscore that earnings momentum captures firm-specific fundamental changes, which price momentum reflects only indirectly and with added noise. This reinforces his assertion that "fundamentally, momentum is fundamental momentum." Expanding this perspective to an international context, Sarwar (2021) demonstrates the universality of the relationship between earnings and price momentum across various markets. His findings confirm that earnings momentum consistently explains a substantial portion of price momentum returns globally, strengthening the case for the primacy of earnings momentum as a driver.

2.4. DEBUNKING THE SIZE FACTOR

The size factor has faced criticism for its instability and susceptibility to methodological biases. Early studies, such as Banz (1981) and Fama and French (1992), had already recognized the distortion caused by micro-cap stocks. Fama and French (1992) sought to mitigate it by excluding the smallest 5% of firms by market capitalization.[5] However, Knez and Ready (1997) showed that this static exclusion was insufficient, as micro-cap outliers continued to bias regression results. Using least trimmed squares (LTS), they demonstrated that large-cap firms outperform small-cap firms, contrary to the outcome in the Fama-French three-factor model (Fama & French, 1992). They found that once you trim influential outliers, the size effect vanishes or even reverses. Hou et al. (2020) further criticized the size factor for its lack of replicability, particularly outside the United States and after accounting for micro-caps and data-snooping biases.

Recent advancements have provided two refined approaches to addressing these issues. First, Martin and Xia (2022) recommended the use of robust regression techniques to systematically address the influence of outliers. Building on Knez and Ready (1997), they demonstrated that applying these methods not only mitigates the distortion caused by micro-cap stocks but also reveals that controlling for outliers reverses the SMB coefficient's sign, highlighting a systematic bias in prior methods. Second, Asness et al. (2018) provided a different perspective by addressing the distortion caused by low-quality stocks, which are characterized by weak profitability, poor growth, and financial instability.

[5] Fama and French (1992) did note that the size effect was concentrated among micro-caps and weakened after controlling for book-to-market (value).

They emphasized that the influence of low-quality stocks on the size factor is not limited to small-cap stocks, even though small-cap stocks are more likely to have these characteristics. Mid- and large-cap stocks can also include low-quality companies, making it necessary to apply quality adjustments across all market capitalization levels. By controlling for quality metrics using the QMJ factor, they demonstrated that the quality-adjusted size factor re-emerges with greater consistency and robustness. Moreover, the quality-adjusted size factor exhibits strong performance across markets and time periods, effectively eliminating the noise introduced by low-quality stocks and isolating the true economic significance of the small-cap premium.

2.5. THE EXPANDING FACTOR ZOO

- **Quality (QMJ).** Asness et al. (2019) formalize quality as a set of firm characteristics that investors should rationally pay more for – specifically profitability, growth, safety, and payout characteristics, standardized and combined into a composite score. They show that a long-short QMJ factor earns economically large, statistically significant risk-adjusted returns across the United States and 24 other countries robust to standard risk factor adjustments (e.g., CAPM, Fama-French three- and four-factor models). The paper builds on classic and modern antecedents such as Graham and Dodd's emphasis on quality and price (margin of safety), Piotroski's accounting-based sorting, and Novy-Marx's profitability premium. The results challenge simple risk-based explanations, as quality stocks tend to have lower market beta yet deliver higher risk-adjusted returns.
- **Low-beta (BAB) and the low-risk anomaly.** Frazzini and Pedersen's 2014 BAB factor highlights the low-risk anomaly

as it pertains to beta, not volatility per se: a portfolio that is long (leveraged) low-beta and short high-beta securities (to be beta neutral) earns positive alphas across multiple asset classes that persist after adjusting for standard risk factors. The mechanism is consistent with classic theory under leverage constraints – most prominently Black (1972) and Black et al. (1972) – which implies an empirically *too flat* SML when investors cannot costlessly lever low-beta assets (Black, 1972; Black et al., 1972; Frazzini & Pedersen, 2014). The mechanism is explained by leverage constraints because most investors are unable or unwilling to lever up low-beta assets to their desired risk level, so they overweight high-beta assets, which therefore trade at a premium with lower subsequent returns. Conversely, low-beta assets trade at a discount and deliver higher risk-adjusted returns when properly leveraged. This leads to an SML that is *too flat* as compared to classic CAPM predictions. The theory is directly linked to Black (1972) and Black et al. (1972). These foundational papers show that, with leverage constraints, the SML flattens, exactly as Frazzini and Pedersen empirically observe in multiple asset classes including stocks, bonds, and futures.

- **RMW (profitability, specifically operating profit).** Fama and French (2015) introduced the RMW factor to capture the "profitability premium" in stock returns associated with firms demonstrating higher operating profitability. The RMW factor is constructed as the difference in returns between portfolios of firms with robust (high) operating profitability and firms with weak (low or negative) operating profitability. Their measure of profitability is operating profitability, which accounts for costs including selling, general, and administrative (SG&A) expenses and interest, making it a more comprehensive reflection of a firm's true profitability. This builds on the earlier work of

Novy-Marx (2013), who found that gross profitability predicts stock returns well.

- **CMA (investment).** The CMA factor, also introduced by Fama and French (2015), reflects the tendency of firms with conservative (low asset growth) investment strategies to outperform those with aggressive (high asset growth) investment strategies. The factor measures the return spread between firms with low and high investment intensity, with investment defined as the change in total assets relative to total assets at the end of the prior year. This factor builds on earlier studies, including Titman et al. (2004), who demonstrated that firms making aggressive investments often underperform due to inefficiencies. By incorporating CMA and RMW, the Fama-French FF5 model represents a significant extension of the original Fama-French three-factor model, which only had beta, size, and style (book-to-market) factors.
- **Supply chain factors.** Supply chain networks serve as a crucial and distinct source of priced risk in asset pricing (Capponi et al., 2024). A graph neural network (GNN) framework was developed that moves beyond traditional linear models by nonlinearly integrating the financial characteristics of neighboring firms within d-hops on the network up to the third order. Up to (d=3) is found to balance bias reduction from higher-order relations with variance resulting from added complexity. This model generates firm-level return estimates that are used to construct a tradable, long-short "supply chain factor," which demonstrates significant Sharpe ratio gains over Fama-French 5 and PCA benchmarks. Ultimately, incorporating this supply chain information improves mean-variance efficiency and therefore merits attention.

2.6. LOW-RISK ANOMALIES: IVOL, BAB, MAX, AND CO-SKEW

The low-risk anomaly traces its origins to empirical work in the 1970s that challenged the CAPM foundational tenet that higher risk, measured by beta, should command higher returns. Studies found the relationship between beta and returns to be flatter (slope of the SML line) than predicted (Black et al., 1972) and, more directly, that low-volatility portfolios historically outperformed high-volatility ones (Haugen & Heins, 1975). The puzzle was deepened further by the discovery that stocks with high idiosyncratic volatility (IVOL) also tend to deliver anomalously low future returns.

Three primary explanations have been proposed for these anomalies. The first centers on leverage constraints, which prevent investors from arbitraging the anomaly by sufficiently leveraging low-beta stocks, causing them to overvalue high-beta assets instead (Frazzini & Pedersen, 2014). The second points to behavioral biases, primarily a preference for lottery-like stocks with high positive skewness, leading investors to overpay for them (Bali et al., 2011). The third involves institutional frictions and agency problems, where benchmark-hugging and incentive structures cause professional managers to systematically prefer higher-volatility stocks (Baker et al., 2011).

The low-volatility anomaly was formalized earlier by Blitz and van Vliet (2007), who showed that portfolios of low-volatility stocks produced superior risk-adjusted returns. However, the independence of this factor is heavily debated, with prominent critiques arguing that the anomaly is partially subsumed by exposures to other well-known factors, such as profitability and value, within a more comprehensive model like the Fama-French FF5 model (Fama & French, 2016) as opposed to the original three-factor model.

The "IVOL puzzle," first identified by Ang et al. (2006), who documented the counterintuitive finding that stocks with high IVOL tend to have lower future returns, contrary to the CAPM and the SML. But the robustness of this finding has been challenged due to methodological sensitivities and the influence of specific market events. Stambaugh et al. (2015) provided a leading synthesis of the puzzle, showing that the negative IVOL-return relationship is not uniform across all stocks. It is particularly concentrated among overvalued stocks, where high IVOL proxies for risk and valuation uncertainty, which deters arbitrage because investors are more willing and able to buy underpriced stocks but face greater risks and costs shorting overpriced stocks, especially those that are hard to short and during periods of high investor sentiment.

Stemming from the theory that investors have a preference for lottery-like payoffs (Kraus & Litzenberger, 1976), researchers have developed factors to capture this phenomenon. The most prominent is the MAX factor, which uses a stock's maximum daily return over the past month as a proxy for its lottery-like characteristics. Stocks with high MAX values tend to be overvalued and subsequently underperform (Bali et al., 2011).

The BAB factor operationalizes the flat SML by going long leveraged low-beta stocks and short high-beta stocks (Frazzini & Pedersen, 2014), as described in the previous section. The BAB debate centers on whether its success is driven by the leverage-constraint mechanism or if it is merely another manifestation of behavioral lottery preferences, which is what the critics argue showing that BAB's returns are significantly diminished after controlling for the MAX factor (Bali et al., 2017).

Most recently, Schneider et al. (2020) proposed a unified explanation for the various low-risk anomalies based on a single priced factor, viz., residual co-skewness. They demonstrate that a factor built to capture this skewness risk subsumes the returns of many other low-volatility strategies, suggesting the puzzle can be explained via rational compensation for bearing exposure to undesirable return distributions.

2.7. WHAT IS MULTIFACTOR INVESTING?

In multifactor models, companies within the estimation universe are ranked according to these factors, with their rankings aggregated via specific functions of each factor. This approach forms the basis of factor investing, where securities are chosen based on certain characteristics to increase exposure to return-driving factors or to optimize risk-adjusted performance. The asset growth in this area has been significant. Global assets pegged to factor-based strategies are now well into the trillions (low single digits). This reflects the tremendous growth and increasingly mainstream appeal of what was once an arcane quant niche in the 1990s when I started implementing factor investing in the 1940 Act context.[6]

What began with the CAPM and the single index model (and its applications in the earliest index funds at Wells Fargo) soon led to Ross's APT (arbitrage pricing theory) for

[6]The 1940 Act refers to the Investment Company Act of 1940 which is the cornerstone US federal law that regulates investment funds, particularly mutual funds, closed-end funds, and ETFs. It was enacted after the 1929 market crash to ensure investor protection and transparency in pooled investment vehicles.

the multifactor case and the earliest implementations of it through quants at Morgan Stanley and subsequently by D. E. Shaw. Our researchers have drawn on their decades of collective experience to identify, clean and test 18 factor cohorts (or style categories) from which we construct the 18 enhanced smart betas (ESBs) as the indispensable building blocks for our MFMs.

For instance, the Book-to-Market (aka HML) factor of Fama-French fame ranks companies cross-sectionally based on this value metric taking the HML book-to-price stock portfolios in order to track the performance of said factor. The assumption is that monotonicity in the out-of-sample performance of factor fractiles would yield positive spread returns and ICs (information coefficient) for the market-neutral construct described herein. While academics often consider terciles or quintiles, we have deliberately chosen 5%-tile equal-weighted spreads to be consistent with industry norms as most fundamental managers would not be able to track or run more than about 150 × 150 names on a long versus short basis.

Typical rationales for the success of investment factors are commonly classified through two primary lenses: risk-based and behavioral-based explanations. The risk-based view gained prominence with Fama and French's (1993) foundational work, which argued that factors like value reflect compensation for bearing systematic risks. By contrast, the behavioral-based view, expanded on by authors like Daniel et al. (1998), attributes anomalies such as momentum to systematic cognitive biases in investor behavior, like herding or underreaction to new information.

Beyond these static rationales, a dynamic approach based on factor timing has gained prominence. Factor momentum, as an extension of traditional factor investing, focuses on the idea that the past returns of factors themselves can predict future performance. This concept leverages both cross-sectional and time-series momentum effects at the factor level, capturing persistent return trends observed across multiple markets (Arnott et al., 2021; Ehsani & Linnainmaa, 2022; Gupta & Kelly, 2019). For instance, while cross-sectional factor momentum involves ranking factors against each other, time-series factor momentum assesses a single factor's historical performance to inform long or short positions. Recent research also shows that factor momentum strategies not only produce significant alpha but also provide stability and defensive characteristics during volatile market conditions (Gu & Mulvey, 2021a). These strategies have demonstrated reliable performance by capitalizing on the persistence of factor returns, offering investors an additional method to enhance risk-adjusted returns within a multifactor framework. We extend the literature with our own contribution to this topic in Chapter 8.

2.8. TAMING THE FACTOR ZOO

Over the past three decades, academic research into factors and anomalies has greatly enhanced our understanding of the market. While many well-established factors have proven their worth, the sheer volume of proposed factors has led to significant challenges. John Cochrane, in his seminal 2011 American Finance Association (AFA) presidential address, raised concerns about this proliferation, famously referring to it as the *factor zoo*. Cochrane's question – "how many of these factors are really important?" – underscored the validity concern and spurred a vigorous debate over whether multifactor models should be sparse or comprehensive.

Cochrane's concerns are reflected in subsequent research surrounding both internal and external validity challenges. Internal validity issues, where results cannot be properly reproduced, were highlighted by Hou et al. (2020), who alerted that "most anomalies fail to hold up to currently acceptable standards for empirical finance." External validity, where results fail in new samples, is another crucial issue. Campbell Harvey, a leading voice in this area, addressed the risks of false discovery from *p*-hacking and multiple testing, suggesting many reported factors would not replicate under stricter statistical scrutiny (Harvey et al., 2016). This sentiment was echoed by Linnainmaa and Roberts (2018), who found many accounting-based anomalies were likely products of data snooping. In his 2017 AFA address, Harvey further argued that academic incentives promote selective reporting, artificially inflating the number of "valid" factors and reinforcing the need for stricter significance thresholds.

In response to the challenges of the factor zoo, researchers developed methodologies that impose sparsity constraints. Feng et al. (2020), in their influential paper, "Taming the Factor Zoo," offered a systematic framework using machine learning and a double-selection LASSO (Least Absolute Shrinkage and Selection Operator) to isolate factors with genuine predictive power. Their results showed that out of 150 candidate factors, only a select few consistently held predictive power, supporting the case for sparse models. A middle-ground approach was proposed by Kozak et al. (2020), who argued that using a greater number of factors, constrained by shrinkage techniques, improved out-of-sample performance. They employed principal component analysis to create a sparse representation from a larger set of factor information, bridging the gap between sparse and complex models.

However, recent research has challenged the prevailing efforts to "tame the factor zoo." Chen et al. (2023) questioned the academic community's systematic bias against data-mined factors, demonstrating that such factors can match or even outperform peer-reviewed factors in out-of-sample performance. At the same time, a series of studies led by Bryan Kelly challenges the pursuit of sparse models, proposing the potential of complex models with proper regularization. Jensen et al. (2023) suggested the replication crisis is less severe than previously portrayed, while Kelly et al. (2024) argued for "the virtue of complexity" in prediction. This perspective is notable, as Dacheng Xiu – a coauthor of the influential Feng et al. (2020) paper advocating for sparsity – also coauthored a book with Bryan T. Kelly titled *Financial Machine Learning (Foundations and Trends in Finance)* (2023), suggesting a nuanced view on the role of model complexity. This recent leaning toward complex factor models has drawn criticism. Harvey (2022) questioned the assumptions underlying the methodology of Jensen et al. (2023), while Jonathan Berk (2023) criticized Kelly et al. (2024) by arguing their results are narrow and that their reliance on shrinkage techniques actually aligns with the principle of parsimony.

The debate over complexity versus sparsity in factor research is likely to continue. Fortunately, the development of standardized datasets, such as those pioneered by Green et al. (2017) in the United States and Jensen et al. (2023) globally, has advanced the goal of promoting consistency and replicability in factor testing. These standardized datasets reinforce the value of factor investing as a disciplined approach to portfolio construction, targeting factors that contribute to stable, risk-adjusted returns across different market conditions.

2.9. WHAT ARE SMART BETAS?

While factor ranks are developed based on a single definition, our enhanced smart betas (ESBs) combine a range of factors within each cohort with the objective of outperforming the naive benchmark factor. Smart betas therefore represent thematic clusters of factors like value or growth and are often also called interchangeably risk-premia in industry parlance, although a priori one need not expect all smart betas to deliver risk-premia. The smart beta label started as a marketing gimmick and has caught on to the extent that it allows for the differentiation of "smarter" fundamental factor-weighted indices versus the default market capitalization-weighted ones.

Continuing the example of value cohort from before, the deep value (DV) smart beta would combine multiple factors, including trailing price-to-book, forward price-to-book, trailing sales-to-enterprise value, forward sales-to-enterprise value, and so on.

2.10. WHY COMBINE FACTORS WITHIN THE SAME COHORT?

The following are the key reasons why one might combine factors intra-cohort to form ESBs:

- **Negate outlier effects.** While there are multiple techniques such as winsorization or trimming out of outliers, these techniques come with their own pros and cons. Outliers need to be dealt with at the single factor level, but on aggregation across factors at the cohort level, outliers usually cancel out due to shrinkage, although occasionally they may be magnified.

- **Capture true risk-premia.** The majority of smart beta exchange-traded funds (ETFs) are based on a few well-known factor definitions within each factor cohort. More recently, researchers have found multiple other factors to be significant related to stocks returns. Popular factors, such as book-to-price, 12-month price momentum, are perhaps not surprisingly the most arbitraged ones, hence not among the most significant ones in their respective cohorts. Our extensive factor library combined with our innovative factor blending techniques enables us to capture the true risk-premia associated with factors while attempting to outperform their better-known naive brethren, which we use as our cohort benchmarks.
- **Enhance performance across market cycles.** Factor cyclicality is now becoming better recognized as a result of the risk-on/risk-off behavior entering the market vernacular. Our affiliated hedge fund was early in the application of regime-based factor investing. Indeed, our regime-based approach to timing and tilting on ESBs truly delivered promising results through the COVID crash of Q1 2020 and the subsequent rebound. Hedging via the "generic crash factor" is a logical extension to this approach where we solve for the optimal combination of our liquid ESBs and sector ETFs to express a bearish view.
- **Harvest factor dispersion within cohorts.** The most obvious and compelling reason to combine factors intra-cohort is to benefit from overweighting the better ones ex ante. Clearly, this can work well to the investor's benefit provided the ex post results confirm the choice of factor weightings. In other words, the historical factor ICs, returns and *t*-stats should have some out sample predictive power.

The box-whisker plot below shows us that different factors within our DV ESB exhibit rather different distributional characteristics. This dispersion allows us to enhance the risk-adjusted performance of our ESBs. The hope is that by ensembling factors within the DV cohort one may obtain better distributional characteristics at the ESB level. Figure 2.1 is a long-short portfolio's monthly returns for 2000–2019 developed using the top 5% and bottom 5% stocks for each factor definition. The litmus test for our approach is of course LIVE performance. Interestingly, our out-of-sample outperformance particularly in 2021 and 2022 has been impressive (matched only by the Nasdaq crash era) and in most cases higher than the in-sample back tests. This has provided live validation of the rigor and conceptual soundness of our approach.

Since we combine information from multiple different factors within each factor cohort to form the ESB ranks we are usually able to generate superior risk-adjusted performance

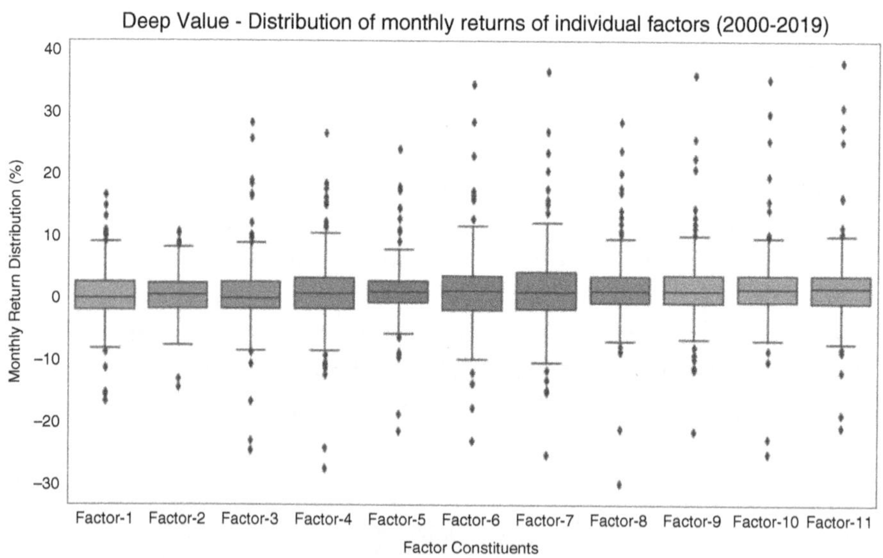

Figure 2.1 DV Distribution of Individual Factors' Monthly Returns.

versus the naive benchmark factor, which in this would be current book-to-price for the DV ESB cohort. The substantial out performance of our DV ESB versus the Fama-French book-to-price (HML factor) naive benchmark is easily verified from the 20-year cumulative returns in Figure 2.2 (as well as the subsequent LIVE period).

We now look at the factor dispersion within the Momentum cohort, where once again it is quite clear that not all factors are equal. This is because the better-known 12-month price momentum (first from left in Figure 2.3) has the worst crashes as compared to our risk-adjusted versions to the right. Not surprisingly, our process tends to overweight the better-behaved proprietary versions, which results in our enhanced momentum ESB faring much better after market inflection points. Indeed, it is during such short covering rallies that the worst momentum crashes occur, which our enhanced momentum ESB, is able to sidestep to a large extent as per Table 2.2. Indeed, we see that our enhanced momentum ESB outperforms in both bull and bear markets as per Tables 2.2 and 2.3 (particularly in the LIVE period).

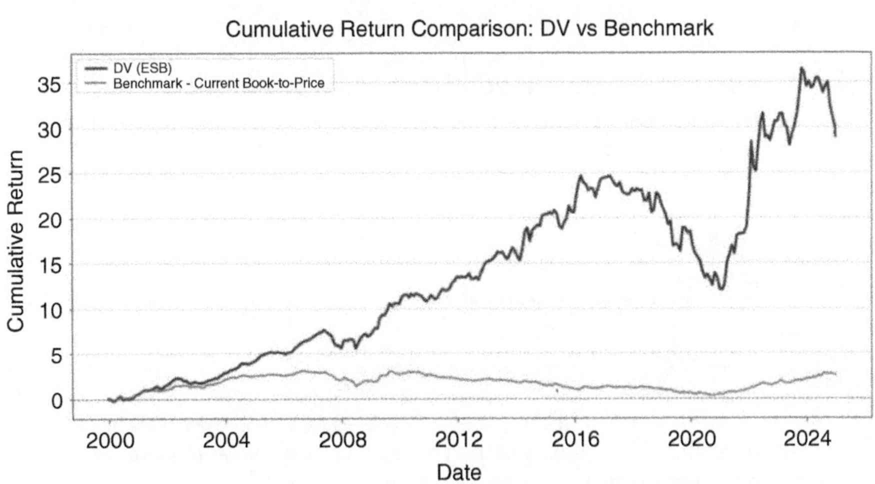

Figure 2.2 DV Cumulative Return – 25Y.

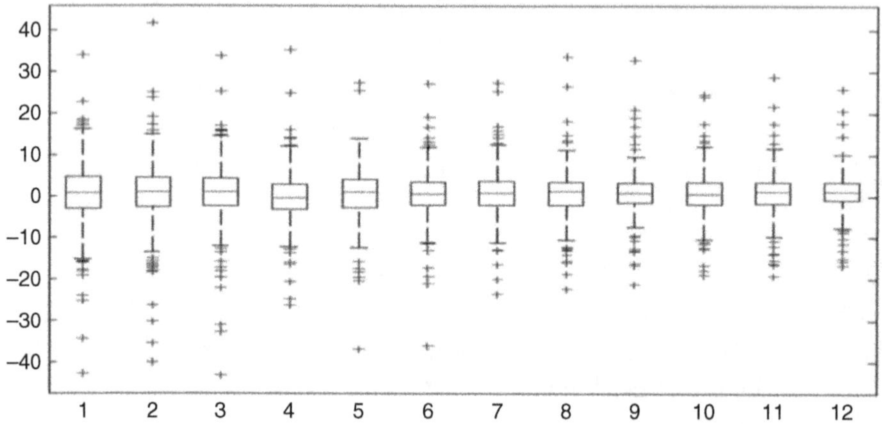

Figure 2.3 Momentum Factor Dispersion.

Table 2.2 Momentum at Inflection Points.[7]

Inflection Points	12Mo Mom	EnMom	EnMom Long	EnMom Short
2008	−8.3%	+24.1%	−35.3%	−45.6%
2009	−72.2%	−36.9%	4.3%	60.8%
2016	−26.3%	−9.4%	9.5%	23.6%

Table 2.3 Enhanced Momentum During Runups.

Momentum Runup	12Mo Mom	EnMom
2000–2008	−11.6%	+123.6%
2009–2015	−25.7%	+3.5%
2017–2018	+8%	+14.1%

[7] It is important to note that since multiplication and addition are not commutative operators, these numbers will not exactly cross-foot or down-foot due to geometric compounding of the spread returns in the multi-period case.

For further evidence of ESB out-of-sample efficacy we need only consider their Sharpe ratios versus the naive benchmark factor as per Figure 2.4 – shown in descending order of Sharpe ratios. In all cases except for SIRF (Short-Interest Ratio/ Short-Interest to Float) – where there are too few factors in the cohort for the ensemble to add value – we find that the QMIT ESBs outperform naive benchmark factors by a wide margin. Further, one can make the analogous observation for Sortino ratios in descending order (Figure 2.5). Visual inspection shows the significant outperformance of QMIT ESBs in both return and risk-adjusted terms particularly for the top performers like leverage, risk, profitability, growth, DV, RV, CSU, stability, and so on. Strikingly true for the LIVE 2021–2022 period in which we saw the dramatic resurgence of factor investing alphas and ICs as financial

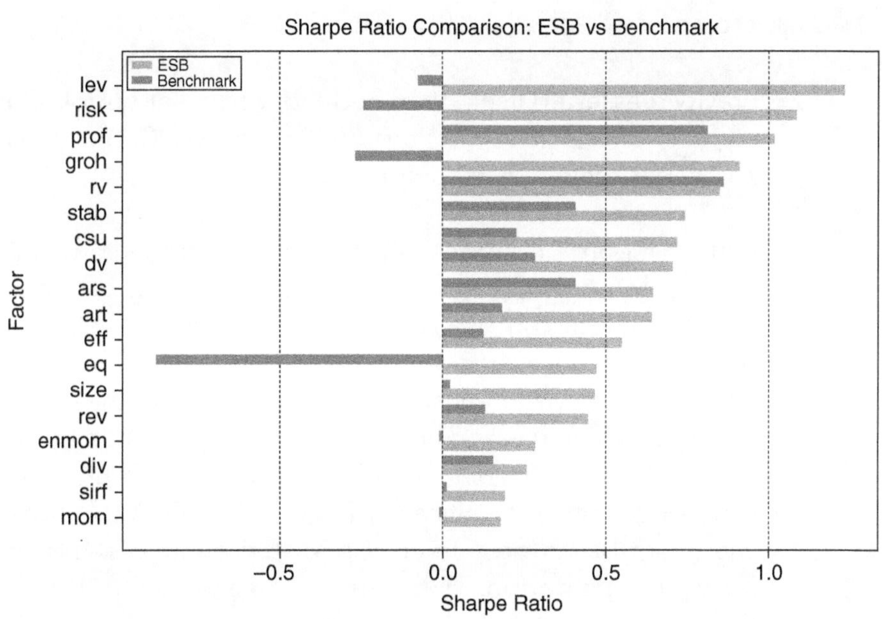

Figure 2.4 ESB BFOM Beta-Neutral Sharpe Ratios 25Y.

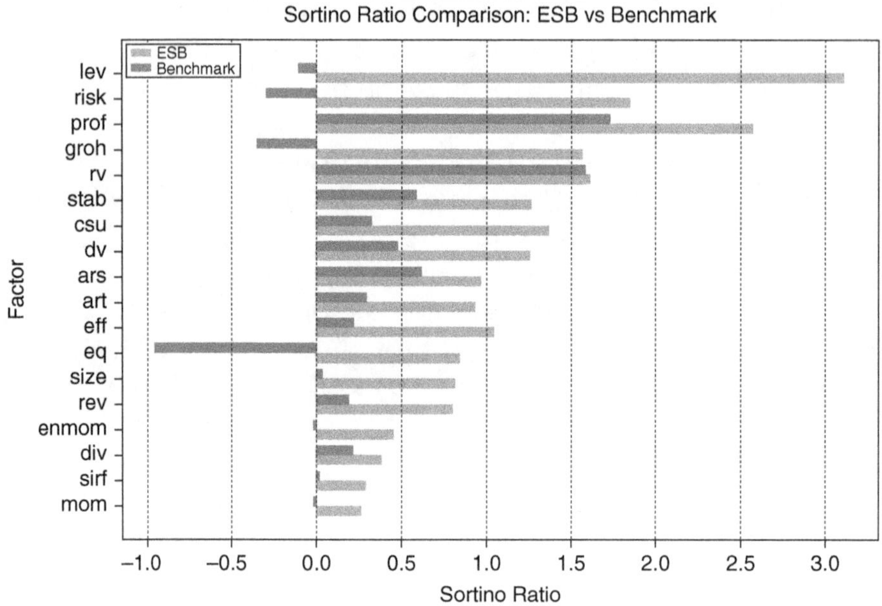

Figure 2.5 BFOM Beta-Neutral Sortino Ratios – 25Y.

gravity reasserted itself upon Fed-induced asset bubbles in cryptos, SPACs (Special Purpose Acquisition Companies) and hyper-growth tech companies.

Further, Figure 2.6 shows QMIT ESBs in descending order of 25Y pooled ICs. ICs are computed as the Spearman rank correlation (but can also be done as a Pearson correlation) of cross-sectional ranks today versus the forward month's return. Hence, the IC encapsulates information for the entire rank order of alphas and not just the information in the top/bottom fractiles. Further, the IC *t*-stats demonstrate a high level of statistical significance (Figure 2.7). Both of these charts are based on pooled ICs for the entire 300-month (25-year) time period. The same can also be computed as the mean of monthly ICs (either Spearman or Pearson correlations).

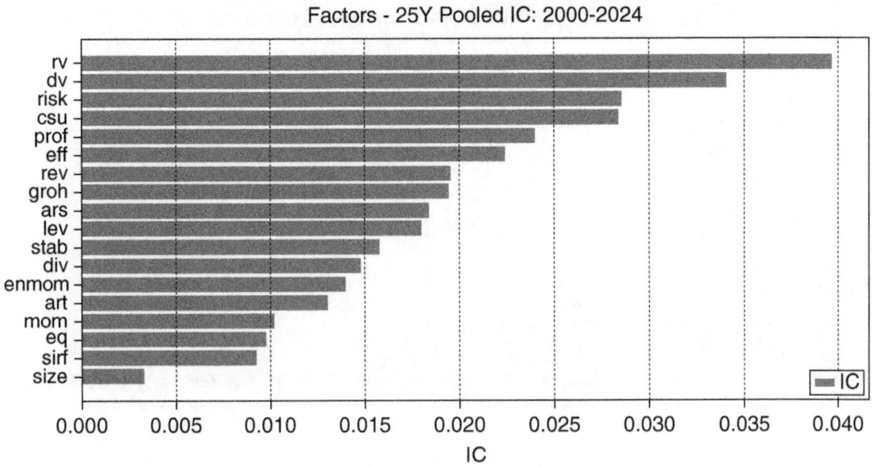

Figure 2.6 25Y Pooled ICs for ESB BFOMs.

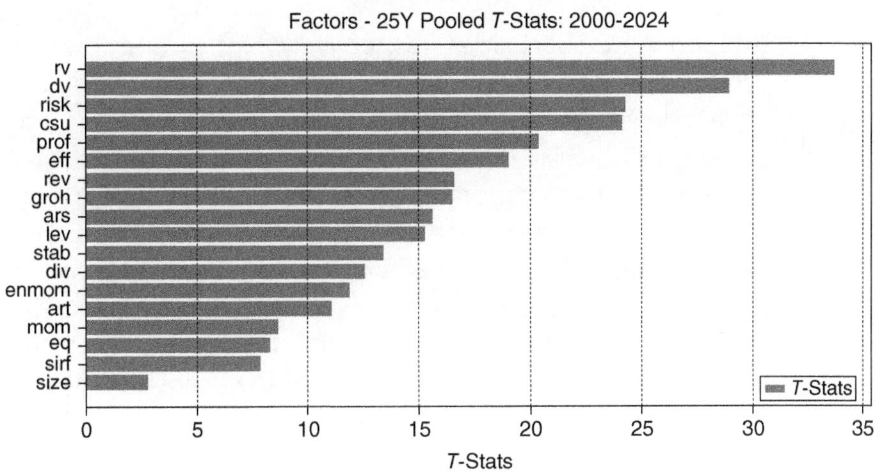

Figure 2.7 25Y Pooled IC *T*-Stats for ESB BFOMs.

Figure 2.8 shows turnover in ascending order for ESB BFOMs since lower turnover is better from the standpoint of transaction costs. We compute two-way turnover[8] showing the sum of average ratios of stocks flipped each month on

[8] The definition of turnover can be found in Chapter 9, Section 9.1.

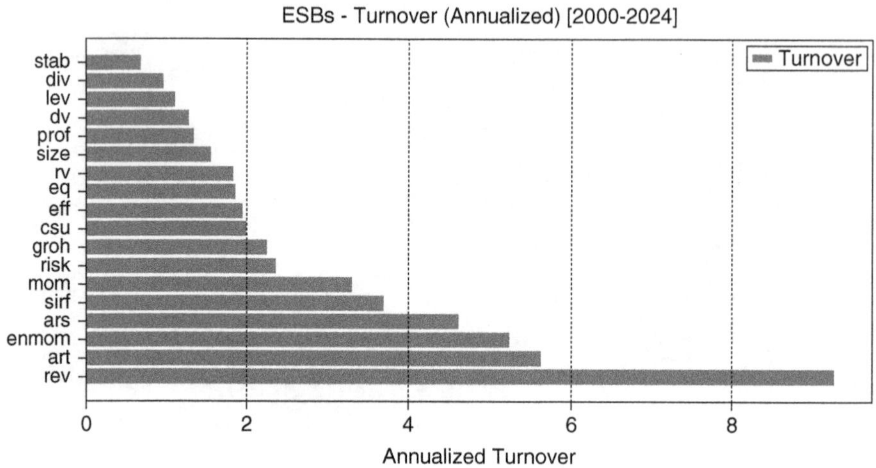

Figure 2.8 ESBS – BFOM Turnover 25Y.[9]

the long and short sides, respectively. Not surprisingly, the slower moving purely fundamental factor cohorts like stability and leverage have the lowest turnover in stark contrast to reversals (which is our mean reversion proxy for statistical arbitrage). Also, consistent with intuition, we find price-based factors like momentum and ARS (Analyst Revisions), ART (Analyst Rating and Targets) (since analysts often update their price targets and estimates) to be among the highest turnover ESBs. In Section 4.4, subsequent to the introduction of composite signals, we shall consider the relative turnover of different composites comprised of ESBs in Figure 4.12.

2.11. FACTOR CYCLICALITY

A topic of much debate in factor investing is the question of factor cyclicality. While most of our factors (smart betas)

[9]The turnover here is calculated based on the monthly rebalanced portfolios of top versus bottom quintile stocks for each ESB.

have exhibited superior risk-adjusted returns over long time periods, over shorter horizons they may exhibit substantial cyclicality reflecting the cyclicality of markets and the underlying economy. Indeed, the value complex had seen substantial underperformance throughout the years of easy money driven by coordinated global central bank easing policies following the GFC. At the time of QMIT signals going live in 2019 many were tempted to significantly underweight value having given up on the factor. Needless to say, the dramatic resurgence of value in 2021–2022 propelled our ESBs and signals to spectacular triple digit gains. In 2022, when nearly all asset classes (except for commodities) and 60/40 were down, we once again saw extraordinary returns across our ESBs and signals both relative to the index and on an EMN basis as per our QUMN hedge fund in a box index presented in Chapter 9. History suggests that factor risk-premia can be monetized in the long run by patient investors, which is why our ensembles learn on an expanding window LTD. For pensions and endowments, it may be advisable to simply buy and hold exposure to factor risk-premia ideally through a multifactor approach as embodied by our composite signals thereby disintermediating the 2/20 hedge fund fees for obtaining factor exposures. A critical decision that institutional investors are often faced with is with respect to dealing with factor cyclicality. Potential approaches include the following:

- Set a longer horizon and weather the drawdowns but benefit from reversion to the LT mean.
- Learn on a shorter trailing window, which may better capture the current regime, but this approach will underperform after inflection points until the window catches up to the new reality, which is what happened in 2021 and 2022 subsequent to the Value resurgence.
- Adopt a multifactor approach thereby harvesting factor diversification.

- Adopt a factor timing/tilting mechanism for entry and exit (Chapters 7 and 8).
- Adopt a RORO (Risk-On/Risk-Off) regime-based framework for factor timing/tilting based on the regime (Chapter 7).

The approach deployed should depend on the investor's investment mandate and philosophy. In Chapter 7, we provide a detailed discussion of mapping ESBs into regimes; the RORO framework and "regime-aware" models based on statistical jumps.

Chapter 3

QMIT's Enhanced Smart Betas

QMIT (QuantZ Machine Intelligence Technologies, LLC) has developed 18 different enhanced smart betas (ESBs) based on extensive factor research over the past 25 years. To prevent look-ahead bias in representing a single 26-year time series for a given ESB, QMIT uses a BFOM (best flavor of the month) trading strategy that picks the "best flavor of the month" based on cumulative LTD (life-to-date) return and risk-adjusted metrics through T-1, ex ante, which preempts look-ahead bias. Finally, QMIT then constructs a series of composite signals based on these ESB BFOMs that we deploy toward testing out our various strategies.

Table 3.1 provides an overview of all QMIT ESBs and composite signals.

Table 3.1 ESBs and Composite Signals.

	ESB	Composite Signals
1	Deep Value (DV)	Famous Five
2	Relative Value (RV)	Sizzling Seven
3	Dividends (DIVS)	Fabulous 14
4	Reversals (REVS)	Enterprise 18
5	Price Momentum (PMOM)	Value Composite
6	Enhanced Momentum (EnMom)	Growth Momentum Composite
7	Analyst Revisions (ARS)	Quality Composite
8	Analyst Ratings and Targets (ART)	Value Momentum Composite
9	Growth – Historical (GROH)	Quality Momentum Composite
10	Quality – Earnings Quality (EQ)	Quality Value Composite
11	Quality – Leverage (LEV)	
12	Quality – Profitability (PROF)	
13	Quality – Capital Usage (CSU)	
14	Quality – Stability (STAB)	
15	Quality – Efficiency (EFF)	
16	Size	
17	Short Interest (SIRF)	
18	Risk (LOW VOL)	

A potential concern in all factor research is data mining, whereby factor formulations are tweaked in search of definitions that deliver the best in-sample performance. Data-mined factors may fail to deliver a comparable performance out-of-sample. We mitigate the chances of data mining by ensuring that only factors that have extensive validation from research as well as a clear economic rationale are selected, as opposed to clearly contrived formulations.

Table 3.2 provides an overview of our ESBs with the corresponding naive factors and academic references.

Table 3.2 Overview of QMIT ESBs.

No	QMIT ESBs	Acronym	Description	Benchmark
1	Deep Value	DV	Captures excess returns to value stocks based on intrinsic value metrics	Book-to-price
2	Relative Value	RV	Captures excess returns to value stocks based on relative valuation metrics	Earnings-to-price
3	Dividends	DIV	Captures excess returns to stocks that pay higher-than-average dividends	Quarterly dividend yield
4	Reversals	REV	Captures excess returns to stocks displaying mean reversion	Trailing 1-month return
5	Price Momentum	MOM	Captures excess returns to stocks experiencing trend continuation	Trailing 12-month return

(Continued)

Table 3.2 *(Continued)*

No	QMIT ESBs	Acronym	Description	Benchmark
6	Enhanced Momentum	EnMom	Captures excess returns to stocks experiencing trend continuation, enhanced to adjust for shorts vulnerable to short covering rallies	Trailing 12-month return
7	Analyst Revisions	ARS	Captures excess returns to stocks due to earnings momentum resulting from analyst revisions, consensus change, and so on	FY0 SUE score
8	Analyst Ratings and Targets	ART	Captures excess returns to stocks due to revisions in analyst recommendations and target prices	Distance to target price
9	Growth Historical	GROH	Captures excess returns to stocks that have higher-than-average historical growth	Three-year sales growth
10	Earnings Quality	EQ	Captures excess returns to stocks that are characterized by low accruals and so on	Total accruals

No	QMIT ESBs	Acronym	Description	Benchmark
11	Quality – Leverage	LEV	Captures excess returns to stocks with low leverage and related credit metrics	Debt-to-equity
12	Quality – Profitability	PROF	Captures excess returns to stocks with high profitability-related metrics	ROE
13	Quality – Capital Structure/Usage	CSU	Captures excess returns to firms owing to better capital structure and capital usage decisions	Cash-to-market cap
14	Quality – Stability	STAB	Captures excess returns to stocks with more stable financial ratios	Five-year EPS dispersion
15	Quality – Efficiency	EFF	Captures excess returns to stocks characterized by better operating efficiency metrics	AR change to NOA
16	Size	SIZE	Captures excess returns to smaller firms	Market cap
17	Short Interest	SIRF	Captures excess returns to stocks with lower short interest–related metrics	Short interest trend
18	Safety/Risk	RISK	Captures excess returns to stocks with lower-than-average volatility, beta, and/or idiosyncratic risk	3-year beta

3.1. QMIT'S ESB RANKING PROCESS

For a visual representation of QMIT's data pipeline and the methodology used to construct its 18 ESBs, please refer to Figure 3.1.

3.2. DATA PRE-PROCESSING

A critical step in the construction of smart beta lies in the pre-processing of input data to eliminate GIGO (garbage in, garbage out). Prior to assigning factor ranks to stocks, the underlying data goes through a thorough internal process that ensures that the factor ranks are not affected by outliers and missing data while dynamically handling issues relating to multiple share classes, adjustments for M&A/ corporate actions. The following describes in detail the steps undertaken by us in the data cleaning process.

- **Handling NA values.** Situations where factor ranks for stocks are unavailable; we fill NA values with a rank of 50 to maintain stock coverage (provided enough other attributes are populated) without affecting the distribution of ranks. One must re-rank once more after all such data pre-processing.
- **"As-was" tickers.** Our historical data, at each point in time, includes all tickers within our universe only at that particular point in time to prevent survivorship bias.
- **Lagged fundamentals.** Company fundamental data are subject to ex post revisions, leading to a common pitfall in back-testing wherein revised data are assumed to be available in advance. Our factor ranks are constructed based on conservatively lagged fundamentals ensuring

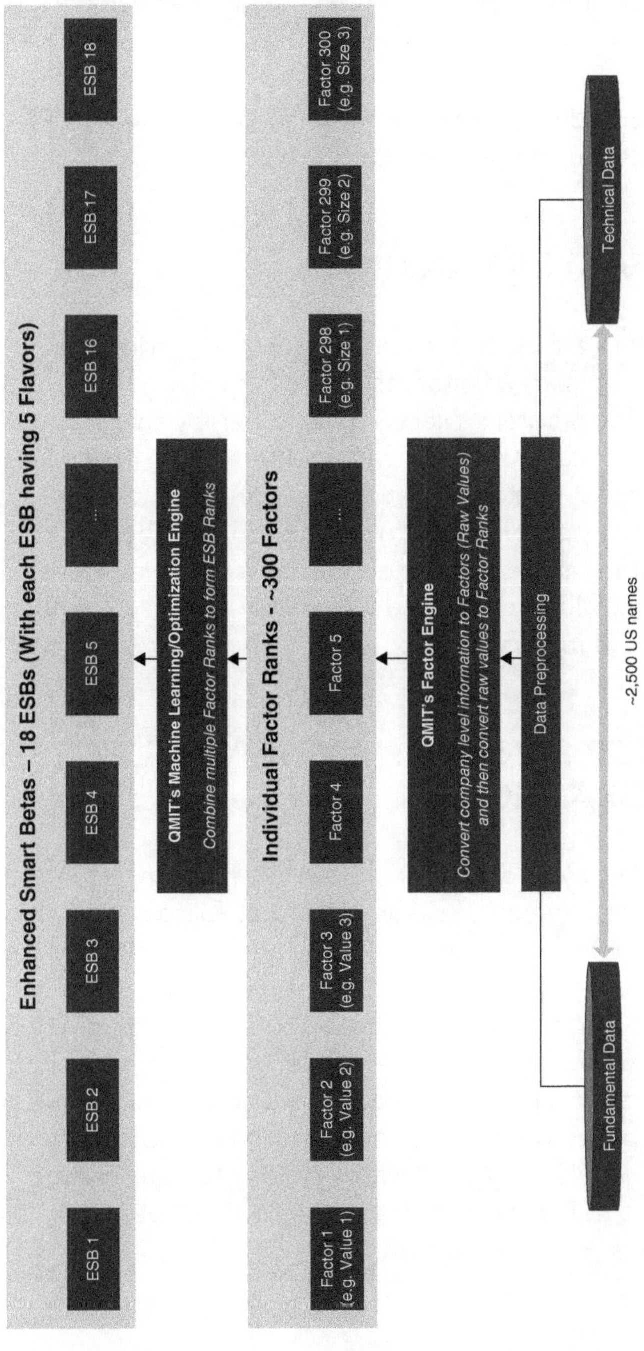

Figure 3.1 QMIT's Process Flow for Constructing ESBs.

that our model does not suffer from look-ahead bias. This does not affect data that was collected "live" by QuantZ since 2009.

- **Other adjustments.** These include the use of USD as numeraire, M&A, splits, corporate actions, and so on.

3.3. FACTOR RANKING

All factors are sorted in descending rank order (100 to 0) based on their raw factor ranks, and it is to be noted that our default factors are not sector neutral thereby enabling investors to tactically switch between sectors based on individual factor ranks. Sector allocation decisions are typically taken during the portfolio construction phase, and therefore, having ranks that are not sector neutralized provides investors flexibility, although we do separately track sector-neutral versions of factors as well.

3.4. ESB RANKING: MIXING VERSUS INTEGRATING

A simple way to diversify across factors is to invest in some linear combination of single-factor portfolios based on the desired weights. However, the academic and the practitioner literature largely agrees that this is an inefficient way of exploiting factor diversification. The more effective alternative is to fully "integrate" different factor ranks into a combined multifactor score and subsequently re-rank the alphas based on it. We follow this second and more robust route. Additionally, by choosing to integrate factors we arrive at ESB ranks rather than a portfolio of factors that facilitates multiple use cases.

- **Bottom-up approach.** We adopt a cross-sectional approach to ESB ranking that involves finding a weighted average factor rank. This bottom-up approach to the ESB portfolio construction is also known as "integrating" in the literature. The alternate methodology, known as "mixing," involves linear combinations of single-factor portfolios.
- **Flexible framework.** The integrating approach, while being computationally expensive, results in ranks for every stock in the universe, thereby making it a highly flexible framework. The mixing approach is an easier and more straightforward approach if the objective were to only develop a factor portfolio. It would enable us to move from individual factor portfolios to the ESB portfolio seamlessly without having to determine ESB ranks, thereby resulting in a large portfolio of stocks with likely conflicting positions that are complex to manage. Using the ESB integrated rank to form a portfolio naturally results in a more concentrated and consistent portfolio since the multifactor ranks represent the best of intersecting multifactor characteristics. Stocks where the multifactor rank characteristics effectively cancel out should land up in the middle with no conviction. Conviction lies in the tails hence the focus on top versus bottom spreads.

3.5. MOVING FROM CONSTITUENT FACTOR RANKS TO ESB RANKS

We employ different proprietary weighting schemas under a multifactor framework for combining individual factors intra-cohort to calculate the ESB ranks. For example, the DV ESB rank is determined based on factors including current book-to-price, current sales-to-price, among other such factors in the DV cohort.

Every stock in our universe has an ESB rank (0 to 100) for each of the ESBs every day. Stocks with lower ESB ranks are expected to have lower future returns, while stocks with higher ESB ranks are expected to have higher future returns. However, while the ordinal ranking reflects the embedded relative value, there is no absolute forecast of expected returns at the single stock level.

The different weighting methodologies require us to determine the performance of the individual factors based on compounding the long-short portfolio spread return of the dollar-neutral top 5% versus bottom 5% of stocks. Of course, one may choose to instead formulate this as a tercile or quintile spread, as is more common in the literature. The rationale for picking 5%-tiles out of a universe of about 3,000 names is that 150 × 150 stocks correspond better to the practicality of quantamental/fundamental manager mind space and attention bandwidth.

Here are the portfolio constructions for determining the performance of individual factors:

- Portfolio: Top 5% and bottom 5% are used for portfolio construction. To handle situations wherein the number of stocks with factor ranks is low, we have the following procedure:
  a. IF the total number of stocks ≥ 500, THEN take the top/bottom 5%-tile of the stocks.
  b. IF the 100 ≤ number of stocks < 500, THEN take the top 25 and bottom 25 stocks.
  c. IF the number of stocks < 100, THEN we set the fractile differential return to be 0% for that date. This is done because the universe of stocks for that date is not sufficiently large.
  d. The above logic leads to tie-breaker situations in some cases while selecting the stocks for top/bottom

portfolios. We handle these situations by choosing all the stocks corresponding to the threshold tie-breaker rank. This is particularly germane for factors like dividends where almost half of the universe pays a zero dividend, which means that the short portfolio may include all such names without the ability to further discern among them.

- Rebalancing discipline:
  a. **Monthly.** Investors worried about the transaction cost implications of excessive turnover ought to use this version of the model. Since one has access to daily ranks, it's worth considering which day of the month to rebalance on.
  b. **Daily.** All historical data available until December 2018 is on a month end basis since we only have "live" daily data from January 2019 onwards.
- All portfolios are tracked on a dollar-neutral basis, although we subsequently also report their beta-neutral performance separately (note that only involves dynamic beta hedge ratio adjustment and has no implications for the alpha ranks).
- Since market impact is really a function of investor assets under management (which we do not know prima facie), we simply leave out the impact of transaction costs as is customary in factor research. Besides, liquid equity commissions are now de minimis with some institutions trading for negative commissions. Even in the retail world zero commissions have become the new normal as a result of PFOF (payment for order flow).
- Transaction cost models and assessing impact would lead us down a different branch of the literature relating to market microstructure and trade execution that is not the central focus of factor investing; hence, we shall resist that digression till later chapters.

Performance estimation is subject to a variety of biases, which usually inflate historical returns. To minimize these biases, we adopt the following measures:

- **Survivorship bias.** QMIT historical data includes both live and dead companies. The inclusion of "as-was" dead tickers is critical to avoiding such bias. This is a typical error that neophytes are vulnerable to, and certainly many of the early industry attempts at long-term studies were flawed due to the lack of good data or attention to such detail. Accidentally (or conveniently) omitting real-life failures can significantly inflate the perception of reality and has led to the failure of many quant strategies in real life. Indeed, this is where the rubber meets the road.
- **Look-ahead bias.** QMIT history only includes data that was available to investors at that point in time or with suitably conservative lags. This bias is especially pernicious in this day and age of large language models and generative artificial intelligence, where it's not possible to easily hide data up to T-1 from models in a given back test.
- **Data mining.** Our objective is not to data mine contrived factors, but to focus only on factors that are supported by our research and trader intuition. In particular, that's why we reject the purely statistical approaches that often result in compelling but contrived back-tests that fail miserably out-of-sample. Recent literature suggests that there may be some merit to datamining nonsensical accounting ratios or factors not supported by investor intuition, but good luck explaining that to your board and investors.
- **Liquidity.** We only include stocks with a minimum market capitalization of $250 million to avoid contamination of results by micro-caps that are not institutionally tradable. In practice, investors may choose to deploy a higher

threshold for their buy list leaving some buffer before they choose to sell in order to minimize turnover.

- **Hindsight bias.** It is critical to only use information that was known ex ante through T-1 at time *T* without the benefit of hindsight else it would be rather convenient (cheating) to simply pick the "best" flavor ex-post with the benefit of hindsight (distinct from lookahead). In particular, this is why we track the BFOM strategy as the investable equivalent best flavor from our ensemble learners (see more in Section 3.6). While one may highlight the best flavor (or any flavor) ex post for the sake of brevity, the BFOM strategy is the obvious investable route that avoids the benefit of hindsight.

As mentioned, our ESBs judiciously combine a plethora of factors based on multiple techniques, which constitute the ensemble of learners from which the BFOM strategy is picked as the atomic unit of disclosure.

While the set of combinations and permutations possible for combining factors is clearly quite large and susceptible to data mining, we find that in practice the methodologies adopted yield robust results due to their being guided by market intuition and experience. Please note that across all ESBs, ranks for the first two years are calculated by equal weighting factors within a cohort since we need that as the anchor to initialize the learning process thereafter on an expanding window LTD. While we formulate multiple variants within each ESB, to succinctly publish the performance of a particular ESB, we show the results of the BFOM which is representative of the factor cohort based on the ensemble learners.

The following are some of the additional assumptions:

- Intra-cohort optimal factor weights are determined on a monthly basis. The month-end optimal factor weights are subsequently used for updating ESB ranks daily intra-month.

- The performance of each of the different techniques for the first 24 months will be identical to the equal-weighted case since all of the ensemble learners must be anchored by the initial 24 months.
- While blending factors (the techniques defined previously) to determine the ESB ranks, we screen out factors that have been determined as "perverse" factors based on these two criteria:
  a. If the annualized factor spread return LTD is less than zero AND
  b. If the LTD factor IC of the signal is less than or equal to zero
- Maximum weight for any factor in a given ESB is 1/3. If hypothetically, there are three or fewer "non-perverse" factors (as may happen in SIRF), then the 1/3 limit does not apply.

3.6. BFOM INVESTABLE STRATEGIES

We have a suite of 18 BFOM investable strategies based on our 18 ESBs, which systematically switch between the alternate ESB flavors as the atomic unit of disclosure as reflected in our ESB heatmaps. These alternate models for the same smart beta can be viewed as an ensemble of learners on an expanding window (to prevent look-ahead bias). Further, these models must re-optimize monthly (using only data through T-1 month-end) to solve for the optimal factor weights, which are used in calculating performance from T to T+1. To prevent look-ahead bias in representing a single LTD time series for a given ESB such as DV we must ensure that such a time series represents the performance of a BFOM trading strategy which picks the BFOM based on cumulative risk and return profile through T-1 ex ante, as we do not know a priori if that BFOM will in fact be the best performer in the coming month.

3.7. CORRELATIONS

The cross-sectional Spearman rank correlations for ESBs tell us how correlated the ESBs are at a given point in time. It's worth noting that cross-sectional factor rank correlations are based on the latest ranks across the entire universe while the historical return correlations are only based on the information in the tails (i.e., the 5%-tile spread returns). Figures 3.2–3.4 show various correlations matrices for perspective. For example, Figure 3.2 shows the rank correlations for QMIT ESBs (as of 12-31-24) cross-sectionally while Figure 3.3 shows three-year time-series returns correlations, and Figure 3.4 shows the same but on a 20-year trailing window.

Figure 3.5 shows ACF plots for dollar-neutral monthly BFOM ESBs and Enterprise 18 combo signal.

	ARS	ART	CSU	DV	Dividends	EQ	Efficiency	EnMOM	Growth	Leverage	PMOM	Profit	RV	Reversals	Risk	SIRF	Size	Stability
ARS	1.0	0.3	0.17	−0.21	−0.11	−0.01	−0.04	0.3	0.25	0.16	0.34	0.19	−0.04	0.01	0.03	−0.07	−0.25	0.09
ART	0.3	1.0	0.04	−0.23	0.03	−0.05	−0.07	0.46	0.08	0.01	0.53	0.03	−0.08	0.0	0.05	0.01	−0.08	−0.02
CSU	0.17	0.04	1.0	0.05	0.09	0.17	0.33	0.12	0.23	0.37	0.04	0.36	0.52	0.1	0.25	0.07	−0.25	0.28
DV	−0.21	−0.23	0.05	1.0	0.16	0.07	0.48	−0.2	−0.08	−0.15	−0.27	−0.19	0.33	0.05	0.05	0.08	0.14	0.24
Dividends	−0.11	0.03	0.09	0.16	1.0	−0.08	0.04	0.15	−0.21	0.11	−0.03	0.27	0.25	0.08	0.52	0.09	−0.17	0.21
EQ	−0.01	−0.05	0.17	0.07	−0.08	1.0	0.3	−0.02	0.05	−0.15	−0.01	−0.29	0.11	−0.03	−0.11	0.04	0.16	−0.09
Efficiency	−0.04	−0.07	0.33	0.48	0.04	0.3	1.0	−0.07	0.01	−0.15	−0.08	−0.17	0.34	0.06	−0.07	0.08	0.22	0.26
EnMOM	0.3	0.46	0.12	−0.2	0.15	−0.02	−0.07	1.0	0.12	0.05	0.86	0.11	−0.04	0.16	0.22	−0.05	−0.25	0.08
Growth	0.25	0.08	0.23	−0.08	−0.21	0.05	0.01	0.12	1.0	0.23	0.2	0.21	0.29	−0.01	−0.02	−0.02	−0.1	0.02
Leverage	0.16	0.01	0.37	−0.15	0.11	−0.15	−0.15	0.05	0.23	1.0	0.03	0.64	0.29	0.09	0.27	−0.0	−0.4	0.21
PMOM	0.34	0.53	0.04	−0.27	−0.03	−0.01	−0.08	0.86	0.2	0.03	1.0	0.05	−0.1	−0.03	−0.03	−0.11	−0.14	−0.07
Profit	0.19	0.03	0.36	−0.19	0.27	−0.29	−0.17	0.11	0.21	0.64	0.05	1.0	0.29	0.07	0.39	0.02	−0.48	0.19
RV	−0.04	−0.08	0.52	0.33	0.25	0.11	0.34	−0.04	0.29	0.29	−0.1	0.29	1.0	0.02	0.25	0.1	0.0	0.17
Reversals	0.01	0.0	0.1	0.05	0.08	−0.03	0.06	0.16	−0.01	0.09	−0.03	0.07	0.02	1.0	0.07	0.06	−0.15	0.21
Risk	0.03	0.05	0.25	0.05	0.52	−0.11	−0.07	0.22	−0.02	0.27	−0.03	0.39	0.25	0.07	1.0	0.11	−0.45	0.41
SIRF	−0.07	0.01	0.07	0.08	0.09	0.04	0.08	−0.05	−0.02	−0.0	−0.11	0.02	0.1	0.06	0.11	1.0	0.07	0.02
Size	−0.25	−0.08	−0.25	0.14	−0.17	0.16	0.22	−0.25	−0.1	−0.4	−0.14	−0.48	0.0	−0.15	−0.45	0.07	1.0	−0.36
Stability	0.09	−0.02	0.28	0.24	0.21	−0.09	0.26	0.08	0.02	0.21	−0.07	0.19	0.17	0.21	0.41	0.02	−0.36	1.0

Figure 3.2 C-S Rank Correlations for QMIT ESBs (12-31-24).

	ARS	ART	CSU	DV	Dividends	EQ	Efficiency	EnMOM	Growth	Leverage	PMOM	Profit	RV	Reversals	Risk	SIRF	Size	Stability
ARS	1.0	0.73	0.37	−0.04	0.1	−0.18	0.14	0.7	0.6	0.5	0.58	0.62	0.31	−0.09	0.61	0.27	−0.61	0.62
ART	0.73	1.0	0.49	0.07	0.33	−0.16	0.31	0.66	0.7	0.54	0.79	0.66	0.53	−0.36	0.69	0.28	−0.53	0.62
CSU	0.37	0.49	1.0	0.68	0.56	−0.03	0.85	0.17	0.37	0.87	0.47	0.81	0.87	−0.18	0.71	0.63	−0.13	0.82
DV	−0.04	0.07	0.68	1.0	0.39	−0.1	0.78	−0.2	0.14	0.62	0.11	0.42	0.71	−0.27	0.29	0.57	0.38	0.43
Dividends	0.1	0.33	0.56	0.39	1.0	0.11	0.42	−0.03	0.2	0.65	0.2	0.58	0.65	−0.53	0.63	0.63	−0.02	0.56
EQ	−0.18	−0.16	−0.03	−0.1	0.11	1.0	0.0	−0.19	−0.39	−0.16	−0.11	−0.21	−0.19	−0.16	0.06	0.02	0.34	−0.06
Efficiency	0.14	0.31	0.85	0.78	0.42	0.0	1.0	−0.03	0.18	0.7	0.31	0.61	0.79	−0.19	0.5	0.55	0.14	0.66
EnMOM	0.7	0.66	0.17	−0.2	−0.03	−0.19	−0.03	1.0	0.7	0.22	0.8	0.33	0.19	0.04	0.31	−0.04	−0.46	0.4
Growth	0.6	0.7	0.37	0.14	0.2	−0.39	0.18	0.7	1.0	0.49	0.78	0.51	0.54	−0.24	0.45	0.2	−0.39	0.47
Leverage	0.5	0.54	0.87	0.62	0.65	−0.16	0.7	0.22	0.49	1.0	0.48	0.88	0.89	−0.23	0.81	0.76	−0.23	0.87
PMOM	0.58	0.79	0.47	0.11	0.2	−0.11	0.31	0.8	0.78	0.48	1.0	0.48	0.53	−0.22	0.5	0.08	−0.31	0.52
Profit	0.62	0.66	0.81	0.42	0.58	−0.21	0.61	0.33	0.51	0.88	0.48	1.0	0.8	−0.27	0.87	0.7	−0.46	0.9
RV	0.31	0.53	0.87	0.71	0.65	−0.19	0.79	0.19	0.54	0.89	0.53	0.8	1.0	−0.35	0.72	0.65	−0.06	0.78
Reversals	−0.09	−0.36	−0.18	−0.27	−0.53	−0.16	−0.19	0.04	−0.24	−0.23	−0.22	−0.27	−0.35	1.0	−0.37	−0.35	−0.02	−0.18
Risk	0.61	0.69	0.71	0.29	0.63	0.06	0.5	0.31	0.45	0.81	0.5	0.87	0.72	−0.37	1.0	0.72	−0.46	0.88
SIRF	0.27	0.28	0.63	0.57	0.63	0.02	0.55	−0.04	0.2	0.76	0.08	0.7	0.65	−0.35	0.72	1.0	−0.17	0.75
Size	−0.61	−0.53	−0.13	0.38	−0.02	0.34	0.14	−0.46	−0.39	−0.23	−0.31	−0.46	−0.06	−0.02	−0.46	−0.17	1.0	−0.39
Stability	0.62	0.62	0.82	0.43	0.56	−0.06	0.66	0.4	0.47	0.87	0.52	0.9	0.78	−0.18	0.88	0.75	−0.39	1.0

Figure 3.3 3Y Return Correlations for QMIT ESBs (12-31-24).

	ARS	ART	CSU	DV	Dividends	EQ	Efficiency	EnMOM	Growth	Leverage	PMOM	Profit	RV	Reversals	Risk	SIRF	Size	Stability
ARS	1.0	0.78	0.29	−0.28	0.03	−0.25	−0.05	0.58	0.56	0.37	0.66	0.49	0.07	−0.44	0.55	0.21	−0.49	0.46
ART	0.78	1.0	0.2	−0.28	−0.07	−0.24	−0.08	0.57	0.53	0.32	0.68	0.38	0.01	−0.33	0.45	0.23	−0.36	0.33
CSU	0.29	0.2	1.0	0.64	0.69	0.39	0.78	−0.02	0.47	0.69	0.1	0.76	0.8	−0.22	0.76	−0.05	−0.3	0.77
DV	−0.28	−0.28	0.64	1.0	0.6	0.42	0.86	−0.43	0.09	0.36	−0.4	0.33	0.79	0.13	0.31	−0.15	0.08	0.43
Dividends	0.03	−0.07	0.69	0.6	1.0	0.36	0.64	−0.2	0.25	0.49	−0.12	0.55	0.69	−0.13	0.67	−0.14	−0.28	0.57
EQ	−0.25	−0.24	0.39	0.42	0.36	1.0	0.49	−0.14	−0.17	0.1	−0.1	0.05	0.28	0.05	0.16	−0.25	0.13	0.17
Efficiency	−0.05	−0.08	0.78	0.86	0.64	0.49	1.0	−0.2	0.19	0.44	−0.14	0.46	0.81	−0.01	0.48	−0.14	−0.02	0.53
EnMOM	0.58	0.57	−0.02	−0.43	−0.2	−0.14	−0.2	1.0	0.29	0.08	0.9	0.14	−0.14	−0.21	0.19	0.22	−0.14	0.07
Growth	0.56	0.53	0.47	0.09	0.25	−0.17	0.19	0.29	1.0	0.58	0.43	0.65	0.45	−0.24	0.57	0.07	−0.34	0.44
Leverage	0.37	0.32	0.69	0.36	0.49	0.1	0.44	0.08	0.58	1.0	0.2	0.84	0.7	−0.3	0.75	0.18	−0.41	0.68
PMOM	0.66	0.68	0.1	−0.4	−0.12	−0.1	−0.14	0.9	0.43	0.2	1.0	0.27	−0.06	−0.38	0.34	0.23	−0.25	0.19
Profit	0.49	0.38	0.76	0.33	0.55	0.05	0.46	0.14	0.65	0.84	0.27	1.0	0.7	−0.3	0.82	0.13	−0.52	0.74
RV	0.07	0.01	0.8	0.79	0.69	0.28	0.81	−0.14	0.45	0.7	−0.06	0.7	1.0	−0.09	0.62	−0.01	−0.16	0.62
Reversals	−0.44	−0.33	−0.22	0.13	−0.13	0.05	−0.01	−0.21	−0.24	−0.3	−0.38	−0.3	−0.09	1.0	−0.39	−0.21	0.35	−0.31
Risk	0.55	0.45	0.76	0.31	0.67	0.16	0.48	0.19	0.57	0.75	0.34	0.82	0.62	−0.39	1.0	0.08	−0.54	0.81
SIRF	0.21	0.23	−0.05	−0.15	−0.14	−0.25	−0.14	0.22	0.07	0.18	0.23	0.13	−0.01	−0.21	0.08	1.0	−0.14	0.06
Size	−0.49	−0.36	−0.3	0.08	−0.28	0.13	−0.02	−0.14	−0.34	−0.41	−0.25	−0.52	−0.16	0.35	−0.54	−0.14	1.0	−0.49
Stability	0.46	0.33	0.77	0.43	0.57	0.17	0.53	0.07	0.44	0.68	0.19	0.74	0.62	−0.31	0.81	0.06	−0.49	1.0

Figure 3.4 20Y Return Correlations for QMIT ESBs (12-31-24).

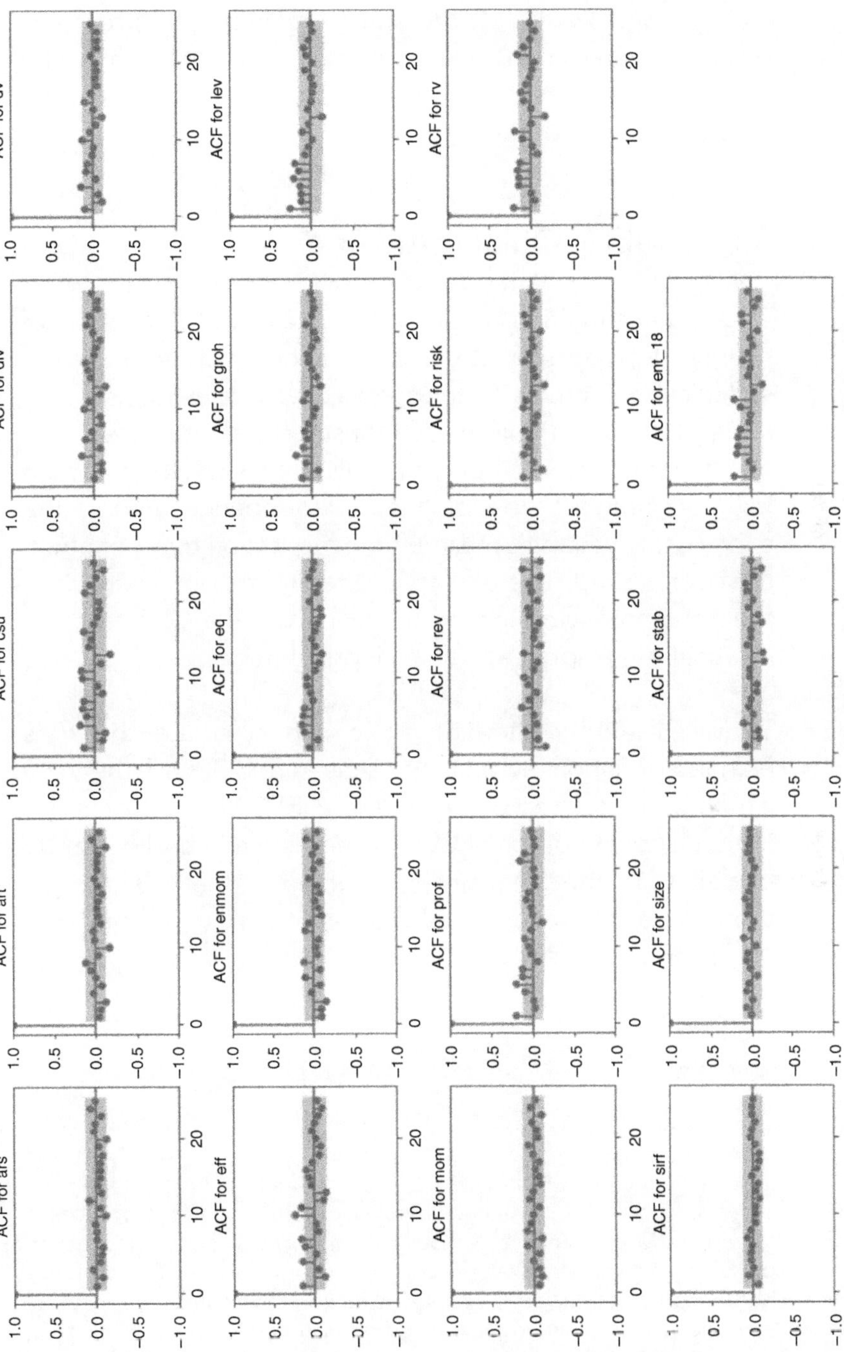

Figure 3.5 24Y ESB ACF Plots (10-31-23).

Figure 3.5 shows that if the autocorrelation coefficient lies outside of the shaded area, it is statistically significant at the 5% significance level. Factor momentum is noted in certain previous fundamentals.

3.8. MULTICOLLINEARITY

The issue of multicollinearity often arises in the analysis of financial time-series data. Given that our ESBs are not pure statistical constructs (orthogonalized by construction) but largely based on the intuitive industry standard clusters, it is worth checking whether multicollinearity may become an issue. A high degree of linear dependence among the explanatory variables in a multiple regression may not affect the overall predictive efficacy of the model, but it can make the estimated coefficients unreliable as they can change erratically in response to small input changes.

To assess multicollinearity, one can calculate the VIFs (Variance inflation factors).[1] For a given ESB BFOM, the $VIF(i)$ would be calculated by taking the ith BFOM and regressing it against every other BFOM to see how much of it can be explained by the other BFOMs. If the R^2 of that OLS is high, then as per the following definition, the $VIF(i)$ will be high, suggesting collinearity:

$$VIF(i) = \frac{1}{1 - R^2(i)}$$

[1] Several alternative approaches have been proposed. One such method is ridge regression, which regularizes the model by shrinking the coefficients especially of correlated features toward (but not exactly) zero thereby reducing variance without eliminating predictors. By contrast, the Least Absolute Shrinkage and Selection Operator (LASSO) performs both regularization and feature selection by constraining some coefficients – often among correlated predictors – down to exactly zero, thereby producing a sparser and more interpretable model.

Table 3.3 VIFs of 18 ESBs.

SIRF	REV	SIZE	EQ	GROH	STAB	DIV	ART	LEV
1.42	1.64	1.95	2.50	3.09	4.11	4.44	4.91	5.04
ARS	PROF	CSU	RISK	**EnMom**	**RV**	**EFF**	**DV**	**MOM**
5.26	6.80	7.83	9.05	***10.26***	***10.45***	***10.73***	***11.89***	***14.47***

A VIF (i) exceeding 10 would indicate unacceptably high multicollinearity for the ith BFOM. The ESB data used are the monthly BFOM returns of the 18 ESBs from December 1999 to December 2019. The corresponding VIFs are shown in Table 3.3.

As per Table 3.3, EnMom, RV, EFF, DV, and MOM constitute five ESBs with VIFs clearly in excess of 10 (bolded items in the table). This is no surprise since RV and DV are closely related (as are MOM and EnMom) but can logically be replaced by the corresponding composites.

To mitigate the multicollinearity evidenced above, we replace DV and RV with the value composite (VAL), as per Table 3.4. In addition, we replace ARS, ART, EnMom, and GROH with the growth-momentum composite (GrowthMo),[2] which leaves us with 14 explanatory variables: CSU, DIV, EFF, EQ, LEV, MOM, PROF, REV, RISK, SIRF, SIZE, STAB, VAL, and GrowthMo. Now, we re-calculate the VIFs for these 14 variables to note that all VIFs are now under 10 with only EFF and VAL over 9 (see Table 3.4).

While some sources consider VIFs < 10 to suffice others are much more conservative in the level of this threshold. Hence, we now investigate VIFs where all corresponding

[2]Please refer to Chapter 4, Section 4.4 for the definition of composite trading signals.

Table 3.4 VIFs After Replacing Highly Correlated ESBs with Composites.

SIRF	REV	SIZE	EQ	STAB	DIV	LEV
1.38	1.42	1.84	2.07	3.64	4.15	4.50
MOM	PROF	GrowthMo	CSU	RISK	VAL	EFF
5.80	6.23	6.76	7.15	8.63	9.14	9.43

ESBs have been replaced with their composites (which incrementally amounts to collapsing six ESBs into Qual). The resulting VIFs are presented in Table 3.5, which shows that all values are now well under 10, with only four (MOM, GrowthMo, RISK, and Qual) exceeding a VIF of 5.

Finally, noting the high correlation between MOM and GrowthMo we recompute VIFs without MOM. As expected, we see that the GrowthMo VIF drops sharply by 52% to 2.90 once we remove MOM given that MOM and EnMom have 0.91 correlation. Table 3.6 shows the logical progression and deflation of VIFs along this journey, which in the end leads us to a set of eight predictors (in ascending VIFs) where collinearity is reasonably under control.

The punchline is that a parsimonious subset of predictors which still encapsulates the most diverse/non-overlapping alphas would be the following eight variables (in order of ascending VIFs–Variance Inflation Factors), of which VAL, Qual, and GrowthMo are composites each with multiple ESBs embedded and several hundred constituent factors therein: *{SIRF, REV, SIZE, GrowthMo, DIV, VAL, RISK, Qual}*

Table 3.5 VIFs After Further Aggregation into Composite Factors.

SIRF	REV	SIZE	DIV	VAL	MOM	GrowthMo	RISK	Qual
1.29	1.34	1.69	3.83	4.99	5.13	6.03	6.77	8.15

Table 3.6 VIFs Across Factor Selection Process *{SIRF, REV, SIZE, GrowthMo, DIV, VAL, RISK, Qual}*.

BFOMs/ Composites	ESBs	BFOM and Composite	BFOM + GroMo + ValC w/o Mom	BFOM + GroMo + ValC + Qual	BFOM + GroMo + ValC + Qual w/o Mom
SIRF	1.42	1.38	1.34	1.29	1.27
REV	1.64	1.42	1.40	1.34	1.32
SIZE	1.95	1.84	1.84	1.69	1.69
EQ	2.50	2.07	1.90		
GROH	3.09				
STAB	4.11	3.64	3.64		
DIV	4.44	4.15	4.10	3.83	3.82
ART	4.91				
LEV	5.04	4.50	4.45		
ARS	5.26				
PROF	6.80	6.23	6.21		
CSU	7.83	7.15	7.09		
RISK	9.05	8.63	8.55	6.77	6.76
EnMom	10.26				
RV	10.45				
EFF	10.73	9.43	9.43		
DV	11.89				
MOM	14.47	5.80		5.13	
GrowthMo			3.15	6.03	2.90
Val		9.14	8.95	4.99	4.82
Qual				8.15	8.15

We deliberately display the parsimonious subset in ascending order of VIFs to highlight SIRF and REV as the most orthogonal ESBs. This analysis is key toward a determination of the minimum set of ESBs and composites that one may wish to include among their set of alphas. *This also presents the rationale for the construction of our flagship Sizzling Seven composite signal.*

Chapter 4

From Smart Betas to Smarter Alphas

QMIT's models encompass 18 enhanced smart betas (ESBs) and 12 composite signals with infinitely many more on a bespoke basis for a universe of about 4,000 stocks (as per Appendix A.1) with history going back to January 1, 2000. These ranks have multiple use cases including the following:

1. **Factor heatmaps**
   a. We have developed factor heatmaps based on our 18 ESBs, which would enable one to keep one's finger on the pulse of factors driving the market beneath the surface.
   b. Such factor heatmaps can be used by traders, asset managers, risk managers, and so on.

2. **Trading signals**
   a. The ESBs/combo ranks have been developed to be used as a trading signal.
   b. We demonstrate the efficacy of our ESBs/combo signals in our factor heatmaps using a simple top 5% versus bottom 5% portfolio construction (with dollar-neutral and beta-neutral versions).
   c. Since portfolio construction would be a function of the investment mandate, one would look at the ESBs and combo signals for the stipulated universe or subset of coverage.

3. **Factor exposures and hedging**
   a. Use QMIT's custom factor exposure framework to measure and monitor one's factor exposures.
   b. Deploy baskets to hedge out unwanted factor exposures.
   c. **Universal crash factor.** Our PCA (principal component analysis) and estimated crash beta-based optimal weights enable one to position for a crash using a combination of our ESBs and liquid sector exchange-traded funds (ETFs).

4. **Other use cases**
   a. **Screening and filtering**

Screen a broad universe of stocks to identify securities with desired characteristics which can be formulated as custom signals.

   b. **Alpha research**
      i. One can also use QMIT signals as an input to alpha research, by leveraging linear combination of our ESBs and combo signals to express any linear view on equities.

ii. One can easily back-test custom strategies in conjunction with other proprietary signals based on the long-term historical data.
iii. White labeled stock research signals for the sell side with cost efficient and instant coverage of a large universe.

c. **Risk and performance attribution**
   i. Use ESB ranks to build custom risk models that directly constrain the alphas without loss of information in going from raw alphas to optimal portfolios by constraining a less precise set of risk factors that are misaligned with the alphas.
   ii. Create performance attribution for manager/strategy evaluation using our factor exposures.

Finally, to take readers the last mile from signal spreads to fully baked hedge fund/mutual fund portfolios we also track the HEDGE FUND IN A BOX, which has substantially outperformed the most prominent factor investing peers in LIVE tracking. This index is being published LIVE daily by Canada's largest exchange (TMX) as the QUMN index for provision of exposure via bank QIS swaps.

4.1. FACTOR HEATMAPS

QMIT's factor heatmaps are intended to provide a real-time view of factor performance as embodied by our ESBs to help asset managers follow the factor narrative as it may affect their equity portfolios.

ESB Portfolio Construction

- **Factor weighting methodology.** As was explained in Chapter 3, Section 3.5, we use multiple weighting methodologies in developing the ESB ranks. Therefore, we have multiple ranks for each stock within each ESB and hence multiple portfolios for each ESB. For the sake of practicality and brevity, and to avoid look-ahead bias, we only display ESB ranks and performance based on best flavor of the month strategies (BFOMs) as proxies for the factor cohorts.

- **Choice of fractiles.** Most academic research on factor investing is based on long-short portfolios that take the top and bottom deciles, quintiles, or even terciles of the universe. Subsequent to liquidity and other criterion, our universe of 4,000 names shrinks down to under 3,000, which means that 30% of these tradable liquid stocks would result in a portfolio of upto 1,000 on either side in the case of terciles. We therefore reduce the top and bottom to 5%, that is, about 150 stocks on either side, which is more practical from a portfolio management perspective.
- **Rebalancing period.** We have both monthly and daily versions of the tracking heatmaps. While this may not matter as much for some purely fundamental ESBs it can be critical to the performance of ESBs where intra-month factor ranks are quite dynamic as with our analyst-based ESBs (such as ARS and ART), price-related ESBs (such as PMOM, EnMom, REV, RISK), short interest (SIRF), and so on. Even fundamental ESBs can benefit from timely updates due to earnings/news flow intra-month, which can substantially reshuffle the ESB factor ranks. It's important to note that while our daily heatmaps enable us to monetize the benefits of daily factor re-ranking intra-month, the *optimal factor weights and factor selection is still static intra-month* in order to prevent excessive turnover and unnecessary noise detracting from the signal.
- **Market neutrality.** We track both dollar- and beta-neutral versions.

- **Dollar neutrality.** On a daily basis, the long and short portfolio are given the same weights.
- **Beta neutrality.** The majority of factor research, including Fama-French factors, are constructed as being dollar neutral. While this may seem to suffice, the actual *net beta drift* of these long-short ESB portfolios can be substantial leading to a dramatic impact on future factor performance due to accidental beta rather than the factor fundamentals. While beta neutralization does not always improve factor performance it does provide us a with purer factor representation with lower volatility and a higher risk-adjusted profile. We have implemented beta neutrality in these ESBs by de-levering the side (long or short leg) with the higher beta to be conservative. We use three-year betas in order to equalize the long versus short legs.
- It behooves portfolio managers to understand and track the impact of dollar versus beta neutrality on factors comprising their combined signals.

Figures 4.1 and 4.2 illustrate these concepts by presenting daily last 12 months (LTM) factor performance heatmaps for dollar-neutral and beta-neutral ESBs.

Multi-period spread returns are not the difference of cumulative top versus bottom returns. Instead, they represent the daily geometrically compounded rebalancing of the market-neutral "active return" differential of the top versus bottom portfolios, which is a more realistic representation. LTD data commences in January 2000 for our life to date heatmaps. The first 19 years through December 2018 are based on monthly rebalancing while the live data from 2019 onwards is based on daily re-ranking of factors but with monthly re-optimization of factor weights within ESB cohorts for a given flavor.

	DTD Long	DTD Short	DTD Spread	MTD Long	MTD Short	MTD Spread	LTM Long	LTM Short	LTM Spread
DV	0.69%	−2.07%	2.76%	−5.66%	−3.36%	−3.12%	9.84%	23.93%	−14.13%
RV	0.84%	−0.77%	1.61%	−3.42%	−4.15%	0.07%	21.23%	17.17%	−1.91%
Efficiency	0.61%	−0.96%	1.57%	−4.57%	−4.96%	0.17%	9.16%	11.43%	−2.81%
Size	−0.16%	−0.32%	0.16%	−2.26%	−5.89%	3.9%	4.36%	22.63%	−14.81%
CSU	0.2%	−0.91%	1.11%	−5.74%	−2.27%	−4.0%	16.23%	21.88%	−8.14%
ARS	−0.15%	0.88%	−1.02%	−5.14%	−5.97%	0.83%	26.91%	−0.48%	25.35%
Profit	−0.08%	−1.54%	1.46%	−4.03%	−3.4%	−1.3%	15.58%	6.38%	2.51%
EnMoM	−0.51%	−0.14%	−0.37%	−6.13%	−5.25%	−1.02%	28.12%	6.33%	17.65%
Leverage	0.08%	−1.5%	1.58%	−4.04%	1.14%	−5.81%	18.73%	11.02%	1.93%
Growth	−0.04%	0.87%	−0.92%	−5.61%	−7.16%	1.6%	36.04%	4.84%	27.88%
ART	−0.21%	0.8%	−1.01%	−5.77%	−5.77%	−0.18%	21.43%	−6.2%	26.89%
Reversals	0.69%	−2.46%	3.14%	−6.23%	−6.66%	0.15%	14.12%	5.93%	6.53%
EQ	−0.57%	−0.01%	−0.56%	−3.27%	−5.07%	1.84%	14.94%	17.41%	−2.29%
PMOM	−1.81%	0.34%	−2.15%	−4.5%	−4.66%	0.06%	29.18%	0.71%	23.86%
Stability	0.41%	−1.8%	2.21%	−7.19%	−0.92%	−6.98%	9.91%	24.15%	−15.84%
SIRF	0.19%	−0.73%	0.92%	−6.12%	−5.23%	−1.06%	19.02%	20.98%	−2.86%
Dividends	0.62%	−0.19%	0.82%	−6.08%	−4.42%	−1.85%	12.61%	12.34%	−1.22%
Risk	0.36%	−2.77%	3.13%	−4.98%	−1.51%	−5.13%	12.38%	19.94%	−17.51%
RiskOn	0.4%	−0.92%	1.32%	−4.84%	−5.34%	0.24%	16.25%	15.27%	−0.3%
RiskOff	−0.15%	−0.62%	0.47%	−5.17%	−3.46%	−2.14%	18.73%	10.32%	4.84%
RORO Spread	0.55%	−0.3%	0.85%	0.33%	−1.88%	2.38%	−2.48%	4.95%	−5.14%

Figure 4.1 Dollar Neutral – Daily Heatmap LTM (12-31-24).

	DTD Long	DTD Short	DTD Spread	MTD Long	MTD Short	MTD Spread	LTM Long	LTM Short	LTM Spread
DV	0.69%	−1.39%	2.08%	−5.66%	−2.22%	−3.86%	9.9%	23.65%	−12.88%
RV	0.84%	−0.45%	1.29%	−3.43%	−2.32%	−1.3%	21.21%	13.49%	5.32%
Efficiency	0.61%	−0.84%	1.45%	−4.56%	−4.47%	−0.31%	8.03%	11.98%	−4.36%
Size	−0.13%	−0.32%	0.19%	−2.12%	−5.9%	4.04%	4.9%	22.48%	−14.54%
CSU	0.2%	−0.6%	0.8%	−5.77%	−1.53%	−4.43%	16.24%	17.68%	−2.58%
ARS	−0.13%	0.88%	−1.0%	−4.67%	−5.96%	1.31%	25.75%	−0.43%	23.99%
Profit	−0.08%	−1.02%	0.94%	−4.04%	−2.21%	−2.06%	15.49%	7.76%	5.01%
EnMoM	−0.47%	−0.14%	−0.33%	−5.96%	−5.02%	−1.07%	22.22%	8.1%	9.97%
Leverage	0.08%	−0.96%	1.04%	−4.05%	0.81%	−5.03%	18.68%	8.89%	6.27%
Growth	−0.04%	0.87%	−0.91%	−4.87%	−7.16%	2.36%	34.9%	4.92%	26.38%
ART	−0.21%	0.79%	−1.0%	−5.71%	−5.46%	−0.39%	20.19%	−4.55%	24.02%
Reversals	0.69%	−2.0%	2.69%	−6.17%	−4.87%	−1.55%	14.57%	5.84%	7.34%
EQ	−0.57%	−0.01%	−0.56%	−3.27%	−4.48%	1.22%	15.61%	15.71%	−0.27%
PMOM	−1.22%	0.34%	−1.57%	−3.43%	−4.68%	1.08%	19.36%	0.76%	13.04%
Stability	0.41%	−0.89%	1.3%	−7.18%	−0.35%	−7.0%	9.91%	15.39%	−5.94%
SIRF	0.19%	−0.53%	0.72%	−6.11%	−3.84%	−2.39%	19.01%	16.52%	1.87%
Dividends	0.62%	−0.12%	0.75%	−6.06%	−2.76%	−3.39%	12.63%	7.54%	4.77%
Risk	0.36%	−0.47%	0.83%	−4.99%	−0.22%	−4.8%	12.45%	4.39%	7.54%
RiskOn	0.41%	−0.67%	1.07%	−4.7%	−4.4%	−0.43%	16.07%	14.13%	1.3%
RiskOff	−0.09%	−0.2%	0.11%	−5.01%	−2.9%	−2.23%	17.14%	7.39%	7.8%
RORO Spread	0.5%	−0.47%	0.96%	0.31%	−1.5%	1.8%	−1.07%	6.74%	−6.5%

Figure 4.2 Beta Neutral – Daily Heatmap LTM (12-31-24).

Following this methodology, Figures 4.3 and 4.4 display the LTD 25-year heatmaps – incorporating 19 years of monthly rebalancing followed by 6 years of daily rebalancing from 2019 onwards – for dollar-neutral and beta-neutral approaches.

	3Y Long	3Y Short	3Y Spread	5Y Long	5Y Short	5Y Spread	LTD Long	LTD Short	LTD Spread
DV	15.16%	−2.34%	14.66%	24.92%	2.33%	18.41%	15.14%	−2.94%	17.11%
RV	17.89%	−3.8%	12.5%	27.4%	10.45%	9.13%	17.47%	0.81%	12.66%
Efficiency	12.82%	−17.83%	31.55%	21.31%	−9.27%	29.46%	11.01%	−1.11%	11.21%
Size	10.0%	3.4%	6.79%	13.0%	13.05%	0.68%	18.0%	6.18%	11.7%
CSU	11.77%	−4.51%	7.93%	17.57%	1.61%	8.08%	12.37%	0.56%	8.15%
ARS	10.81%	−1.55%	8.88%	20.14%	3.34%	10.57%	14.97%	2.83%	8.5%
Profit	5.98%	−13.35%	12.67%	13.29%	−2.83%	6.47%	10.37%	−3.11%	8.1%
EnMoM	7.69%	−4.67%	8.99%	16.19%	3.65%	7.69%	10.67%	1.14%	6.08%
Leverage	9.07%	−9.85%	11.53%	14.48%	−0.18%	6.37%	10.84%	−2.06%	8.24%
Growth	18.41%	1.69%	13.23%	25.65%	14.68%	6.1%	14.82%	4.39%	7.63%
ART	7.44%	−2.33%	4.41%	12.63%	4.21%	1.65%	13.62%	3.66%	6.11%
Reversals	12.37%	−6.82%	20.26%	25.19%	−2.27%	26.89%	12.14%	1.68%	10.2%
EQ	0.48%	−3.36%	3.49%	8.45%	3.13%	4.87%	8.55%	1.6%	6.6%
PMOM	8.14%	−8.13%	5.94%	15.49%	3.63%	−0.32%	10.03%	−0.69%	3.22%
Stability	6.83%	2.77%	−3.26%	12.93%	1.33%	3.66%	12.31%	4.63%	3.39%
SIRF	10.66%	6.02%	2.67%	12.72%	14.34%	−3.32%	12.45%	8.64%	2.75%
Dividends	11.82%	3.56%	4.3%	14.27%	12.0%	0.22%	10.04%	10.16%	−1.77%
Risk	3.31%	−1.13%	−13.49%	6.41%	9.2%	−21.74%	9.87%	−0.17%	−4.04%

Figure 4.3 Dollar-Neutral 19Y Monthly and Daily (Thereafter) Heatmap LTD (12-31-24).

	3Y Long	3Y Short	3Y Spread	5Y Long	5Y Short	5Y Spread	LTD Long	LTD Short	LTD Spread
DV	11.38%	−2.4%	9.97%	18.27%	2.27%	9.87%	11.8%	−1.53%	11.55%
RV	17.34%	−6.44%	16.69%	28.22%	6.27%	14.22%	17.14%	1.98%	12.53%
Efficiency	10.16%	−17.55%	26.77%	15.53%	−9.09%	20.63%	7.85%	0.27%	6.19%
Size	8.28%	3.36%	3.82%	7.74%	12.96%	−5.41%	10.69%	6.43%	3.62%
CSU	11.17%	−5.23%	10.03%	18.5%	−1.12%	13.7%	12.46%	1.81%	8.7%
ARS	10.82%	−1.12%	9.51%	19.99%	2.55%	14.31%	14.2%	3.34%	9.22%
Profit	5.88%	−9.61%	12.42%	13.22%	−7.08%	17.58%	10.34%	−3.0%	11.88%
EnMom	6.0%	−2.45%	5.31%	15.36%	1.48%	10.2%	9.39%	1.94%	5.52%
Leverage	8.79%	−8.15%	12.13%	14.3%	−2.22%	12.18%	10.66%	−2.65%	11.66%
Growth	17.53%	0.74%	12.82%	24.92%	13.33%	7.25%	14.06%	4.13%	7.93%
ART	7.46%	−3.77%	7.51%	11.28%	2.39%	5.31%	12.56%	3.56%	7.24%
Reversals	7.48%	−4.08%	11.89%	20.07%	−1.21%	20.49%	10.31%	1.26%	8.08%
EQ	0.75%	−1.52%	2.75%	5.18%	5.15%	−0.45%	5.61%	2.76%	2.2%
PMOM	7.16%	−8.61%	6.55%	13.19%	−3.78%	8.53%	7.83%	−1.02%	5.49%
Stability	6.88%	3.76%	0.79%	12.94%	0.15%	10.28%	12.32%	2.36%	8.81%
SIRF	10.69%	5.92%	4.22%	12.91%	9.17%	3.14%	11.31%	7.59%	2.94%
Dividends	11.83%	3.08%	6.76%	12.51%	13.1%	−1.0%	9.75%	8.74%	0.79%
Risk	3.34%	1.85%	1.32%	6.43%	2.21%	4.15%	9.88%	0.94%	8.87%

Figure 4.4 Beta-Neutral 19Y Monthly and Daily (Thereafter) Heatmap LTD (12-31-24).

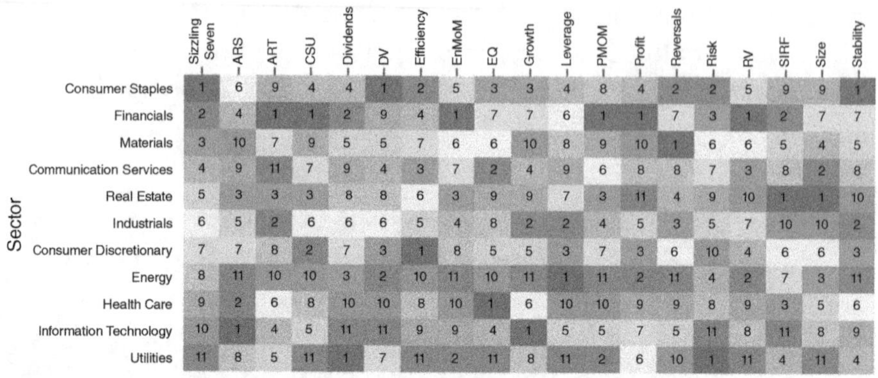

Figure 4.5 Sector Ranks Based on QMIT ESBs (12-31-24).

Figure 4.5 is based on the bottom-up aggregation of QMIT's ESB ranks within sectors cross-sectionally on that date (12-31-24).

4.2. FACTOR TIMING VERSUS TILTING

Some industry participants have made the case that one ought to maintain core diversified exposure to certain key factors in order to monetize risk-premia that are rewarded in the long run. With notable exceptions, most nimble managers recognize the benefits of opportunistically tilting around this core factor allocation to further enhance their risk-adjusted return profile. While the difference between timing versus tilting may seem to be one of degree it isn't just playing with semantics given that our regime-dependent approach suggests much more extreme posturing including possibly shorting the risk-on or risk-off ESBs, which are expected to underperform in certain regimes. This, however, leaves open the key question of regime identification, which we deal with in Chapter 7, Section 7.2.

4.3. FACTOR TIMING AND META-FACTOR CONSIDERATIONS

Separate from the regime-based approach one may consider a host of factors applied to the ESBs (essentially a meta-factor model) to drive the timing decision. The most important considerations for timing from a meta perspective are as follows:

- **Valuation.** One can apply a rich-cheap analysis to the top versus bottom 5% portfolios of a given ESB relative to its own history to determine whether that ESB is now trading rich (cheap) suggesting an under-(over)weight of that ESB. This is done by simply assessing spread in metrics like the PE, PB, and so on (or better still our value composite score) for the top versus bottom 5% portfolios. In other words, the valuation spread of value itself.
- **Quality.** One may compute the analogous spread for our quality composite to see if the ESBs are historically stretched based on those metrics or not. In other words, the quality spread of value or quality or momentum itself.
- **Momentum.** One can evaluate the average momentum spread of top versus bottom 5% names for a given ESB relative to its own history to determine whether that ESB displays relative strength or not for it to be over-(under) weighted. Further, one may interpret extreme overbought/oversold conditions in that ESB as a contrarian signal indicative of factor crowding and suggestive of factor liquidation risk. In other words, the momentum of value or quality or momentum itself.
- **Factor crowding.** One can investigate pair-wise correlations, auto-correlations, and the previous metrics, to look for signs of factor crowding and the potential for liquidation risk. For those who have the vivid institutional

muscle memory of August 2007 or February 2016 and related momentum crash episodes, this is a key consideration.

4.4. TRADING SIGNALS

In this section we discuss the construction of multifactor composite trading signals that leverage the best of our suite of 18 individual ESBs.

4.4.1. ESB Trading Signals

As per Chapter 3, Section 3.6, we have a suite of 18 BFOMs investable strategies based on our 18 ESBs that systematically switch between the alternate ESB models. The portfolio construction for the BFOMs is similar to the one explained in the factor heatmaps. These are the atomic units or Lego building blocks for our composite signals.

4.4.2. Composite Trading Signals

Our main findings are that smart betas enable us to harvest risk-premia over the long haul and diversify given the low correlation among them. Additionally, as we have seen, smart betas exhibit cyclicality over shorter horizons despite the long-term outperformance. To mitigate the impact of cyclicality while taking advantage of the attractive properties of smart betas (such as low correlation and positive alpha), one needs to build multifactor portfolios.

One way of building a multifactor portfolio is to simply invest in several factor portfolios. An alternative to building a portfolio of factors is to design a multifactor model, which selects stocks based on how they rank according to several factor metrics at the same time. An example would be a value and momentum model that selects stocks that rank highly on a combined rank of value and momentum. While a portfolio of value and momentum factors tends to contain stocks with the highest rank on one of these two metrics separately (but may rank poorly on the other), a multifactor model tends to have stocks that rank favorably on both metrics (i.e., the highest combined ranking). E.g., the implosion of asset bubbles in 2021–2022 led to extraordinary returns (about +250% cum) actualized by our ValMo (GARP[1]) multifactor signal spreads.

QMIT has constructed a series of composite signals that leverage the best of individual ESB BFOMs as outlined in Table A.1 of Appendix A.2. As per the heatmaps in Figures 4.6 and 4.7, we show their performance LTM and

	DTD Long	DTD Short	DTD Spread	MTD Long	MTD Short	MTD Spread	LTM Long	LTM Short	LTM Spread
Fabulous Fourteen	0.26%	−1.97%	2.22%	−3.56%	−3.86%	−0.53%	27.76%	19.61%	1.34%
Sizzling Seven	0.34%	−2.56%	2.9%	−4.49%	−4.15%	−1.21%	21.97%	19.49%	−3.21%
Famous Five	0.27%	−1.78%	2.05%	−4.39%	−4.55%	−0.64%	18.31%	8.12%	3.03%
Q-GARP	0.05%	−1.72%	1.77%	−4.39%	−3.52%	−1.55%	26.82%	13.13%	6.91%
ValMo	0.18%	−1.49%	1.66%	−5.08%	−4.46%	−1.09%	35.27%	14.68%	13.15%
Enterpise Eighteen	0.14%	−1.77%	1.91%	−5.25%	−4.44%	−1.62%	25.42%	12.45%	4.61%
Value	0.88%	−1.91%	2.78%	−2.95%	−2.57%	−1.48%	10.13%	23.88%	−15.26%
QualMo	−0.17%	−0.52%	0.35%	−5.84%	−2.36%	−3.84%	24.18%	8.29%	10.15%
QualVal	0.46%	−1.89%	2.35%	−3.98%	−2.49%	−2.6%	13.33%	19.43%	−10.32%
Quality	0.05%	−1.59%	1.63%	−5.23%	−2.06%	−3.96%	12.57%	19.67%	−10.62%
GrowthMo	−0.47%	0.7%	−1.16%	−6.34%	−7.49%	1.1%	30.88%	−0.85%	28.32%

Figure 4.6 Dollar-Neutral – Daily Heatmap LTM – 12-31-24.

[1]GARP stands for growth at reasonable price.

	3Y Long	3Y Short	3Y Spread	5Y Long	5Y Short	5Y Spread	LTD Long	LTD Short	LTD Spread
Fabulous Fourteen	17.68%	−9.52%	17.43%	23.86%	−2.24%	17.06%	18.49%	−8.86%	24.0%
Sizzling Seven	14.61%	−9.17%	15.79%	21.56%	−3.02%	16.67%	20.04%	−5.84%	22.62%
Famous Five	11.74%	−10.59%	11.09%	14.73%	−1.86%	6.5%	17.58%	−8.61%	21.6%
Q-GARP	18.68%	−11.13%	20.84%	22.8%	−6.25%	21.34%	16.61%	−7.31%	20.63%
ValMo	19.88%	−9.74%	21.98%	24.38%	−5.31%	23.64%	16.59%	−5.46%	19.7%
Enterpise Eighteen	12.98%	−12.6%	14.22%	18.72%	−4.07%	12.17%	16.77%	−7.48%	19.27%
Value	15.44%	−8.0%	17.19%	25.5%	−1.61%	19.93%	16.44%	−2.34%	15.78%
QualMo	11.92%	−10.18%	12.68%	16.97%	−5.97%	13.75%	13.25%	−6.12%	14.22%
QualVal	13.23%	−10.87%	16.37%	20.03%	−2.58%	13.52%	15.57%	−2.82%	14.36%
Quality	8.32%	−7.52%	6.47%	14.97%	1.11%	4.38%	13.15%	−1.12%	9.49%
GrowthMo	10.67%	−4.08%	9.25%	19.72%	2.74%	9.08%	15.13%	0.56%	9.73%

Figure 4.7 Dollar-Neutral – 19Y Monthly and Daily Onwards Heatmap LTD – 12-31-24.

LTD on a dollar-neutral basis. These include popular combinations such as GARP (aka Val-Mo), Q-GARP, Qual-Val, GrowthMo, Qual-Mo, and so on, as well as our proprietary combinations such as Sizzling Seven, Fabulous 14, and so on, which are meant to demonstrate the merits of combining our high-octane ESBs toward formulating turnkey signals for hedge funds. One can further customize these signals as per one's investment mandate. Further, as per Chapter 6, we can back out the ESB exposures or style signature of a given manager and run them forward to meet or likely beat the manager's style returns. Such is the power of this framework built with the ESB building blocks.

As per Figures 4.8–4.13, one can see that QMIT's proprietary composite signals such as Sizzling Seven have the highest Sharpe and Sortino ratios as well ICs (followed by Famous Five, Fabulous 14, and Enterprise 18). The better-known combinations, such as GARP (Val-Mo), Growth-Momentum, etc., are significantly lower. Clearly, there are benefits to diversifying across our high-octane ESB BFOMs to leverage the best of the ensemble learners as embodied by Sizzling Seven. However, Sizzling Seven does come with the highest turnover (which can be constrained at the portfolio construction stage) as opposed to the Value composite at the low end of the turnover and risk-adjusted performance range.

Further details on the performance characteristics of these composite signals are presented in Figures 4.8–4.13. These figures illustrate 25-year beta-neutral Sharpe and Sortino ratios (Figures 4.8 and 4.9), 25-year information coefficients and their corresponding *t*-stats (Figures 4.10 and 4.11), 25-year annualized turnovers (Figure 4.12), and autocorrelation function (ACF) plots for 24-year composite multifactor models as of October 31, 2023 (Figure 4.13). Information Coefficients (ICs) are computed as the Spearman rank correlation of cross-sectional ranks today versus the forward month's return.

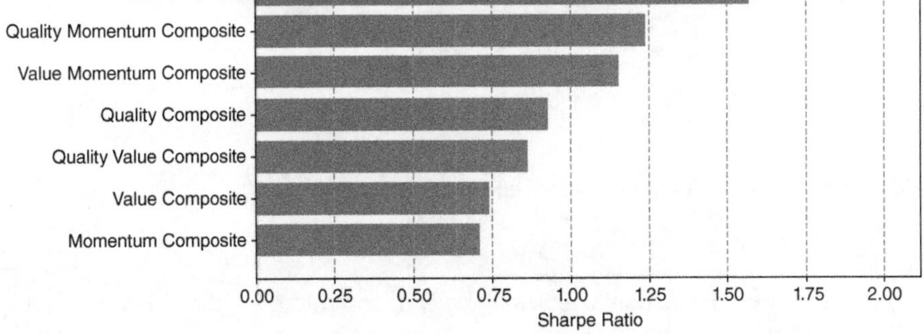

Figure 4.8 Composite Signals (Beta Neutral) – 25Y Sharpe Ratios.

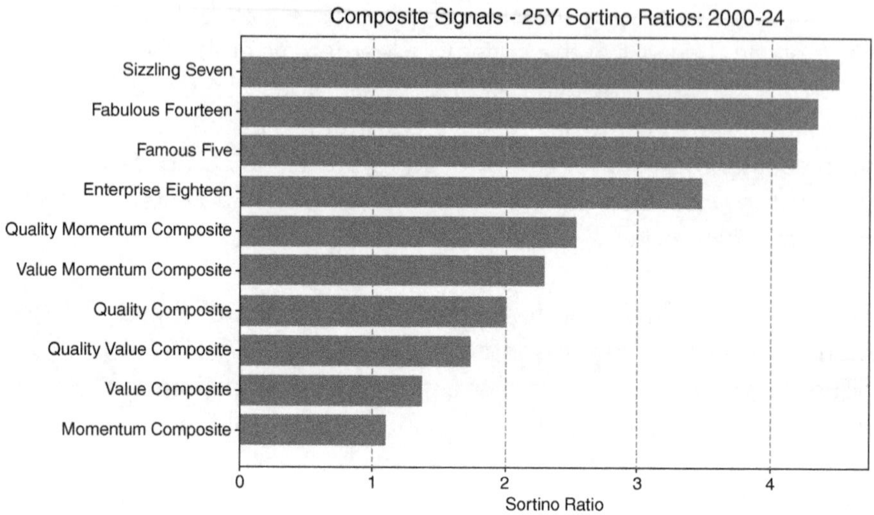

Figure 4.9 Composite Signals (Beta Neutral) – 25Y Sortino Ratios.

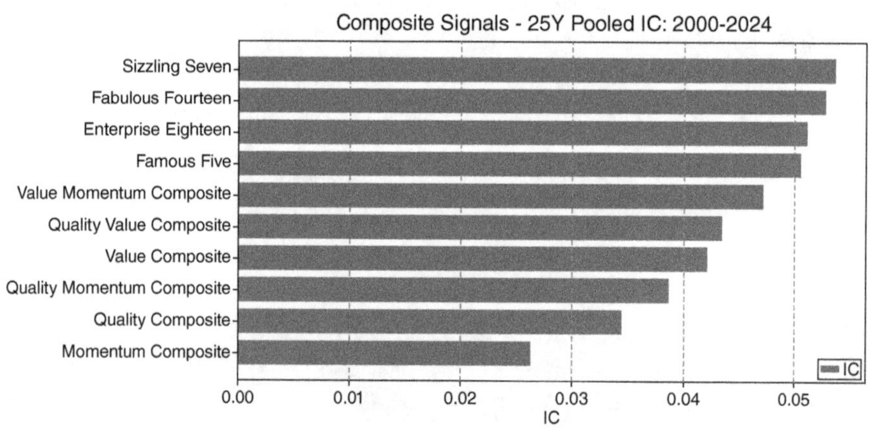

Figure 4.10 Composite Signals – 25Y Information Coefficients.[2]

[2]The information coefficient here is computed as the Spearman rank correlation of cross-sectional ranks today versus the forward month's return. Further, all 25 years are pooled.

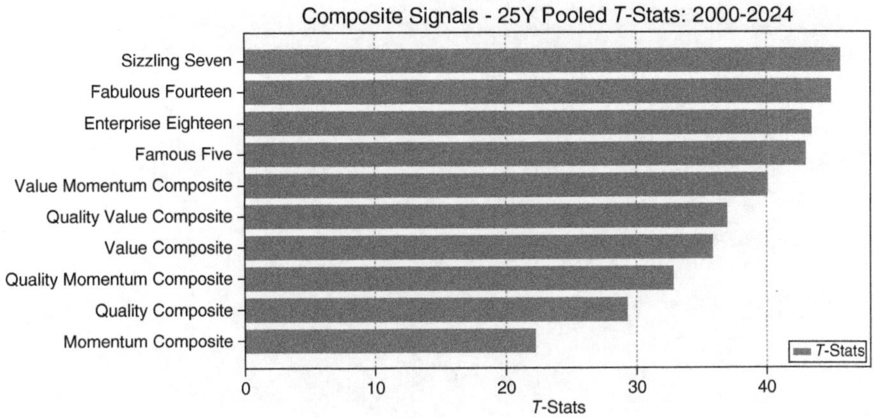

Figure 4.11 Composite Signals – 25Y IC *T*-Stats.

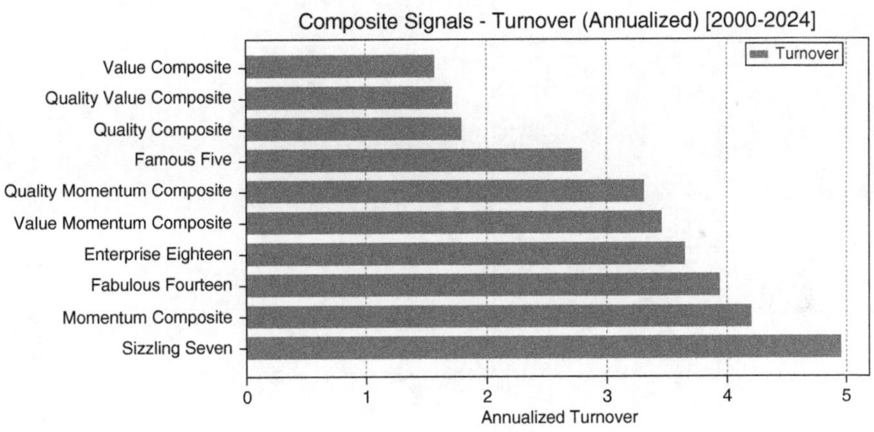

Figure 4.12 Composite Signals – 25Y Annualized Turnovers.[3]

[3] The turnover here is calculated based on monthly rebalanced top versus bottom quintile stocks for each composite trading signal.

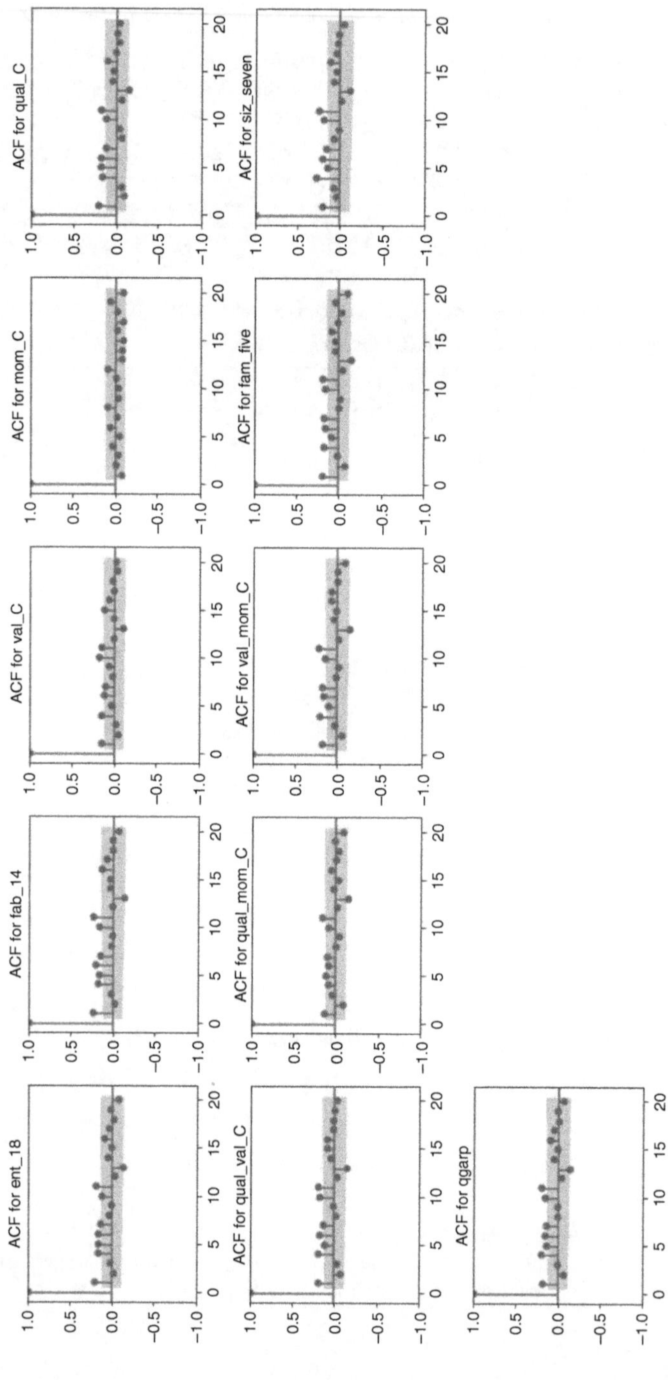

Figure 4.13 24Y Composite MFMs – ACF Plots (10-31-23).

4.5. FAMA-FRENCH ALPHAS OF COMPOSITE SIGNALS

The alpha-generating capabilities of these composite signals are further examined using CAPM and Fama-French models. Figures 4.14 and 4.15 detail the 24-year CAPM and

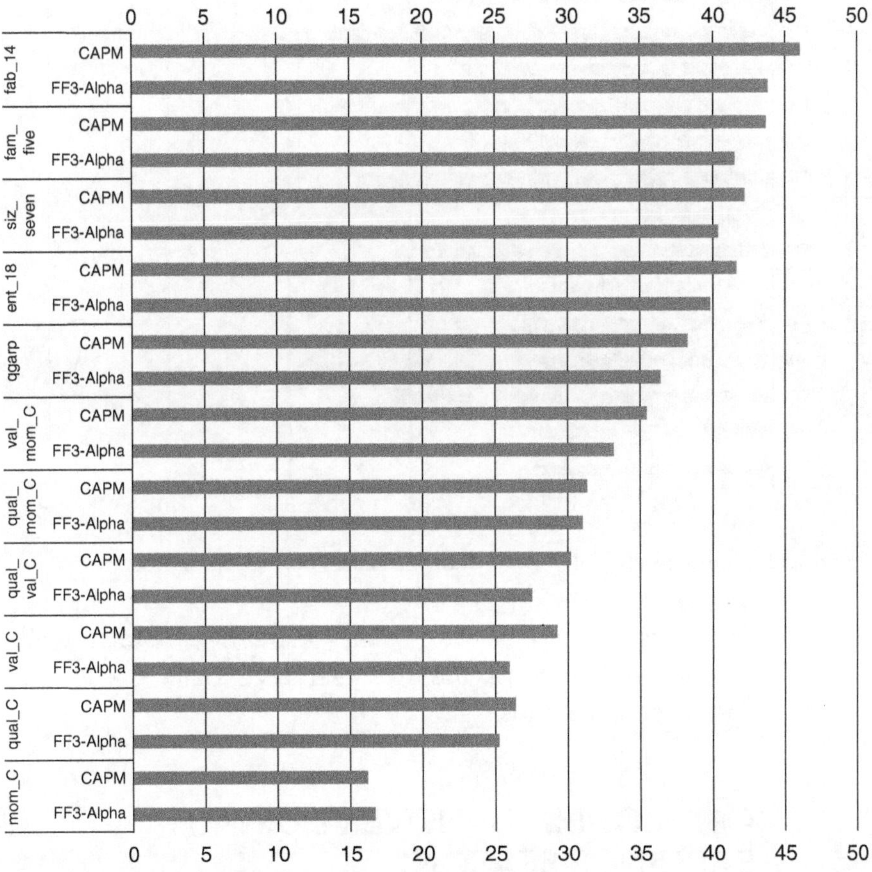

Figure 4.14 Composite Signals – 24Y CAPM and Fama-French Alphas.

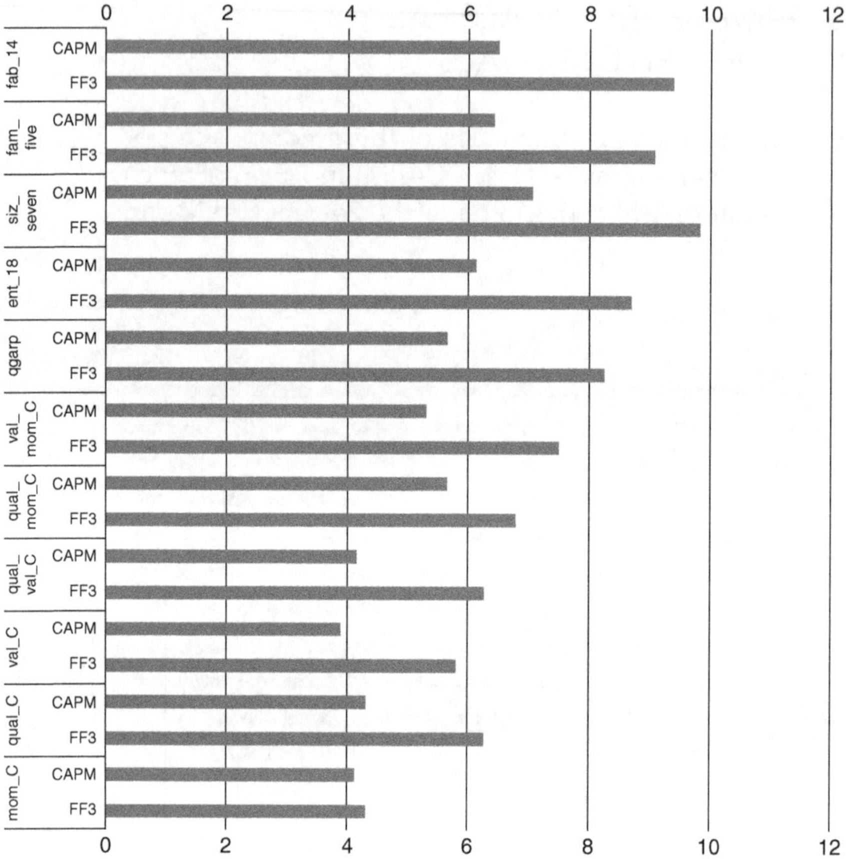

Figure 4.15 Composite Signals – 24Y CAPM and Fama-French Alpha *T*-Stats.

Fama-French alphas and their respective *t*-stats, while Figure 4.16 presents the five-year LIVE daily CAPM and Fama-French alphas.

4.6. MODEL TURNOVER DURING EARNINGS SEASON

For intuition on the impact of earnings season on our combo signals we look at four of our flagship models in January 2020 (prior to earnings) versus April during earnings season and

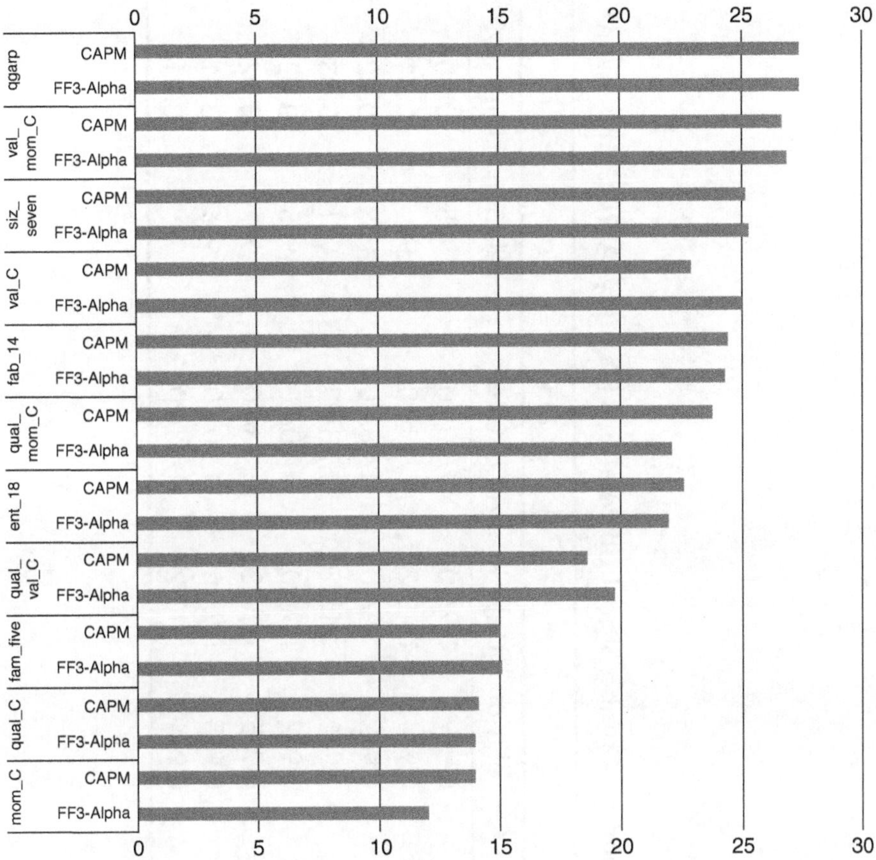

Figure 4.16 Composite Signals – 5Y LIVE Daily CAPM and Fama-French Alphas.

investigate the rank volatility on consecutive days (Table 4.1). To do this we simply ran the rank correlations of, for example, Famous 5 from one day to the next in versus out of earnings season to give you some sense of that (based on the intersecting set of names because there are 2,238 names/day in January pre-COVID crash versus only 2,115 names/day in April). Correlations are indeed *lower in April* reflecting *more rank changes during earnings season* versus early January, which makes sense (although since all correlations are quite high it may be harder to discern at the margin).

Table 4.1 Impact of Earnings Season on Combo Signal Correlations (January–April Comparison).

	Apr			Jan			
Combo	**Date From**	**Date to**	**Correlation**	**Date From**	**Date to**	**Correlation**	**Jan–Apr**
fam_five	4/28/20	4/29/20	0.989	1/9/20	1/10/20	0.995	**0.006**
fam_five	4/29/20	4/30/20	0.984	1/10/20	1/13/20	0.997	**0.013**
siz_seven	4/28/20	4/29/20	0.932	1/9/20	1/10/20	0.953	**0.021**
siz_seven	4/29/20	4/30/20	0.941	1/10/20	1/13/20	0.971	**0.03**
fab_14	4/28/20	4/29/20	0.962	1/9/20	1/10/20	0.985	**0.023**
fab_14	4/29/20	4/30/20	0.965	1/10/20	1/13/20	0.987	**0.022**
ent_18	4/28/20	4/29/20	0.975	1/9/20	1/10/20	0.986	**0.011**
ent_18	4/29/20	4/30/20	0.974	1/10/20	1/13/20	0.99	**0.016**

Table 4.2, which illustrates the difference in average correlations for January versus April (on two consecutive days for each), confirms our intuition:

1. The average correlations across the two consecutive sets of days is higher for the lower turnover signals like Famous Five versus Sizzling Seven as one might expect due to fewer rank changes.
2. The difference in average correlations (January versus April) is also higher for higher turnover signals like Sizzling Seven.

Table 4.2 Impact of Turnover Signals on Correlation Differences During Earnings Season.

	Avg Apr	Avg Jan	Difference Jan–Apr
fam_five	0.987	0.996	0.009
siz_seven	0.937	0.962	0.026
fab_14	0.963	0.986	0.023
ent_18	0.974	0.988	0.014
Overall	0.968	0.986	0.018

4.7. FACTOR EXPOSURES

QMIT's factor exposure framework provides visualization designed to easily compare factor exposures between one's portfolio and its respective benchmark. It is based on our putatively spanning set of 18 QMIT ESBs. This may help one make better decisions regarding their factor exposures once they are empowered to measure, monitor, and manage them better.

Figure 4.17 displays the style exposure of QMIT's LBO Top 100 signal against the Russell 2000 Value benchmark as

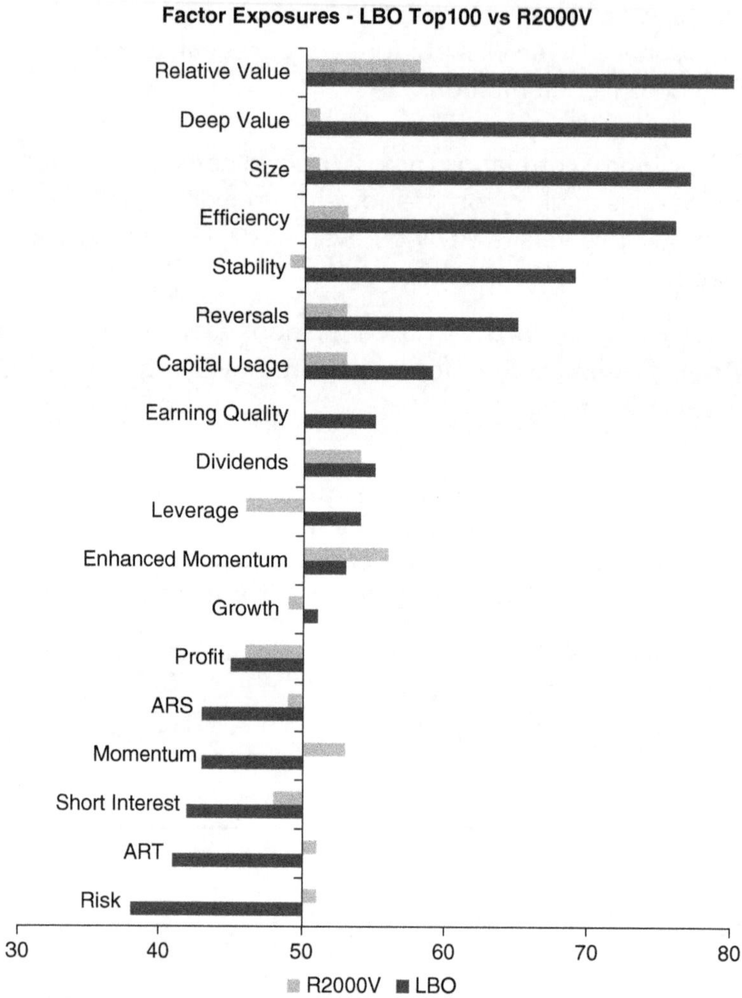

Figure 4.17 LBO Top 100: Style Exposures to ESBs.

an example. It clearly indicates that the LBO Top 100 model portfolio has a significant value tilt (both deep value and relative value) and is composed of smaller size companies with higher-quality financials (efficiency, stability, capital usage and structure, leverage, and earnings quality) while being negatively exposed to the momentum cohort (enhanced momentum, growth, analyst revisions, momentum, analyst ratings, and targets). This is entirely consistent with what one may expect LBO targets to typify as per Chapter 10.

Clearly, one can extend this methodology to any portfolio to display factor exposures based on our more granular ESBs as compared to typical risk models. Further, as we demonstrate in our HF in a Box portfolio, one can entirely dispense with risk models by directly constraining to the ESBs in order to control for net factor exposures. There is evidence from the literature in support of aligning alphas with risk in order to prevent the risk model from potentially destroying the MFM alphas.

4.8. PLATINUM HEDGE – CRASH BASKETS

Analogous to QMIT's factor exposure framework, this analysis could serve as a tool for investors to measure, monitor, and manage their portfolios' exposure to crash-related risks. By visualizing how different factors behaved during crash periods, investors can make more informed decisions about their hedging strategies.

The key takeaway here is that by understanding these factor exposures, particularly Figure 4.18 which details the "crash factor" portfolio managers can design strategies

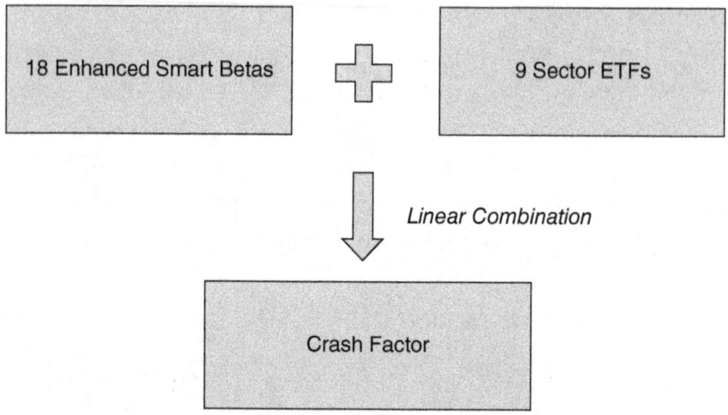

Figure 4.18 Construction of Crash Factor Basket Based on ESBs and Sector ETFs.

that are better suited to withstand similar future events. They can adjust their exposure to sectors and factors that are historically known to either mitigate or exacerbate losses during market crashes. This methodology extends beyond traditional risk models by using a more nuanced set of factors (ESBs) and directly incorporating them into portfolio construction to control risk and potentially preserve alpha. It also quite distinct from single stock crash beta sensitivities often used by risk vendors. Figure 4.19 presents the estimated crash betas for the 18 ESBs and 9 sector ETFs. The "no COVID" estimated betas are based on the specific historical crash periods shown in Figure 4.20 excluding the COVID crash, which was observed live in Figure 4.21. The betas were subsequently recalculated inclusive of the COVID episode (full period) in order to have the crash factor basket recalibrated and ready for the next crash. This can be done on an equity market-neutral (EMN) basis as well as long only by simply taking the long side of ESBs.

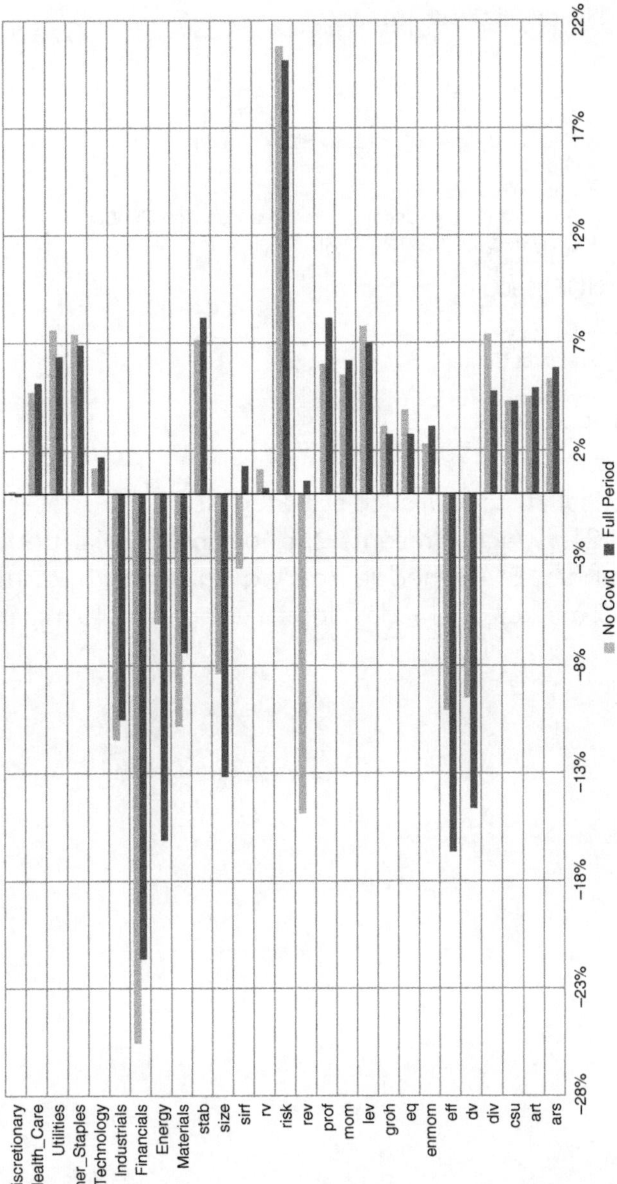

Figure 4.19 Crash Beta Weights for ESBs and ETFs During COVID and Full Period.

Historical Crash Periods

- Apr 2000 - Oct 2002 (Nasdaq Crash)
- Oct 2007 - Feb 2009 (2008 Financial Crisis)
- May 2011 - Oct 2011 (US Debt-Ceiling Crisis)
- Sep 2018 - Dec 2018 (2018 Stock Market Crash)
- Feb 2020 - Mar 2020 (COVID Crash)
- 30 months excl Nasdaq; 28 months excluded COVID
- Daily data-24 TDs for COVID Crash

UCF Hedging portfolios

- Long Only
- Market Neutral

Figure 4.20 Crash Period.

The practical efficacy of such a strategy is demonstrated in Figure 4.21, which presents the out-of-sample performance of an EMN hedge (during the month of the COVID-19 market crash), developed using this crash factor methodology.

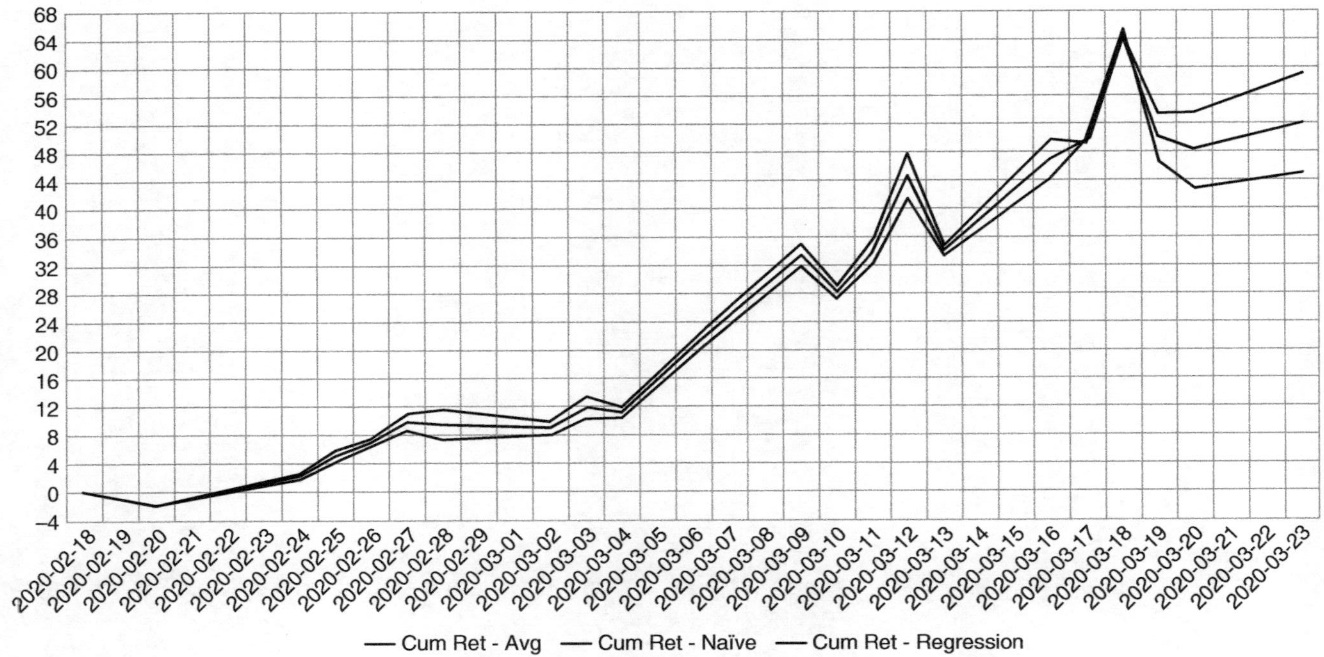

Figure 4.21 Out-of-Sample Performance of an EMN Hedge During the COVID-19 Market Crash.

Chapter 5

Sector Rotation

5.1. EXECUTIVE SUMMARY

- Our objective was to test the efficacy of a sector rotation strategy based on QMIT's flagship Sizzling Seven signal.
- We studied two sector rotation strategies. In the first study, we tested the sector rotation strategy using sector exchange-traded funds (ETFs) as a proxy for the sectors.
- In the second study, we enhanced the strategy based on ETFs by choosing the stocks with highest/lowest Sizzling Seven ranks from the sectors that were chosen to be bought/shorted.
- We tried various long/short combinations and found that top versus bottom two-sector strategy is the best strategy in terms of hit rates and risk-adjusted metrics for ETFs while 5 × 5 sectors each dominate in the single stock case that maximizes the distance between intra and inter

cluster stock picks. In both phases a strategy based on single sectors (1 × 1 or top versus bottom) has the highest concentration risk resulting in the highest volatility and maximum drawdowns.

- This strategy could have helped investors sit out the financials sector during the GFC (great financial crisis) of 2008 and the energy sector through the commodity crash of 2015, suggesting efficacy on the short side.

5.2. WHY SECTOR ROTATION STRATEGIES?

Sector rotation is a prominent investment strategy used by investors to maximize returns by timing sector exposures based on their performance outlook. This strategy capitalizes on the fact that different sectors of the economy often exhibit varying performance patterns during different phases of economic cycles, business cycles, and secular trends.

The fundamental premise behind sector rotation is that sectors will reflect the cyclicality of the respective industry groups. For example, defensive sectors like utilities and consumer staples tend to perform well during economic downturns, while cyclical sectors like information technology and consumer discretionary often lead during economic expansions due to increased consumer and business spending and their higher beta to the business cycle.

Sector rotation can be implemented through various means, including ETFs, mutual funds, or direct investments in individual stocks within targeted sectors. The effectiveness of sector rotation strategies is supported by academic research. For instance, Fabozzi et al. (2002) provided an overview of the evolution of portfolio theory, including sector rotation strategies within the broader context of portfolio management. Moskowitz and Grinblatt (1999) examined the role of industry and sector momentum in explaining stock performance, offering insights into sector-based strategies. Fama and French (1997) explored the cost of equity across different industries, providing a basis for understanding the varying risk and return characteristics of sectors.

5.3. QMIT'S FACTOR LIBRARY AND ENHANCED SMART BETAS

Figure 5.1 shows that there's substantial performance dispersion (as embodied by the best-worst spread) across sectors to be monetized given that sector leadership changes almost every year – driven by secular trends, business cycles, and market cycles.[1] In this chapter, we investigate whether one can use QMIT's Sizzling Seven bottom-up stock-based signals to generate high risk-adjusted return long/short sector-level strategies. The application of bottom-up stock-based signals in investment strategies also has been well studied. Piotroski (2000) discusses the effectiveness of fundamental analysis in identifying high book-to-market firms and their subsequent performance.

5.4. QMIT'S SIZZLING SEVEN COMPOSITE SIGNAL

For this chapter, we focus on deploying the Sizzling Seven multifactor model (MFM) composite signal, which is QMIT's

---

[1] Based on SPDR Sector Select ETF. For communication services, where there is insufficient data, we use the Communication Services Select Sector Index as a tradable proxy.

2011	2012	2013	2014	2015	2016	2017	2018	2019	
Utilities 19.62%	Financials 28.42%	Consumer Discretionary 42.74%	Utilities 28.73%	Communication Services 10.81%	Energy 28.02%	Information Technology 34.25%	Health care 6.28%	Information Technology 49.86%	
Consumer Staples 14.08%	Communication Services 24.70%	Health care 41.40%	Health care 25.14%	Consumer Discretionary 9.92%	Financials 22.60%	Communication Services 24.47%	Utilities 3.92%	Financials 31.88%	
Health care 12.39%	Consumer Discretionary 23.60%	Communication Services 40.77%	Information Technology 17.85%	Consumer Staples 6.89%	Industrials 20.01%	Materials 24.01%	Consumer Discretionary 1.59%	Communication Services 31.39%	
Communication Services 6.78%	Health care 17.37%	Industrials 40.55%	Consumer Staples 15.72%	Health care 6.84%	Materials 16.80%	Industrials 23.97%	Information Technology −1.66%	Industrials 29.09%	
Consumer Discretionary 5.99%	Information Technology 15.29%	Financials 35.52%	Financials 15.05%	Information Technology 5.49%	Utilities 16.05%	Consumer Discretionary 22.82%	Communication Services −6.88%	Consumer Discretionary 28.39%	
Energy 2.84%	Industrials 14.92%	Consumer Staples 26.30%	Industrials 10.36%	Financials −1.74%	Information Technology 15.02%	Financials 22.00%	Consumer Staples −8.07%	Consumer Staples 27.43%	
Information Technology 2.61%	Materials 14.70%	Energy 26.25%	Consumer Discretionary 9.46%	Industrials −4.30%	Communication Services 11.61%	Health care 21.77%	Financials −13.04%	Utilities 25.92%	
Industrials −1.11%	Consumer Staples 10.74%	Information Technology 26.25%	Materials 7.17%	Utilities −4.91%	Consumer Discretionary 5.97%	Consumer Staples 12.98%	Industrials −13.24%	Materials 24.13%	
Materials −10.93%	Energy 5.20%	Materials 26.00%	Communication Services 7.08%	Materials −8.67%	Consumer Staples 4.98%	Utilities 12.03%	Materials −14.87%	Health care 20.44%	
Financials −17.15%	Utilities 1.04%	Utilities 13.05%	Energy −8.70%	Energy −21.47%	Health care −2.76%	Energy −0.90%	Energy −18.21%	Energy 11.74%	
36.77%	27.38%	29.69%	37.43%	32.28%	30.78%	35.15%	24.49%	38.12%	Best Minus Worst

Figure 5.1 Calendar Year Sector Returns.

proprietary combination of ESBs meant to demonstrate the merits of combining QMIT's high-octane ESBs toward formulating turnkey signals for hedge funds.

QMIT's Sizzling Seven composite multifactor model includes the following:

Quality Composite

- Quality – Leverage (LEV)
  - Captures excess returns to stocks with low leverage
- Quality – Profitability (PROF)
  - Captures excess returns to highly profitable stocks
- Quality – Capital Structure/Use (CSU)
  - Captures excess returns to firms with better usage of capital
- Quality – Stability (STAB)
  - Captures excess returns to stocks with stable financial ratios
- Quality – Efficiency (EFF)
  - Captures excess returns to stocks that are characterized by high operating efficiency
- Quality – Earnings Quality (EQ)
  - Captures excess returns to stocks that are characterized by low accruals

Value Composite

- Deep Value (DV)
  - Captures excess returns to value stocks based on intrinsic value metrics
- Relative Value (RV)
  - Captures excess returns to value stocks based on relative valuation metrics

Growth + Momentum Composite

- Analyst Revisions (ARS)
  - Captures excess returns of stocks with momentum on account of analyst revisions
- Analyst Ratings (ART)
  - Captures excess returns to stocks that track analyst recommendation and target
- Enhanced Momentum (EnMom)
  - Captures excess returns to stocks experiencing trend continuation
- Growth (GroH)
  - Captures excess returns to stocks that have higher-than-average historical growth

Risk (RISK)

- Captures excess returns to stocks with lower-than-average volatility, beta, and/or idiosyncratic risk

Size (SIZE)

- Captures excess returns to smaller firms

Reversals (REV)

- Captures excess returns to stocks with lackluster past performance that is due for a rebound

Short Interest (SIRF)

- Captures excess returns to stocks with lower short interest

5.5. METHODOLOGY

5.5.1. Sector Choice

The first step is aggregating bottom-up single stock ranks to determine the descending rank order of sectors, which would then yield the top versus bottom sectors for back-testing the spread returns based on ETFs as sector proxies. We use QMIT's Sizzling Seven month-end (single stock level) signal ranks to determine the descending rank order of the sectors. QMIT's signal data includes monthly factor scores from [0–100] for about 2,500 tickers from 12/31/1999 to 12/31/2019. We make the prediction as per the following steps:

1. We labeled each ticker based on QMIT's sector labeling, which includes utilities, energy, communication services, consumer discretionary, financials, consumer staples, information technology, materials, industrials, and health care.
2. QMIT's sector labeling is based on a mapping table maintained by the firm using FactSet industry codes.[2]
3. For every month, we will calculate a sector signal score based on the average rank for stocks labeled in that sector. We exclude real estate because it is not as suitable in a generic quant model. We then rank the 10 sectors from 1 to 10 based on signal strength.
4. We now have a prediction each month as to which sector is going to perform best/worst in the next month.

5.6. PHASE 1: STRATEGY BASED ON SECTOR ETFs

The simplest way to reflect bullish or bearish views on a sector is to utilize liquid, institutionally tradable sector ETFs. For

[2]We exclude some tickers that we cannot find the right labels for, which accounts for less than 1% of total date-ticker combinations. Each date has no more than 2% of missing tickers, and most dates have 0–1% of missing ticker labels.

each of the 11 sectors, SPDR provides a corresponding sector ETF (e.g., XLF, XLU) that one can use.[3] Subsequent to the exclusion of real estate (XLRE), we then obtain the adjusted prices to compute monthly total returns for the remaining 10 sectors. We implement the strategy by going long the sectors with the highest scores and shorting the sectors with the lowest scores. Next, we present the back-test results of long/short cases ranging from one to five sectors in each direction with a starting capital of $100 million as the assets under management. We have the following assumptions:

- Gross exposure of 200% = GMV = 100% LMV + 100% SMV with a Net MV = 0% at each rebalancing month-end date ensures dollar neutrality.
- Month-end rebalancing on, for example, formation date 03/31/00 ranks would be utilized for monetizing the strategy returns in the calendar month of April 2000.[4]
- Each sector is equally weighted at the time of rebalancing based on the cum VAMI. We present the results of long/short portfolios of one to five sectors in each direction.[5]

---

[3] SPDR: A Standard & Poor's Depositary Receipt, or SPDR, is a type of exchange traded fund that began trading on the American Stock Exchange (AMEX) in 1993 when State Street Global Advisors' investment management group first issued shares of the SPDR 500 Trust (SPY). XLF: The Financial Select Sector SPDR® Fund; XLU: The Utilities Select Sector SPDR Fund are examples of some of the ETF we used. We removed real estate because of its insufficient data, and it is unsuitable in a generic quant framework. The SPDR communication sector ETF (XLC) has a short history due to a change of GICS classification system in 2018, but the underlying index has 20+ years of data. Hence, we instead use the underlying index, which is the Communication Services Select Sector Index instead as our proxy.

[4] To be careful one would take the 03/30/00 rank file available pre-open on 03/31/00 order to enter the trade at the close of 03/31/00, not that the sector ranks would be likely change much intra-day.

[5] For instance, long/short one sector means that for every month end, we rebalance the portfolio to 100% weight long the highest score sector, and 100% weight short the lowest score sector. Choosing five sectors means that we long the top five sectors with 20% weight each, and short the bottom five sectors with 20% weight each.

5.6.1. Result Highlights

Picking fewer sectors consistently yields higher returns given the more concentrated bets, which suggests predictive efficacy of the underlying Sizzling Seven signal. Given that higher signal scores are supposed to imply higher predicted stock returns, implementing this at the aggregated sector level should yield similar results. This hypothesis is confirmed by the results presented herein.

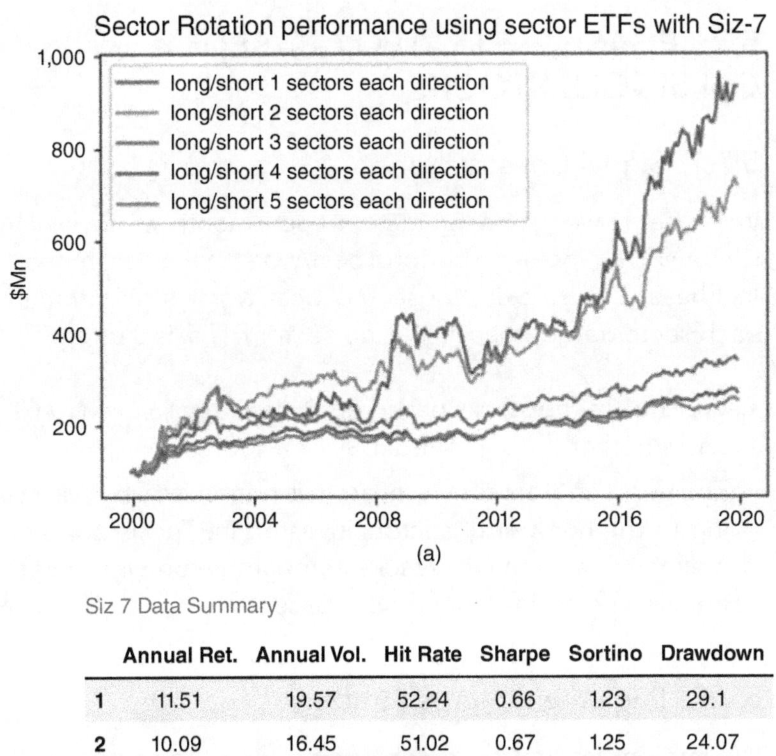

(a)

Siz 7 Data Summary

	Annual Ret.	Annual Vol.	Hit Rate	Sharpe	Sortino	Drawdown
1	11.51	19.57	52.24	0.66	1.23	29.1
2	10.09	16.45	51.02	0.67	1.25	24.07
3	6.08	12.2	54.29	0.55	0.96	18.2
4	4.87	9.39	52.24	0.56	0.98	19.83
5	4.54	8.03	53.06	0.6	1.09	14.76

(b)

Figure 5.2 Sector Rotation Performance Using Sector ETFs with Sizzling Seven.

However, picking one sector each yields much higher annual volatility and drawdown than picking two sectors at a time. The two-sector strategy appears to be the optimal choice with the highest hit rate, Sharpe and Sortino ratios, due to significantly reduced drawdowns from the one-sector strategy per Figure 5.2.[6] This shows the benefits of diversification although drawdowns decrease going from 1×1 to 5×5 as one might expect.

5.7. PHASE 2: STRATEGY BASED ON SINGLE STOCKS

5.7.1. Signal Construction

In Phase 1, we got a prediction each month as to which sector(s) is/are going to perform best/worst in the next month. In Phase 2, we now choose the best/worst stocks within each sector rather than just using sector ETFs as a proxy.

- We choose the stocks based on their Sizzling Seven ranks and whether the sector is a buy or a short.
- The number of stocks we invest in is normalized by adjusting to the number of sectors invested in. This is done to make the performance results comparable between strategies using a different number of sectors.

5.7.2. Implementing the Strategy

We implement the strategy by going long the sectors with the highest scores and shorting the sectors with the lowest scores. Within the best sectors we go long the best stocks

[6]We define hit rate here as the percentage of months that the strategy yields positive returns, which necessarily means that the long sectors outperform the short sectors.

with highest Sizzling Seven ranks (in the top decile or quintile) and, analogously, we must short the worst stocks (bottom decile or quintile) in the worst sectors while ensuring a minimum of 35 stocks on each side. However, given the varying sector sizes, the total number of top decile or quintile names picked on each side may differ subject to the minimum. For the case of 5×5 sectors, if the intra-sector number of stocks is less than seven then we must ensure a minimum of seven stocks with equal weights to satisfy the minimum of 35 names.

Next, we present the back-test results of long/short cases ranging from one to five sectors in each direction with a starting capital of $100 million. We have the same assumptions as Phase 1 with the following additional assumption, namely, that all stocks are also equally weighted within each sector (where the sectors themselves are equally weighted on each side).

5.7.3. Results

- Picking more sectors consistently yields higher returns (counterintuitively) and lower volatility (intuitive) with monotonically better risk-adjusted outcomes whether we consider deciles or quintiles.
- Picking 1×1 sector results in much higher volatility and drawdowns than picking two or more sectors at a time. This shows the benefits of diversification.
- Comparing the top decile versus top quintile scenarios, we see that performance metrics and returns are better for the top decile case. Given the 5.33 Sortino for the top decile with 5 x 5 sectors, it's clear that's the winning strategy. Thus, in Figure 5.3, we see that our sector rotation implemented with single stocks provides much better risk-adjusted performance by virtue of maximizing the intra- and inter-cluster distances of scores.

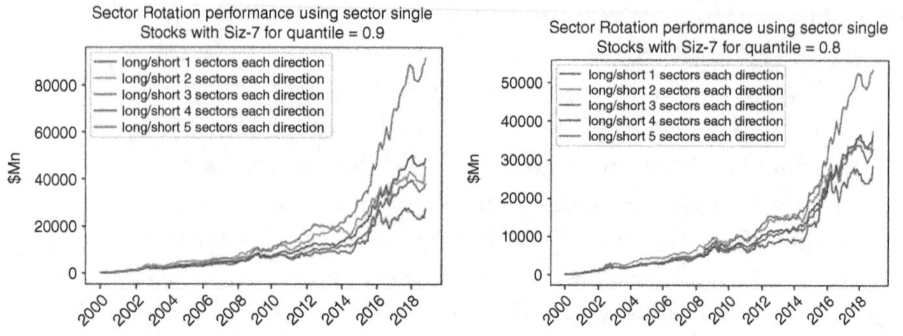

(a) (b)

Siz7 summary for 0.9 quantile

	Annual Ret.	Annual Vol.	Hit Rate	Sharpe	Sortino	Drawdown	Weighted siz7
1	34.29	31.88	59.47	1.05	2.21	41.87	72.64
2	37.66	30.06	61.23	1.14	2.93	26.34	84.8
3	36.45	25.22	63.88	1.29	3.24	23.09	89.41
4	38.47	23.26	64.76	1.44	3.91	22.74	91.71
5	43.56	22.23	67.84	1.63	5.33	18.09	92.68

(c)

Siz7 summary for 0.8 quantile

Annual Ret.	Annual Vol.	Hit Rate	Sharpe	Sortino	Drawdown	Weighted siz7
34.67	31.34	61.23	1.07	2.28	37.98	69.71
36.43	29.88	59.47	1.12	2.81	28.8	83.03
35.36	24.38	62.56	1.3	3.33	21.66	88.04
36.21	22.45	63.44	1.42	3.87	23.06	90.56
39.45	21.55	66.52	1.57	4.61	20.51	91.76

(d)

Figure 5.3 Sector Rotation Performance Using Single Stocks with Sizzling Seven.

5.8. COMPARISON OF PHASE 1 AND PHASE 2

We see that the strategy based on single stocks results in risk-adjusted performance that is higher than the one based on ETFs by a multiple. In Phase 1, the best risk-adjusted performer was the two-sector case with a Sharpe ratio of 0.67. In Phase 2, the best risk-adjusted performer for choosing top versus bottom 20% and 10% stocks was the five-sector case, not the two-sector case with a Sharpe of 1.57 and 1.63, respectively. Thus, we see that our sector rotation implemented with single stocks provides much better risk-adjusted performance by virtue of maximizing the intra- and inter-cluster distances of scores. Given the *5.33 Sortino for the 90% quantile with* 5×5 sectors it's clear that's the winning strategy since it is not only better than other single stock cases but also 4.9× better risk-adjusted than the 1.09 Sortino for the best ETF case. This is because in the ETF scenarios, the returns decay in tandem with the volatility despite greater diversification across more sectors resulting in not much of a risk-adjusted gradient whereas in Phase 2, we see the best of both worlds. *Not only do the returns increase significantly as we monetize the top-ranked stocks across multiple sectors but also with lower strategy volatility due to greater diversification across more sectors.*

5.9. REGRESSIONS

For each signal, we would like to assess how well it explains returns. To do so, we performed the following steps:

1. Since we are trying to capture relative returns, we normalized the sector returns each month by the mean of the 10-sector returns.
2. Similarly, we also normalized the 10-sector scores each month.
3. For each month, we have 10 *x-y* pairs. We pooled 240 months (20 years) together and now we have 2,400 *x-y* pairs, with *x* as a sector score, and *y* as *next month's sector return.* With these data points, we then performed an OLS regression as per Table 5.1, and observed the following:
   - There is clear statistical significance in Sizzling Seven ranks predicting relative sector returns in the following month.
   - The IC (information coefficient) is highly significant in the quantitative finance context.

Table 5.1 Regression Results: Sizzling Seven Ranks.

R-square	0.049
T-stat	10.79
IC (information coefficient)	0.22

5.10. TOP SECTOR PICKS – FREQUENCY

Figure 5.4 shows for each sector the percentage of times that it receives a certain score in the past 20 years. For instance, communication services has a score of 1 (worst sector) for 19.6% of the months in the past 20 years for Sizzling Seven. Additionally, Figure 5.5 presents dot plots illustrating the time series of these Sizzling Seven sector scores, which lead to the following observations:

- The sector that is most frequently held long happens to be consumer staples followed by utilities, due to consistently high Sizzling Seven scores on average over time. The preference for most defensive sectors may be a reflection of the success of low volatility investing as well as a function of the two crashes in the 20-year dataset.
- Financials were rarely shorted except near the GFC.
- The most frequently shorted sector is energy, reflecting poor Sizzling Seven scores on average over time. Looking at the plot, we observe that the strategies shorted energy consistently before and after the commodity crash of 2015. However, industrials, staples, and discretionary are rarely at the bottom of the sector ranks.

5.11. CONCLUSION

- QMIT's Sizzling Seven MFM signal clearly has some predictive content in being able to sort sector winners versus sector losers over the past 19 years.
- For the case of investing in single ETFs, picking two sectors top versus bottom yields slightly lower returns in comparison to picking just the best versus worst sector, but the diversification benefits dramatically outweigh the

Percentage of sector score in 20 years for each sector for Sizzling Seven										
Rank	Com. Services	Consumer Discretionary	Consumer Staples	Energy	Financials	Health Care	Industrials	Materials	Technology	Utilities
1[worst]	19.6	0	0	52.9	1.7	7.9	0	14.2	0.4	3.3
2	22.5	0.4	0	8.8	6.2	18.3	0	30.8	6.7	6.2
3	14.6	3.8	0	15	3.8	26.7	1.2	21.2	7.5	6.2
4	15.8	8.3	0.4	9.2	3.3	24.2	4.6	16.2	10.8	7.1
5	11.2	19.6	1.2	3.8	10.4	8.3	13.3	9.6	12.9	9.6
6	7.9	22.5	4.6	4.6	9.6	6.2	18.8	4.2	14.2	7.5
7	3.3	17.9	5	3.8	13.8	3.3	26.7	2.5	15.0	8.8
8	3.3	15	11.2	1.2	16.2	3.8	22.5	1.2	15.4	10
9	1.2	10.8	30.8	0.8	10.4	1.2	11.2	0	11.2	22.1
10 [best]	0.4	1.7	46.7	0	24.6	0	1.7	0	5.8	19.2

Figure 5.4 Percentage of Scores (20Y) for Each Sector: Sizzling Seven.[7]

---

[7] N.B. Aggregate sector ranks will be the same whether one implements the strategy based on ETFs or single stocks.

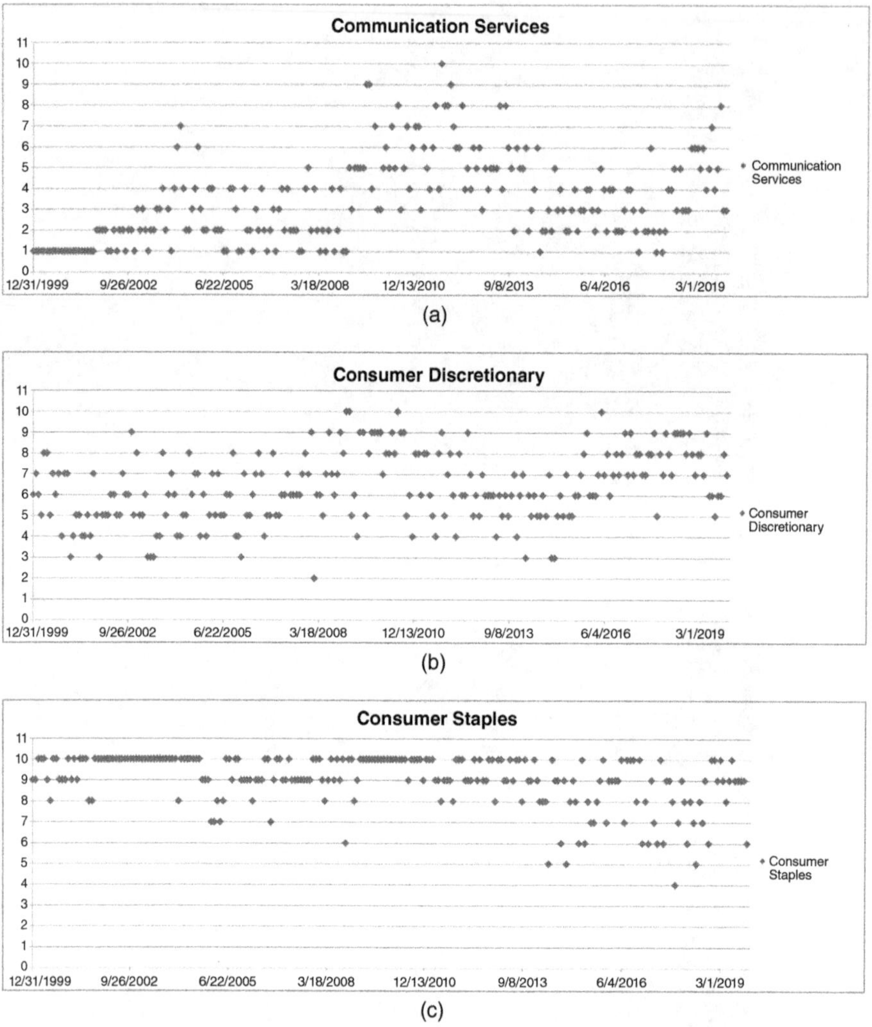

Figure 5.5 Sizzling Seven Sector Ranks.

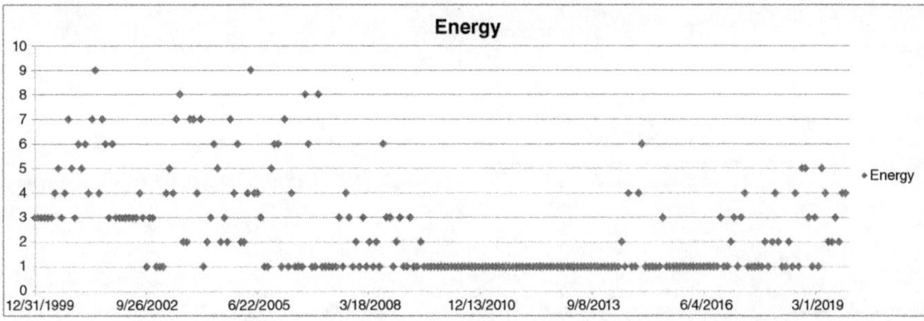

(d)

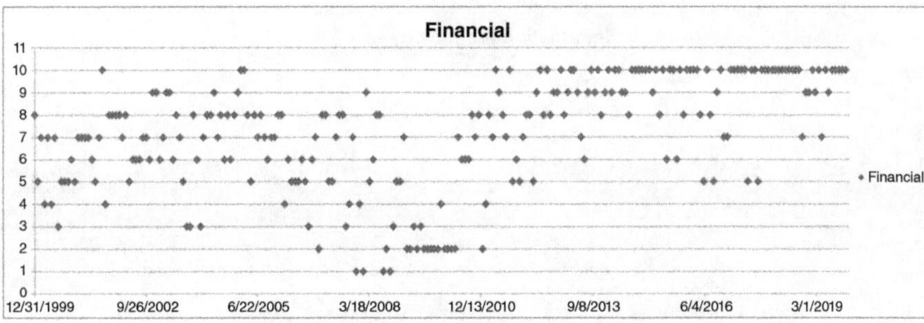

(e)

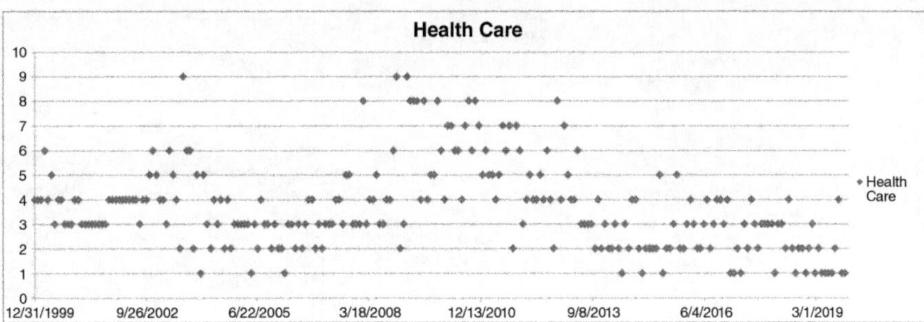

(f)

Figure 5.5 (Continued)

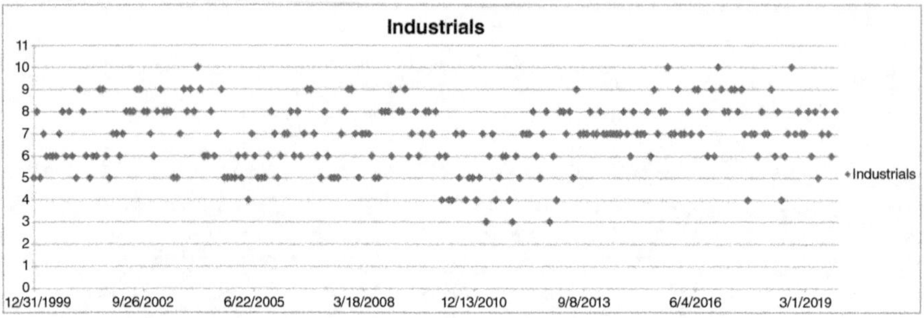

(g)

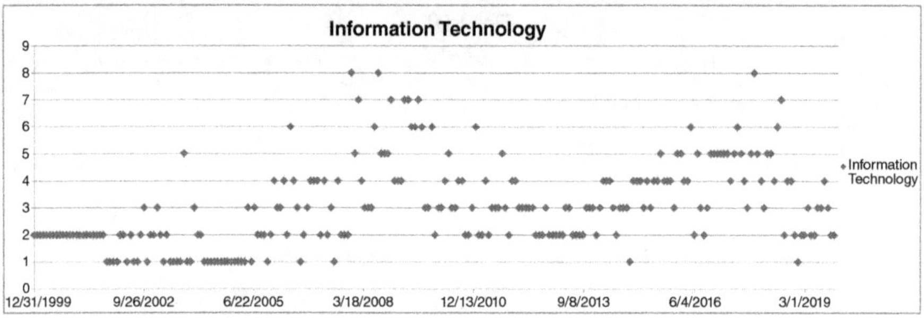

(h)

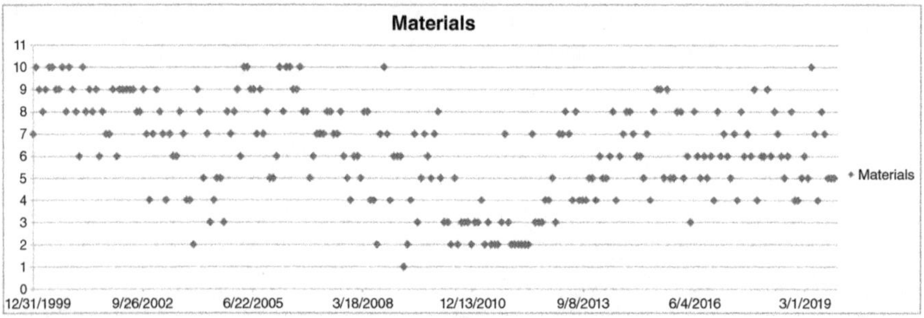

(i)

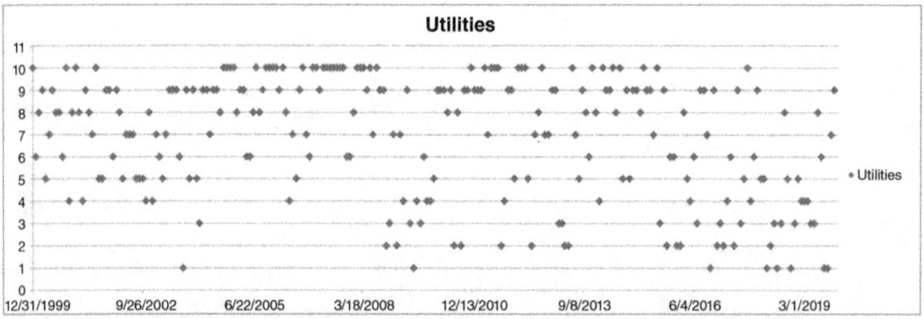

(j)

Figure 5.5 (Continued)

return trade-off given the much lower volatility and max drawdowns.

- For the case of investing in single stocks, picking the top five versus bottom five sectors yields higher returns in comparison to picking just the best versus worst sector. Moreover, we also get the diversification benefits.
- Using top/bottom 10% stocks within the sectors yields better performance results than using 20%. Overall, volatility is a bit higher, which shows the benefits of diversification, but these benefits are not that high. To conclude, there is no significant difference in performance results for the top 10% versus 20% cases, but based on risk-adjusted metrics we should take 0.9 quantile (top 10% of stocks) for 5×5 sectors.
- Our final implementation of the rotation strategy uses single stocks within the sectors that substantially outperform the case using ETFs in both risk-adjusted and nominal performance.

Chapter 6

Style Analysis

6.1. FUND: STYLE AND PERFORMANCE MEASUREMENT

In this study, we seek to attribute the performance of select mutual and hedge funds by using style analysis based on a putatively spanning set of enhanced smart betas (ESBs) that constitute our explanatory factor model. These ESBs are further combined into various indices. To reduce collinearity, we use five ESBs, and three composites toward the attribution of fund performance due to "style," while the remainder of the excess return is attributed to the managers' "selection."

Our approach employs a framework analogous to that outlined by Sharpe (1992) for returns-based style analysis. We seek to answer the following questions: Given a return stream of a mutual fund, how much of its return can be attributed to style, which is proxied by using the return's exposure to a list of our ESBs versus how much can be attributed to the manager's selection (as proxied by the residual return)?

In Sharpe's study, the return of a fund is allocated into several major asset classes. Sharpe used an asset class factor model to measure fund's exposures to variations in returns of major asset classes. Specifically, the asset class factor model is a special case of a generic factor model. In this model, each factor represents the return on an asset class and the sensitivities (exposures) are required to sum to 100%. As a result, a fund's return is represented as the return on a portfolio invested in the asset classes plus a residual component. Sharpe attributed the return driven by these systematic factor exposures to style. The remaining non-factor returns, assumed to be uncorrelated across different assets' residuals, are attributed to manager's selection. Sharpe contended that this decomposition facilitates an evaluation of individual fund managers' effectiveness and quantifies the value, if any, added through active management decisions.

To measure how well the return is explained by asset classes, Sharpe used R^2 to measure the proportion of return variance explained by the selected asset classes, or style, and the remaining $1-R^2$ to measure the proportion of return variance explained by manager's selection.

Sharpe selected 12 asset classes, each represented by a market capitalization-weighted index of the returns on many securities (each index represents a strategy that could be followed at low cost using an index fund). Sharpe (1992) argued that much of the variation in fund returns "can be attributed to the combined effects of their exposures to these asset classes and the realized returns on those classes."

In our study, we believe that QuantZ QMIT's ESBs can achieve the same goal of capturing common variations of returns across equities. Therefore, we follow similar procedures as per Sharpe's study and replace the 12 asset classes with eight QMIT factors (five ESBs and three composite signals) to do fund attribution and style analysis on two long-only equity mutual funds and one long/short equity hedge fund.

6.2. METHODOLOGY

6.2.1. Data

We select two long-only funds and one long/short fund. All three funds invest in equities. We selected the two mutual funds because they have clear investment theses – they have consistent exposure to several styles. LMOPX is a long-term value fund with a focus on mid-cap stocks. MALVX is a large-cap value fund. QMNIX is a market-neutral fund with changing exposures. We argue that our attribution results should indicate such fund characteristics.

- Miller Opportunity Trust Class C: LMOPX monthly return
    - We chose this share class because this class has the longest return history among all Miller Opportunity Trust share classes.
- BlackRock Advantage Large Cap Value Fund: MALVX monthly return
- AQR Equity Market Neutral Fund Class I: QMNIX monthly return

- We chose this share class because this class has the longest return history among all AQR Equity Market Neutral Fund share classes.

6.2.2. Multiple Linear Regression Using Long-Only ESBs

From a multi-collinearity perspective, as per Section 3.8, we select eight ESBs and composite signals including SIRF, REV, SIZE, GrowthMo, DIV, VAL, RISK, Qual. We conduct two forms of regressions in each iteration: unconstrained and constrained. Unconstrained regression is a multiple ordinary least squares (OLS) linear regression. Constrained regression is the same with one additional constraint: the regression coefficients (i.e., exposures) must add up to 100%. There will be a more detailed explanation in later sections.

For long-only mutual funds (LMOPX, MALVX):

$$R_i = b1 * DIV + b2 * REV + b3 * RISK + b4 * SIRF + b5 * SIZE$$
$$+ b6 * VAL + b7 * QUAL + b8 * GrowthMo + e_i$$

R_i = Monthly Fund Return

- *DIV:* Long-only return of stocks that have higher-than-average dividends (top 5% in estimation universe)
- *REV:* Long-only return of stocks that constitute the top reversals candidates based on mean reversion
- *RISK:* Long-only return of stocks with lower-than-average volatility, beta, and/or idiosyncratic risk
- *SIRF:* Long-only return of stocks with lower short interest-related metrics
- *SIZE:* Long-only return of smaller firms' stocks

- *VAL:* Long-only return of value composite
- *QUAL:* Long-only return of quality composite
- *GrowthMo:* Long-only return of growth momentum composite
- e_i: Residual or non-factor return. e_i is assumed to be uncorrelated with the returns of every other explanatory ESB variable e_j. We interpret this residual return to the manager's stock selection, which cannot be attributed to QMIT's ESBs.

For long/short funds (QMNIX) using long-only ESB regressors:

$$R_i + R_{SPY} = b1 * DIV + b2 * REV + b3 * RISK + b4 * SIRF + b5 * SIZE +$$

$$b6 * VAL + b7 * QUAL + b8 * GrowthMo + e_i$$

$R_i + R_{SPY}$ = Monthly long/short fund return plus return of SPY

The remaining variables are the same as previously stated.

The reason we add the market return to the long/short fund return is that the fund is supposed to be market neutral (i.e., it does not have exposure to the market), whereas the ESB regressors are long-only return. Thus, the SPY (SPDR® S&P 500® ETF Trust) return is added back to the fund's return, to make both sides of the equation comparable so that we can run the regression on a pari passu basis.

6.2.3. Market-Neutral Regressions

In a market-neutral context, we seek to remove the market beta embedded in mutual funds returns (note that the market-neutral fund QMNIX has no market exposure to start with). Hence, we must subtract the SPY return from the mutual fund returns on left-hand side. Then, we can use the EMN (Equity Market Neutral) spread returns of our ESBs or composites, which are analogous to the market-neutral versions of factor returns.

For mutual funds (LMOPX, MALVX):

$$R_i - R_{SPY} = b0 + b1 * DIV + b2 * REV + b3 * RISK + b4 * SIRF$$

$$+ b5 * SIZE + b6 * VAL + b7 * QUAL + b8 * GrowthMo + e_i$$

$R_i - R_{SPY}$ = Monthly long/short fund return minus return on SPY

- *DIV:* Spread return of stocks that have higher-than-average dividends
- *REV:* Spread return of stocks with lackluster past performance that is due for a rebound
- *RISK:* Spread return of stocks with lower-than-average volatility, beta, and/or idiosyncratic risk
- *SIRF:* Spread return of stocks with lower short interest
- *SIZE:* Spread return of smaller firms' stocks
- *VAL:* Spread return of value composite
- *QUAL:* Spread return of quality composite
- *GrowthMo:* Spread return of growth momentum composite

We seek to remove the market effect on mutual funds' return. Therefore, we subtract return of SPY on the left-hand side. On the right-hand side, we use the spread returns of our ESBs to keep it pari passu.

For long/short funds (QMNIX) both side are already EMN:

$$R_i = b0 + b1 * DIV + b2 * REV + b3 * RISK + b4 * SIRF + b5 * SIZE$$
$$+ b6 * VAL + b7 * QUAL + b8 * GrowthMo + e_i$$

R_i = Monthly long/short fund return

The remaining variables are the same as previously stated.

6.2.4. Minimization Problem

(a) Unconstrained regression (OLS):

$$\underbrace{argmin}_{b_0 - b_8} \sum_{i=0}^{T} \left(Fund\ Return - b_0 - \sum_{j=1}^{8} b_j * factor_j \right)^2$$

- *Fund Return* refers to the dependent variable in this regression.
- $factor_j$ refers to the return for the jth ESB or composites. (It can be either long-only ESB returns for long-only regressions, or spread ESB returns for market-neutral regressions.)
- $b_1 ... b_8$ are exposures to the respective ESBs. b_0 is the regression intercept.
- We force the intercept to be zero. The reason is that we attribute the residual return as the manager's selection. While a non-zero intercept is central to performance evaluation metrics like the Jensen (1968) alpha, where the intercept explicitly represents the value added by active management, in this context, the proportion of active management, or manager's stock selection, is attributed to the variance not explained by the ESBs, or $1 - R^2$.

(b) Constrained regression:

$$\underbrace{argmin}_{b_0-b_8} \sum_{i=0}^{T} \left(Fund\ Return - b_0 - \sum_{j=1}^{8} b_j * factor_j \right)^2$$

$$subject\ to\ constraints:$$

$$\sum_{j=1}^{8} b_j = 1$$

The idea of a constrained regression is quite simple. This procedure imposes one additional constraint on an otherwise multiple OLS regression: all the b_j values (factor exposure) must add up to 1. The reason for this additional constraint is that our measure of factors exposures is comparable across funds. The problem with this constrained regression procedure is that, once additional constraints are applied, the resulting exposures are no longer best linear unbiased estimators. And the R^2 of the regression will consequently decrease. However, this is a small price to pay for a uniform measure across funds.

Performance evaluation:

$$R^2 = 1 - \frac{RSS}{SST} = 1 - \frac{\sum_i (y_i - \hat{y}_i)^2}{\sum_i (y_i - \bar{y})^2}$$

$$R^2_{adj} = 1 - \frac{RSS/(n-k)}{SST/(n-1)} = 1 - \frac{\sum_i \left(y_i - \hat{y}_i \right)^2 /(n-k)}{\sum_i (y_i - \bar{y})^2 /(n-1)}$$

where n = number of data points (number of monthly returns); k = number of explanatory variables (in our case, $k = 8$ ESBs or composites).

R^2 measures the proportion of the variance of fund's return explained by the QMIT ESBs. R^2_{adj} , often attributed to Raju et al. (1997), achieves the same goal but with penalties for the number of independent variables to take into account model parsimony. Arguably, this adjustment dates back to the Ezekiel estimator of Ezekiel (1930).

We attribute the R^2_{adj} value to the fund's style, and the remainder $\left(1-R^2_{adj}\right)$ to manager's selection. The reason we use R^2_{adj} is because of the penalty else the R^2 is monotonic in the number of predictors selected.

We summarize our results in the following manner: the first chart lists exposures to each of our factors while the second graph plots the amount attributable to our factors versus the manager's stock selection.

6.3. RESULTS

6.3.1. LMOPX (Miller Opportunity Trust Class C): Mid-Cap Value[1]

Let's start by putting Bill Miller's Legg Mason Opportunity Trust (LMOPX) under the style analysis microscope to see if the attribution is consistent with its historically distinctive tilts toward mid-cap and value stocks, with a flexible approach that often-included prominent growth names such as Amazon, Alphabet, Meta, and Nvidia. LMOPX is categorized by Morningstar in the mid-cap value style box, which means that it tends to invest in stocks considered

[1] Fund characteristics according to Morningstar: https://www.morningstar.com/funds/xnas/lmopx/quote, MarketWatch: https://www.marketwatch.com/investing/fund/lmopx, and Miller Opportunity Trust: https://millervaluefunds.com/miller-opportunity-trust/.

undervalued relative to their fundamentals (e.g., low price-to-earnings ratios, high dividend yields, etc.). For such a fund, we would expect it to have positive exposure to the long-only value ESB (as it invests in cheap, value stocks), positive exposure to the growth-momentum composite, positive exposure to size (since Miller invests in mid-caps), and positive exposure to dividends as well. There is no explicit mention of a systematic quality tilt in the mandate although one may infer that from the preponderance of mega-cap high-quality aforementioned technology names. The long-only LMOPX regression against the long side of our ESBs is summarized in Table 6.1.

Results. We see positive exposures to value, GrowthMo, and quality in the unconstrained case. We suspect the low

Table 6.1 Long-Only LMOPX Regression (Monthly from 01/00 to 05/21).

LMOPX Long Only	Unconstrained Regression (t-stat)	Constrained Regression (%)
div	37.96% (2.22)	44.88
rev	10.89% (1.95)	10.10
risk	11.21% (0.94)	–4.04
sirf	10.9% (0.75)	5.02
size	13.58% (1.49)	13.29
val	8.98% (0.51)	12.10
qual	9.98% (0.57)	–0.93
GrowthMo	14.36% (1.39)	19.56
Total	117.87%	100.00
R-Squared	78.80%	78.11
Adj R-Squared	77.80%	77.40%

exposure number to value is due to the disproportionately large attribution to the correlated dividends ESB because the 30-day US Securities and Exchange Commission yield and trailing 12-month yields are both reported as zero, indicating little to no income generation from dividends, which justifies re-running the analysis without dividends. In the long-only case, market beta results in a rather high R^2 of 77.4% and a corresponding lower 22.6% attributed to the manager's selection as in Figure 6.1.

To assess the impact of the dividends ESB, the long-only regression for LMOPX was re-run excluding it. These results (monthly data from January 2000 to May 2021) are presented in Table 6.2.

Results. Indeed, after removing the dividends ESB, the exposure to value is much higher in line with our expectations and the long-only attribution makes more sense overall.

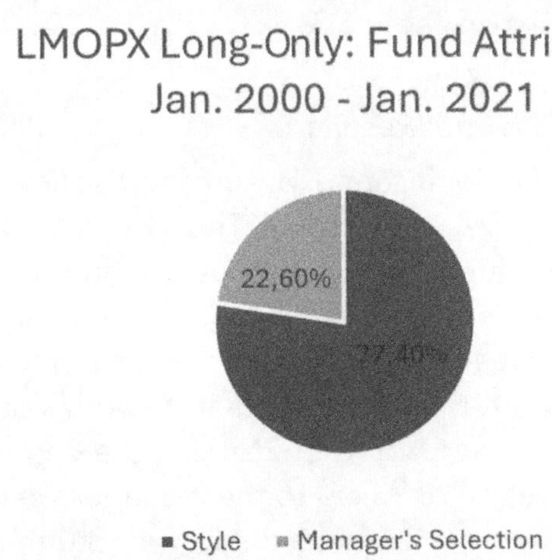

Figure 6.1 Long-Only LMOPX Fund Attribution.

Table 6.2 Long-Only LMOPX Regression – No Dividends Case.

LMOPX Long, no div	Unconstrained Regression (*t*-stat)	Constrained Regression (%)
rev	12.58% (2.25)	11.98
risk	12.82% (1.06)	−6.15
sirf	14.31% (0.98)	7.64
size	16.71% (1.84)	17.07
val	40.38% (3.87)	51.60
qual	16.93% (0.97)	4.70
GrowthMo	8.03% (0.80)	13.16
Total	121.76%	100.00
R-Squared	78.38%	77.48
Adj R-Squared	77.46%	76.75

The style analysis for LMOPX on a market-neutral basis, with the regression results (monthly data from January 2000 to May 2021), is shown in Table 6.3.

6.3.1.1. Market-Neutral Results

We see statistically significant exposures to risk (low volatility), short interest, size, and value. This is in line with our intuition given the fund's mid-cap value orientation and no explicit quality tilt as previously noted. The market-neutral regression gives cleaner results than the long-only regression by stripping out the market beta from both sides. This results in a much lower Adj R^2 of 26.4% and a correspondingly larger attribution of 73.6% to the manager's selection, as visualized in Figure 6.2. Interestingly, we note that while dividends still dominate (and that can be fixed in an analogous manner by dropping that ESB), the key difference is the much larger exposure to size and a correspondingly

Table 6.3 Market-Neutral LMOPX Regression Results.

LMOPX-SPY

Market Neutral	Unconstrained Regression (t-stat)	Constrained Regression (%)
div	5.88% (0.70)	43.62
rev	−3.34% (−0.92)	4.00
risk	−25.11% (−5.41)	−30.16
sirf	−25.73% (−3.21)	10.97
size	17.54% (2.8)	39.88
val	15.8% (2.64)	11.67
qual	−0.29% (−0.03)	−0.30
GrowthMo	5.5% (0.92)	20.32
Total	−9.76%	100.00
R-Squared	42.70%	28.68
Adj R-Squared	40.68%	26.37

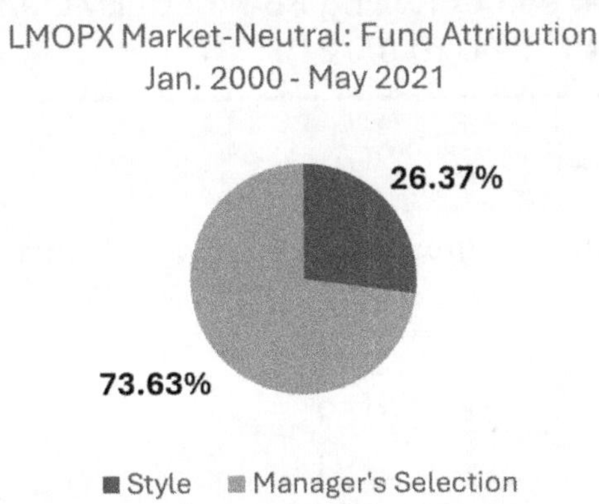

Figure 6.2 Market-Neutral LMOPX Fund Attribution.

larger negative exposure to risk (low volatility), which would be consistent with the tilt toward higher beta riskier growthy names.

In the next section we continue with this train of thought but using rolling regressions to tease out any style drift over time and unmask cross-sectional variations over time that may have averaged out in a single-shot 21.5-year regression.

Table 6.4 summarizes the mean coefficients from these 36-month rolling LMOPX regressions (January 2000 to May 2021), and Figure 6.3 graphically depicts the resulting time-varying long-only smart beta exposures.

We see that the sum of weights is indeed equal to one and that the exposures do vary dramatically over time hinting at style drift that makes the mean coefficients from 36-month rolling windows potentially quite misleading. As before, the

Table 6.4 Mean of Rolling 36-Month LMOPX Regressions (01/00 to 05/21).

LMOPX Long Only – Mean of Rolling	Unconstrained Regression (%)	Constrained Regression (%)
div	62.45	67.04
rev	0.89	4.27
risk	28.93	6.60
sirf	7.94	7.68
size	12.01	13.78
val	6.17	5.55
qual	−30.48	−37.47
GrowthMo	31.29	32.55
Total	119.21	100.00

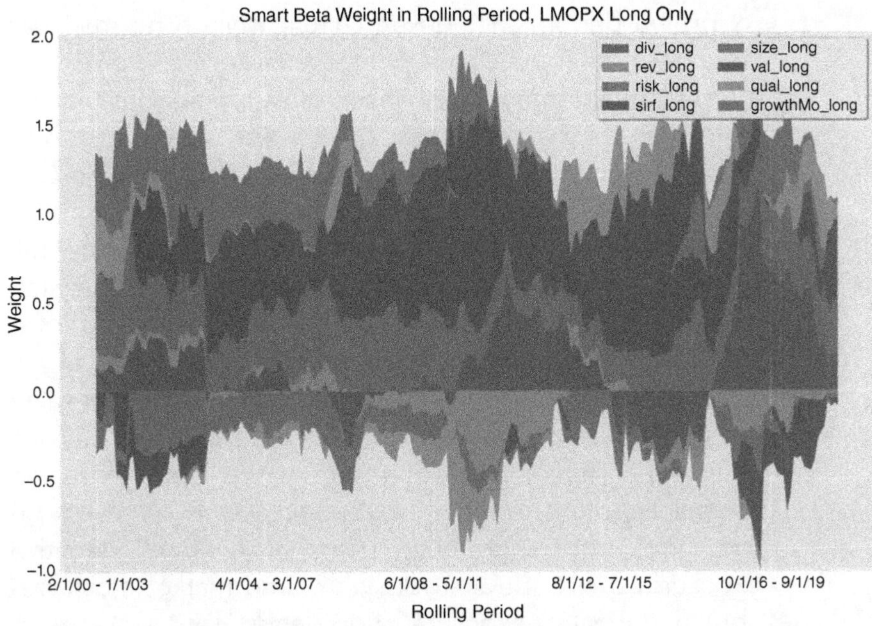

Figure 6.3 Long-Only LMOPX Smart Beta Rolling Exposures.

exposure to value (including dividend ESB) and GrowthMo is substantial but now the average quality has become substantially negative.

6.3.2. MALVX (Blackrock Advantage Large Cap Value Fund): Large-Cap Value[2]

In June 1999, Bob Doll joined Merrill Lynch Investment Managers (MLIM) as chief investment officer (CIO), having previously served as CIO at Oppenheimer Funds. Bob Doll was recruited by then-head of MLIM, Jeffrey Peek, to bring new leadership and investment discipline to the firm's equity offerings. Doll's approach emphasized a combination of fundamental research and disciplined risk management, aiming

[2] Fund characteristics from Morningstar: https://www.marketwatch.com/investing/fund/malvx.

to instill a performance-driven culture while tying manager compensation to benchmark outperformance and profitability. His "quantamental" philosophy was embodied in the "judicious combination of art and science" mantra. In short order, he set about launching the Merrill Lynch Large Cap Series funds with me as the senior quant on the team. These funds were part of a strategic effort to strengthen Merrill Lynch's presence in the large-cap equity space and to revitalize its mutual fund lineup. The LC Series grew to over $30 billion (assets under management) by the time of my departure from the firm in 2004. The MALVX large-cap value fund continues under the BlackRock umbrella over 25 years later as a fund that seeks long-term growth, with a focus on risk management. We therefore expect MALVX to have positive exposure to value (buys cheap, value stocks), negative exposure to size (buys stocks with large market capitalization), and positive exposure to dividends (value stocks tend to issue dividends). The results are summarized in Table 6.5.

Table 6.5 Long-Only MALVX Regression Results (Monthly Data from 01/00 to 05/21).

MALVX Long Only	Unconstrained Regression (*t*-stat)	Constrained Regression (%)
div	8.38% (1.15)	4.49
rev	0.99% (0.41)	1.42
risk	20.68% (4.04)	29.23
sirf	24.3% (3.90)	27.60
size	−16.46% (−4.22)	−16.30
val	21.06% (2.81)	19.31
qual	11.19% (1.48)	17.31
GrowthMo	19.84% (4.49)	16.92
Total	89.98%	100.00
R-Squared	87.72%	87.06
Adj R-Squared	86.97%	86.64

Given that dividend exposure is small, –4.5%, we don't expect value exposure to increase that much as in the case of LMOPX.

The fund attribution for this long-only MALVX analysis is illustrated in Figure 6.4.

Results. Consistent with the fund's mandate we see positive exposures to large cap (negative to size ESB), value, GrowthMo, low volatility (risk), and the quality composite in the unconstrained case. We suspect the low exposure number to value is due to the disproportionately large attribution to the correlated dividends ESB, which justifies running it without dividends as we did in the LMOPX case. As with the LMOPX analysis, the regression for MALVX was re-estimated without the dividends ESB; these results are presented in Table 6.6.

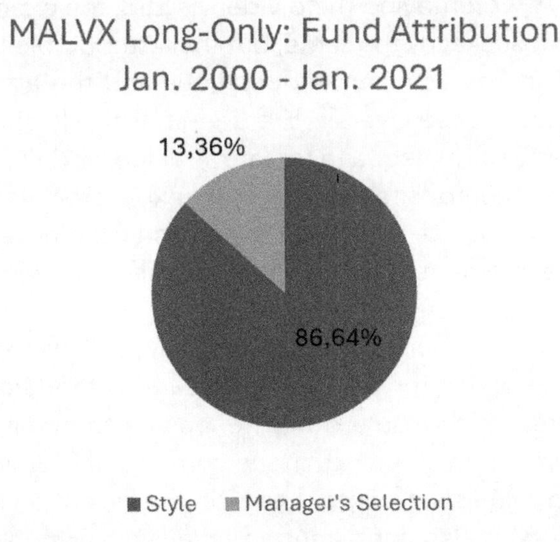

Figure 6.4 **Long-Only MALVX Fund Attribution.**

Table 6.6 Long-Only MALVX Regression – No Dividends Case.

MALVX Long, no div	Unconstrained Regression (t-stat)	Constrained Regression
rev	1.36% (0.57)	1.61%
risk	21.03% (4.12)	29.04%
sirf	25.05% (4.04)	27.83%
size	−15.77% (−4.09)	−15.91%
val	27.99% (6.31)	23.27%
qual	12.73% (1.71)	17.86%
GrowthMo	18.44% (4.34)	16.30%
Total	90.84%	100.00%
R-Squared	87.66%	87.04%
Adj R-Squared	86.96	86.62

Results. After removing the dividends ESB, the exposure to size is almost exactly the same, but that attributable to Value is higher in line with our expectations and the attribution makes more sense overall. We see statistically significant exposures to size (negative for large), value, and the growth momentum composites as one might expect for a large-cap value fund that used multifactor alphas including earnings and price momentum. From the author's involvement on the fund management team as the quant for the Merrill Lynch Large Cap Series funds (of which MALVX was the flagship), I can vouch for the high exposure to the GrowthMo composite, which resulted from exposure to earnings and price momentum albeit within the confines of Morningstar's large and value style boxes. The high coefficient on low volatility (RISK) is also consistent and plausible with the quantamental mandate while that from SIRF may be spurious, as there was no explicit short interest component in the long-only MFMs. Given that this is a single-shot regression over 21.5 years during which time there was complete turnover of the management team, it's conceivable that there may have been significant style drift as verified in the next section. The single-shot view over such a long time period can result in potentially misleading exposures. The time-varying exposure to ESBs dominates with 13.36% remaining as manager selection versus 22.6% for Bill Miller in the long-only style analysis for the same period.

In Table 6.7, we see that the sum of weights is indeed equal to one albeit with a substantially time-varying style signature similar to what was observed in the case of LMOPX. Figure 6.5 reveals that on average long exposures to SIRF and RISK have positive weights, while SIZE has negative weights. For other parameters we see sign changes indicative of style drift, which is to be expected over a period of decades with complete turnover of the portfolio team.

Table 6.7 MALVX – Mean of 36-Month Rolling Regressions (01/00 to 05/21).

MALVX		
Long Only – Mean of Rolling	**Unconstrained Regression (%)**	**Constrained Regression (%)**
div	20.59	15.48
rev	–5.73	–6.10
risk	20.10	29.90
sirf	32.02	35.58
size	–11.41	–11.91
val	12.40	12.50
qual	–0.15	5.94
GrowthMo	20.81	18.61
Total	88.63	100.00

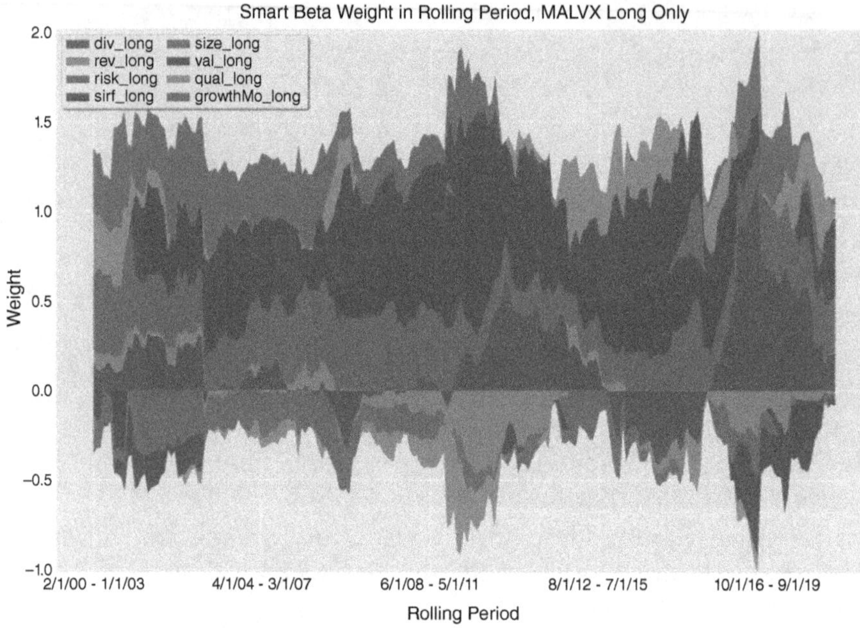

Figure 6.5 MALVX Long Only: 36-Month Rolling Coefficients (01/00 to 05/21).

6.3.3. QMNIX – AQR Equity Market Neutral Fund[3]

We shall now move on to extend Sharpe's style analysis framework to the market-neutral context. Given that AQR Capital Management has played a pivotal role in the evolution of the quant equity space and remains a behemoth in the factor space (despite some visibly deep drawdowns and fund liquidations), we showcase their liquid alternative QMNIX (1940 act) fund since its returns are readily available to anyone through almost any financial data source including Yahoo Finance. The AQR Equity Market Neutral Fund (QMNIX) appears to be the primary liquid alternatives fund managed by AQR as of 2025 (inception in 2014) as opposed to several related funds that may have been liquidated.

[3] Fund characteristics according to Morningstar: https://www.morningstar.com/funds/xnas/qmnix/quote.

QMNIX seeks to deliver positive absolute returns by taking long and short positions in equity and equity-related instruments. The fund is market neutral, whereby positions are chosen such that the long-side exposure is offset by the short side as per Morningstar. It employs factors such as value, momentum, and quality toward security selection and is classified as "alt style correlation/relative value" by Morningstar.

For QMNIX, we expect to plausibly see net positive exposures (on a market-neutral basis) to value as well as dividends, growth momentum, and the quality ESBs, which is confirmed by glancing at the 6Y daily single-shot regression in Table 6.8. This fund does not have history going back to 2000 (unlike MALVX and LMOPX), which is why we take the 6Y daily window, which is also used for peer comparison with QMIT strategies subsequently in Chapter 9, Section 9.1

Table 6.8 QMNIX – Market-Neutral Style Decomposition (6Y Daily 2019 to 2024).

QMNIX-Daily Beta Neutral	Unconstrained Regression (t-stat)	Constrained Regression (%)
div_spread	3.42% (1.8)	7.27
GrowthMo_spread	14.62% (15.2)	20.27
qual_spread	10.88% (5.3)	17.70
rev_spread	−5.42% (−6.2)	−3.77
risk_spread	1.37% (0.6)	10.98
sirf_spread	1.92% (0.8)	17.56
size_spread	13.16% (9.1)	27.35
val_spread	8.81% (5.9)	2.64
Total	48.77%	100.00
R-Squared	41.00%	29.94
Adj R-Squared	40.72%	29.57

along with market-neutral funds from other prominent firms like J.P. Morgan and Vanguard.

6.3.4 Results

R^2 of 29.6% is lower for QMNIX than that for the long-only mutual fund regressions due to the lack of market beta in the EMN case but well in line with the 26.4% for LMOPX when considered in market-neutral terms. That results in an analogously larger 70.4% attributable to the manager's selection (active management) as depicted in Figure 6.6. As per Table 6.8, QMNIX has statistically significant exposures to GrowthMo, size, quality, value and (negative exposure to) mean reversion [REV] over the full 6Y daily

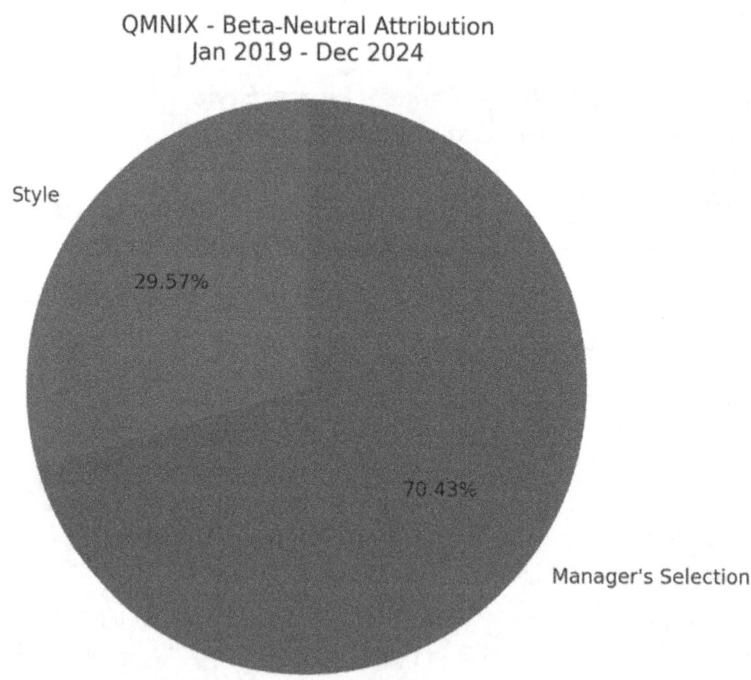

Figure 6.6 Market-Neutral QMNIX Fund Attribution.

window here. These style tilts appear to be consistent with AQR's published philosophy based on papers such as Asness et al. (2013) and Asness et al. (2019). Table 6.9 presents the six-year beta-neutral ESB regression results excluding the dividends ESB (daily data from 2019 to 2024).

Given the typically dynamic exposure of hedge funds to various style factors over time (as opposed to coefficients, which may wash out in a single-shot regression), we should also consider the beta-neutral 60-day rolling regressions of QMNIX over the 6Y window.

Table 6.10 provides the mean coefficients from these 60-day rolling QMNIX regressions (January 2019 to December 2024), and Figure 6.7 graphically displays these dynamic rolling ESB exposures.

Table 6.9 QMNIX – 6Y Beta-Neutral ESB Regression – No DIV (2019 to 2024).

QMNIX-Daily No Div Beta Neutral	Unconstrained Regression (t-stat)	Constrained Regression (%)
GrowthMo_spread	14.69% (15.3)	20.56
qual_spread	11.00% (5.4)	18.15
rev_spread	−5.49% (−6.3)	−3.88
risk_spread	2.67% (1.3)	14.05
sirf_spread	1.95% (0.8)	18.04
size_spread	13.82% (9.9)	29.15
val_spread	9.48% (6.6)	3.92
Total	48.13%	100.00
R-Squared	40.87%	29.37
Adj R-Squared	40.64%	29.04

Table 6.10 Mean of Rolling 60-Day QMNIX Coefficients (01/19 to 12/24).

QMNIX-Daily Rolling Mean	Unconstrained Regression (*t*-stat)	Constrained Regression (%)
div_spread	9.18%	17.91
GrowthMo_spread	11.41%	21.75
qual_spread	11.69%	15.51
rev_spread	−1.77%	0.43
risk_spread	−4.72%	5.08
sirf_spread	−5.25%	6.87
size_spread	13.53%	27.14
val_spread	7.89%	5.32
Total	41.96%	100.00

We see that the sum of weights is equal to one (cross-sectionally) and that there is evidence of dynamic exposure to various style factors over time.

6.4. CONCLUSION

We conclude that the set of eight QMIT explanatory factors (five ESBs and three composite signals) serve as a good representation of the style of the three funds examined. The output of our regression analysis matches the general expectation of the fund's characteristics as per public disclosure.

Thus, one may conclude that our QMIT ESBs can be used to conduct top-down returns-based style analysis on equity mutual funds and long/short equity funds to glean insights on their realized factor exposures and style drift over time. In so doing, we have extended the analysis of Sharpe (1992) to a richer set of explanatory factors (as embodied by QMIT ESBs) and to the market-neutral setting as well as going

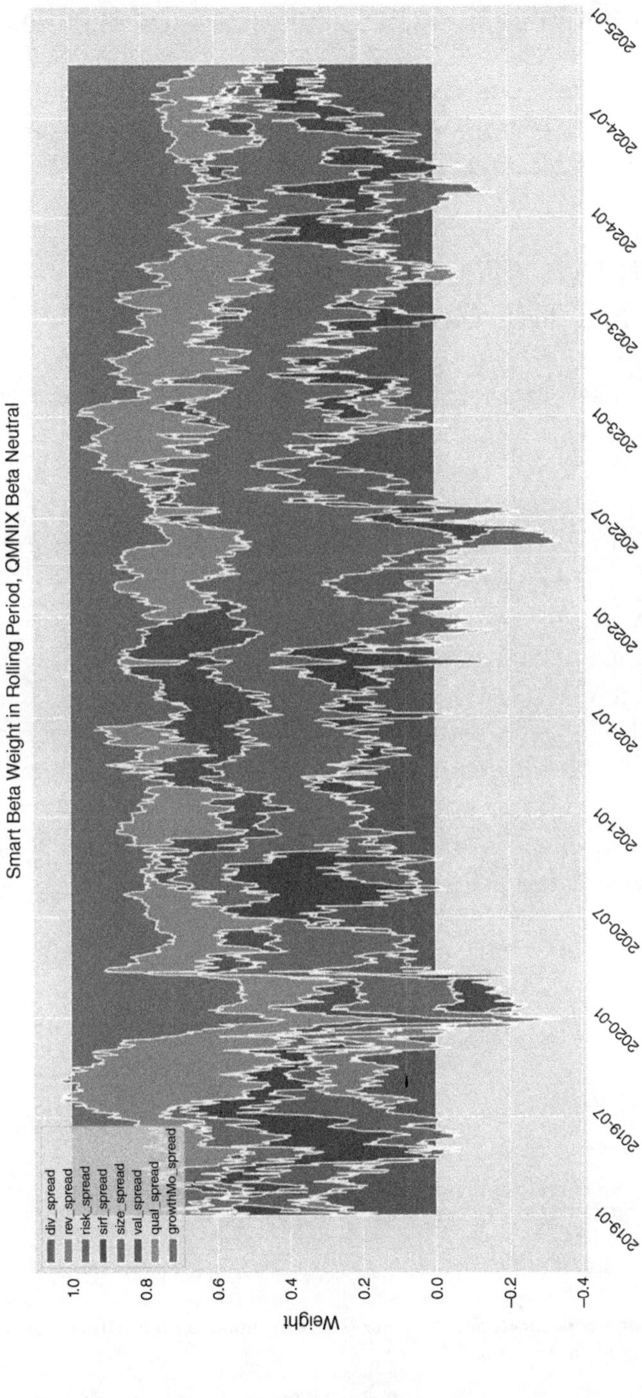

Figure 6.7 QMNIX – Rolling 60-Day ESB Regressions.

beyond the original long-only framework. Additionally, in Chapter 4, Section 4.7, and Chapter 10, Section 10.2, we also show how one can obtain the bottom-up aggregate style exposures from actual fund holdings as opposed to that surmised from its returns top-down.

6.5. REPLICATING AND BEATING THE GURUS

The required regulatory 13F disclosures of gurus and the ability to easily web scrape information has led to a cottage industry of copycat funds. While the idea seems plausible and appealing it has had limited success in practice because of the time lags involved by which point either the thesis is fully priced into the stock or the manager has quite possibly moved on, monetized, or even flipped their position in the specific name.

Given the large idiosyncratic risks associated with such an approach we suggest that the better way to emulate the greats would be to engineer the guru fund based on style replication, which is likely to be far more stable and with far less idiosyncratic risk (see Figure 6.8).

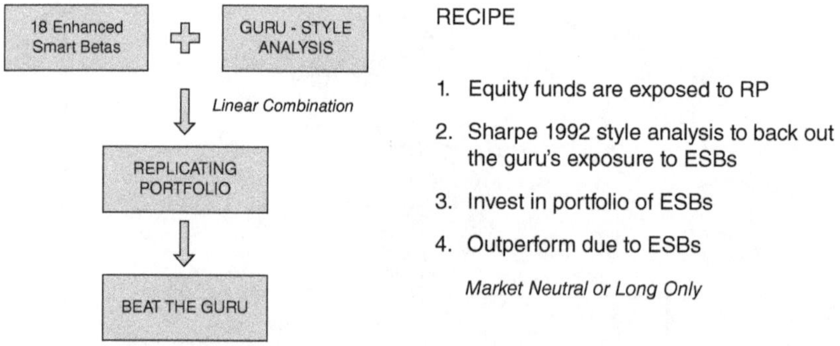

Figure 6.8 Framework for Replicating and Outperforming Guru Portfolios Using ESBs and Sharpe-Style Analysis.

Chapter 7

Regime Dependence

Regime dependent approaches have been the holy grail of factor investing. Certain factors/company attributes are more favored during risk-on (offensive) environments while others are more in vogue during risk-off (defensive) environments, as mentioned in Chapter 4. Indeed, it should seem eminently plausible that the cyclicality of factors merely reflects the cyclicality of markets and, in turn, that of the underlying economy. While it may be difficult to predict regimes, one should at least be able to contemporaneously guess the existing regime based on a RORO (risk-on/risk-off) spread indicator proposed herein. But first we need to map our enhanced smart betas (ESBs) into the risk-on/risk-off regimes in order to track the RORO spread returns.

We determine the regime dependence of our ESBs based on their correlation to the S&P 500, VIX, and 10-year yields. While computing the correlation to VIX and 10-year yields we remove the effect of change in S&P 500 on VIX and 10-year yields by regressing the change in S&P 500 against the change in VIX and change in 10-year yields. While most of the ESBs are negatively correlated to S&P 500 on account of them being market neutral, typically, risk-off factors have a negative correlation to VIX and 10-year yields as well in addition. We also looked at ESB performance during multiple market downturns in order to arrive at the classification.

Figure 7.1 presents the classification of ESBs into risk-on and risk-off categories, based on their 20-year correlations with the S&P 500 and VIX and 10-year yields. Complementing this classification, Figure 7.2 illustrates the 20-year cumulative returns for these distinct risk-on and risk-off ESB groups, providing insights into their long-term performance characteristics.

ESBs		S&P500	VIX*	10Y Yields*	Risk ON/OFF
		Full Period Correlations (20 Years)			
Momentum Cohort	Analyst Revisions	-0.39	-0.08	-0.10	OFF
	Analyst Ratings	-0.37	-0.07	-0.16	OFF
	Enhanced Momentum	-0.33	-0.11	-0.17	OFF
	Momentum	-0.39	-0.11	-0.14	OFF
	Growth	-0.36	-0.07	-0.05	ON
Quality Cohort	Capital Structure and Use	-0.36	-0.02	-0.07	OFF
	Efficiency	-0.10	-0.03	0.03	ON
	Earnings Quality	-0.07	-0.05	0.00	OFF
	Leverage	-0.47	-0.09	-0.14	OFF
	Profitability	-0.49	-0.01	-0.15	OFF
	Stability	-0.50	0.00	-0.08	OFF
Value Cohort	Deep Value	0.02	-0.02	0.07	ON
	Relative Value	-0.22	-0.05	-0.01	ON
Others	Reversals	0.36	0.03	0.00	ON
	Dividend	-0.43	0.02	-0.01	OFF
	Risk	-0.64	-0.02	-0.15	OFF
	Size	0.20	-0.14	0.17	ON
	Short Interest	0.51	-0.02	0.04	ON

Figure 7.1 Risk-On Versus Risk-Off ESBs – 20Y Correlations and Classification.

ESBs		Oct-07 Feb-09	Apr-10 Jul-10	May-11 Oct-11	Sep-18 Dec-18	Risk ON/OFF
		Cumulative Returns				
Momentum Cohort	Analyst Revisions	44.7%	0.3%	10.9%	4.0%	OFF
	Analyst Ratings	52.8%	0.3%	10.4%	-3.2%	OFF
	Enhanced Momentum	9.2%	2.0%	11.4%	-0.3%	OFF
	Momentum	23.4%	-4.5%	7.2%	2.0%	OFF
	Growth	35.9%	0.1%	5.4%	0.2%	ON
Quality Cohort	Capital Structure & Usage	41.8%	3.2%	17.1%	12.5%	OFF
	Efficiency	-11.5%	-3.1%	1.4%	-1.1%	ON
	Earnings Quality	24.3%	-1.4%	12.2%	7.3%	OFF
	Leverage	71.6%	2.8%	20.8%	10.4%	OFF
	Profitability	41.6%	2.1%	35.3%	16.0%	OFF
	Stability	32.8%	3.7%	17.7%	18.5%	OFF
Value Cohort	Deep Value	23.3%	-3.9%	8.8%	0.1%	ON
	Relative Value	34.4%	3.7%	5.9%	4.7%	ON
Others	Reversals	1.0%	-7.0%	-1.9%	-5.2%	ON
	Dividend	17.1%	11.7%	22.7%	12.5%	OFF
	Risk	109.4%	14.1%	52.7%	39.0%	OFF
	Size	24.0%	5.0%	-8.1%	-4.2%	ON
	Short Interest	-19.3%	-12.8%	-15.1%	6.5%	ON
Regime Summary						
No. of months		16	3	5	4	
S&P500		-50.2%	-11.4%	-16.3%	-13.8%	
VIX Change		28	17	28	15	
10Y Yield Change (bps)		-157	-87	-140	-14	

Figure 7.2 Risk-On Versus Risk-Off ESBs – 20Y Cumulative Returns.

*VIX represents residual of monthly change in VIX levels regressed on monthly S&P 500 returns. 10Y yields represent residuals of monthly change in 10Y yields regressed on monthly S&P 500 returns.

While Figures 7.1 and 7.2 provide justification for the mapping of our ESBs into RORO regimes, Figure 7.3 shows the remarkable success of the RORO regime-based paradigm of tilting our factors (ESBs) during the COVID (S&P) crash episode from February 19 (when Italian contagion was on the front page news) until March 23, 2020, when the Fed stepped in to put a floor under risk assets. The mean RORO spread during this one month was about +22%, thereby quantifying the upper bound on the opportunity set for one who could have bet with perfect foresight. Figure 7.4 lends further credibility to this RORO framework given that the live out-sample returns for ESBs flip as the markets rebound

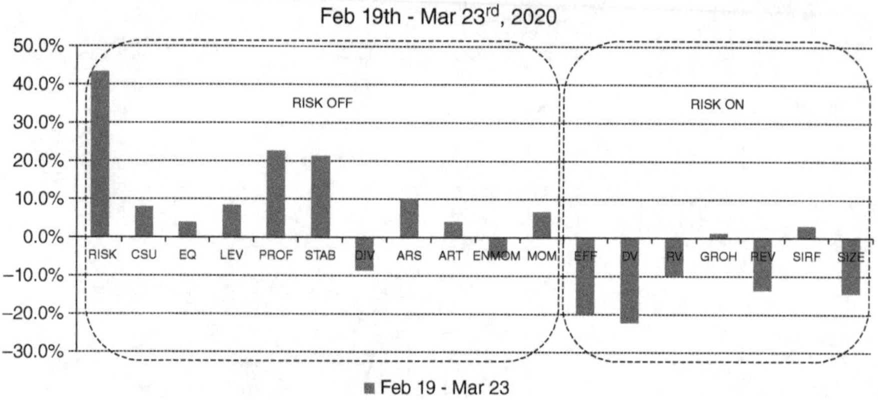

Figure 7.3 Risk-On Versus Risk-Off ESBs – COVID Crash.

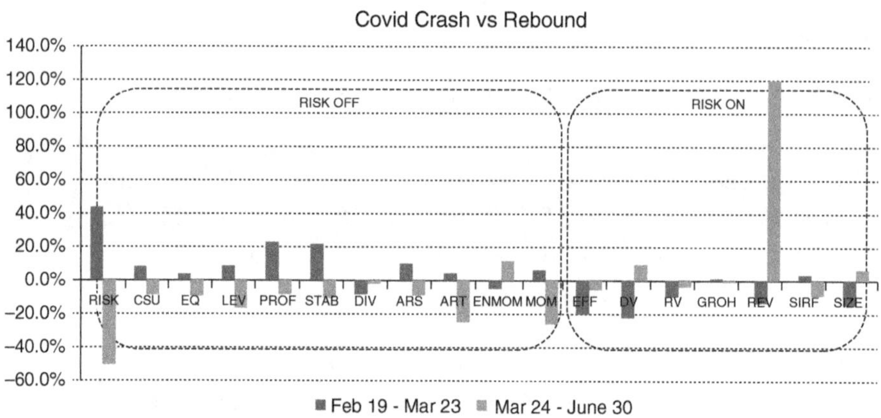

Figure 7.4 Risk-On Versus Risk-Off ESBs – COVID Crash Versus Rebound.

sharply after March 24, 2020, in light of stimulative monetary and fiscal policy. Visual inspection of the RORO ESB evolution in Figure 7.5 over Q1 of 2020 provides further evidence in favor of this RORO framework not to mention Figure 7.6 which documents the +24.8% RORO spread for FY2021 reflective of the bullish tape.

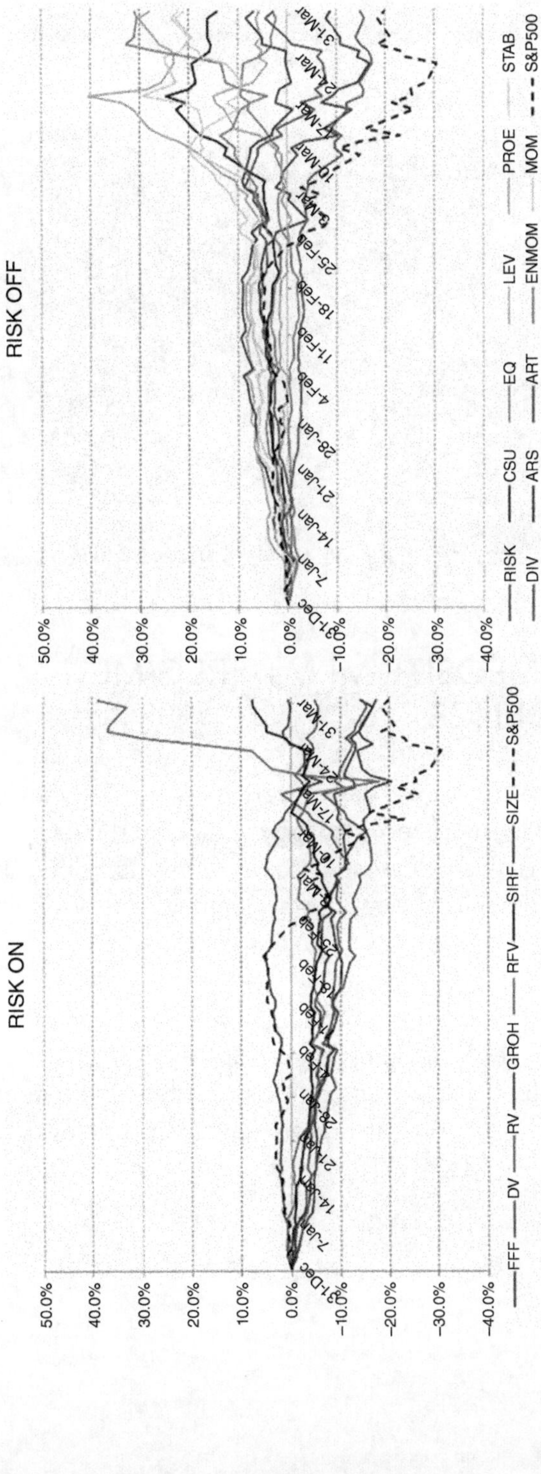

Figure 7.5 Risk-On Versus Risk-Off ESBs – Q1 2020.

	DTD Long	DTD Short	DTD Spread	MTD Long	MTD Short	MTD Spread	YTD Long	YTD Short	YTD Spread
DV	0.16%	−0.55%	0.71%	5.89%	−12.86%	20.62%	54.55%	−31.47%	109.31%
RV	0.13%	−0.98%	1.1%	5.52%	−6.85%	12.25%	66.5%	−4.55%	67.65%
Profit	−0.12%	−1.22%	1.1%	2.06%	−10.55%	12.85%	20.89%	0.35%	10.3%
Size	−0.48%	−0.31%	−0.17%	−7.15%	1.69%	−8.5%	−2.68%	16.85%	−16.19%
CSU	0.02%	−1.24%	1.26%	5.3%	−13.11%	19.52%	36.26%	−10.54%	40.06%
Efficiency	0.2%	−1.2%	1.4%	4.66%	−11.57%	17.16%	54.8%	−33.97%	122.47%
Leverage	−0.13%	−1.18%	1.05%	2.08%	−5.95%	7.37%	17.77%	−24.19%	42.05%
Reversals	−1.56%	0.43%	−1.99%	2.06%	0.81%	1.37%	7.53%	15.2%	−8.35%
EQ	−0.75%	−0.55%	−0.2%	−6.45%	−5.88%	−0.67%	14.86%	−10.92%	27.87%
Growth	0.25%	−0.58%	0.83%	3.77%	−0.18%	3.81%	50.52%	24.6%	19.22%
ART	0.28%	−0.82%	1.1%	3.13%	−1.25%	4.16%	30.5%	10.46%	17.04%
EnMoM	0.24%	−0.19%	0.44%	1.6%	1.11%	0.53%	11.93%	6.1%	5.05%
ARS	0.05%	−0.39%	0.44%	4.02%	−2.17%	5.98%	42.68%	5.41%	32.4%
Stability	0.3%	−1.14%	1.44%	6.93%	−6.72%	13.46%	29.57%	−8.15%	29.33%
PMOM	0.29%	−1.09%	1.38%	−3.0%	−6.45%	3.16%	14.53%	−1.74%	15.42%
SIRF	0.15%	−0.3%	0.45%	6.78%	1.02%	5.38%	23.62%	16.46%	2.95%
Risk	0.19%	−1.03%	1.22%	6.22%	−11.98%	18.26%	16.41%	2.92%	−4.39%
Dividends	0.27%	−0.08%	0.35%	5.16%	5.14%	−0.42%	40.25%	34.1%	2.97%
RiskOn	−0.16%	−0.5%	0.33%	3.08%	−3.99%	7.44%	36.41%	0.45%	42.44%
RiskOff	0.08%	−0.78%	0.85%	2.5%	−5.19%	7.68%	25.79%	2.8%	17.6%
RORO Spread	−0.24%	−0.28%	−0.52%	0.58%	1.2%	−0.24%	10.62%	−2.35%	24.84%

Figure 7.6 ESB Heatmaps 2021 YTD (Daily Rebalanced, $ Neutral) – RORO Spread.

7.1. COMPOSITE MFMs – REGIME DEPENDENCE

The observed regime dependence of the 24-year dollar-neutral Sizzling Seven strategy, particularly its behavior conditioned on up versus down markets, different VIX environments, and recessionary periods, is visualized in Figure 7.7.

Following this regime analysis, Table 7.1 details the coefficients for the 24-year dollar-neutral composite MFMs under these different conditions. Table 7.2 presents the corresponding five-year dollar-neutral coefficients for the composite MFMs.

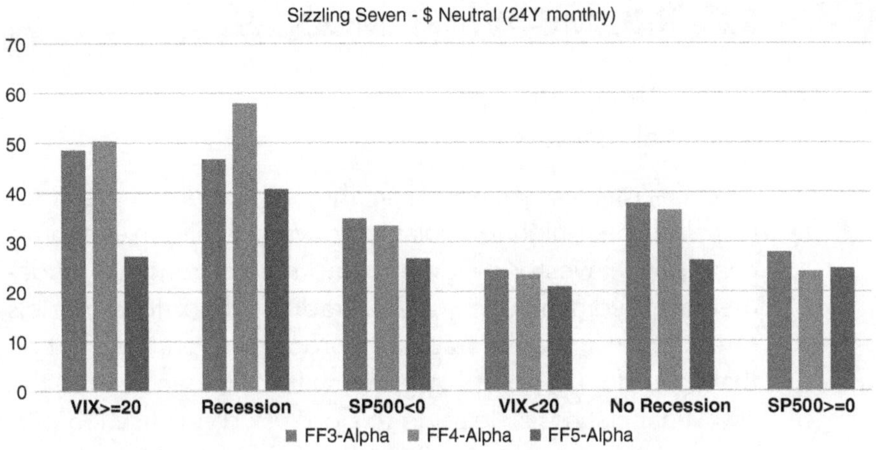

Figure 7.7 Anti-Fragility: Dollar-Neutral Sizzling Seven Regimes – 24Y (Monthly).

Table 7.1 Dollar-Neutral Combo MFMs Coefficients – 24Y (Monthly).

	Mkt-Beta	SMB	HML	RMW	CMA	F-stats
ent_18	−0.48	−0.17	0.41	1.61	0.57	198.83
fab_14	−0.34	−0.14	0.49	1.58	0.60	191.65
siz_seven	−0.34	−0.16	0.53	1.28	0.35	153.87
qgarp	−0.26	−0.20	0.50	1.63	0.56	204.37

Table 7.2 Dollar-Neutral Combo MFMs Coefficients – 5Y (Daily).

	Mkt-Beta	SMB	HML	RMW	CMA	F-stats
ent_18	−0.15	−0.65	0.36	1.05	0.69	262.85
fab_14	−0.10	−0.46	0.43	0.99	0.50	245.96
siz_seven	−0.13	−0.44	0.55	0.83	0.27	228.08
qgarp	−0.03	−0.46	0.42	1.13	0.55	315.28

7.2. REGIME-AWARE MODELS

7.2.1. The Challenge: Nonstationary Financial Markets

Financial markets are not static; they exhibit distinct regimes (e.g., bull, bear, high/low volatility) driven by shifts in economic conditions, investor sentiment, and macroeconomic fundamentals (Aydınhan et al., 2024). Traditional portfolio models often assume stable statistical properties, an assumption that fails during abrupt regime shifts (as seen during the 2008 financial crisis), leading to poor risk diversification precisely when it is most needed. Identifying these hidden market states is a critical challenge for improving risk management and asset allocation (Gu & Mulvey, 2021b). For investment management, an effective model must identify regimes that are not only statistically distinct but also persistent and economically interpretable. While HMMs provide a familiar Markovian scaffold for regime switching, the JM family (statistical jump models) used by the team (Aydinhan, Kolm, Mulvey, and Shu) enforces regime persistence directly and, with sparse/probabilistic extensions, offers cleaner regime learning and feature parsimony, which they argue translates into more robust regime-aware portfolios.

In practice, the *real pain point has always been persistence and interpretability*. It's not enough to know that regimes exist – quants need regimes that are *stable enough to trade on* and that can be explained in economic terms.

7.2.2. The Traditional Approach: Hidden Markov Models

For decades, the hidden Markov model (HMM) has been a popular choice for modeling regime switches. An HMM is a probabilistic model that assumes the market transitions between a set of unobservable states, with each state generating asset returns according to a specific probability distribution. It attempts to infer the most likely sequence of hidden states from observed data.

However, HMMs present several challenges in real-world financial applications. Their core structure assumes that the time spent in any given state follows a "memoryless" geometric distribution, as a consequence of the Markov property. This is at odds with the strong persistence of financial regimes. This and other limitations cause HMM-based regimes to be overly sensitive to noise, often "flickering" between states. This makes them unreliable for guiding trading strategies, particularly from the standpoint of high turnover and excessive transaction costs. As Nystrup et al. (2020) demonstrate, HMMs frequently produce "jittery" regime sequences, leading to signals that change faster than a portfolio can realistically be rebalanced. Ask any quant who has implemented an HMM and the result is often more churn than conviction.

7.2.3. A Modern Solution: The Statistical Jump Model

To address the shortcomings of HMMs, recent research has introduced the statistical jump model (JM), a modern alternative that reframes regime detection as an optimization problem. The model's core innovation is an objective function that balances two goals as per Table 7.3. The authors have proposed JMs to learn regimes with high persistence, based on clustering of temporal features while explicitly penalizing jumps across regimes:

- **Goodness-of-fit.** Grouping time periods with similar data characteristics into clusters.
- **Jump penalty.** Applying an explicit, tunable cost (λ) for every change in regime.

Table 7.3 HMM Versus Jump Model Comparison.

Aspect	Hidden Markov Models (HMM)	Statistical Jump Models (JMs + Sparse and Probabilistic Extensions)
State dynamics	Markov chain with transition matrix P; persistence via Pkk	Penalized segmentation; persistence enforced directly via jump penalty (few switches)
Distributional setup	State-conditional parametric emissions (Gaussian/ *t*- distribution)	Piecewise-stationary segments; fit loss + jump penalty; no Markov assumption
Feature handling	Typically fixed feature set; risk of noisy inputs	Joint feature selection (sparse JM) to keep only regime-discriminative variables
Outputs	Posterior state probs; Viterbi path	Regime labels and/or probability vector; mode-loss sharpens identification
Interpretability	Clear: states via means/vols and transition matrix	Clear: explicit persistence control; selected features highlight regime drivers
Estimation	EM/Baum-Welch; sensitive to KK, local maxima, label switching	Convex/DP-style solvers; tune jump penalty; probabilistic SJM adds differentiable loss
Regime persistence	Indirect (via P); can be "jittery" if P mis-estimated	Directly controlled; tends to produce stickier, economically plausible regimes

Aspect	Hidden Markov Models (HMM)	Statistical Jump Models (JMs + Sparse and Probabilistic Extensions)
Feature selection	Not available – all features treated equally	Sparse JM (SJM) selects informative features; irrelevant ones are down weighted
Turnover	High regime flicker -> excessive trading	Lower turnover thanks to stickier regimes; more tradable signals

The objective function for a Sparse JM (SJM) with K states is to find the set of state parameters (or centroids) Θ and the state sequence S that minimizes the total cost:

$$\underset{\Theta,S}{\operatorname{argmin}} \sum_{t=0}^{T-1} l\left(y_t, \theta_{s_t}\right) + \lambda \sum_{t=1}^{T-1} I_{\{s_{t-1} \neq s_t\}}$$

where $l(y_t, \theta_{st})$ is the loss from assigning data point y_t to the centroid θ_{st} of its assigned state s_t, and $I\{\cdot\}$ is an indicator function that equals 1 if the state changes between time $t-1$ and t.

The jump penalty λ is a tunable parameter that controls the model's preference for persistence. At one extreme, if $\lambda = 0$, there is no cost to switching, and the model simply clusters each time point without regard for temporal structure. At the other extreme, a very large λ makes any switch prohibitively expensive, forcing the model to assign the entire dataset to a single regime. By calibrating λ between these extremes, JMs can identify regimes that are persistent yet responsive to meaningful changes.

By directly penalizing state changes, the JM is structurally designed to produce the persistent, stable regimes that HMMs struggle to capture, making its output more robust and economically meaningful. The model is typically fitted using an efficient coordinate descent algorithm, which alternates between updating the state centroids and finding the optimal state sequence via dynamic programming.

It is important to emphasize that JMs have nothing to do with jump-diffusion processes in continuous-time finance, a confusion one often encounters when discussing these models with students and practitioners. Instead, they are temporal clustering models that penalize regime switching. Extensions such as the Sparse JMs (SJMs) go further by jointly selecting the most relevant features, ensuring that regime classifications are not polluted by noisy predictors as per Nystrup et al. (2021). This is a big deal in practice, since quants can rarely resist the temptation to throw every macro and sentiment variable into the mix.

In this formulation, a new sparsity hyperparameter κ controls how many features are retained.

A smaller κ value forces the model to be picky, keeping only the strongest predictors, while a larger κ enables more features to remain in play.

7.2.4. Recent Advances and Practical Applications

The SJM framework has been extended to enhance its flexibility and power for financial applications.[1]

- **Continuous jump models (CJMs):** This extension generalizes the discrete hard clustering of the SJM into a continuous probability vector for each time point (e.g., 80% bull, 20% bear). This allows for smoother transitions and provides a more nuanced view of market uncertainty,

[1] We've been fortunate to have Professors Petter Kolm and John Mulvey present their latest insights on this topic at QWAFAxNEW.

which is crucial for downstream tasks like portfolio construction and risk management. Its objective function replaces the discrete penalty with a term based on the squared L_1-norm of the difference between consecutive probability vectors $\| s_{t-1} - s_t \|_1^2$, a choice that promotes persistence. To ensure the results remain distinct, an additional regularizer, often called mode loss, is included to nudge the probability vectors toward the corners of the simplex (e.g., toward a clear [0.9, 0.1] state rather than an ambiguous [0.5, 0.5]), making the regimes smooth but still interpretable. Empirical studies show the CJM can identify subtle patterns, such as brief rebound periods during a major market crash, that discrete models miss.

- **Sparse jump model (SJM).** This version integrates feature selection directly into the optimization, automatically identifying the most important economic or technical indicators that drive regime shifts from a high-dimensional feature space. This removes the assumption that input features have a static importance over time, allowing the model to adapt to changing market drivers.

In practice, these models are used within a systematic framework for dynamic portfolio management:

- **Model fitting and feature selection.** A JM is trained on a historical window of data. If using the SJM or an adaptive approach, the optimal set of predictive features (e.g., market data, macroeconomic indicators) is selected.
- **Regime identification (in-sample).** The fitted model is used to label the historical data within the training window, identifying persistent regime states.
- **Regime forecasting (out-of-sample).** With regimes identified, a supervised machine learning model (e.g., random forest, gradient boosting) is trained to predict the probability of future regimes using the selected

features – such as recent returns, volatility, yield curve data, and sentiment indices – as inputs.

- **Portfolio construction and testing.** The regime forecasts are used to dynamically adjust asset allocations. For example, a portfolio might reduce leverage or shift into defensive assets when a high-volatility regime is predicted, or the covariance matrix and expected return inputs for an optimizer can be conditioned on the forecasted regime.

Empirical studies consistently show that strategies guided by the JM framework significantly outperform static buy-and-hold benchmarks and HMM-guided approaches. These regime-aware strategies deliver higher risk-adjusted returns (Sharpe ratios) and, most important, provide superior downside protection by reducing volatility and maximum drawdowns, particularly in multi-asset and factor-based portfolios. By effectively de-risking during impending crash regimes, they protect capital, and because the identified regimes are more stable, the strategy trades less frequently, reducing turnover and transaction costs.

The evolution from the probabilistic HMM to the optimization-based JM represents a significant advance in AI-driven finance. By explicitly enforcing persistence, the JM framework produces more robust and interpretable market regimes. This translates directly into more effective dynamic asset allocation strategies that can better navigate changing market environments and improve long-term investment outcomes. Whereas there are alternative regime detection methods (threshold models, smooth transition models, etc.), for the purposes of this exposition and for the sake of brevity, we have deliberately presented one viable option in detail – the reader can choose to look up the rest.

7.2.5. Parameter Selection

A key question that always comes up is: how do you actually fine-tune the knobs – the jump penalty λ, the sparsity level κ, and the number of states K? In theory, the textbook answer is cross-validation or information criteria like AIC and BIC. In practice, quants need something that works out of sample without endless parameter fiddling. Think of λ as your "stickiness dial." Set it too low and the model jumps around like a caffeinated day trader, switching regimes at every wiggle. Set it too high and you get one giant regime that looks like the S&P 500 since 1950. In between is the sweet spot, persistent but still reactive to major shocks such as 2008 and COVID. For κ, the sparsity control, the idea is to avoid letting every macro-series or sentiment index into the party. Sparse SJMs automatically filter out the junk and keep the few features that really drive regime changes (Nystrup et al., 2021). As for K, when more than three or four states are allowed, the model tends to invent one-off "regimes" that nobody can trade on. Cortese et al. (2024) provide a principled approach using generalized information criteria (FTIC) that often beat AIC/BIC in high-dimensional settings. Many practitioners may just choose to cross-validate λ on a simple strategy's Sharpe ratio (like the 0/1 strategy) and call it a day.

7.2.6. Sensitivity Analysis

If there is one thing that quants are guilty of it's falling in love with their favorite parameter settings. Run it once, see a pretty back-test, and declare victory. The problem is that financial markets have a way of humbling any solution that isn't robust and causing maximal pain out-sample. Sensitivity analysis is the antidote. Change λ a little, move the training window around, try a different set of features. Do you still see the 2008 crisis pop out as a distinct bear regime? Does

COVID-19 still look like a separate event? If not, you may have overfit your way into a ghost story.

Cortese et al. (2024) show that FTIC is fairly reliable at picking stable parameters, and Cortese et al. (2023) find that sparse SJMs often recover the same drivers across subsamples (e.g., volatility and correlations dominate in equities, Google search trends matter in crypto). But the sanity check is simple – if your model's bear regime disappears when you extend the sample by six months, it's time to worry.

7.2.7. Regime Stability and Interpretability

The key benefit of JMs over HMMs is that the regimes are stickier and easier to explain. Traders don't want 17 micro-regimes. They want a handful they can map to real conditions like markets melting down, business-as-usual, and maybe exuberant bubbles. Empirical results back this up. JM-guided strategies deliver lower turnover and more stable signals than HMMs, which means lower costs and fewer whipsaws (Shu et al., 2025).

The continuous jump model adds nuance by letting you say "we're 80% in a bull, 20% in a bear," which is useful in transitional periods like the rebound phases after big crashes (Aydinhan et al., 2024).

Interpretability is the kicker – sparse JMs highlight which features matter in each regime. Instead of a black-box ML forecast, you can say "volatility spikes and credit spreads drove the shift into the bear regime." That's something a PM (portfolio manager) or risk committee can actually understand and trade on. Voila!

Chapter 8

Longing for Winners: Evidence of Persistence in QMIT ESBs

8.1. INTRODUCTION

This chapter aims to replicate, validate, and extend the existing literature on factor momentum using a proprietary dataset that has been deployed in live trading for the past 5.75 years in addition to the full 24.75-year history used in documenting the existence of factor momentum via time series momentum (TSMOM) strategies applied to the 18 QuantZ enhanced smart beta (ESB) composites.

We demonstrate that TSMOM improves risk-adjusted returns when applied to these ESBs. Such outperformance is corroborated by testing the TSMOM strategies with 5.75 years of live trading data.

The best-performing ESB-based TSMOM strategies outperform both the equal-weighted QuantZ ESBs benchmark and the QuantZ Enterprise 18 composites in terms of risk-adjusted returns (i.e., Sharpe, Sortino, and Calmar ratios) in our 24.75-year full history of back-testing. Further, we validate that excluding cross-sectional momentum ESBs can enhance the performance of TSMOM strategies as previously documented in the literature. The litmus test is outperformance in the 5.75-year live trading data, which also exhibits the defensive, downside protection characteristics noted in the TSMOM literature by Gu and Mulvey (2021a).

The QMIT founder has been part of multiple pioneering industry applications of factor investing in the quantamental realm since 1997. QMIT pioneered the application of machine learning (ML) ensembles toward the formulation of a spanning set of ESB composites in its attempt at taming the factor zoo. I have employed these ESB composites to combine hundreds of factors in various hedge and mutual fund strategies since the 1990s. In this chapter, we deploy ESBs as the ingredients of TSMOM strategies to ascertain whether they outperform a baseline equal-weighted ESB benchmark as evidence of persistence in such ESBs.

8.2. LITERATURE REVIEW

8.2.1. Cross-Sectional Momentum (XSMOM)

The study of momentum started with the cross-sectional momentum (XSMOM) effect, which refers to the tendency of stocks that have performed well relative to their peers to continue to perform well in the near future. XSMOM strategies focus on the cross-sectional ranking of past returns ("relative performance") across assets in order to construct long-short decile, quintile, or tercile portfolios possibly with a double sort. Jegadeesh and Titman (1993) showed that buying recent top quintiles ("winners") and selling recent bottom quintiles ("losers") among individual stocks in NYSE and AMEX can yield significant positive returns when using equal holding and lookback periods (the latter also referred to as "portfolio formation period" in some of the literature) ranging from 3 to 12 months, with reversals observed in the short term (out to 1 month) (Jegadeesh, 1990; Lehmann, 1990) as well as the long term (ranging from three to five years) (De Bondt & Thaler, 1985). Carhart (1997) constructed a four-factor model by adding the one-year individual stock-level XSMOM effect to the original Fama-French three-factor model (FF3), which was based purely on size (small minus big), style (high minus low as the Value metric), and market beta (Fama & French, 1993). The resulting Carhart four-factor model greatly improved on the average pricing errors across mutual fund portfolios compared to both the CAPM (capital asset pricing model) and FF3.

8.2.2. Time Series Momentum (TSMOM)

The TSMOM literature focuses on nominal past performance instead of cross-sectional rankings as in the XSMOM case. TSMOM strategies go long the assets with positive returns ("winners") in the lookback period and short the ones with negative returns ("losers") in the lookback period. Moskowitz et al. (2012) presented evidence of positive TSMOM effects in all 58 financial instruments they tested (including equity index futures), and 52 of them were significantly non-zero at a 5% significance level. They noted that

TSMOM has a payoff profile similar to an option straddle on the market, as per Fung and Hsieh (2001) observed in trend-following strategies, given the significantly positive coefficient on squared market returns. Namely, TSMOM performs well during extreme market conditions (both up and down), as it typically takes long positions during significant market upswings, and goes short during market downturns (Moskowitz et al., 2012). In particular, their TSMOM strategy outperformed the S&P 500 during the crash periods (Moskowitz et al., 2012). Unlike XSMOM strategies, the TSMOM effects usually do not come with short-term reversals. Thus TSMOM studies, like Gu and Mulvey (2021a), do not exclude the most recent month from the lookback period like the implementation of the XSMOM strategies. For example, consider a TSMOM strategy with a six-month lookback period and monthly rebalancing at the rebalancing date; the strategy determines if an asset or a factor is a winner or a loser based on the sign of the cumulative return of the past six months.

8.2.3. Factor Momentum

Researchers have discovered that both the XSMOM and TSMOM effects are present not only at the single asset level but also at the industry and factor levels. In the US equity market, they find that factor-level momentum not only subsumes single asset- or industry-level momentum effects but also actually drives them. Arnott et al. (2021) demonstrated that factor XSMOM strategy retained highly significant and positive alphas (of +70 bps and +66 bps per month, with *t*-stats of 6.60 and 6.12, respectively) despite controlling for the FF5 model and FF5 plus Carhart's single stock-level momentum factor (Carhart, 1997). Remarkably, the profitability of the short-term factor momentum XSMOM effect does not stem from single-stock level XSMOM effect and is a stand-alone phenomenon. Arnott et al. (2021) also showed that industry XSMOM momentum is a by-product of the factor XSMOM. Gupta and Kelly (2019) and Ehsani and Linnainmaa (2022) found that momentum at the individual stock level is largely driven by factor TSMOM persistence, and documented significant positive returns for factor momentum strategies (due to the positive autocorrelation in returns of most factors). Thus, momentum may not represent a unique risk factor but rather an interplay of existing factors' continuation patterns.

8.2.4. Factor Time Series Momentum

Gupta and Kelly (2019) and Ehsani and Linnainmaa (2022) demonstrate that strategies based on factor TSMOM are purer, more robust, and more reliable approaches for capturing the persistence in factor performance compared to factor XSMOM strategies. Gupta and Kelly (2019) observed that factor TSMOM yields more stable returns than factor XSMOM and exhibits positive alpha when controlling for factor XSMOM, while factor XSMOM generates negative alpha when controlling for factor TSMOM, indicating that factor TSMOM subsumes factor XSMOM. Ehsani and Linnainmaa (2022) further confirm this subsumption. Inspired by the straddle-like qualities of TSMOM strategies observed in asset classes beyond equities (Moskowitz et al., 2012), some researchers have explored whether market-neutral equity factor TSMOM could demonstrate defensive characteristics during market crashes. Gu and Mulvey (2021a) investigated the potential for crash protection using a dollar-neutral factor TSMOM strategy. Their findings showed that buy-winner TSMOM strategies achieved a Sharpe ratio exceeding 2.0 during crash periods, and incorporating these strategies into their diversified core portfolios significantly enhanced risk-adjusted returns.

8.2.5. Road Map

We follow the framework and procedures in Ehsani and Linnainmaa (2022) and Gu and Mulvey (2021a) to implement TSMOM strategies and test for persistence among the "winners leg" and "losers leg" portfolios of equal-weighted factors. The factor dataset is composed of QuantZ's 18 ESBs defined next. Thereafter, we try combinations of parameters such as lookback periods, rebalancing frequencies, and dollar versus beta neutrality. Section 8.4 confirms the persistence of TSMOM in the returns of ESBs and documents the extent of autocorrelation therein. Section 8.5 shows the back-tested performance on our full 24.75-year history (January 2000–September 2024) highlighting the strong performance of TSMOM strategies across different configurations and identifies the top performers. Finally, Section 8.6 validates the effectiveness of these strategies in 5.75 years of live trading, demonstrating their strong risk-adjusted returns and defensive performance during volatile periods. It is noteworthy that the factor construction methodology and the history of our dataset are different from Gu and Mulvey (2021a) who only used 48 out of 55 factors (each constructed with a single explicitly defined ranking characteristic) from Ehsani and Linnainmaa (2022) and Kozak et al. (2020), covering the period from 1975 to 2019, while we use the 18 ESBs (based on hundreds of raw factors) from QuantZ, spanning January 2000 to September 2024.

Since our implementation of the Gu and Mulvey (2021a) factor TSMOM strategy is based on QuantZ's ESBs, it's important to describe our foundational building blocks (viz., the ESBs) which are used to establish factor persistence. QuantZ provides ML-enhanced smart betas allowing one to express almost any linear view on equities based on ensemble learners that determine the optimal combination of raw factors intra-cohort. The ESBs were designed to be higher-octane composites that could outperform naive well-known factor representatives of each cohort. Definitions are presented in the Appendix 2, Section A.2.

Our researchers have drawn on their decades of collective experience to identify, clean, and test 18 factor cohorts from which we construct the 18 ESBs so that you may directly deploy these indispensable building blocks cost effectively toward the creation of quant equity strategies for which our composite signals (based on such ESBs) are good proxies. Given that the binomial coefficient results in combinatoric explosion in the number of possible outcomes, it's particularly instructive to focus on the curated signal composites we have created as opposed to the larger set of all hypotheticals.

8.3. METHODOLOGY

8.3.1. Data

We use the monthly ESB returns data between January 2000 and September 2024. The data from 2000 to 2018 are from back-testing, and the data since 2019 pertain to the live trading history. Following the tradition of momentum research, including Jegadeesh and Titman (1993) and subsequent literature, such as some notable works in factor TSMOM, like Ehsani and Linnainmaa (2022) and Gu and Mulvey (2021a), we do not account for the impact of transaction costs or rebates.

While this analysis excludes transaction costs, it is worth noting that they can be incorporated. For instance, an important paper on factor TSMOM by Gupta and Kelly (2019) considers transaction costs. They assume, based on Frazzini et al. (2015), that an incremental 1% of factor-level turnover incurs a 10 basis point transaction cost. However, since most major studies do not account for commissions or short rebates, we have chosen to exclude these from our analysis.

8.3.2. Implementation

We follow the framework and procedure in Ehsani and Linnainmaa (2022) and Gu and Mulvey (2021a) to implement TSMOM strategies. For a TSMOM strategy of *k*-month lookback, at the beginning of each holding period, all the factors are classified into either winners or losers based on previous cumulative returns over the most recent *k* months before this holding period, and we construct a winners leg portfolio as an equal-weighted portfolio of winner ESBs, and a losers leg as an equal-weighted portfolio of loser ESBs:

Previous cumulative return: $r_{f,t-k\to t-1} = \prod_{i=1}^{k}\left(1+r_{f,t-i}\right)-1$

Winners: $r_{f,\,t-k\to t-1} \geq 0$

Losers: $r_{f,\,t-k\to t-1} < 0$

Return on the winners leg: $R_{WINNERS,\,t} = \dfrac{\sum_{f\in WINNERS}\left(1+r_{f,\,t}\right)}{|WINNERS|}$

Return on the losers leg: $R_{LOSERS,\,t} = \dfrac{\sum_{f\in LOSERS}\left(1+r_{f,\,t}\right)}{|LOSERS|}$

where *k* is the length of the lookback period.

We back-test the factor TSMOM strategies based on our 18 ESBs (not on their constituent factors or single stocks), and as Gu and Mulvey (2021a) did, we include three ways of implementation:

- Long-short (LS), in which we go long the winner's leg and short the loser's leg

- Long winners (LW), in which we buy and hold the winner's leg only
- Long losers (LL), in which we buy and hold the loser's leg only

Since each ESB is constructed as a market-neutral LS portfolio of the individual stocks in QuantZ's investment universe, the long-only portfolios consisting of the ESBs are also market-neutral LS portfolios of these individual stocks.

The primary benchmark is the equal-weighted portfolio across all ESBs in the investment universe. We also bring in Enterprise 18, a plug-and-play composite signal composed of all ESBs, as an alternative goalpost based on an active quantamental multifactor model strategy. Instead of being a portfolio of the 18 ESBs, the Enterprise 18 signal captures the overlap among the underlying ESBs, resulting in a LS market-neutral portfolio that is higher-octane and more diversified, enabling higher returns and improved risk-adjusted performance compared to each individual ESB. While most factor studies such as Gu and Mulvey (2021a) limit the analysis to dollar neutrality we also show the beta-neutral case for contrast given that the latter is bona fide market neutral, particularly since some ESBs like Risk (aka low volatility which is akin to the BAB factor) and momentum can have substantial and time-varying net betas.

We evaluate and rank the strategies predominantly by their risk-adjusted returns, assessed in terms of the Sharpe ratio, the Sortino ratio, and the Calmar ratio. For all tables of performance metrics in this study, we rank the strategies based on their Sharpe ratios.

It is noteworthy that the factor construction methodology and the history of our dataset is rather different from Gu and Mulvey (2021a). Gu and Mulvey used 48 out of 55 factors (each constructed with a single explicitly defined raw ranking characteristic) from Ehsani and Linnainmaa (2022) and Kozak et al. (2020), covering the period from 1975 to 2019, while we use the spanning set of 18 ESBs from QuantZ, covering the most recent about 24.75 years of (January 2000 to September 2024). The last 5.75years were collected live (hence no possibility of look-ahead or survivorship biases) with daily granularity that would be rare in the academic literature. Furthermore, the QuantZ ESBs are not single company characteristics, but dynamic factor composites generated by the ensemble learners. These differences may account for the resulting differences in the performance and optimal lookback periods.

8.3.2.1. Choice of Lookback Period and Rebalancing Frequency

The lookback period used to compute the past absolute performance is crucial in determining the winner and loser factor portfolios while the rebalancing frequency determines the holding period. Moskowitz et al. (2012) used the 12-month lookback period to determine winners and losers while Gu and Mulvey (2021a) tried lookbacks of 1/3/6/12/24 months. In this study, we use lookback periods of 1/3/6/12 months, with monthly or quarterly rebalancing.

8.3.2.2. With and Without Momentum

Gu and Mulvey (2021a) suggested excluding XSMOM factors in time-series factor momentum strategies to avoid the impact of the correlation between factor momentum

TSMOM and individual stock momentum XSMOM. Their approach is in line with the observation of Ehsani and Linnainmaa (2022), viz., that the individual stock-level XSMOM factor does not have significant returns persistence. This study will contrast the performance of the factor TSMOM strategy with and without the individual stock-level XSMOM ESBs, which are momentum (MOM) and enhanced momentum (EnMom).

8.3.2.3. Dollar Neutral Versus Beta Neutral

As previously noted, certain ESBs like Risk (aka low volatility which is similar to the BAB factor) and momentum (EnMom or MOM) can have substantial and time-varying net betas, which means that inferences made using the academic default of dollar neutrality can often be substantially misleading as shown by Gu and Mulvey (2021a) and Ehsani and Linnainmaa (2022). Therefore, we show both dollar-neutral and beta-neutral results allowing the reader to make contrasting inferences. In particular, we note that deploying beta-neutral ESBs can improve risk-adjusted returns, which extends the existing strand of literature.

8.4. CORRELATION ANALYSIS

The success of TSMOM requires persistence of the winner/loser factor portfolios, which entails a statistically significant and positive correlation between the lookback and holding period returns. The correlation charts in Figures 8.1–8.6 are based on the full 24.75 years of our history (i.e., partially in-sample), which means that they cannot be used directly to select the optimal lookback period or the rebalancing frequency.

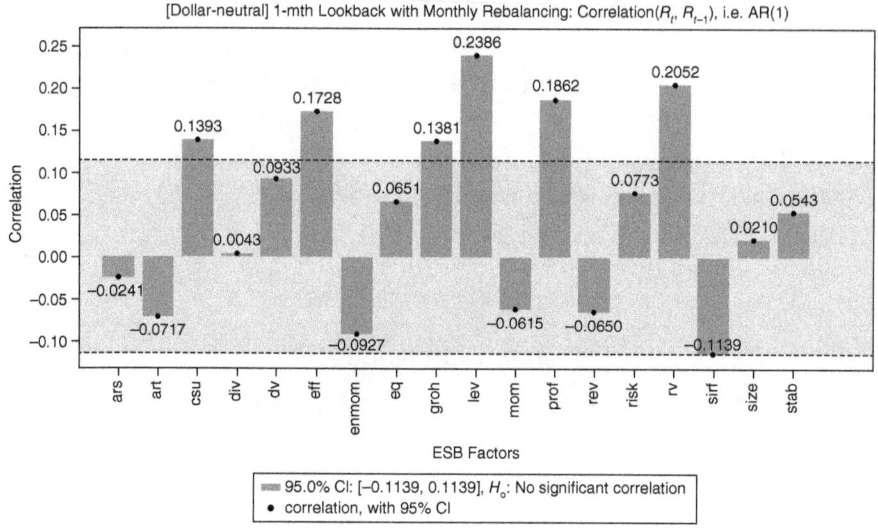

Figure 8.1 Correlation Between Holding Period Returns and Lookback Period Returns, with the 1-Month Lookback Period, Rebalanced Monthly; AR(1) (Dollar-Neutral ESBs).

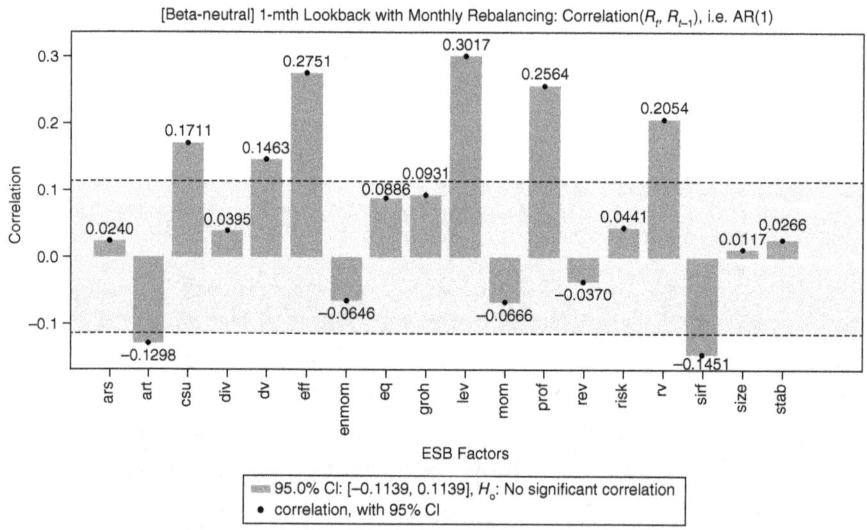

Figure 8.2 Correlation Between Holding Period Returns and Lookback Period Returns, with the 1-Month Lookback Period, Rebalanced Monthly; AR(1) (Beta-Neutral ESBs).

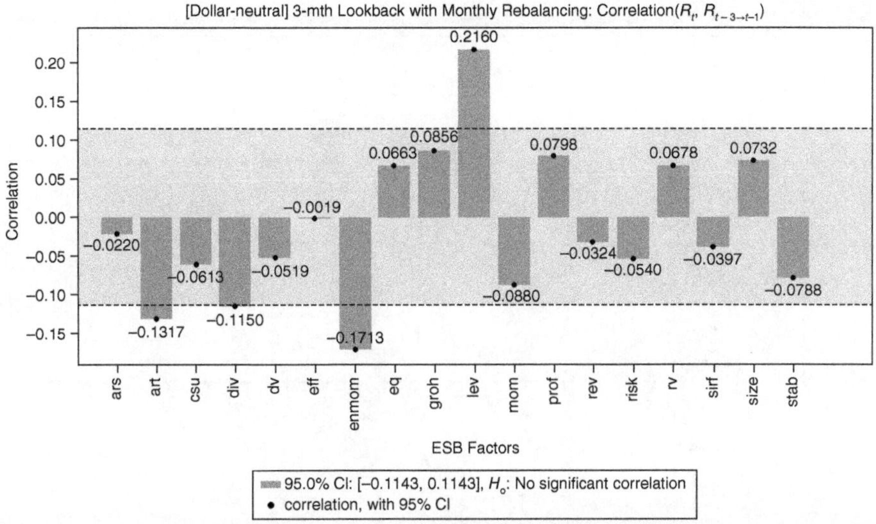

Figure 8.3 Correlation Between Holding Period Returns and Lookback Period Returns, with the 3-Month Lookback Period, Rebalanced Monthly (Dollar-Neutral ESBs).

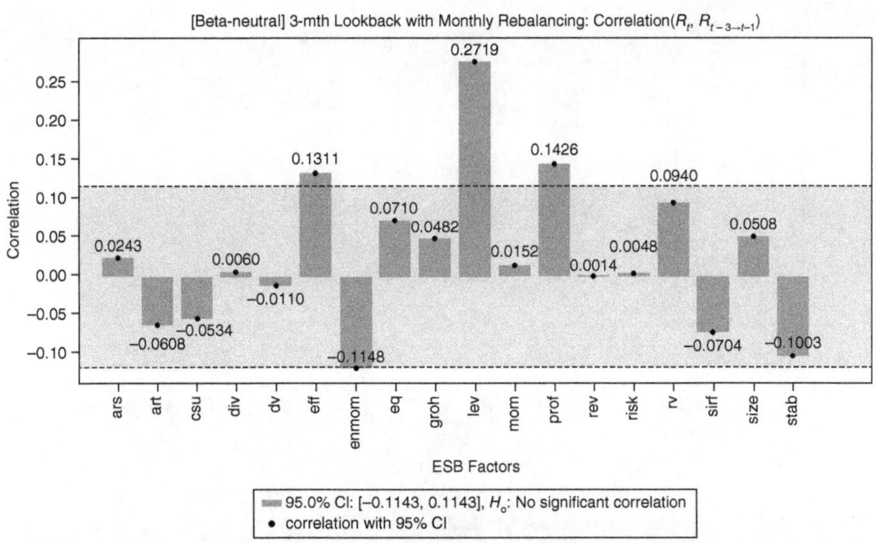

Figure 8.4 Correlation Between Holding Period Returns and Lookback Period Returns, with the 3-Month Lookback Period, Rebalanced Monthly (Beta-Neutral ESBs).

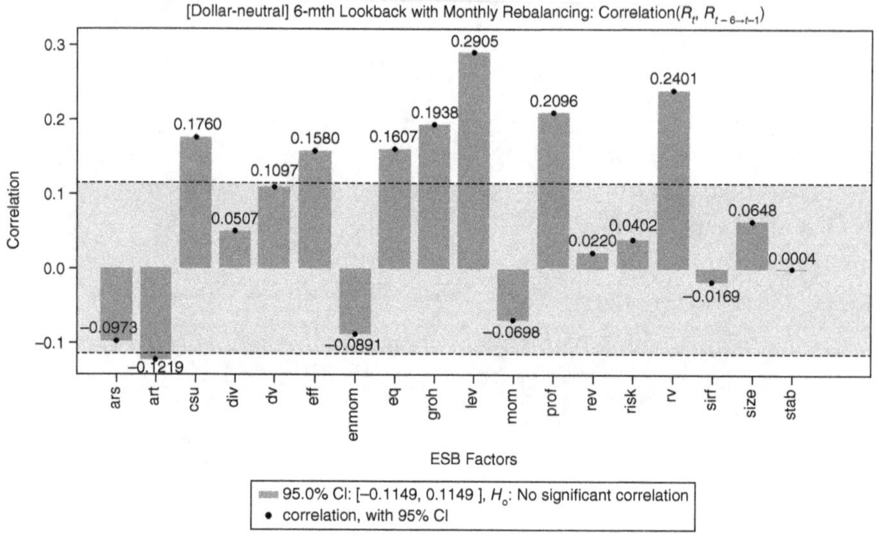

Figure 8.5 Correlation Between Holding Period Returns and Lookback Period Returns, with the 6-Month Lookback Period, Rebalanced Monthly (Dollar-Neutral ESBs).

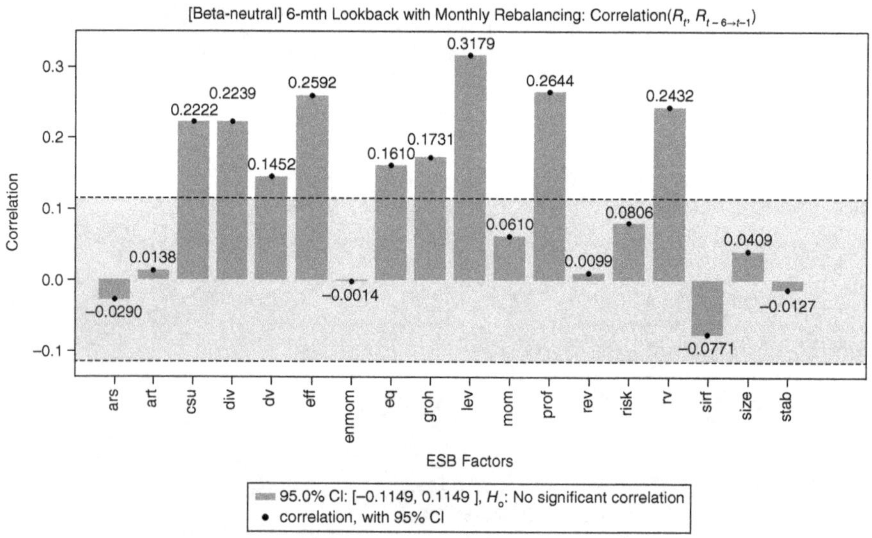

Figure 8.6 Correlation Between Holding Period Returns and Lookback Period Returns, with the 6-Month Lookback Period, Rebalanced Monthly (Beta-Neutral ESBs).

We first display the first-order autoregression, AR(1) coefficients below, in line with Gu and Mulvey (2021a). Among the 18 dollar-neutral (or beta-neutral) ESBs, 12 (or 13) ESBs have a positive AR(1) coefficient, and in both dollar-neutral and beta-neutral cases, six of the ESBs are statistically significant at a 95% confidence level. This is suggestive of factor persistence, that is, profitably going long the winners while reducing exposure to (or even shorting) the losers. Indeed, the 1-month dollar-neutral (monthly rebalance) chart (Figure 8.1) shows *fundamental ESBs* like leverage, relative value, profitability, efficiency, growth, and CSU exhibit serial correlation while some of the technical ones like EnMom, MOM, reversals, and short interest mean revert (with only SIRF being statistically significant). With beta neutrality the statistical significance is even more pronounced with analyst ratings and targets (ART) as well as deep value coefficients becoming significant as well.

However, Moskowitz et al. (2012) noted that only using autocorrelation tests to evaluate the validity of the TSMOM effect can miss some significant predictability because for monthly data AR(1) only shows the correlation between the 1-month lookback versus look-forward period. Given the various combinations of {lookback × holding} periods used in the literature we generalize the notion to simply consider correlations between the lookback {1/3/6/12 months} versus the out-sample holding periods {1 or 3 months}. As we vary the combinations of {lookback × holding} periods the correlations and their significances change – as one might expect – with the occasional flip in sign as noted for CSU, DV and stability.

Among all combinations, the {6-month × 1-month} seems most promising given the largest number of ESBs that have a significantly positive correlation in both dollar-neutral and beta-neutral configurations. Among the 18 dollar-neutral ESBs, 12 ESBs have a positive correlation, 7 of them are statistically significant at a 95% confidence level, and only the ART ESB has a negative correlation that is narrowly significant. Under beta neutrality, 15 of 18 ESBs have a positive correlation, 9 of them are statistically significant at a 95% confidence level, and none of the ESBs has a significantly negative correlation. This result indicates that the 6-month lookback with monthly rebalancing configuration may be the optimal setup for TSMOM strategies based on ESBs.

8.5. PERFORMANCE OF TSMOM STRATEGIES (JANUARY 2000–SEPTEMBER 2024)

We noted the formulation of various TSMOM strategy combinations in Section 8.3.2. In this section, we back-test TSMOM strategies over 24.75 years across four distinct scenarios using either dollar-neutral or beta-neutral ESBs, and either including or excluding the two XSMOM ESBs. Each scenario is coupled with three possible implementations (LS, LW, and LL) for a total of 12 cases further multiplied by lookback periods (1, 3, 6, and 12 months) and two rebalancing frequencies (monthly and quarterly), which results in a total of 96 configurations. To recap, that's 24 configurations × 4 scenarios.

The cumulative performance of each strategy is visualized as the value-added monthly index (or VAMI pegged at $1 at inception) as shown in Figures 8.7–8.9 for the top two Sharpe ratio performers in each of the three ways of implementation <LS, LW, LL>. Since one of our benchmarks, Enterprise 18, has much higher returns and volatility than any ESB, its VAMI may seem to dominate all other ESBs (see Figure 8.7). Thus, to evaluate the strategies based on their risk-adjusted performance, we scale their VAMIs to match the volatility level of the 18-ESB equal-weighted portfolio (EW18) benchmark in all other VAMI plots

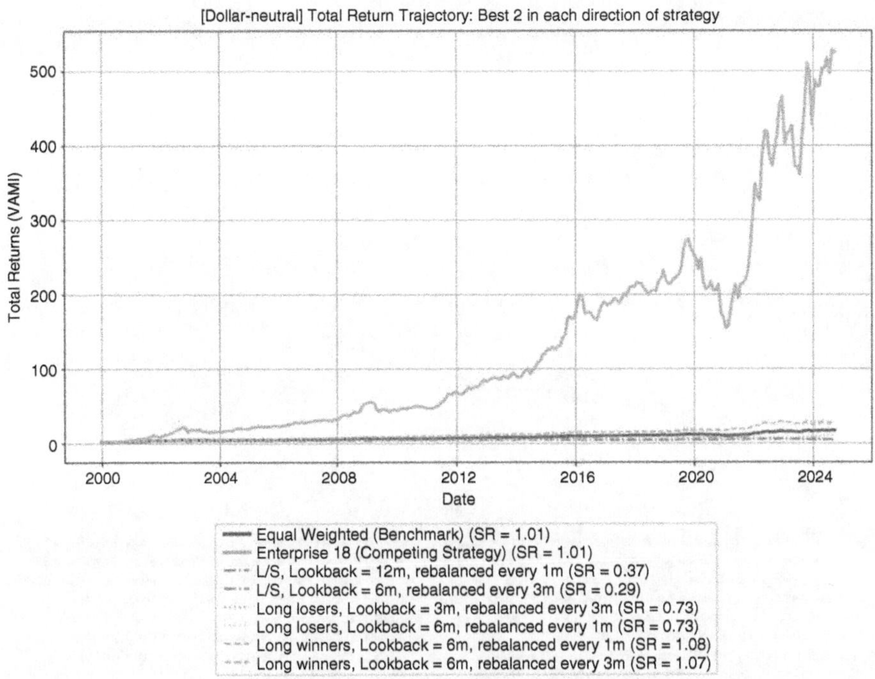

Figure 8.7 Dollar Neutral: Best Two in Each Direction of Strategy (Without Volatility Scaling).

hereafter, which also visually brings Enterprise 18 down to a comparable volatility scale.

The TSMOM strategies (like their ESB brethren) need to be anchored or initialized with enough history (for the lookback) to get started. For ESBs that means equal weighting constituent factors for the first 24 months before the ensembles can start learning. Similarly, each TSMOM strategy sits in the EW18 benchmark portfolio until it accumulates enough data for its lookback period to start picking winners and losers. Ironically, the NASDAQ crash years at the beginning of the 24.75-year period are in fact the strongest for our ESBs, hence any methodology such as sitting in cash would dramatically handicap longer lookbacks.

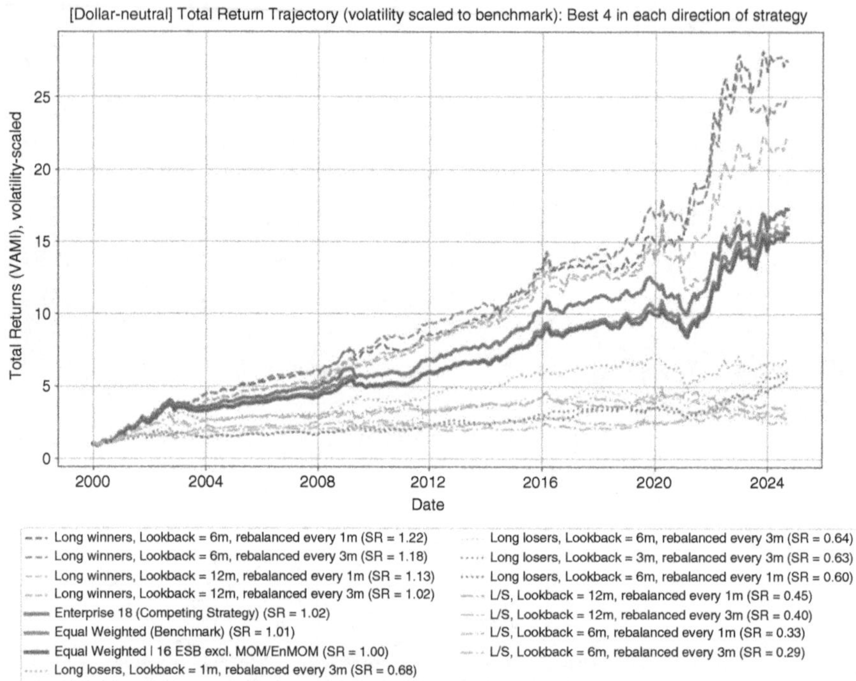

Figure 8.8 VAMI of TSMOM Strategies – 16 ESBs (Dollar Neutral; ex-XSMOM) for 24.75Y (Volatility Scaled).

Implementation (LS/LW/LL). In all four scenarios {BN/DN × with/without XSMOM ESBs}, we observe that the LW implementation of TSMOM strategies systematically outperforms all others, with the LL trailing significantly behind. This highlights the dominance of the TSMOM effect over the 24.75-year history. However, it's noteworthy that even the laggard LL generated positive returns with the best of the cohort being as high as 0.88 Sharpe (LL, BN, 3m/3m, with XSMOM) which is quite good on a stand-alone basis. That's why the long/short implementation is stymied by the strength of the shorts. After all, the market neutral ESBs were designed to outperform in absolute terms – even the Losers.

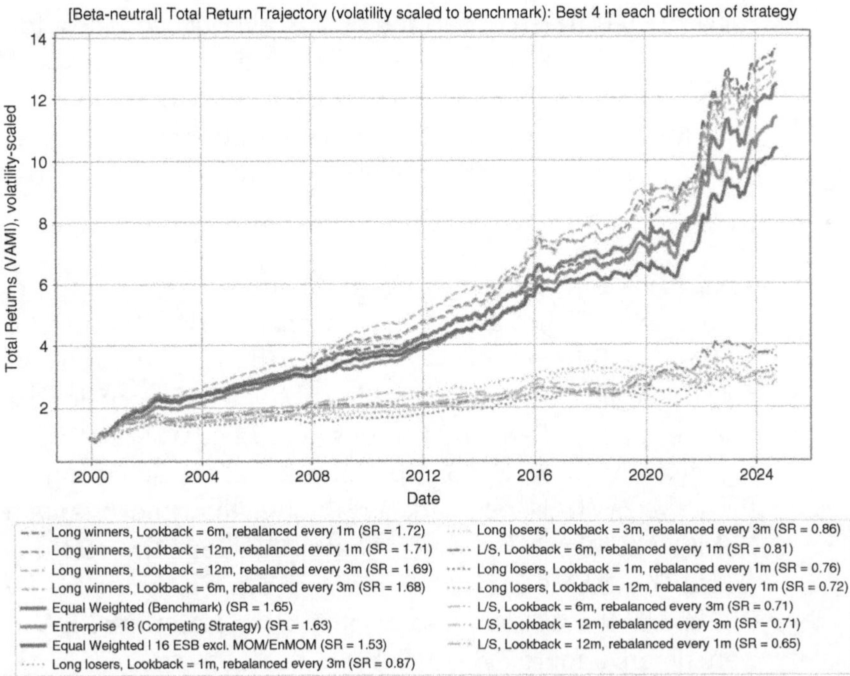

Figure 8.9 VAMI of TSMOM Strategies – 16 ESBs (Beta-Neutral; ex-XSMOM) for 24.75Y (Volatility Scaled).

Beta versus dollar neutrality. We also observe that beta-neutral configurations generally exhibit much higher risk-adjusted returns for the top-performing strategies than the dollar-neutral ones, ceteris paribus, due to significantly lower volatility and downside deviations.

With/without XSMOM. Furthermore, in both dollar-neutral and beta-neutral configurations, the exclusion of XSMOM ESBs resulted in an overall increase in the risk-adjusted returns for TSMOM strategies, especially for dollar-neutral cases.

Best strategy (Lookback × Rebalance period). Among all TSMOM strategies, the LW TSMOM strategies with a 6-month lookback period and rebalanced monthly

(LW 6m/1m) performed the best in all four scenarios, followed by LW TSMOM strategies with a 6-month lookback period and rebalanced quarterly (LW 6m/3m). LW 6m/1m TSMOM strategy outperformed both benchmarks in all four scenarios under all three risk-adjusted metrics as per Table 8.1.

Take the top risk-adjusted TSMOM strategies, LW 6m/1m, for instance. In the dollar-neutral scenarios, the Sharpe ratio of the EW18 benchmark is 1.01. For the dollar-neutral LW 6m/1m strategies, the one with XSMOM ESBs obtained a Sharpe ratio of 1.08, and the one excluding XSMOM ESBs significantly raised the Sharpe ratio to 1.22 (which is higher than the EW18 benchmark and higher than the one with XSMOM ESBs). The dollar-neutral LW 6m/1m strategy (excluding XSMOM) also improved the Sortino ratio by 26.1% and the Calmar ratio by 50% compared to the EW16 benchmark (Figure 8.8 and Table 8.2).

Although using TSMOM is also helpful in beta-neutral scenarios, it is noteworthy that the relative improvement in the Sharpe ratio for the top TSMOM strategies is much higher in the dollar-neutral scenarios because the benchmark has a much lower Sharpe ratio to start with. In the beta-neutral scenarios, the Sharpe ratio of the equal-weighted benchmark (EW16) is 1.53 (a tough bar to clear). For the beta-neutral LW 6m/1m strategies, the one with XSMOM ESBs obtained a trivially higher Sharpe ratio of 1.65, and the one excluding XSMOM ESBs further raised the Sharpe ratio to 1.72 and increased the Sharpe ratio by about 12.4% relative to the EW16 benchmark. The relative improvement in the other two risk-adjusted return metrics, Sortino and Calmar, is also lower than in the dollar-neutral case, but the magnitude in each case is close to 30%, which is substantial. The corresponding VAMI, illustrating the cumulative performance trajectory of these beta-neutral TSMOM strategies over the 24.75-year period, is presented in Figure 8.9.

Table 8.1. Performance of the TSMOM Strategy for 24.75Y.

(a) Dollar-Neutral ESBs

Strategy	Mean (%)	Std (%)	DownDev (%)	MDD (%)	Sharpe	Sortino	Calmar	CumRet (%)
Enterprise 18	28.88	28.35	13.80	43.82	1.02	2.09	0.66	52,336.32
Equal Weighted	11.88	11.81	5.77	19.73	1.01	2.06	0.60	1,497.56
EW16 ex-XSMOM	12.33	12.39	5.88	20.09	0.99	2.10	0.61	1,664.76
Optimal TSMOM strategy: LW strategies (6-month lookback period, rebalanced monthly)								
with XSMOM	14.30	13.20	6.71	19.62	1.08	2.13	0.73	2,606.71
without XSMOM	15.57	12.79	5.86	17.34	1.22	2.65	0.90	3,456.52

(b) Beta-Neutral ESBs

Strategy	Mean (%)	Std (%)	DownDev (%)	MDD (%)	Sharpe	Sortino	Calmar	CumRet (%)
Enterprise 18	24.17	14.80	6.62	16.10	**1.63**	3.65	1.50	20,831.24
Equal Weighted	10.74	6.52	2.58	7.85	**1.65**	4.16	1.37	1,139.05
EW16 ex-XSMOM	11.16	7.30	2.94	8.46	**1.53**	3.80	1.32	1,261.73
Optimal TSMOM strategy: LW strategies (6-month lookback period, rebalanced monthly)								
with XSMOM	13.28	8.04	3.08	8.27	**1.65**	4.31	1.61	2072.20
without XSMOM	13.56	7.89	2.74	7.92	**1.72**	4.94	1.71	2,208.66

The detailed performance metrics for these top 10 beta-neutral TSMOM strategies (using 16 ESBs, excluding XSMOM) over the same 24.75-year period are summarized in Table 8.3.

The back-test shows that using monthly rebalanced LW TSMOM strategies on the 16 non-XSMOM ESBs with a 6-month lookback period can help investors significantly improve the Sortino ratio and the Calmar ratio of their ESB-based strategies in comparison to the EW16 strategy and the Enterprise 18 composite, and with Sharpe ratios at a comparable level or even better (especially in the dollar-neutral cases). The desirable characteristics in terms of downside deviation and maximum drawdown (MDD) are in line with other studies such as Gu and Mulvey (2021a).

8.5.1. Robustness Checks

Considering that the extraordinarily profitable NASDAQ crash episode may distort the full period performance of the strategies, we first re-evaluate the performance of the strategies with beta-neutral ESBs (without XSMOM ESBs) using the 22.75-year data starting with the 25th month (January 2002) as a robustness check in order to (1) remove the impact of the positive outlier NASDAQ crash episode and (2) omit the anchoring period of the ensembles when they simply match the equal-weighted benchmark (EW16) as with our TSMOM strategies. The LW TSMOM strategies on the 16 non-XSMOM ESBs with a six-month lookback still performed the best among all TSMOM strategies. However, it obtained a Sharpe ratio of 1.55, which is slightly higher than the one of the EW16 (1.54) but lower than the Sharpe ratio of the Enterprise 18 composite (1.57). However, using the top TSMOM strategy still helps investors

Table 8.2 Performance of Top 10 Strategies – 16 ESBs (Dollar Neutral; ex-XSMOM) for 24.75Y.

Strategy	Mean (%)	Std (%)	DownDev (%)	MDD (%)	Sharpe	Sortino	Calmar	CumRet (%)
LW, 6m/1m	15.57	12.79	5.86	17.34	1.22	2.65	0.90	3,456.52
LW, 6m/3m	14.87	12.64	5.82	17.34	1.18	2.55	0.86	2,959.62
LW, 12m/1m	13.98	12.35	5.81	18.41	1.13	2.41	0.76	2,424.71
LW, 12m/3m	12.96	12.68	6.32	29.81	1.02	2.05	0.43	1924.69
Enterprise 18	28.88	28.35	13.80	43.82	1.02	2.09	0.66	52,336.32
EW18	11.88	11.81	5.77	19.73	1.01	2.06	0.60	1,497.56
EW16 ex-XSMOM	12.33	12.39	5.88	20.09	0.99	2.10	0.61	1,664.76
LL, 1m/3m	9.64	14.24	7.45	34.53	0.68	1.29	0.28	868.64
LL, 6m/3m	8.57	13.43	7.24	27.44	0.64	1.18	0.31	660.41
LL, 3m/3m	8.28	13.20	6.90	29.40	0.63	1.20	0.28	612.54

Table 8.3 Performance of Top-10 Strategies – 16 ESBs (Beta Neutral; ex-XSMOM) for 24.75Y.

Strategy	Mean (%)	Std (%)	DownDev (%)	MDD (%)	Sharpe	Sortino	Calmar	CumRet (%)
LW, 6m/1m	13.56	7.89	2.74	7.92	1.72	4.94	1.71	2,208.66
LW, 12m/1m	12.13	7.08	2.86	9.08	1.71	4.25	1.34	1,587.97
LW, 12m/3m	12.19	7.20	3.00	9.96	1.69	4.07	1.22	1,611.06
LW, 6m/3m	12.39	7.39	2.98	9.44	1.68	4.15	1.31	1,685.23
EW18	10.74	6.52	2.58	7.85	1.65	4.16	1.37	1,139.05
Enterprise 18	24.17	14.80	6.62	16.10	1.63	3.65	1.50	20,831.24
EW16 ex-XSMOM	11.16	7.30	2.94	8.46	1.53	3.80	1.32	1,261.73
LL, 1m/3m	7.74	8.91	4.55	18.60	0.87	1.70	0.42	529.83
LL, 3m/3m	7.20	8.40	4.77	18.60	0.86	1.51	0.39	456.63
LS, 6m/1m	8.93	11.05	5.79	19.42	0.81	1.54	0.46	725.21

manage the downside deviation and drawdowns much better, cutting down both by more than 50% resulting in a much higher Sortino ratio (3.89) and Calmar ratio (1.34) than the ones of the EW16 and the Enterprise 18 composite (see Appendix A.5).

8.5.2. Drivers of Performance

The dynamic regime-dependent choice of ESBs in the trending <LW, LL, LS> portfolios may explain why the top TSMOM strategies have downside deviations and MDDs comparable to the equal-weighted benchmark, yet monetize a higher return. To further evaluate the potential drivers of performance we consider how the TSMOM strategy bets on each ESB. In Figures 8.10 and 8.11, we visualize the number of ESBs in the winners leg for each period and the winning rate of each ESB in the beta-neutral LW 6m/1m strategies. To aid visualization, we use the risk-off risk-on spread (RORO), which is the difference between the mean return of all risk-off ESBs and the mean return of all risk-on ESBs, as a contemporaneous proxy for the market regime. A lower contemporaneous RORO spread (like in 2008) is indicative of a risk-off episode.

From Figure 8.10, we can observe that the winners leg of the LW 6m/1m strategy encompasses nearly all ESBs (EW16) during the risk-on periods when most ESBs will likely be positive over the lookback period. Empirically, the strategies based on a 6-month lookback period seem to be sufficiently responsive to market changes without excessive turnover.

For the given horizon in Figure 8.11, leverage (lev), risk (risk), profitability (prof), and stability (stab) ESBs register a winning rate of about 80% in the 24.75-year history, consistent with the correlation analysis (Figure 8.6) and the positive hit

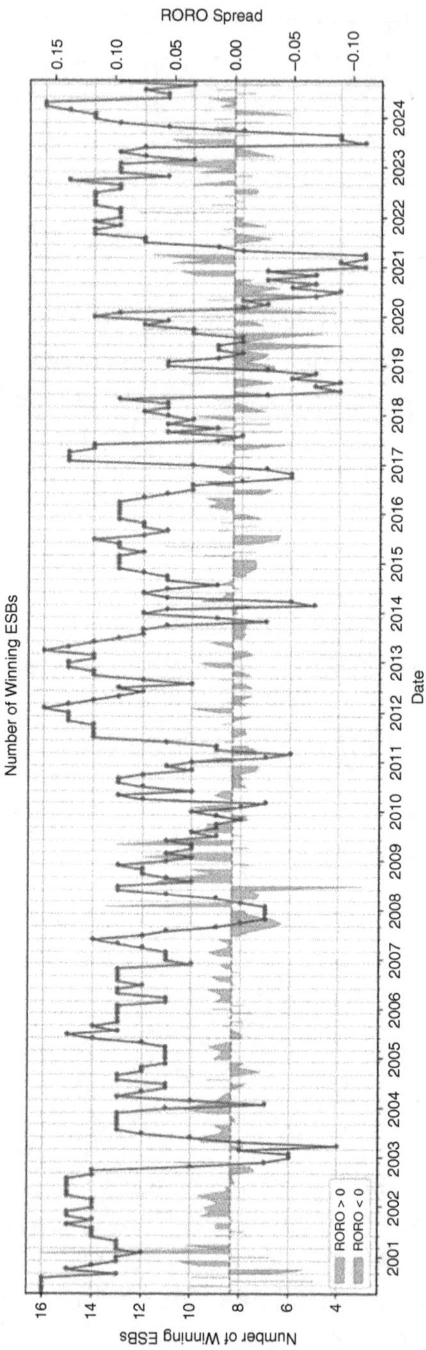

Figure 8.10 Number of ESBs in the Winners Leg of the LW 6m/1m Strategy, 16 ESBs (Beta Neutral; ex-XSMOM) for 24.75Y.

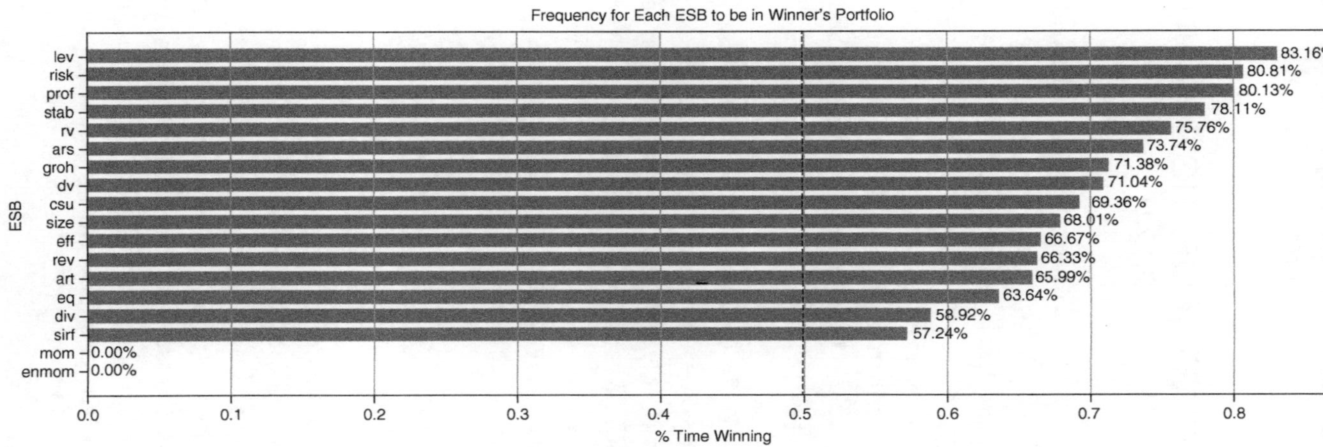

Figure 8.11 Winning Rate of Each ESB in the LW 6m/1m Strategy, 16 ESBs (Beta Neutral; ex-XSMOM) for 24.75Y.

rate for these ESBs. The winning 6-month lookback balances turnover with reaction time to regime changes.

8.6. LIVE CORROBORATION (JANUARY 2019–SEPTEMBER 2024)

We have 24.75 years of returns for our ESBs with the recent 5.75 years post-2019 being a live-trading record (while the prior 19 years are back-tested). To corroborate the validity of the strategy, we re-evaluate the TSMOM strategies with the 5.75-year live-trading data. Figure 8.12 and Table 8.4 visualize the performance of TSMOM strategies based on beta-neutral ESBs (excluding XSMOM ESBs) over the live trading history.

As with the 24.75-year and 22.75-year history, the LW TSMOM strategies with a 6-month lookback period and rebalanced monthly (LW 6m/1m) still performed the best among all TSMOM strategies once again over the 5.75-year live-trading data, with a Sharpe ratio of 1.47, which is higher than the Sharpe ratio of the EW16 benchmark (1.21) and is higher than that of the Enterprise (1.24).

We also observe that the outperformance of long-winner TSMOM strategies compared to the benchmarks was largely established between March 2020 and early 2021 when COVID (for obvious reasons) resulted in significant strategy dispersion whereas subsequent performance has marched more in tandem. Relative to the benchmark, the best TSMOM (LW, 6m/1m) strategy essentially doubles the cumulative return with a similar MDD resulting in a far superior risk-adjusted profile showing good downside protection during volatile periods similar to what Gu and Mulvey (2021a) observed.

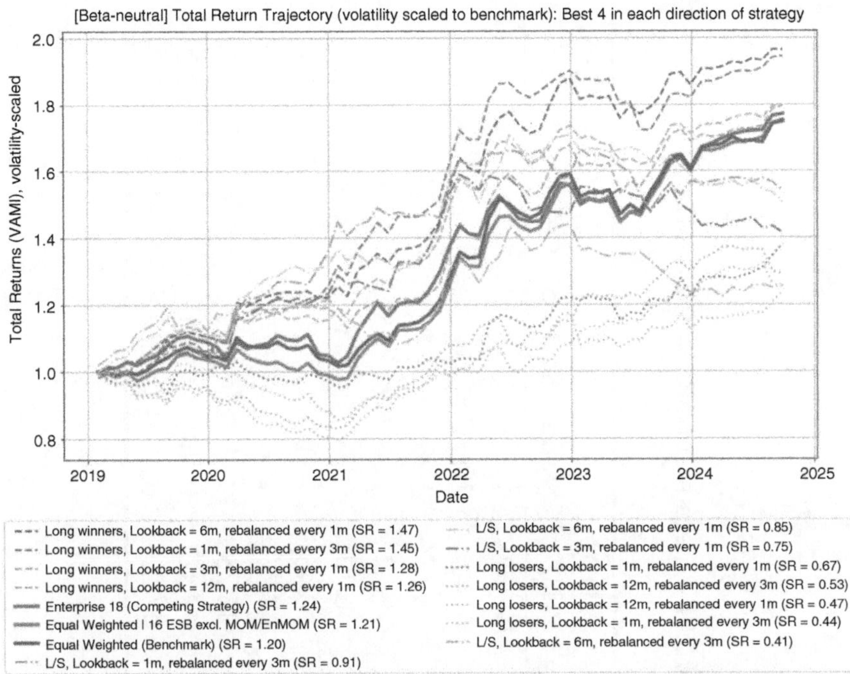

Figure 8.12 VAMI of TSMOM Strategies – 16 ESBs (Beta Neutral; ex-XSMOM) for LIVE 5.75Y (Volatility Scaled).

In Table 8.4, we observe that, compared to the outcome on a longer history, the annualized returns of long-winner TSMOM strategies (LIVE 5.75Y) are now a bit higher in magnitude and are closer to 70% of Enterprise 18 now (in comparison to about 50% in the longer horizons discussed previously). Also, we observe that the LW strategies outperform the benchmarks in trend between early 2020 and 2021 (the heavily COVID-impacted period).

8.7. PUBLICATION DECAY

The publication of a strategy may result in performance decay, as noted by McLean and Pontiff (2016), potentially diminishing the strategy's alpha or lowering its Sharpe ratio.

Table 8.4 Performance of Top-10 Strategies – 16 ESBs (Beta Neutral; ex-XSMOM) for LIVE 5.75Y.

Strategy	Mean (%)	Std (%)	DownDev (%)	MDD (%)	Sharpe	Sortino	Calmar	CumRet (%)
LW, 6m/1m	16.15	10.96	4.02	7.92	1.47	4.02	2.04	131.03
LW, 1m/3m	17.06	11.73	4.73	12.45	1.45	3.61	1.37	141.28
LW, 3m/1m	14.78	11.52	3.83	8.63	1.28	3.85	1.71	116.13
LW, 12m/1m	11.73	9.34	4.38	9.08	1.26	2.68	1.29	85.93
Enterprise 18	23.03	18.63	9.67	16.10	1.24	2.38	1.43	218.65
EW16 ex-XSMOM	10.43	8.63	3.89	8.46	1.21	2.68	1.23	74.14
EW18	10.49	8.77	4.06	7.85	1.20	2.58	1.34	74.66
LS, 1m/3m	11.56	12.66	6.10	15.75	0.91	1.89	0.73	84.32
LS, 6m/1m	12.41	14.57	6.87	19.42	0.85	1.81	0.64	92.37
LS, 3m/1m	10.37	13.74	6.41	17.20	0.75	1.62	0.60	73.59

For factor TSMOM strategies, the most closely related and frequently cited works, such as Gupta and Kelly (2019) and Ehsani and Linnainmaa (2022), use US equity factor data spanning from 1963 to 2016 (for the latter) or 2017 (for the former). Additionally, their initial working papers were likely released before their formal journal publications, suggesting that the market could have started to incorporate the strategies' insights before their official release.

The first draft of Ehsani and Linnainmaa (2022) was published in March 2017, while the earliest available version of Gupta and Kelly (2019) appeared as a Yale ICF working paper in November 2018. Following McLean and Pontiff (2016), who argue that the dissemination of research ideas likely begins when the first working paper is released – and potentially even earlier due to conference presentations or discussions – we therefore hypothesize that publication decay (if any) ought to gradually manifest from 2017 onwards. Based on this, we divide the historical data into two distinct periods:

- **Pre-publication history.** January 2002–December 2016 (to exclude the NASDAQ crash period, during which QuantZ ESBs perform particularly well through the history and there was insufficient history for the lookback periods of the TSMOM strategies)
- **Post-publication history.** January 2017–September 2024
- The analysis then focuses on assessing the post-publication decay of these three beta-neutral, TSMOM strategies:
  - **LW 6m/1m.** This is the best performer during our 24.75/22.75/5.75-year history.
  - **LW 1m/1m.** This is the best performer in our history from back-testing (2002–2018) and was mentioned as the best strategy in Gu and Mulvey (2021a).

- **LW 12m/1m.** Considered the paradigm of the TSMOM strategies in the late 2010s, this strategy is the most researched and frequently mentioned. It was central to the construction of factor TSMOM strategy by Gupta and Kelly (2019), Arnott et al. (2021), and Ehsani and Linnainmaa (2022).

We assess the performance decay by comparison against two benchmarks (EW18 and EW16) and Enterprise 18, giving precedence to the EW18 and EW16, which themselves show the post-publication Sharpe decays of −45.0% and −50.5%, down to Sharpe ratios of 1.10 and 1.08, respectively. Interestingly, of the three TSMOM strategies considered, the most-researched LW 12m/1m shows a decay of −45.8%, which is pretty much in line, while the LW 1m/1m decay of −58.2% is much worse in contrast to the much milder decay of only −39.4% for the LW 6m/1m case. Hence, while there is prima facie strong evidence of post-publication decay; it is just as strong for the benchmarks, which means that risk-adjusted decay is structural, pervasive, and may not be specific to a post-publication effect at least based on Sharpe ratios. Based on alphas there is not much evidence of decay in the nominal intercept values either for the EW18 benchmark or the best strategies like LW 6m/1m.

Table 8.5 illustrates the performance decay in key investment strategies, comparing metrics from the pre-publication period (January 2003–December 2016) and the post-publication period (January 2017–September 2024). Percentage changes are reported as positive (e.g., +X%) for post-publication increases and negative (e.g., −X%) for decreases.

Table 8.5 Performance Decay: Pre- and Post-Publication Analysis (2003–2024 September).

Strategies	FF5 Alpha (%)	FF5 + WML Alpha (%)	Sharpe Ratio (%)	Sortino Ratio (%)	Calmar Ratio (%)
LW 6m/1m	+20.6	+14.7	−39.4	−26.9	−22.0
LW 1m/1m	0.0	+1.6	−58.2	−59.0	−55.1
LW 12m/1m	−6.3	−11.1	−45.8	−49.5	−40.2
EW18	+9.1	+1.8	−45.0	−45.6	−28.6
EW16	+1.8	0.0	−50.5	−53.1	−47.1
Enterprise 18	−13.3	−21.3	−47.1	−55.5	−46.0

The LW 6m/1m strategy stands out with a less pronounced performance decline in risk-adjusted return ratios compared to other strategies, despite its declines in the Sharpe, Sortino, and Calmar ratios (−39.4%, −26.9%, and − 22%, respectively). This strategy maintains positive FF5 alpha (+20.6%) and FF5 + WML alpha (+14.7%), indicating a relatively resilient performance post-publication.

Table 8.6 provides a comprehensive comparison of alpha generation and risk-adjusted returns for key TSMOM strategies and benchmarks across several distinct historical periods. These include the full 22.75-year history (January 2002–September 2024), the pre-publication period (January 2002–December 2016), the post-publication period (January 2017–September 2024), and the recent 5.75-year live trading history (January 2019–September 2024), allowing for a detailed assessment of performance consistency and potential publication decay effects.

Table 8.6 Alphas and Risk-Adjusted Returns in 22.75-Year/Pre-publication/Post-publication/5.75-Year History[1].

Strategies	History	FF5 Alpha	FF5 + WML Alpha	Sharpe Ratio	Sortino Ratio	Calmar Ratio
LW 6m/1m	Jan 2002–Sept 2024 (22.75-year)	0.73 (6.83) [0.27]	0.72 (6.76) [0.29]	1.55	3.89	1.34
	Jan 2002–Dec 2016 (Pre-Publication)	0.68 (6.56) [0.07]	0.68 (6.61) [0.10]	2.08	4.58	2.00
	Jan 2017–Sept 2024 (Post-Publication)	0.82 (3.71) [0.49]	0.78 (3.52) [0.49]	1.26	3.35	1.56
	Jan 2019–Sept 2024 (5.75-year)	1.05 (3.89) [0.55]	1.04 (3.81) [0.55]	1.47	4.02	2.04
LW 1m/1m	Jan 2002–Sept 2024 (22.75-year)	0.64 (6.02) [0.24]	0.64 (5.97) [0.24]	1.41	3.21	0.94
	Jan 2002–Dec 2016 (Pre-Publication)	0.63 (6.95) [0.12]	0.63 (6.96) [0.13]	2.25	5.15	2.07
	Jan 2017–Sept 2024 (Post-Publication)	0.63 (2.59) [0.39]	0.64 (2.60) [0.38]	0.94	2.11	0.93
	Jan 2019–Sept 2024 (5.75-year)	0.72 (2.26) [0.39]	0.74 (2.32) [0.38]	1.05	2.39	1.16

[1] Where alphas are in % and *t*-statistics are written in the parenthesis (). All adjusted R-Squareds are in squared brackets []. Both are under the alpha values.

Strategies	History	FF5 Alpha	FF5 + WML Alpha	Sharpe Ratio	Sortino Ratio	Calmar Ratio
LW 12m/1m	Jan 2002–Sept 2024 (22.75-year)	0.64 (6.64) [0.30]	0.62 (6.57) [0.32]	1.52	3.34	1.05
	Jan 2002–Dec 2016 (Pre-Publication)	0.64 (6.29) [0.17]	0.63 (6.33) [0.19]	2.01	4.57	1.69
	Jan 2017–Sept 2024 (Post-Publication)	0.60 (3.17) [0.49]	0.56 (2.97) [0.51]	1.09	2.31	1.01
	Jan 2019–Sept 2024 (5.75-year)	0.74 (3.18) [0.54]	0.72 (3.08) [0.54]	1.26	2.68	1.29
EW18	Jan 2002–Sept 2024 (22.75-year)	0.58 (6.98) [0.34]	0.57 (6.96) [0.38]	1.48	3.24	1.05
	Jan 2002–Dec 2016 (Pre-Publication)	0.55 (6.36) [0.14]	0.55 (6.49) [0.18]	2.00	4.39	1.54
	Jan 2017–Sept 2024 (Post-Publication)	0.60 (3.95) [0.61]	0.56 (3.73) [0.63]	1.10	2.39	1.10
	Jan 2019–Sept 2024 (5.75-year)	0.69 (3.72) [0.66]	0.67 (3.58) [0.66]	1.20	2.58	1.34

(Table 8.6 Continued)

Table 8.6 *(Continued)*

Strategies	History	FF5 Alpha	FF5 + WML Alpha	Sharpe Ratio	Sortino Ratio	Calmar Ratio
EW16	Jan 2002–Sept 2024 (22.75-year)	0.58 (7.42) [0.39]	0.58 (7.38) [0.39]	1.54	3.49	1.00
	Jan 2002–Dec 2016 (Pre-Publication)	0.57 (6.98) [0.17]	0.57 (6.96) [0.17]	2.18	5.07	1.87
	Jan 2017–Sept 2024 (Post-Publication)	0.58 (4.00) [0.65]	0.57 (3.89) [0.65]	1.08	2.38	0.99
	Jan 2019–Sept 2024 (5.75-year)	0.66 (3.63) [0.67]	0.66 (3.60) [0.67]	1.21	2.68	1.23
Enterprise 18	Jan 2002–Sept 2024 (22.75-year)	1.25 (6.55) [0.31]	1.21 (6.53) [0.35]	1.57	3.25	1.21
	Jan 2002–Dec 2016 (Pre-Publication)	1.28 (6.16) [0.13]	1.27 (6.32) [0.18]	2.08	4.81	2.11
	Jan 2017–Sept 2024 (Post-Publication)	1.11 (3.27) [0.58]	1.00 (3.03) [0.62]	1.10	2.14	1.14
	Jan 2019–Sept 2024 (5.75-year)	1.28 (3.08) [0.63]	1.21 (2.93) [0.64]	1.24	2.38	1.43

8.8. CONCLUSION

Our study documents TSMOM persistence in QuantZ's proprietary live factor set of ESBs, which demonstrates the superior risk-adjusted profile of the LW (long-only) TSMOM strategy with a 6-month lookback period and monthly rebalancing particularly during crashes such as the COVID period of 2020. Notably, the LW portfolios also did remarkably well amid the November 2020 momentum crash and the LS 1m/3m did even better. Among all three horizons evaluated (24.75/22.75/5.75 years until September 2024), the LW 6m/1m not only performs the best among all TSMOM strategies but also outperforms both benchmarks in 24.75-year and 5.75-year horizons. As for the 22.75-year horizon, although it obtains nearly identical Sharpe as the Enterprise 18 composite, it reduces the downside deviation and MDD by more than 50% and thus it obtains higher Sortino and Calmar ratios.

You may notice that our top lookback period (6 months) is different from the optimal lookback period in Gu and Mulvey (2021a), which is 1 month. This could be due to differences in the factors in our pool (as well as ensembling at the ESB level) versus their formulation of the factor zoo (since they do not ensemble), and the different horizons used. Finally, we postulate that the factor timing of TSMOM strategies could reflect a potentially regime-aware quality: it benefits from holding a well-diversified set of ESBs similar to the equal-weighted portfolio during normal risk-on periods, and when a crash happens, the strategy rapidly pivots toward the subset of risk-off ESBs (given monthly rebalancing), which should continue to be the winners in a tumultuous tape. The strategies based on a 6-month lookback period seem to strike the right balance of controlled turnover despite responsiveness to changing markets particularly in a downdraft.

In conclusion, we have replicated, validated, and extended the existing literature on factor momentum to QMIT's proprietary dataset of smart betas, which includes 5.75 years of live data.

Chapter 9

HEDGE FUND IN A BOX (HFIB) as the Archetypal EMN Construct

To take our readers the last mile from LIVE signal spreads to fully baked, realistically risk-optimized hedge fund (HF) portfolios, we present the HEDGE FUND IN A BOX (HFIB) strategy daily index tracker in Tables 7.1–7.4. For perspective, we show the cum VAMI (value-added monthly index) of our HFIB index tracker and its substantial outperformance LTD as compared to prominent hedge fund peers with daily performance data available (January 2019–present, daily rebalanced). For the longer perspective, we also show the back-tested summary stats based on monthly rebalancing from the inception date of January 2000. Given the lack of longer-term history on peer funds we use the HFR EMN index as the benchmark. Nota Bene – Gross signal spreads and HFIB returns are a representation of the model portfolio published live as a strategy index or in the longer-term simulation. This is not meant to be an SEC (Securities and Exchange Commission) compliant track record of an investment vehicle as per the disclaimers in the appendix. While this representation benefits from the absence of fees or impact, it is also substantially handicapped by the lack of leverage typically employed by HFs or the benefit from securities lending and so on. Without knowing the parameters of the specific mandate such as assets under management (AUM) and fee structure, one cannot accurately model all such costs. The index construction based on our flagship composite signals enables the portfolio to capitalize on various market inefficiencies in addition to the hundreds of factors embedded within the ensemble of 18 enhanced smart betas (ESBs). The strategy enforces tight controls on net sector and industry exposures (±2.5%) and maintains beta neutrality within a narrow range of [–0.01, 0.01], ensuring minimal sensitivity to market movements. Individual stock weights are capped at 1.5% on both the long and short sides, reducing idiosyncratic risk. Additionally, by enforcing naive factor neutrality across five key common factors (typical of risk models like Axioma), the strategy focuses on purer (idiosyncratic) alpha generation. The resultant optimal portfolio typically holds 75 long versus 75 short positions, providing robust diversification. The underlying composite signal benefits from diversification across ESBs and exposure to exotic risk-premia across approximately the most liquid 3,000 North American stocks and American Depositary Receipts (ADRs). While there does exist 25Y of HFIB history (including 19 years of back-tested returns from 2000 to 2018), for the purposes of this study we only focus on the 6Y LIVE daily published returns for HFIB and peer funds. QMIT's HFIB strategies are net of commissions and short rebates but gross of fees (as is the norm for an index). The three prominent peers used for this study are as follows (based on publicly available returns data):

- JMNAX (JPMorgan Market Neutral Fund)
- QMNNX (AQR Market Neutral Fund)
- VMNFX (Vanguard Market Neutral Fund)

Our flagship strategies like the HFIB EMN and LBO are now being tracked as indices by banks in Bloomberg as well as by index providers as the underlying for swaps and notes in order to facilitate QIS exposure via AA-rated bank counterparties. The 6-year index tracker of our top versus bottom flagship signal spreads and the corresponding risk-optimized HF portfolio (HFIB) compares rather favorably with prominent quant EMN hedge fund peers. The index profile of the HFIB EMN strategy is shown in Table 9.1 with the corresponding 6Y summary statistics shown in Table 9.2.

Table 9.1 HFIB EMN Profile – 6Y Daily Rebalanced.

$ Neutrality	100 long × 90–100 short
Net Sector & Industry Exposure	2.5%
Beta neutrality	[–0.01, 0.01]
Long-side single stock weight	<1.50%
Short-side single stock weight	<1.50%
Naive factor neutrality	0 based on 5 factors

Table 9.2 Summary Stats – 6Y Daily Rebalanced HFIB EMN as of 2024-12-31.

	HFIB	QMNNX	VMNFX	JMNAX
Annualized Ret	27.32%	7.71%	3.89%	5.59%
Annualized Vol	13.77%	9.55%	6.99%	5.51%
Sharpe Ratio	1.98	0.81	0.56	1.01
Annualized Sortino Ratio	3.17	1.16	0.75	1.41
Max DD	16.61	29.5	21.53	7.58

The HFIB strategy index presents a promising annualized return profile of 27.32% (gross), which is a multiple of the returns of QMNNX at 7.71%, VMNFX at 3.89%, and JMNAX at 5.59%. When considering risk-adjusted returns, HFIB's potential becomes more pronounced. The strategy achieves a gross Sharpe ratio of 1.98, indicating efficiency in converting risk into returns compared to the net Sharpe ratio of 0.81 for QMNNX, 0.56 for VMNFX, and 1.01 for JMNAX. Similarly, the gross Sortino ratiofor HFIB is 3.17, versus the ratios for QMNNX (+1.16), VMNFX (+0.75), and JMNAX (+1.41), highlighting better downside risk management. In terms of capital preservation, HFIB exhibits a maximum drawdown of 16.61%, which is notably lower than the maximum drawdown experienced by QMNNX (29.5%). Higher returns with controlled risk underscores HFIB's robustness and its potential for delivering superior, risk-adjusted performance over the period analyzed with the important caveat that the HFIB index is gross of fees and *t*-costs.

Reviewing Table 9.3, the annual returns from 2019 to 2024 YTD, it's clear that the HFIB EMN strategyhas consistently outperformed its peers – QMNNX, VMNFX, and JMNAX. Over the cumulative period, HFIB more than QUADRUPLED

Table 9.3 6Y Daily Rebalanced as of 2024-12-31.

HFIB Performance	HFIB (%)	QMNNX (%)	VMNFX (%)	JMNAX (%)
2019	4.49	−11.55	−9.57	0.97
2020	13.26	−19.79	−11.58	11.93
2021	79.1	17.39	23.24	3.79
2022	29.95	27.08	13.48	−2.38
2023	19.64	16.3	12.23	11.13
2024 YTD	29.27	26.84	0.19	8.87
Total Cumulative	326.0	56.11	25.74	38.56

at +326.0% (gross), far exceeding the cumulative net returns of 56.11% for QMNNX, 25.74% for VMNFX, and 38.56% for JMNAX.

The comparative cumulative growth trajectories of the HFIB EMN strategy and its peers over the 6-year live period are visually depicted by their VAMIs in Figure 9.1. Table 9.4 shows the detailed performance of the 25-year monthly rebalanced HFIB profile.

Examining the monthly summary statistics over a 19-year back-test period, supplemented with over sixyears of live index data as of the latest month-end, the HFIB long/short strategy demonstrates promising outperformance as compared to both the benchmark and the broader market represented by the S&P 500. The HFIB long/short strategy achieved an annualized return of 25.98% with an annualized volatility of 11.48%, resulting in a robust Sharpe ratio of 2.26, which is consistent with the LIVE 6Y period for the index. Additionally, the strategy maintained a relatively low Max DD of −15.91% (monthly rebalance for 19Y of the back-test).

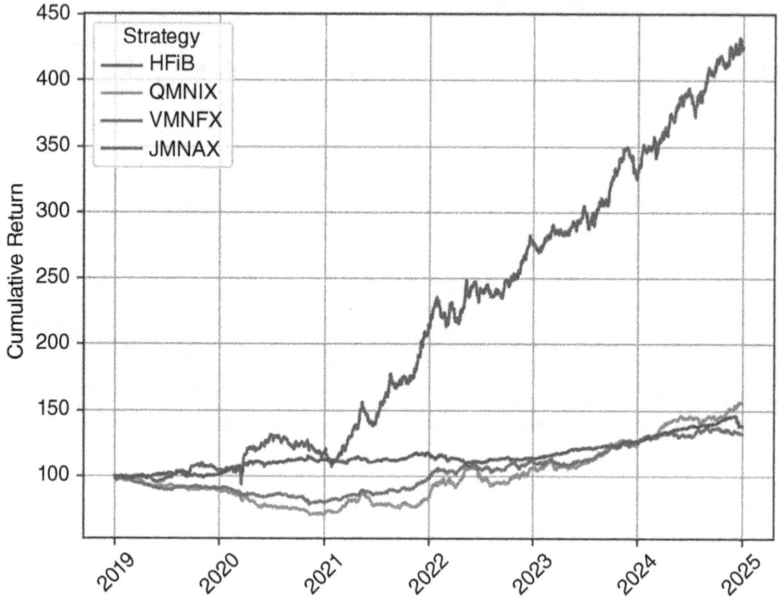

Figure 9.1 **HFIB VAMIs (Daily Rebalanced) – 6Y LIVE as of 2024-12-31.**

Table 9.4 25Y Monthly Profile (19Y Back-Test with 6Y LIVE) as of 2024-12-31.

	HFIB – Long/ Short	Benchmark	HFIB – Long Only	S&P 500
Annualized Return	25.98	0.93	20.99	7.61
Annualized Volatility	11.48	3.68	19.02	15.26
Sharpe	2.26	0.25	1.10	0.50
Sortino	5.92	0.34	1.91	0.74
Max Drawdown	15.91	20.06	39.45	50.80

By contrast, the benchmark (HFRXEMN Index) recorded a modest annualized return of 0.93% with a lower volatility of 3.68%, leading to a Sharpe ratio of 0.25 and a Sortino ratio of 0.34. The maximum drawdown for the benchmark was 20.06%, higher than that of the HFIB long/short strategy. The HFIB *long-only* strategy also outperformed the S&P 500, with an annualized return of 20.99% and a Sharpe ratio of 1.10. Although it experienced higher volatility (being fully exposed to beta) its maximum drawdown was much lower than that of the S&P 500. Meanwhile, the S&P 500 delivered an annualized return of 7.61% with a volatility of 15.26%, a Sharpe ratio of 0.50, and a maximum drawdown of 50.80%.

It bears reiterating that all HFIB EMN index returns presented above are *gross of fees and transactions costs* (de minimis commissions in the monthly rebalancing case) at this juncture (as would be typical of any other index). On the flip side, the HFIB index is also substantially handicapped by the lack of leverage typically employed by peer EMN funds or the benefits accrued due to securities lending and so on. In Section 9.1, we therefore incorporate the impact of turnover, transaction costs (explicit commissions only), and short rebates. Finally in Section 9.4, we go the last mile toward market impact and the decomposition of implementation shortfall (IS) across various indices for context. Remaining performance nuances are addressed in the Disclaimers at the end of the book.

9.1. HFIB EMN PEER COMPARISONS, TURNOVER, AND TRANSACTION COSTS

The QMIT HFIB index is a fully risk-optimized equity market-neutral hedge fund portfolio accessible via bank QIS swaps or structured products. Published daily (6Y LIVE), it is based on our flagship composite multifactor models constructed by combining 18 machine learning (ML) ESBs via ensemble learners. The composite signal benefits from diversification across uncorrelated ESBs and exposure to exotic risk-premia on the most liquid of about 3,000 North American stocks and ADRs. Figure 9.2 shows the Sizzling Seven composite MFM signal underlying the HFIB construct decomposed into its constituent ESBs and subcomposites like Quality, Value, GrowthMo, and so on. The benefits of diversifying across uncorrelated smart betas are evident. The HFIB risk-optimization setup ensures dollar and beta neutrality while controlling for earnings torpedoes and meme stock squeezes in order to presumably deliver a better risk-adjusted outcome. QMIT also neutralizes the most common five naive factors in order to accentuate the idiosyncratic alpha. While there does exist 25 years of HFIB history

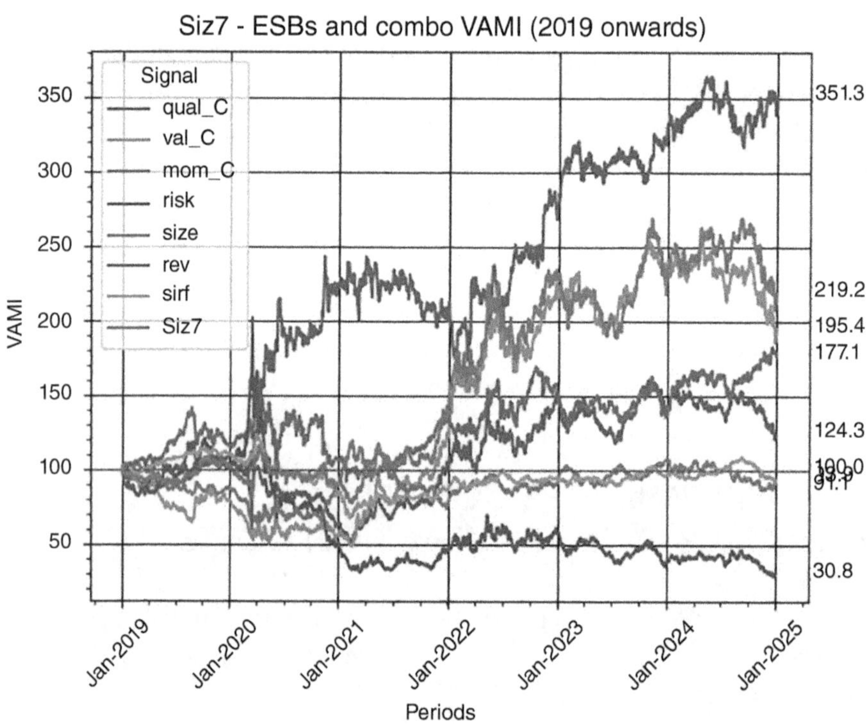

Figure 9.2 ESBs and Combo VAMI as of 2024-12-31.

(including 19 years of back-tested returns from 2000 to 2018), for the purposes of this study we only focus on the 6Y LIVE daily published returns (based on either a daily or a weekly rebalance) for HFIB and peer funds.

9.1.1. Transaction Cost and Turnover

Historical price data and daily portfolio weights are based on a T−1 convention. To avoid look-ahead bias we assume trading on T + 0 using the alphas available on T + 0 based on the T−1 closing prices and fundamentals (the formation date). Further, for the QMIT strategies we assume all executions are done at the close at a rate of 5 mills (i.e., $0.0005/share) on an AUM of $100 million. The average daily transaction cost estimate is based on the six-month period (January 2021–June 2021), which is then annualized in basis points (bps) of AUM.

Turnover is defined as the four-way absolute sum of shares traded on the assumed $100 × $100 million exposure and underlies the corresponding *t*-cost estimates shown in Table 9.5. As one might expect, daily rebalancing results in a 2.5× higher daily flip rate of over 105% (four-way) of AUM, while the imputed daily turnover in the weekly case is much lower at only 40%. The annualized turns are high but consistent with the profile of active quant equity strategies in the EMN space.

Daily Rebalanced Turnover: 105.2% per Day Versus 26,510% Annualized (265x/Y)

Table 9.5 Daily and Weekly Rebalance Transaction Cost.

	Daily Rebalance	Weekly Rebalance
t-cost	44 bps	16 bps

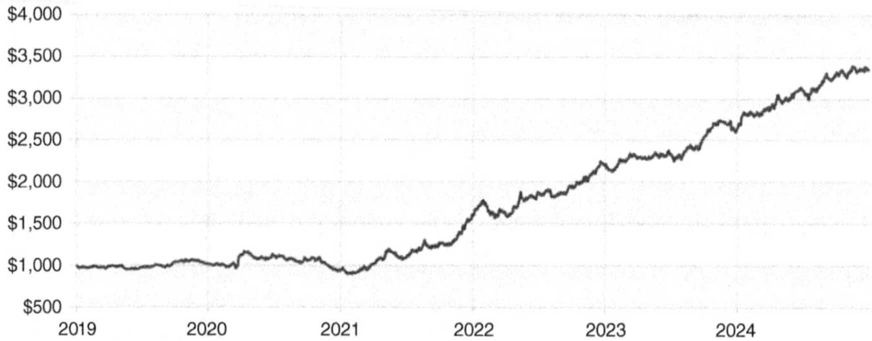

Figure 9.3 QUMN Index (Weekly) VAMI on TMX VettaFi.

Weekly Rebalanced Turnover: 40.25% per Day Versus 10,130% Annualized (101x/Y)

The VAMI for the QUMN index, which represents the HFIB strategy with weekly rebalancing (not daily rebalanced as in Figure 9.1) over the live period as published by TMX (Toronto Montreal stock exchange), is presented in Figure 9.3.

9.1.2. Risk Versus Returns Analysis

Comparing the performance metrics reveals that both HFIB index variations substantially outperform the peer funds on both absolute and risk-adjusted bases. The HFIB strategy detailed in Section 9.1, which utilizes **daily rebalancing**, demonstrates the highest terminal value, concluding the 6-year period close to four times the initial investment. The QUMN index on TMX, based on **weekly rebalancing** as shown in Table 9.6, also delivers strong performance, finishing at just over three times the initial value, while benefiting from interest earned on short proceeds and despite incurring transaction costs.

Table 9.3 shows both of the HFIB indices substantially outperform peers in returns as well as risk-adjusted terms with

Table 9.6 QUMN TMX Index (Weekly) Performance[1].

					Annualized		
	3 Month	6 Month	YTD	1 Year	3 Year	5 Year	ITD
Total Return	1.6%	8.2%	27.3%	27.3%	28.0%	26.9%	22.4%
Excess Return	0.4%	5.7%	21.3%	21.3%	23.4%	24.2%	19.8%
Volatility					11.8%	14.0%	13.2%
Sharpe Ratio					2.38	1.92	1.69

the daily rebalance VAMI ending far ahead of the pack and close to 4× the initial investment while the weekly rebalance HFIB index finishes at just over 3× despite *t*-cost but with the benefit of interest earned on short proceeds. Other peers all end up below 1.5× terminal value partly due to their high TERs (total expense ratios). The key observation based on the return differential would be that the incremental *t*-cost of +28 bps for daily rebalancing (versus weekly rebalancing) still leaves us with an extra +533 bps/annually largely due to the outperformance during the choppier markets of 2019–2020. HFIB annualized 6Y returns are in the +22.7 to 28% range which is a significant (about 5×) multiple of peers which are clustered in the +5 to 7% range.

Given that the HFIB volatility (about 13.5–14%) is also much higher than the peer 5.5% (JMNAX) to 7.0% (VMNFX) range, the litmus test will be the realized Sharpe and Sortino ratios, which do turn out to be as much as 2.85× higher. QMNNX has a much higher volatility than similar peers at 9.6% (but lower than HFIB), which is reflective of an extended and deep drawdown (of which only the last about −30% DD is visible in this

[1] TMX index link: https://www.vettafi.com/indexing/index/qumn.

six-year period) suffered by the AQR fund. This may have been due to AQR's premature bet on Value, which remained out of favor until 2021. Indeed, most peer funds had ill-timed and outsized bets on well-known naive factors such as Value while QMIT ensembles bet on more exotic risk-premia. The QMIT strategies also exhibited volatility near the March 2020 COVID episode but ended up with a positive outlier return of +14% to +15% in March 2020. This was after the Fed (and the usual plunge protection team) stepped in on March 23, 2020. Needless to say, the peer de-leveraging had culminated with statistical arbitrage funds (like that at Jefferies) completing their liquidation just in time for a historic about +110% rally in QMIT's mean reversion ESB, which powered the dramatic resurgence of the Sizzling Seven signals and thereby the HFIB EMN index. While HFIB had a drawdown episode after the US elections on Pfizer Monday (November 9, 2020) as a result of the historic one-day momentum crash precipitated by Pfizer's announcement of the COVID vaccine, it actually had a sizable run up around the COVID crash delivering on the EMN value proposition. However, the most dramatic peer outperformance for HFIB came during 2019–2020 (when quant was left for dead amid the Value doldrums) and in 2021 due to the double alpha resulting from the Cathy Wood/crypto crash amid an otherwise raging bull market, which resulted in triple-digit alphas for QMIT's raw signal spreads. Not only did QMIT model longs beat the ebullient market by double digits in 2021, but the short side also delivered substantial alpha as the air came of out correlated bubbles in cryptos and unprofitable growth names.

For a closer look at the HFIB drawdown profile, please see Table 9.7. The key observation is that the Max DD for HFIB did not occur near the COVID episode. Rather, it was a slow drip as the mean reversion played out post-COVID and was later exacerbated by the momentum crash in November–December 2020, which resulted from the simultaneous resolution of uncertainty surrounding the arrival of the COVID vaccine as well as the post-election (denial) uncertainty.

Table 9.7 HFIB 6Y Daily Versus Weekly Rebalance (QUMN).

Metric	HFIB Daily Rebal	HFIB Weekly Rebal (QUMN)
Number of Years	6.00	6.00
Initial VAMI	100.00	100.00
Final VAMI	426.00	335.91
Ann Return (%)	27.32	22.38
Ann Stdev (%)	13.77	13.21
Sharpe	1.98	1.69
Sortino	3.17	2.70
MDD (%)	16.61	22.48

At the end of the day, investors eat returns not Sharpe or Sortino ratios, but the risk-adjusted metrics are critical to any institutional evaluation of such funds. Based on the risk-adjusted metrics, AQR and Vanguard bring up the rear with similarly low Sharpes about 0.75 versus 2 for HFIB daily rebalance. Analogously, HFIB's 3.2 Sortino is over 3× that of AQR and Vanguard and 2× that of J.P. Morgan's at 1.6. The much higher Sortino versus Sharpe suggests that much of the higher HFIB volatility is actually upside volatility. Hence, the risk/return trade-offs highlight the value proposition of QMIT's HFIB portfolios relative to peers. Furthermore, the HFIB returns over six years are substantially higher than even SPX despite beta neutrality.

9.2. DIVERSIFICATION IS THE ONLY FREE LUNCH

Our LBO models (see Chapters 10 and 11), particularly the Sizzling 35 LBOs (leveraged buyouts), have shown promising returns by identifying potentially undervalued companies suitable for leveraged buyouts. Concurrently, our HFIB EMN strategy index has proven effective in delivering substantial gains over a six-year period. This section explores the benefits of combining these distinct approaches. By blending the market-neutral stability of HFIB (represented by the QUMN TMX index variant here) and the event-driven alpha generation of the LBO strategies in a 50/50 allocation, we aim to harness the best of both. The following analysis details the performance over a six-year period, comparing HFIB (QUMN), the LBO strategies (QLBO and Sizzling LBO), and their combined portfolios. Table 9.8[2] presents the YTD performance metric, for these individual strategies QUMN, QLBO, Sizzling LBO, and their combined portfolios, providing an initial snapshot for this comparative analysis.

The 50/50 combination of QUMN and Sizzling LBOs in Table 9.9 shows an annualized return of 13.90%, lower than QUMN's 27.32% while significantly outperforming both LBO strategies individually. More impressively, the combined portfolio achieves a Sharpe ratio of 2.08 and a Sortino ratio of 3.46, substantially higher than either strategy alone. This indicates superior risk-adjusted returns, making the combined strategy more efficient in converting risk into return.

Table 9.8 YTD Performance Metrics as of 2024-12-31.

QUMN	QLBO	Sizzling 35 LBO	50/50 LBO	50/50 Sizzling LBO
27.32%	−4.99%	1.47%	10.15%	13.90%

[2]Worth noting that the QLBO index moniker is now being subsumed by a version of the prior Top 100 LBOs which is being whittled down to the Top 50 names based on additional constraints.

Table 9.9 50/50 Combo of HFIB EMN + LBOs HEDGED (6Y LIVE Till 12/31/24).

Metric	QUMN	QLBO	Sizzling LBO	50/50 (QLBO)	50/50 (Sizzling LBO)
Number of Years	6.00	6.00	6.00	6.00	6.00
Initial VAMI	100.00	100.00	100.00	100.00	100.00
Final VAMI	335.91	192.66	275.87	258.39	310.29
Daily Std	0.83	0.60	0.78	0.56	0.63
Ann Return	22.38	11.55	18.43	17.14	20.77
Ann Stdev	13.21	9.45	12.37	8.93	9.98
Sharpe	1.69	1.22	1.49	1.92	2.08
Sortino	2.67	1.90	2.43	3.07	3.46
MDD	22.48	14.27	16.83	11.74	12.96

The detailed six-year performance metrics presented in Table 9.9 underscore the compelling diversification benefits achieved by combining the QUMN (HFIB EMN) strategy with the LBO strategies. While the stand-alone QUMN strategy yielded the highest absolute annualized return (22.38%), the 50/50 blend with Sizzling LBO produced a competitive return (20.77%) alongside significantly reduced volatility (9.98% annualized standard deviation compared to QUMN's 13.21%). Most important, the combined portfolios demonstrated markedly superior risk-adjusted performance, with the 50/50 Sizzling LBO mix achieving the highest Sharpe (2.08) and Sortino (3.46) ratios, substantially exceeding those of the individual components. Furthermore, this blend offered enhanced capital preservation, evidenced by a significantly lower maximum drawdown (12.96%) compared to QUMN (22.48%). Collectively, these results highlight the effectiveness of the 50/50 combination, particularly with Sizzling LBO, in creating a more efficient and robust investment profile through reduced risk and enhanced risk-adjusted returns, reinforcing the principle that diversification is advantageous, albeit with the prior caveats regarding returns gross of fees and market impact.

The correlation matrix over the six-year LIVE period, presented in Table 9.10, provides critical insights into the diversification potential when combining the strategies. Most notably, the correlation between the market-neutral QUMN strategy and both LBO strategies (QLBO and Sizzling LBO) is very low at 22%. This limited statistical relationship signifies that their return streams behave largely independently, which is the fundamental driver behind the enhanced risk-adjusted returns and reduced drawdowns observed when they are combined (as shown in Table 9.9). The high correlation of 82% between the two LBO variants is due to their construction since the Sizzling LBOs are composed of 35 out of the Top 100 in the QLBO index. Overall, this correlation structure strongly validates the rationale for combining the distinct QUMN strategy with an LBO strategy to improve portfolio efficiency through diversification.

Table 9.10 HFIB EMN Versus LBOs HEDGED Correlations (6Y LIVE).

	QUMN	QLBO	Sizzling LBO	50/50 (QLBO)	50/50 (Sizzling LBO)
QUMN	1.00				
QLBO	0.22	1.00			
Sizzling LBO	0.22	0.82	1.00		
50/50 (QLBO)	0.86	0.69	0.59	1.00	
50/50 (Sizzling LBO)	0.80	0.66	0.76	0.94	1.00

Figure 9.4 shows the VAMI chart visually confirms the findings from the tables. While the stand-alone QUMN strategy (QUMN VAMI) achieves the highest terminal wealth, the combined portfolios (50/50 (QLBO) VAMI and 50/50 (Sizzling) LBO VAMI) demonstrate considerably smoother growth paths with less volatility and shallower drawdowns, particularly compared to the stand-alone LBO strategies (QLBO VAMI and Sizzling LBO VAMI). The final wealth levels of the combined 50/50 strategies are quite compelling, particularly from a risk-adjusted standpoint. It is important to recall that the QUMN strategy shown here (as per TMX index publication) employs weekly rebalancing, whereas other HFIB EMN analyses in prior sections used daily rebalancing. The difference in rebalancing frequency is important when interpreting performance metrics. Figure 9.5 shows the 50/50 combination of the two weekly QMIT indices in TMX as tracked by the Sandbox system.

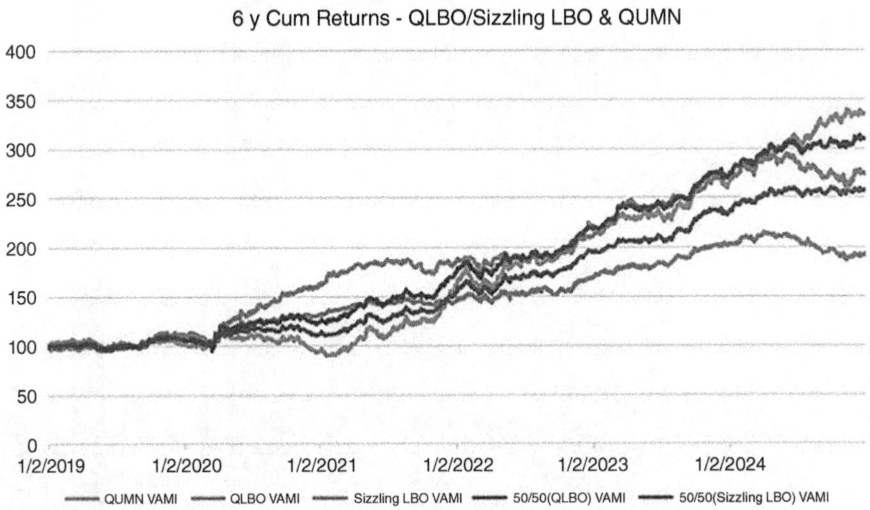

Figure 9.4 6Y Returns VAMI (Cumulative Returns).

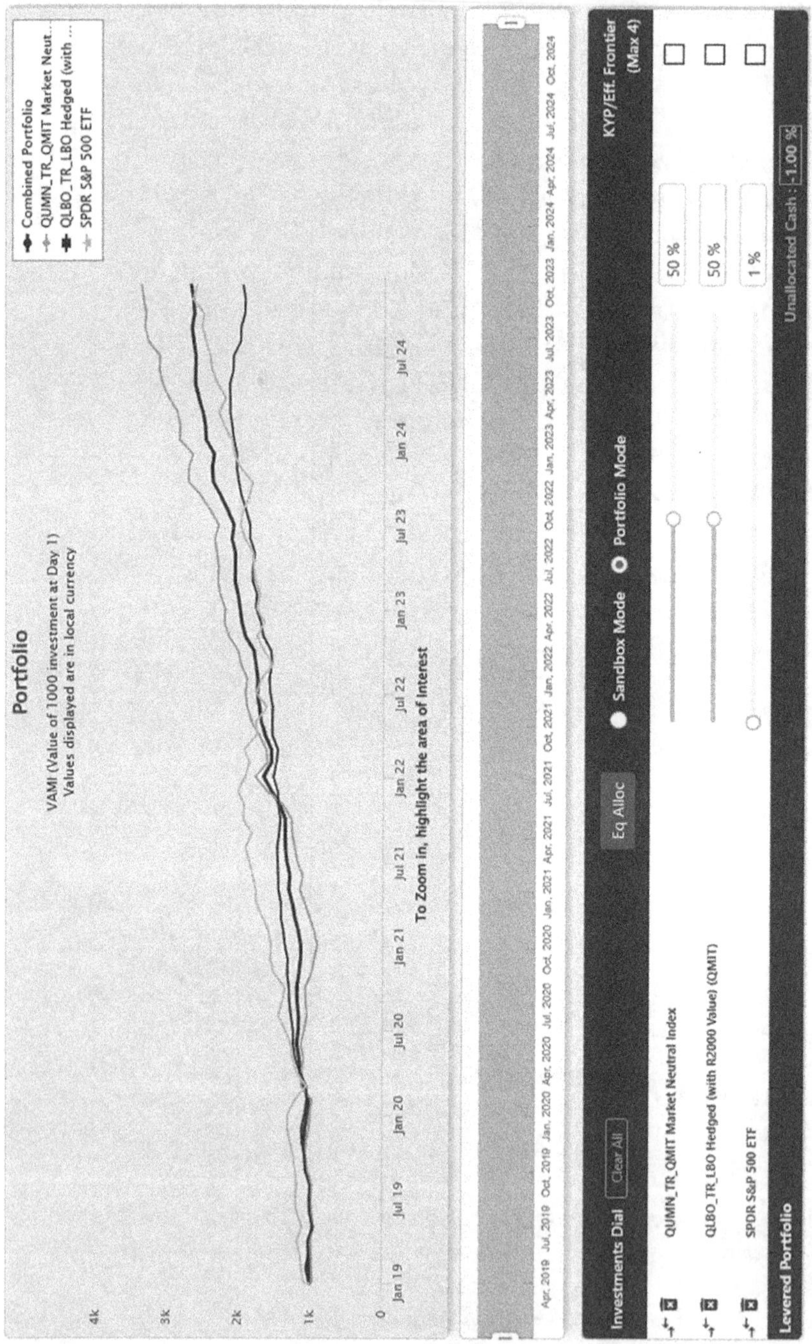

Figure 9.5 Monthly Return VAMI.

9.3. TCA: DELUSIONS OF GRANDEUR

As one of the earliest adopters of fully algorithmic equity execution near the turn of the millennium, I had a front row seat to the disruptive advances in fully automated execution via algorithms such as VWAP, TWAP, Guerilla, Iceberg, Sniper, and many others that have shaped the modern landscape of equity execution. Friends and trade counterparties at firms like ITG and later Credit Suisse AES led the charge on these tectonic shifts that reshaped the industry.

The study of transaction costs, a cornerstone of market microstructure, has evolved significantly from its foundational principles. While the concept of IS (Perold, 1988) and the theoretical underpinnings of market impact (Kyle, 1985) remain central, recent research has leveraged new technologies and data to build far more sophisticated models. The literature now focuses on capturing the complex, nonlinear, and dynamic nature of trading costs in a fragmented electronic market.

A primary driver of recent innovation has been the application of ML and artificial intelligence. Traditional pre-trade models often relied on linear regressions against liquidity proxies like volume and volatility. However, modern research demonstrates that ML techniques, such as gradient-boosted trees and neural networks, can provide more accurate cost estimates by capturing complex interactions and nonlinearities in the data. For instance, Lehalle and Laruelle (2018) showcase how such models can better predict the cost of executing large meta-orders by learning from vast datasets of historical trades. These models move beyond simple proxies to incorporate deeper features of the limit order book, such as order imbalances, book depth at multiple levels, and the flow of high-frequency order cancellations and submissions.

The changing market structure itself has become a major research theme. The rise of high-frequency trading and the fragmentation of liquidity across dozens of "lit" exchanges and off-exchange "dark pools" (alternative trading systems; ATS) complicate cost analysis. Research by Foucault et al. (2013) explores how fragmentation affects liquidity and price discovery. Modern transaction cost analysis (TCA) must therefore account for where liquidity is sourced. Work by Zhu (2014) on dark pools highlights the trade-off they present: lower explicit costs and potential for reduced price impact, but with the risk of adverse selection.

Finally, the field of optimal execution has advanced toward more dynamic and adaptive strategies. While the Almgren and Chriss (2001) framework established the fundamental trade-off between impact and timing risk, recent studies explore how algorithms can learn and adapt in real time. The application of reinforcement learning, as explored in early work by Nevmyvaka et al. (2006) and more recent studies, aims to create execution agents that can dynamically adjust their trading speed and venue selection based on evolving market conditions, effectively learning an optimal execution policy rather than following a static schedule.

At the heart of this entire field lies the concept of IS, a framework so influential that its principles remain the bedrock of modern TCA. André Perold's seminal 1988 paper, "The Implementation Shortfall: Paper Versus Reality," elegantly defined IS as a unified cost metric: the difference between the paper return of a portfolio at the decision price and its actual, realized return. This single number encapsulates all elements of slippage. Crucially, Perold introduced a decomposition of this total cost into distinct components: delay, execution, and opportunity costs, enabling managers to pinpoint where value is lost. The framework's power comes from its decision-price benchmark – using the price that prevailed at the moment of the investment decision (prior to any impact due to the orders interaction with the market), which avoids the hindsight bias of other benchmarks like VWAP. In the extreme situation where our order is 100% of volume the VWAP as a benchmark becomes rather contrived. There is an analog here to the observer participatory nature of the universe in quantum mechanics. The act of being in the market moves the prices we wish to observe. By linking IS directly to portfolio alpha, it makes explicit that every basis point of shortfall is performance forfeited and creates powerful managerial incentives to trade efficiently. Finally, it crystalizes the classic trader's dilemma: the trade-off between execution speed (which minimizes opportunity cost but increases market impact) and patience (which does the opposite).

Building on the foundational understanding provided, in Section 9.4, we seek to quantify the drivers of these costs in today's market and provide an insightful decomposition of IS across various indices for context and comparison.

9.4. TCA: TAMING THE BEAST[3]

Efficient trade execution is a critical determinant of realized performance for quantitative investors and portfolio managers, as excessive trading costs can materially erode alpha. To quantify these effects, we examine estimated execution costs for approximately 2,600 US equities within the QMIT universe as of June 30, 2025, using FactSet's BEAST transaction cost model. For each stock, a standardized $1 million parent order was simulated over the regular trading session (9:30 a.m.–4:00 p.m. EST), excluding the opening and closing auctions. The objective is to derive empirical insights into the distribution and determinants of

[3]Thanks to Brian MacSweeney and Sendoh Xu for their contributions to this section as well as Chris Sparrow of FactSet BEAST for providing the data and critical feedback.

execution costs – specifically the influence of volume, liquidity, and volatility – and to consider the trade-off between execution patience and opportunity cost.

9.4.1. Structure and Components of Trading Costs

The BEAST model decomposes total Implementation Shortfall (IS) – expressed in cost per share – as follows:

$$\text{Total Cost} = \text{Spread Cost} + \text{Liquidity Cost}$$

- **Spread cost:** the explicit, deterministic cost of crossing half the bid-ask spread; directly linked to instantaneous market liquidity.
- **Liquidity cost:** the implicit, temporary market-impact cost of consuming displayed depth (i.e., "eating the book") during order execution.
- **Market impact:** reported separately, denotes the permanent shift in mid-price between the order's initiation and completion. While related to cost, it differs conceptually: if purchases begin at $10 and end at $11 with a volume-weighted execution price of $10.51, the cost is $0.51 per share, whereas the market impact is $1.

  By disentangling these components, the BEAST framework enables practitioners to attribute execution slippage to distinct drivers and to formulate targeted mitigation strategies.

9.4.2. Scope and Definitions

Throughout this analysis, the terms IS, cost, and slippage are used interchangeably to denote total trading cost (spread + liquidity). Estimates exclude brokerage commissions and other explicit fees, focusing solely on implicit trading costs derived from lit-market liquidity, with no adjustment for off-exchange or alternative-trading-system activity.

9.4.3. Cross-Sectional T-Cost Profile for QMIT Universe (June 30, 2025)

We show the cross-sectional *t*-cost profile for the entire QMIT universe (as of June 30, 2025) as summarized in Table 9.11 for *t*-cost in bps (based on one $ million trade size).

Our analysis (as per Figure 9.6) revealed trading costs are highly skewed across stocks. For the majority of stocks, predicted costs are minimal – a few bps or less – reflecting little more than the cost of crossing the bid-ask spread. However, a small subset of stocks incurs extremely high costs, creating a pronounced long tail in the distribution. While the vast majority of stocks can be traded with negligible cost, the presence of these outliers introduces significant tail risk to transaction costs.

In our one-day sample, at the 90th percentile, costs rise sharply, and only in this upper decile of highest-cost names do we observe execution costs climbing into the dozens or even hundreds of bps. In the most extreme cases, the model predicted costs exceeding 1,000 bps for certain illiquid stocks implying that a single trade could move the price by more than 10%. Though infrequent, these extreme outcomes exert a disproportionate influence on the overall distribution of trading costs. In the decile histograms shown in Figure 9.7, we use the right end point (maximum) of the interval. Costs are reported in dollars per share or in bps (where 1 bps is 0.01%).

Unsurprisingly (as per Figure 9.7), the low-cost group is dominated by highly liquid, large-cap stocks. Mega-cap names like Apple, Amazon, and NVIDIA often incur virtually no market impact for a trade of $1 million.

These stocks trade tens of millions of shares daily, so a $1 million order hardly dents the order book. In our data, 550 stocks show no liquidity cost at all but on average show

Table 9.11 Summary of *T*-Cost in BPs (Based on $1 Million Trade).

	Count	Mean	std	min	25%	50%	75%	max	Skew	kurtosis	IQR
costPerShareBps	2,593.0	24.72	58.47	0.39	5.70	11.53	23.89	1,672.34	13.42	295.29	18.19
liquidityCostPerShareBps	2,593.0	11.44	47.13	0.00	0.16	1.25	6.43	1,406.70	15.21	357.15	6.27
spreadCostPerShareBps	2,593.0	13.28	15.81	0.39	5.10	8.99	16.04	286.99	6.19	73.16	10.94

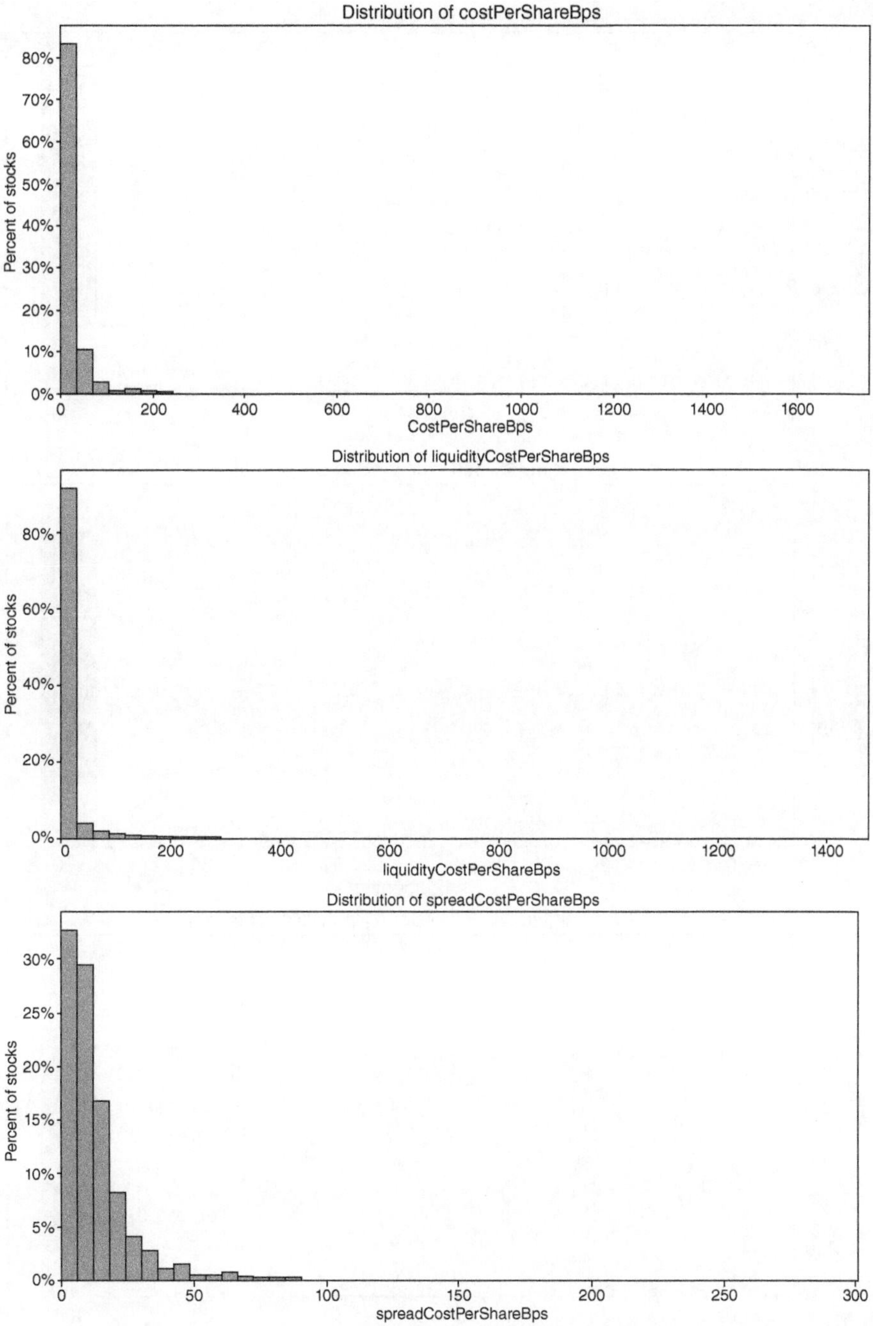

Figure 9.6 Distribution of Costs (Bps) Across the Universe.

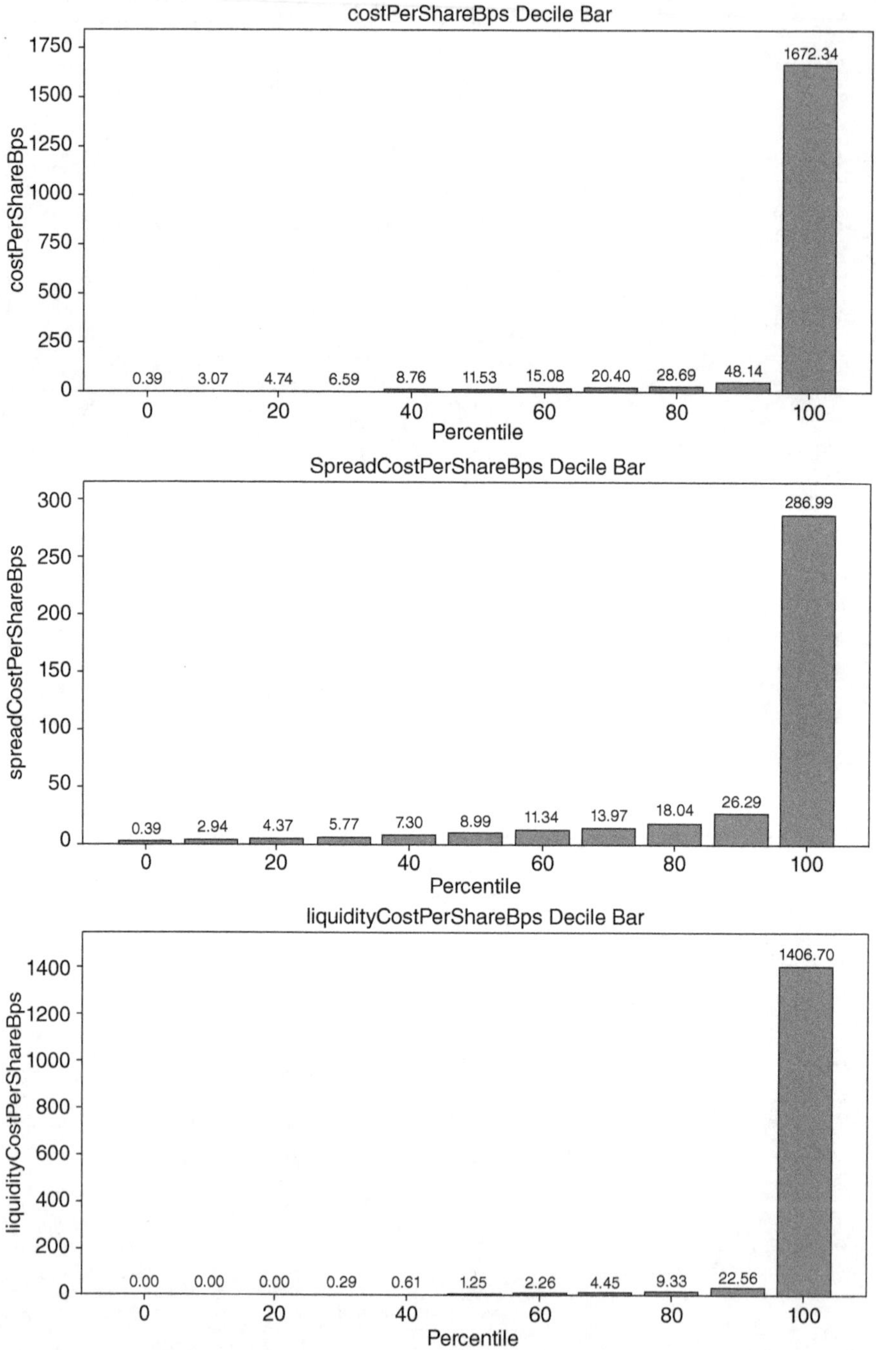

Figure 9.7 BPs of Liquidity Cost by Decile.

5.3 bps of *t*-cost, which is substantial. For these names, trading costs are limited to the bid-ask spread, which is typically just a few bps in highly liquid markets.

However, the high-cost tail consists almost entirely of low-volume, small-cap stocks where even modest trades can push deeply into the order book and generate significant costs. Poor liquidity in these names means that sizable orders can easily move prices, creating a stark divide in trading costs across the universe of stocks.

As a result, while the majority of a typical portfolio can be traded at minimal cost, a small number of illiquid positions can disproportionately drive up overall transaction costs. This skew suggests that trading cost budgets are often dictated by a handful of problematic names rather than the broader portfolio. Even otherwise cost-efficient strategies can be significantly distorted by just one or two expensive-to-trade stocks, making it essential to proactively identify and manage these outliers.

9.4.4. Anatomy of Trading Costs: Spread Versus Liquidity

Every trade's implementation cost consists of two parts: spread cost and liquidity cost. Spread cost reflects the immediate expense of crossing the bid-ask spread – typically half the spread if using the mid-price as a benchmark. Liquidity cost captures slippage from moving the mid-price, driven by order book depth and other price dynamics.

Spread cost is essentially a fixed cost per share for a given stock and time, while liquidity cost grows with the order's size relative to available liquidity. Model outputs display a near-perfect correlation (about 0.98) between total cost (in bps) and the liquidity cost component, and a strong correlation (about 0.78) with the spread component. This result further confirms that trading costs are largely determined by these two factors putting aside momentum costs, which are not considered herein.

Furthermore, spread costs and liquidity costs are strongly positively correlated ($\rho \approx 0.64$) among themselves (Tables 9.12 and 9.13). Stocks that exhibit high market impact often also have wider bid-ask spreads, reflecting their shared illiquidity characteristics. Thinly traded stocks typically feature both wide spreads and shallow order books, which can be quickly depleted by even moderately sized trades.

These cost components behave differently across stock types. Large-cap, actively traded stocks tend to have very tight bid-ask spreads (often 1–2 bps) and deep liquidity, while smaller or less liquid stocks tend to show wider spreads and shallower order books. Spread cost serves as a baseline cost for any trade – relatively stable and low for large caps, but significantly higher for small- and micro-cap names. In our universe, major stocks exhibited spread costs in the range of 1–5 bps, whereas some smaller names showed spreads of several tens of bps.

Liquidity cost becomes significant when an order starts to exhaust the order book. For highly liquid stocks (e.g., top-decile volume) a $1 million order barely penetrated the first few levels of the book, causing minimal market impact. By contrast, for the least liquid names, the same order could represent multiple days of average trading volume, quickly consuming the available liquidity and triggering large price swings. In these cases, liquidity dominates the total trading cost.

This pattern is evident when analyzing cost component breakdowns by liquidity decile (Figure 9.8). In the lowest

Table 9.12 Correlation Matrix (Pearson).

	MarketCap	ADTV	market-Impact	costPer-ShareBps	liquidityCost-PerShareBps	spreadCostPer-ShareBps
MarketCap	1.000	0.719	−0.061	−0.064	−0.042	−0.108
ADTV	0.719	1.000	−0.062	−0.062	−0.043	−0.101
marketImpact	−0.061	−0.062	1.000	0.650	0.562	0.726
costPerShareBps	−0.064	−0.062	0.650	1.000	0.978	0.783
liquidityCostPer-ShareBps	−0.042	−0.043	0.562	0.978	1.000	0.636
spreadCostPer-ShareBps	−0.108	−0.101	0.726	0.783	0.636	1.000

Table 9.13 Correlation Matrix (Spearman).

	MarketCap	ADTV	market-Impact	costPer-ShareBps	liquidityCost-PerShareBps	spreadCostPer-ShareBps
MarketCap	1.000	0.877	–0.814	–0.810	–0.913	–0.682
ADTV	0.877	1.000	–0.877	–0.792	–0.941	–0.655
marketImpact	–0.814	–0.877	1.000	0.874	0.886	0.803
costPerShareBps	–0.810	–0.792	0.874	1.000	0.818	0.957
liquidityCostPer-ShareBps	–0.913	–0.941	0.886	0.818	1.000	0.662
spreadCostPer-ShareBps	–0.682	–0.655	0.803	0.957	0.662	1.000

trading-volume decile, most trading cost comes from liquidity cost, with spreads contributing to only a small share of the cost. Pie charts for these stocks are heavily weighted toward liquidity cost (deciles 1 and 2). This indicates that trades are expensive mainly because the market cannot absorb size without significant price disruption. For larger cap names (deciles 9 and 10), however, orders of the same amount have a negligible impact on liquidity, so we observe that spread costs account for nearly all transaction costs in this scenario.

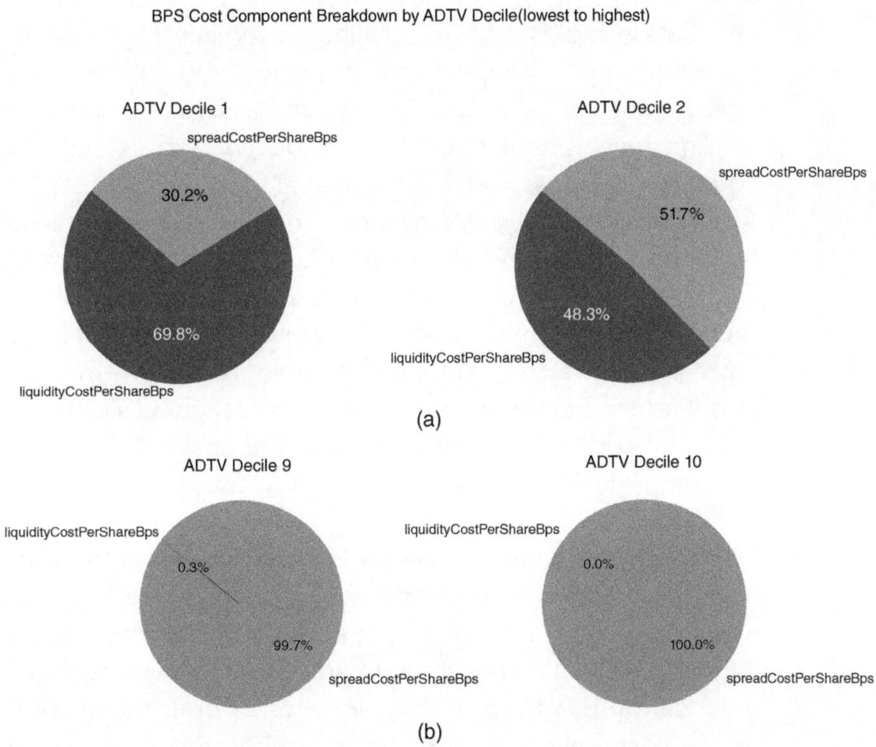

Figure 9.8 Cost Component Breakdown.

9.4.5. The Dominant Driver of Cost

Perhaps the single most important insight from the analysis is the critical role of liquidity in explaining variability in trading costs. Traditional liquidity measures such as market capitalization and 30-day average daily trading volume (ADTV) show a clear relationship with trading costs (Figure 9.9).

Intuitively, a strong inverse relationship exists between a stock's liquidity and its trading cost (Figure 9.10). Securities with higher ADTV and larger market capitalizations have deeper order books and tighter bid-ask spreads. Consequently, executing trades in these stocks is cheaper as they can absorb larger orders with less price impact. This fundamental relationship is confirmed when examining rank-order correlation or grouped comparisons, the relationship strengthens considerably. Ranking stocks by market cap or volume reveals that trading costs decline consistently as liquidity increases. Scatterplots of cost versus market cap or ADTV show a clear downward trend: as stocks become larger and more liquid, total cost decreases. A simple trend line fitted to log10 data suggests that ADTV alone explains roughly 60% of the variation in cost ranks, which is slightly more predictive than market cap. In short, ADTV emerges as one of the best predictors of trading cost. Stocks with low ADTV tend to incur higher-than-average costs, while those with high ADTV are typically low-cost trades.

Grouping stocks into deciles by liquidity illustrates this pattern. The lowest-liquidity decile (by ADTV) had a much higher median transaction cost and a long tail of extreme (higher-cost) outliers, with many trades incurring dozens or even hundreds of bps in costs very long upper tail of even higher-cost outliers. By contrast, as liquidity increases across deciles, the entire cost distribution shifts lower and tightens. By the highest volume decile, median costs were near

OLS Regression Results

Dep. Variable:	log10costPerShareBps	R-squared:	0.612
Model:	OLS	Adj. R-squared:	0.611
Method:	Least Squares	F-statistic:	4080.
Date:	Thu, 24 Jul 2025	Prob (F-statistic) :	0.00
Time:	00: 37:07	Log-Likelihood:	−538.41
No. observations:	2593	AIC:	1081.
Df Residuals:	2591	BIC:	1093.
Df Model:	1		
Covariance Type:	nonrobust		

	coef	std err	t	P> |t|	[0.025	0.975]
const	5.8346	0.075	78.162	0.000	5.688	5.981
log_MC	−0.4941	0.008	−63.874	0.000	−0.509	−0.479

Omnibus:	285.367	Durbin-Watson:	2.055
Prob (Omnibus) :	0.000	Jarque-Bera (JB) :	540.311
Skew:	0.716	Prob (JB) :	4.71e-118
Kurtosis:	4.718	Cond. No.	124.

(a)

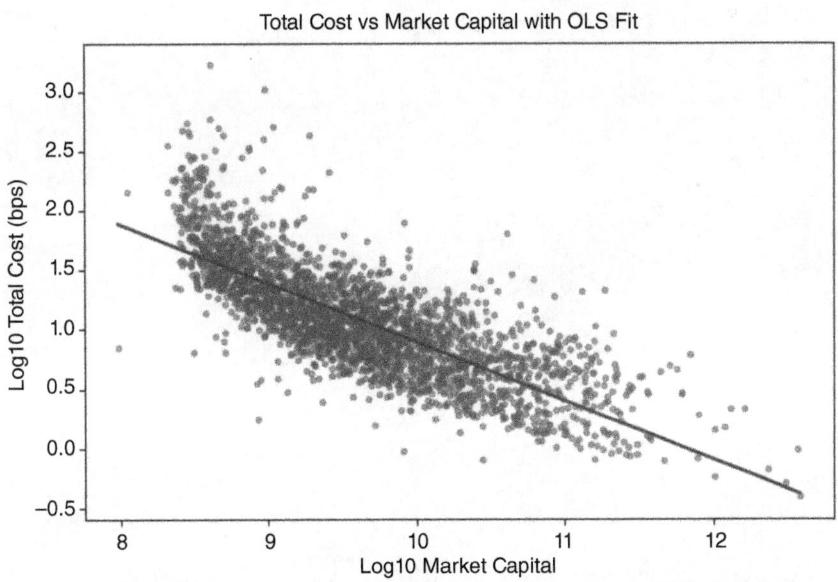

(b)

Figure 9.9 Scatterplot and OLS Fit (Log10 Cost Versus Log10 Market Cap).

OLS Regression Results

Dep. Variable:	log10costPerShareBps	R-squared:	0.633
Model:	OLS	Adj. R-squared:	0.633
Method:	Least Squares	F-statistic:	4474.
Date:	Thu, 24 Jul 2025	Prob (F-statistic) :	0.00
Time:	00: 37:08	Log-Likelihood:	−464.03
No. observations:	2593	AIC:	932.1
Df Residuals:	2591	BIC:	943.8
Df Model:	1		
Covariance Type:	nonrobust		

	coef	std err	t	P> ltl	[0.025	0.975]
const	4.8413	0.057	85.682	0.000	4.731	4.952
log_ADTV	−0.4947	0.007	−66.886	0.000	−0.509	−0.480

Omnibus:	58.669	Durbin-Watson:	2.056
Prob (Omnibus) :	0.000	Jarque-Bera (JB) :	83.634
Skew:	0.248	Prob (JB) :	6.90e-19
Kurtosis:	3.727	Cond. No.	77.2

(a)

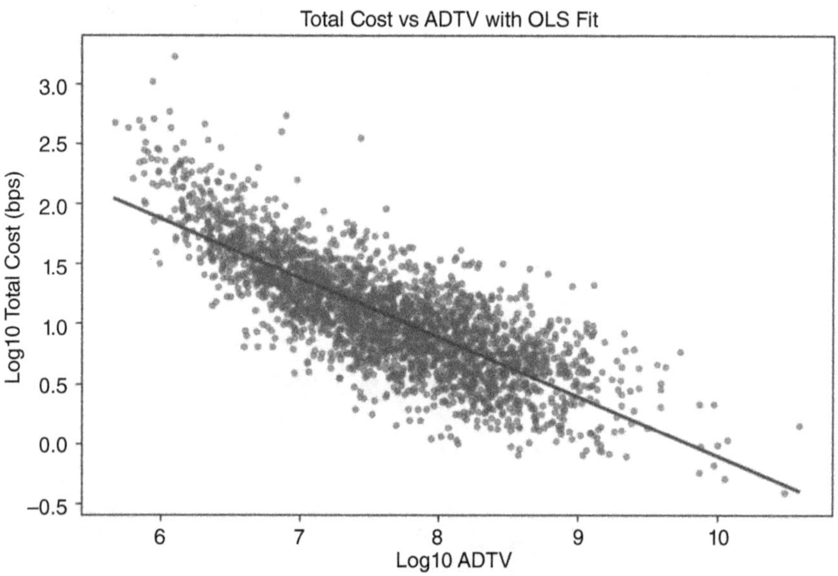

(b)

Figure 9.10 Scatterplot and OLS-Fitted Line (Log10 Cost Versus Log10 ADTV).

zero and high-cost outliers were rare. A similar pattern (as per Figure 9.11) holds when grouping by market cap: trades in small-cap stocks are not only more expensive on average but also far less predictable, showing high variance and occasional spikes to punitive cost levels.

These findings highlight that liquidity is the dominant force in determining trading costs.

From a practical standpoint, average daily volume is a direct proxy for how easily a stock can be traded. High-ADTV stocks provide consistent, low-cost execution strategies – a significant advantage for strategies that trade frequently or in size. Conversely, strategies that venture into low-volume stocks in search of higher alpha must be prepared for sporadic, but at times substantial trading costs.

The practical implication is clear: maintaining sufficient liquidity in portfolio holdings is essential for keeping transaction costs low and predictable. In practice, many institutional investors manage this risk by filtering or weighting investments based on ADTV, often applying minimum

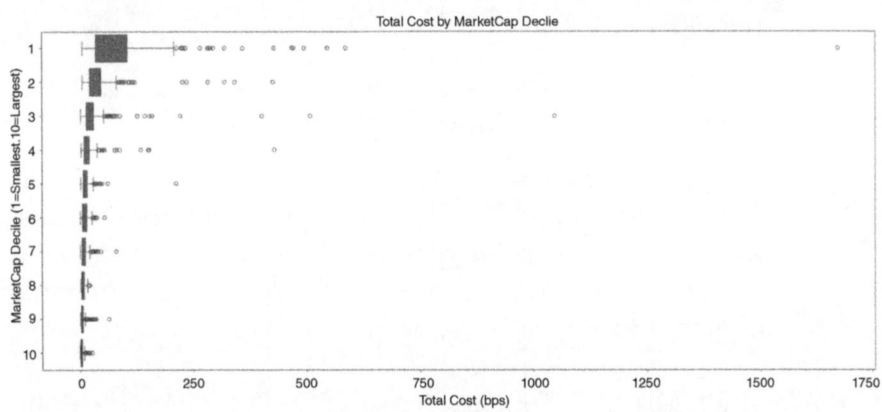

Figure 9.11 Boxplot of Transaction Costs (Bps) by Liquidity Group (Deciles of ADTV).

liquidity thresholds – such as excluding stocks that trade below a certain dollar volume per day.

Our data supports this approach. Simply avoiding the least liquid names eliminates the most extreme cost outliers and leads to a meaningful reduction in overall execution costs. ADTV-based filtering serves as an effective and scalable tool for managing transaction cost risk.

Market capitalization, which often correlates with volume, can also serve as a useful guide – large-cap stocks generally cost less to trade. However, size alone isn't a perfect proxy for liquidity. Many mid-cap stocks trade heavily and are inexpensive to execute, while some large-cap stocks may trade less frequently and incur meaningful costs.

The analysis showed market cap and ADTV are strongly correlated (Pearson $\rho \approx 0.72$ in our sample). Size alone is not a reliable predictor of trading costs. Direct liquidity measures such as bid-ask spread or ADTV are more actionable. For example, there were cases of mid-sized companies with high turnover that were cheap to trade, alongside some large but thinly traded stocks that carried nontrivial costs (as per Figure 9.12).

9.4.6. Benchmark Index Cost Analysis

We now compare five indices {Dow 30, S&P 500, LBO 100, QUMN} and the full universe of securities (both equal weighted and cap weighted) to contrast the total cost decomposition into spread and liquidity components (Figure 9.13).

The QMIT LBO Top 100 Index (LBO 100) tracks the alpha of an equally weighted market-neutral portfolio whose

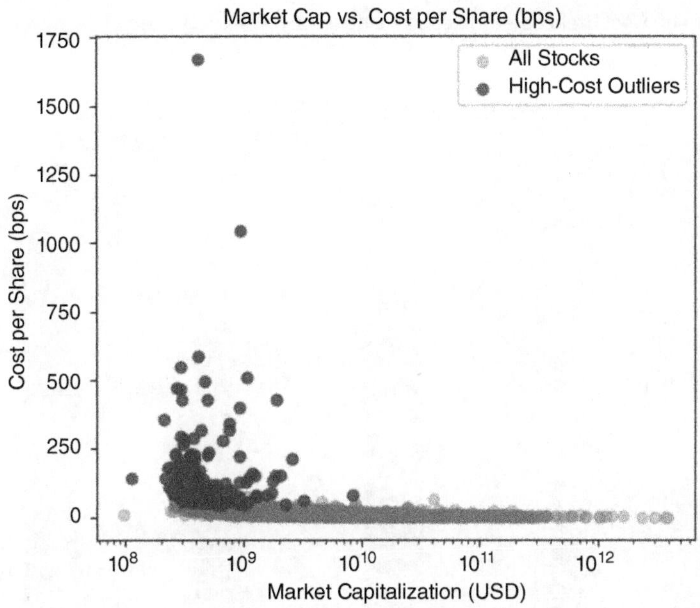

Figure 9.12 Scatterplot of Cost per Share (Bps) Versus Market Capitalization.

holdings are approximately the Top 100 ML-based LBO candidates hedged by a dollar-neutral short position in the IWN ETF (Russell 2000 Value). The index is rebalanced and reconstituted weekly.

The QMIT Equity Market Neutral Index (QUMN) seeks to track the performance of QMIT's EMN (Equity Market Neutral) hedge fund model. The model creates market neutral long/short portfolios based on a universe of the largest approximately 2,500 US + dually listed Canadian stocks + ADRs. The underlying long and short portfolios leverage multifactor alpha signals employing 18 ESBs, which are distilled from hundreds of factors via ML ensemble methods. The index is rebalanced and reconstituted weekly.

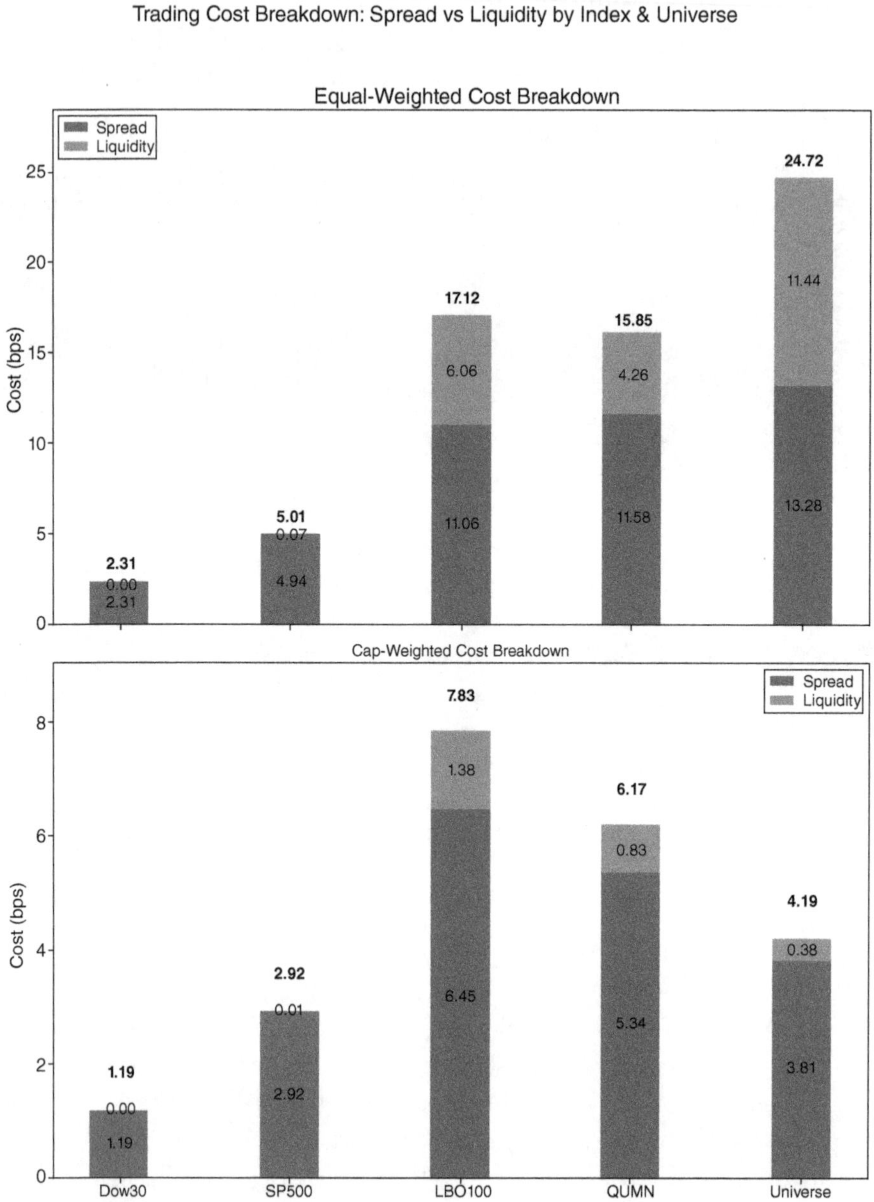

Figure 9.13 Weighted Average Cost of Indices.

Under equal weighting, the Dow 30 remains the cheapest at 2.31 bps of total cost (2.31 bps spread, 0 bps liquidity), reflecting its deep, liquid constituents. The S&P 500 jumps to 5.01 bps total cost (4.94 bps spread, 0.07 bps liquidity), given the inclusion of less liquid names as we go further down the cap spectrum. The LBO 100 – composed of the top 100 deep value small-cap leverage buyout targets – registers 17.12 bps (11.06 bps spread, 6.06 bps liquidity), underscoring the outsized drag from liquidity demand. The QUMN index, however, registers 15.85 bps (11.58 bps spread, 4.26 bps liquidity). This dollar- and beta-neutral index monetizes our flagship composite alphas across the full universe, which is why it's quite as high. The full universe is much higher cost averaging 24.72 bps (13.28 bps spread, 11.44 bps liquidity), driven by the long tail of illiquid, small-cap names outside of the S&P 500.

With cap weighting, costs compress significantly. The Dow 30 falls to 1.19 bps (1.19 bps spread, 0 bps liquidity) by emphasizing its most liquid mega caps. The S&P 500's total halves to 2.92 bps (2.92 bps spread, 0 bps liquidity), while the LBO 100 drops to 7.83 bps (6.45 bps spread, 1.38 bps liquidity) and QUMN drops to 6.17 bps (5.34 bps spread, 0.83 bps liquidity) – illustrating how a few larger cap LBO names can materially reduce average cost. Even the full universe cost shrinks to 4.19 bps (3.81 bps spread, 0.38 bps liquidity), as the largest, most liquid stocks dominate the index weighting.

This plot highlights two key insights: Market-capitalization is extremely lopsided, hence weighting by capitalization at the universe level is going to dramatically lower the liquidity cost. Second, decomposition-wise, liquidity (not spread) impact overwhelmingly drives cost in broad or small-cap heavy universes. Cap-weighted exposures recapture most of the liquidity premium by tilting toward the largest, most tradable names.

9.4.7. Analysis via BEAST GUI

To complement our cross-sectional index comparisons, we also pulled single-stock analytics directly from the BEAST GUI (Date: 2025-06-30, Time: 9:30–16:00, Amount: $1 million), disabling momentum to isolate the core cost drivers and then comparing a high-liquidity large-cap name (Apple) versus a small-cap (AMWD, one of our LBO 100 constituents).

For Apple (AAPL-US), the GUI reports a total IS of 0.49 bps (as per Figures 9.14 and 9.15), with the total-cost line perfectly overlaid by the spread-cost line, indicating that spread alone accounts for the entirety of expected slippage and that liquidity impact, signaling, and momentum costs are all effectively zero. In other words, trading $1 million dollars of Apple under this scenario incurs only the cost of crossing the tight bid-ask spread.

By contrast, for AMWD-US the GUI estimates a 45.87 bps total cost (≈$0.2378 per share). Here the breakdown reveals a dominant spread component (≈41 bps) and a smaller but meaningful liquidity component (≈4 bps), with signaling and momentum costs still negligible when momentum is turned off. This stark divergence between the tiny, spread-only cost for a mega cap versus the large, mixed spread + liquidity cost for a small cap, visually underscores how liquidity profiles drive IS. Including these selected GUI screenshots in our write-up vividly illustrates the contrasting cost decomposition across capital-size regimes.

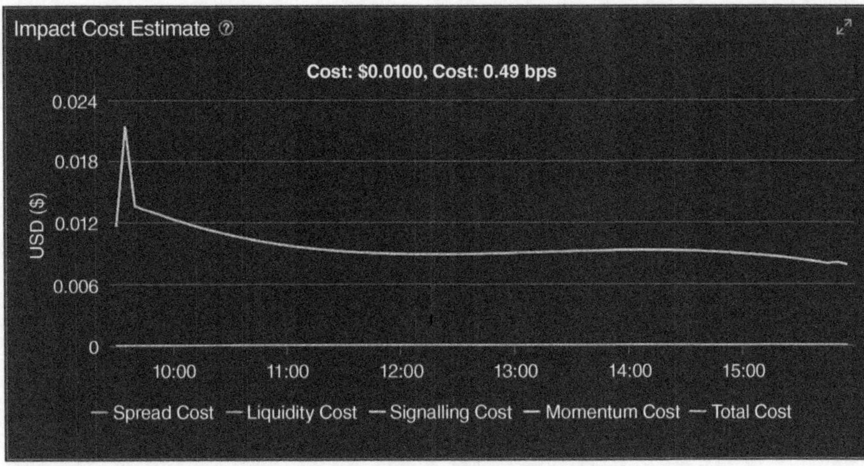

Figure 9.14 Cost Estimate of APPLE in the BEAST GUI.

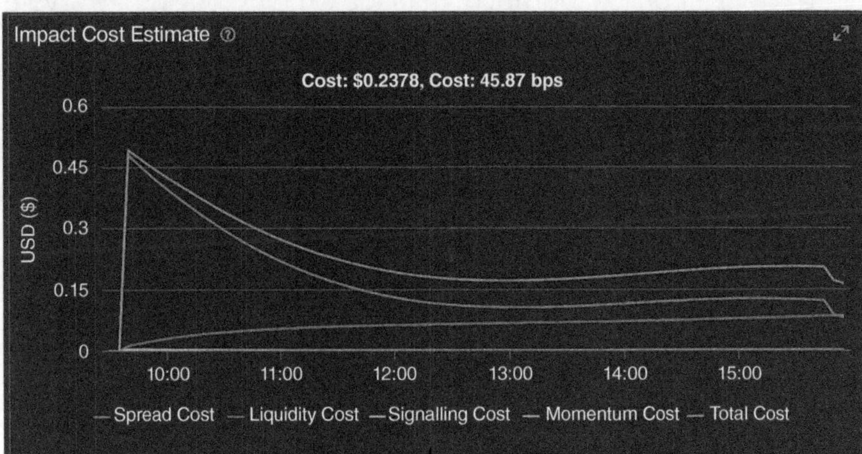

Figure 9.15 Cost Estimate of AMWD in the BEAST GUI.

9.4.8. Managing the High-Cost Outliers

Identifying the handful of high-cost outliers is only half the battle – the next step is managing them. For a quant portfolio, trading cost outliers pose a risk to performance and need special attention. Our analysis suggests a couple of practical approaches to tame these cost drivers:

- **Flag and potentially exclude extremely costly names.** We set a threshold at the 90th percentile of cost (and impact) and defined any stock above that as a high-cost outlier. This cutoff effectively isolated the bottom approximately 10% of names that contributed a disproportionate share of aggregate trading cost. The implication is that by excluding the top decile of costliest stocks, one could eliminate the bulk of extreme transaction cost events, leading to a far more predictable cost profile. In fact, our study found that *removing those outliers would significantly reduce the overall transaction costs and yield a more controlled execution cost distribution.* A portfolio manager might decide to avoid these tickers entirely, or replace them with more liquid substitutes, unless their return contribution is so high that it justifies the cost.
- **Prefer large-cap, high-liquidity names.** This sounds obvious, but it's worth reiterating. Since the outliers were predominantly low-ADTV, small-cap stocks, a portfolio skewed toward larger, more liquid equities will naturally have much lower transaction costs. For example, an equity long-short strategy might choose to confine its universe to the Russell 1000 (large/mid-cap) rather than the entire Russell 3000, as a way to control trading frictions. The trade-off is potentially fewer alpha opportunities outside the most liquid names. But our data clearly shows the execution cost benefits of focusing on liquid names – portfolios of liquid stocks exhibit tight spreads and minimal impact, lowering overall cost.
- **Mitigate costs for necessary illiquid positions.** There may be cases where high-cost names *do* appear in the portfolio – perhaps a niche small-cap stock with

exceptional alpha potential that passes your filters. In those instances, trading should be handled with extra care. One might use smaller position sizes or trade in smaller batches over a longer time to reduce impact. Another tactic is to rebalance less frequently on those names (since each trade is expensive) – effectively accepting a bit more tracking error to avoid the repeated cost of execution. The key is to not treat a low-liquidity stock the same way as a blue chip in trading plans. If you *must* engage with some higher-cost stocks, plan for it: employ liquidity-seeking algorithms, work the order passively if possible, and anticipate materially higher costs (and uncertainty) in your trading schedule. In short, adjust your execution strategy for the assets' liquidity.

- **Review and adjust the universe periodically.** If you do exclude the worst offenders, it's prudent to recompute your cost metrics after those exclusions to quantify the improvement. We found that dropping the top decile outliers dramatically improved portfolio average cost statistics (e.g., the new 90th percentile cost might drop to what was previously the 70th percentile). Regularly monitoring which names fall into the high-cost bracket (since liquidity can change over time) and updating the exclusion list or trading protocol is a good practice. This before-and-after analysis provides tangible evidence of cost efficiency gains, which is valuable for strategy evaluations and for communicating to stakeholders that trading costs are under control.

It's also insightful to examine the characteristics of the high-cost group as a whole. In addition to low liquidity, some common themes emerged. Many of these names were small-cap stocks, often with high volatility and wide spreads, as expected. Some were companies going through distress or special situations (which typically reduces liquidity). We also observed the dispersion *within* the outlier group itself: many had cost estimates on the order of 50–150 bps (high, but perhaps manageable relative to sufficiently compelling alpha); a subset was far worse, in the several-hundred bps range. This suggests that one could implement an additional tier of risk control – for example, setting an even higher cost cutoff (e.g., the 99th percentile) to identify the few worst offenders among outliers and eliminate those as well. The overarching point is that a small number of stocks can dominate your execution cost risk, so you should *know who they are* and have a plan for them.

In conclusion, TCA of our simulated trades highlights that "liquidity, liquidity, liquidity" is the mantra for cost-efficient trading. Volume and trading activity are the lifeblood that keeps execution costs low and predictable. While factors like volatility and spreads matter, they often go hand-in-hand with liquidity. For quant professionals, the practical message is clear: *incorporate liquidity considerations at every step – from universe selection and alpha modeling to trade execution.* By doing so, you'll navigate the trade cost landscape with much more confidence, ensuring that hard-earned alpha isn't eaten away on the execution table. As our analysis showed, a thoughtful approach to liquidity can mean the difference between a strategy that navigates smoothly and one that gets bogged down by hidden costs.

Chapter 10

QMIT's Leveraged Buyout (LBO) Model

10.1. MERGERS AND ACQUISITIONS (M&A), LEVERAGED BUYOUTS (LBOS), AND RISK ARBITRAGE

The traditional risk arbitrage strategies examined by Mark Mitchell and Todd Pulvino[1] have had their challenges of late, but perhaps there is another way to profit from

[1] Mitchell and Pulvino (2001) examined a sample of 4,750 stock swap mergers, cash mergers, and cash tender offers from 1963 to 1998 to suggest that the return profile of the risk arbitrage hedge fund category is typified by that from selling uncovered index put options.

leverage buyout (LBO) events without resorting to a short volatility posture? Interestingly, a trading strategy based on anticipating buyout deals as evidenced by the QMIT LBO Top 100 model (introduced in Section 10.2) turns out to be almost completely uncorrelated with risk arbitrage as a hedge-fund style. This is because the QMIT LBO trading signal is based entirely on speculation prior to deal announcement, whereas risk arbitrage typically bets on deal convergence via its short volatility posture post-announcement.

The rest of this chapter is structured as follows. Section 10.2 introduces the QMIT LBO Top 100 with an exposition of its risk and return profile when formulated as trading signal. Salient features of the LBO prediction and the merits of a trading signal based on it are explored therein. Section 10.3 considers optimal hedge ratios for this model over 6Y live while Section 10.4 extends the same analysis to 24Y. The LBO discussion is continued in Chapter 11 with Section 11.1 providing historical perspective on NLP based Sentiment while Chapter 11, Section 11.2, describes RavenPack's Sum Excess Sentiment Indicator (SESI) signal. Section 11.3 investigates the central thesis of combining alternative data signals (SESI) with traditional factor-based trading signals such as the QMIT LBO Top 100 by overlaying the SESI sentiment on an equal-weighted composite of the LBO Top 100 predictions. Finally, we draw our conclusions based on a series of thought experiments designed to back-test enhancements resulting from such a combination of signals.

An LBO involves acquiring a company but with a significant amount of borrowed money (leverage) to meet the cost of acquisition. The expectation is that the subsequent improvements in performance and strategic restructuring will yield returns that outweigh the interest expense and provide substantial profits on exit, typically through a sale or initial public offering. Leverage can either magnify returns or, once the cycle turns, the debt burden can often bankrupt the underlying businesses while the PE partners extract rich dividends for themselves while rank-and-file employees get laid off. While the private equity (PE) industry and the corporate raiders (as epitomized by Michael Douglas in the iconic movie *Wall Street*) have done rather well for themselves with carried interest, one must ask, where are the customers' yachts? That remains unclear, after one is done with the long lock ups, lack of MTM transparency, layers of fees, "volatility laundering" and other accounting shenanigans such as the mirage of internal rate of returns masquerading as actual realized returns. QMIT's LBO strategy is a liquid proxy for PE style returns without the PE shenanigans. A public market proxy means one has the benefit of daily mark to market (MTM) and liquidity without the lockups or accounting shenanigans. In fact, decades after we started trading this strategy, some academics have suggested that PE style exposure is tantamount to levered exposure to small-cap value.

M&A as a corporate strategy in the United States has been prevalent since the late 1800s. While the purpose early on was to build monopolies in their respective industries (as per Gaughan, 2015, subsequent to the introduction of the Sherman Antitrust Act of 1890, which prohibited anticompetitive agreements), companies started using M&A for customer acquisition, geographical/product expansion, supply chain efficiencies, cost synergies, among other reasons.

Successful M&A led to the emergence of a new breed of companies during the 1950–1970 era, such as Buffet's Berkshire Hathaway and T. Boone Pickens's Mesa Petroleum (Gaughan, 2015), wherein these publicly traded companies were used as holding companies to invest in/acquire corporate assets. Not to be left behind, investment bankers at bulge brackets like Bear Stearns started acquiring companies during the 1960s. They pioneered what was then known as *bootstrapped acquisitions*, since they were highly levered (Gara et al., 2019). They targeted family-owned businesses that were facing succession issues (Cassel et al., 2018). Many of these businesses lacked a viable or attractive exit for their founders as they were too small to be taken public and the founders were reluctant to sell out to competitors. Therefore, selling to a financial buyer proved attractive (Cassel et al., 2018).

Henry Kravis and George Roberts left Bear Stearns to start KKR & Co. Inc. along with Jerome Kohlberg. KKR marked the beginnings of the PE revolution and pioneered the earliest LBOs with deals such as RJR Nabisco (1988), leading to mainstream infamy as memorialized in the book and subsequent HBO movie entitled, *The Barbarians at the Gate*.

Carl Icahn made his mark on the landscape with high-profile deals like the "asset stripping" of TWA Airlines, thereby cementing his reputation as a "corporate raider." The 1970s and 1980s also saw the rise of management buyouts, wherein the acquirers were the managers of the entity themselves (Gaughan, 2015). None of this would have been possible without the concurrent growth of the high-yield market spurred by Michael Milken at Drexel Burnham Lambert. The rather incestuous relationship between the LBO firms like KKR, the so-called greenmailers and a highly confident letter from Drexel allowed them to secure the necessary junk financing through the burgeoning high-yield market for such LBOs. All of this culminated in the "greed is good" mantra, a zeitgeist well encapsulated by Michael Douglas as Gordon Gekko in the epochal 1987 *Wall Street* movie.

As per Renneboog and Vansteenkiste (2017), the sources of value creation in LBOs may include reduction in agency costs, stakeholder wealth transfers, tax benefits, transaction costs savings, and takeover defense strategies, not to mention corporate undervaluation. LBOs required highly levered financing structures that enabled investors to fund the M&A with limited equity, thereby enhancing return on equity while the usual M&A financing options were cash offers or stock swaps.

Hedge funds and investment banks since the mid-1940s (Stefanini, 2006) have taken directional positions in M&A situations by trading the stocks of the companies involved in the deal. Popularly known as risk arbitrage, the strategy involves taking a market-neutral position on the spread: (1) in the case of an acquisition, between the value offered for the acquisition and the current market value of the company to be acquired and (2) in the case of a merger, between the theoretical exchange ratio of the stock of the two merging entities and the exchange ratio currently expressed by the market. In its purest manifestation, hedge funds put on the position post-announcement then wait for spread convergence. The seminal Mitchell and Pulvino (2001) paper deployed a sample of 4,750 stock swap mergers, cash mergers, and cash tender offers during the 1963–1998 period, as well as active hedge funds during the 1990–1998 period to characterize the profile of risk arbitrage. The key finding was that the strategy returns are akin to those obtained from selling uncovered index put options, that is, they fall into the class of other short volatility strategies such as writing insurance that is susceptible to the peso problem[2] of periodic catastrophic losses due to the hidden higher moment risks.

[2]The peso problem in short volatility strategies refers to the tendency for these strategies to show consistently high returns because they do not encounter rare, severe loss events in-sample. This means historical performance looks artificially strong (even when risk adjusted) based on the first two moments, thereby understating hidden risks of an infrequent but extreme loss. The high kurtosis is only visible after the catastrophic losses have been materialized ex post.

10.2. QMIT's LBO TOP 100 MODEL

QMIT's LBO Top 100 model is composed of daily predictions of the 100 most viable LBO candidates among liquid US equities based on the following constraints that ensure that they are institutionally investable:

- Country of domicile must be the United States or Canada.
- They must be listed on a major US exchange like NYSE, NASDAQ, PHLX (hence only dually listed Canadian stocks qualify).
- Price > $3 (minimal liquidity and price eliminates penny stocks and pink sheets).
- Market cap > $250 million (eliminates micro-caps).
- No banks since many key financial ratios are ill-defined for certain sub-industries other than non-bank financials, which are allowed.
- Few utilities; the anomalous TXU deal (largest LBO till 2025) aside, LBOs are uncommon in this sector, and we do not expect them to be significant contributors to the strategy returns.
- No real estate investment trusts (REITs) (we do not have an industry-specific model, and LBOs are infrequent in this industry), but we do have some real estate entities that may qualify.
- No biotechs; this industry is not amenable to modeling in the usual quantamental framework given the preponderance of event risk.
- OTC (over-the-counter)/pink sheets are effectively ruled out by the previous logic.
- While the model does not explicitly remove buyout names with an offer (until the deal is consummated and the identifier is phased out), in the vast majority of

instances the price appreciation post-announcement suffices toward model expulsion. If not, then the prospective target may continue to show up on the Top 100 as still being sufficiently undervalued to be worthy of further speculation – particularly if the deal subsequently falls through.

While daily returns data is available since January 2000[3] this model is a long-only weekly rebalanced portfolio of the Top 100 equally weighted LBO predictions. The model presents the most viable LBO candidates in descending order based on a multifactor model (MFM) construct, but it does not provide a timeline for their acquisition. In other words, the model makes a relative prediction cross-sectionally at a given point of time without prior memory each day. Any forecast of the take-out timeline or post-announcement spread evolution involves game theoretic considerations beyond the scope of this discussion. The model is also agnostic as to whether the exit is due to a strategic buyer or an LBO per se, as the signal benefits from the buyout premium in either scenario as does its hit rate of successful predictions. The model's out-of-sample trading success is not exclusively contingent on an LBO materializing. In fact, only about one-third of the total gains are attributable to buyouts with the rest deriving from related catalysts.

Turnover of the Top 100 portfolio determines the degree to which the top candidates persist in their attractiveness as feasible LBO candidates until changes in the key MFM factors are pushed beyond certain thresholds.

For the purposes of this study, we used the 19-year LBO Top 100 model history from 2000 to 2018, which has a

[3] It's 26 years of history now but was 19.5 at the time of writing.

long-term buyout hit rate of 41% (based on the set of all prior predictions). The number of buyout predictions that came to fruition each year since inception is shown in Figure 10.1 (based on cumulative outstanding predictions).

In particular, the 41 names bought out in 2017 are shown in Table 10.1.

This hit rate does not include other scenarios such as an attractive LBO candidate using a spinoff to monetize its undervaluation or possibly buying out another firm to make use of its excess cash being generated. Indeed, there have been cases where one attractive LBO name ends up buying another one in the same industry.

While the cumulative hit rate based on a subsection of the universe can be benchmarked to a broad universe (like Russell 3000), studies show our hit rate to be 5× higher than if a random stock was selected from the universe. This makes sense (assuming any predictive power), given that we start

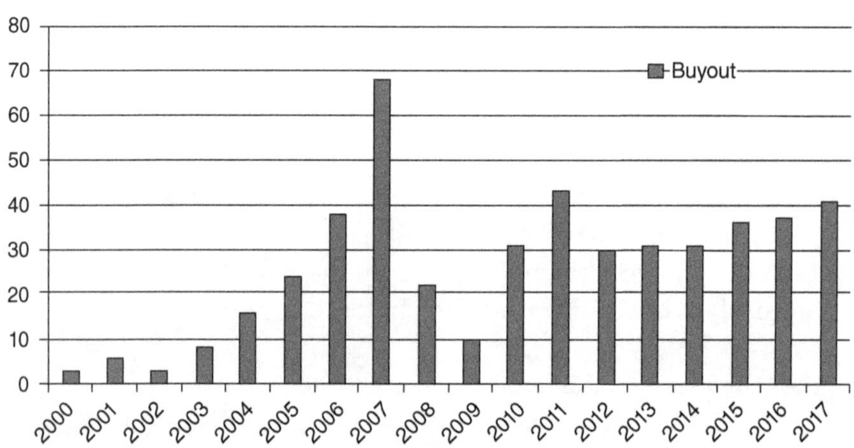

Figure 10.1 Annual Number of Realized Buyout Predictions from the QMIT LBO Top 100.

Table 10.1 List of 41 Companies from the QMIT LBO Top 100 Model Acquired in 2017.

KATE	STJ
PRXL	BEAV
AEPI	SWFT
NSR	BRCD
SWC	MED
ELNK	PMC
WOOF	CDI
VAL	HAR
OME	ISIL
RT	WNR
CYNO	HSNI
MENT	FTI
CAB	SPLS
CLC	LIOX
APOL	HW
CWEI	TESO
GK	ALI
XXIA	EXAR
ENOC	JOY
HNR	WMAR
TRR	

from a comparable universe and filter it down to only the Top 100 buyout candidates.

Figure 10.2 and Table 10.2 demonstrate the remarkable long-term, key performance metrics of the LBO Top 100 model. While the 20.87% return per annum (p.a.) is staggeringly high, so is the long-only volatility of 25.42% p.a. (albeit quite consistent with the 24% p.a. volatility of the Russell Small Cap Value index [R2000V]). Since the LBO

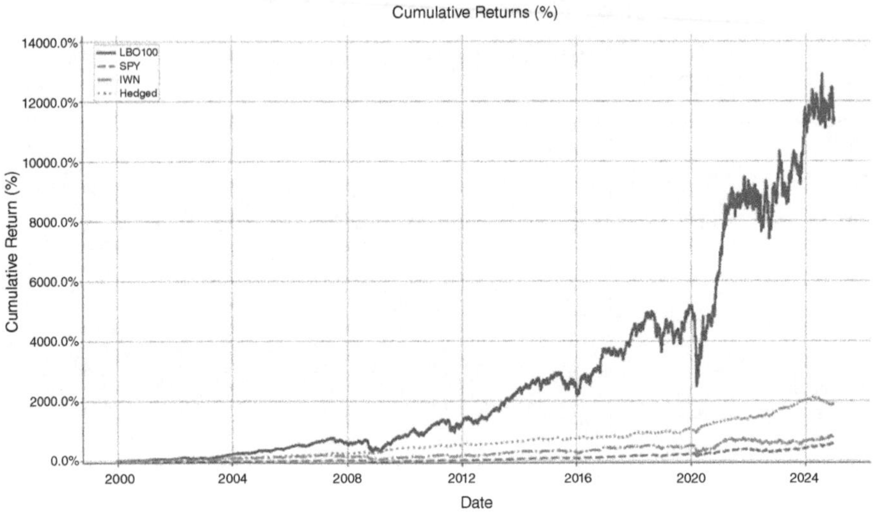

Figure 10.2 Cumulative Returns of the QMIT LBO 100 Versus Benchmarks.

Table 10.2 Key Performance Statistics for LBO 100, Benchmark, and Hedged Strategy.

	LBO100	R2000 Val	LBO–R2000 Val
Annualized Ret	20.87%	8.9%	12.69%
Annualized Vol	25.42%	24.0%	8.21%
Sharpe Ratio	0.82	0.37	1.55
Annualized Sortino Ratio	1.2	0.53	2.4
Max DD	57.48	61.75	16.05

Top 100 constituents are by design small-cap value names it stands to reason that the appropriate factor hedge would be the R2000V index as proxied by the live IWN (ETF) on that index. Indeed, the R2000V hedge results in volatility collapsing all the way from 25.42% down to 8.21% even before any risk optimization or portfolio construction. While the volatility collapses by two-thirds, the hedged returns only decline by 39% to 12.69%, thereby resulting in the hedged Sharpe ratio of {LBO Top 100 – IWN} spiking to 1.55 and the Sortino to 2.4 from 1.2. Most notably, the maximum drawdown declines from a brutal approximately 57.5% for the long-only LBO Top 100 down to only roughly 16% versus R2000V, thereby making the signal investable out of the box!

Calendar performance, as detailed in Table 10.3, indicates no down years on hedging with the R2000V index till 2024.

Table 10.3 Annual Calendar Year Returns for LBO 100, SPY, IWN, and Hedged Strategy.

LBO Performance	LBO100	R2000 Val	LBO–R2000 Val
2000	29.01%	22.68%	10.82%
2001	39.37%	14.0%	26.77%
2002	12.4%	−11.42%	29.26%
2003	60.2%	46.0%	10.7%
2004	39.71%	22.14%	15.33%
2005	19.3%	4.64%	17.24%
2006	35.82%	23.45%	14.81%
2007	−2.33%	−9.8%	12.2%
2008	−27.63%	−28.96%	1.53%
2009	84.1%	20.5%	50.3%
2010	34.98%	24.49%	8.15%
2011	0.11%	−5.5%	6.3%
2012	27.59%	18.05%	8.35%
2013	51.58%	34.52%	12.75%
2014	12.71%	4.21%	8.46%
2015	−6.74%	−7.47%	1.11%

(Continued)

Table 10.3 *(Continued)*

LBO Performance	LBO100	R2000 Val	LBO–R2000 Val
2016	41.59%	31.72%	8.15%
2017	19.35%	7.82%	11.53%
2018	–11.27%	–12.84%	3.87%
2019	33.97%	22.01%	12.03%
2020	21.38%	4.66%	17.12%
2021	42.65%	27.96%	10.81%
2022	–2.93%	–14.75%	15.93%
2023	32.33%	14.57%	20.31%
2024 YTD	–1.94%	7.64%	–4.99%

Unlike many quant MFM models, we do not see marked alpha degradation post–global financial crisis as per Table 10.3. If anything, we see substantially higher long-only returns aided by the Fed's largesse and the globally coordinated central bank easing cycle post-crisis. But the index returns are understandably higher post-crisis as well, resulting in the hedged returns being lower.

The LBO Top 100 model predictions are fairly lopsided across sectors (Figure 10.3) with about 75% of the Top 100 predictions being clustered in consumer discretionary, industrials and information technology sectors while the remainder are spread out across consumer staples, health care and energy. Banks are excluded as are REITS, biotechs and utilities as per the aforementioned constraints. Telecommunications is too small a sector with too few predictions to register in this analysis.

Low turnover means that the explicit transaction cost (TCost) for most institutions would be effectively negligible at

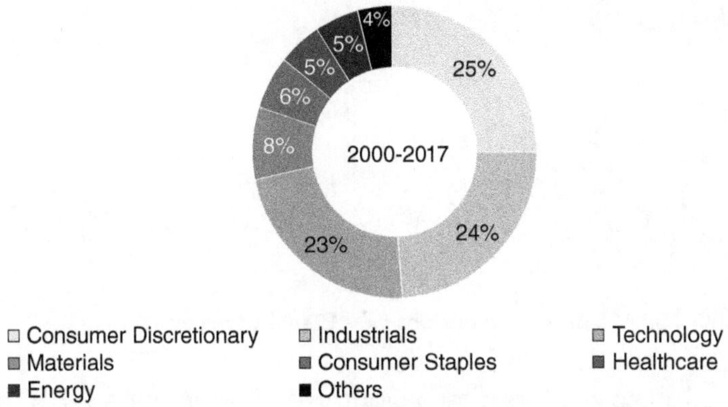

Figure 10.3 LBO TOP 100 Sector Wise Attribution (% of Buyouts).

today's rates putting aside market impact. The portfolio exhibits low turnover of about 15% (monthly). We witness only 6% of the maximum possible turnover based on all predictions made – life to date (LTD) versus the total number of distinct tickers observed (since the remainder of those tickers repeat). *T*-cost assumptions are already embedded in these results. We assume 0.05% annualized for this level of turnover based on institutional execution rates (at 0.05 cents per share) and an average share price of $30/share.

It's worth noting that takeouts (LBO or strategic) only contribute to about one-third of the total strategy gains over the 19 years while the remainder of the returns are propelled by various catalysts such as activists agitating in the name or buybacks or dividend hikes, and so on.

As previously mentioned, there is no specific timeline to the model predictions. Indeed, we show the example in Figure 10.4 of RCII (Rent a Center), which was in the model for 47% of the 18 years until it finally got bought out in June 2018. However, even if one was hypothetically not fortunate

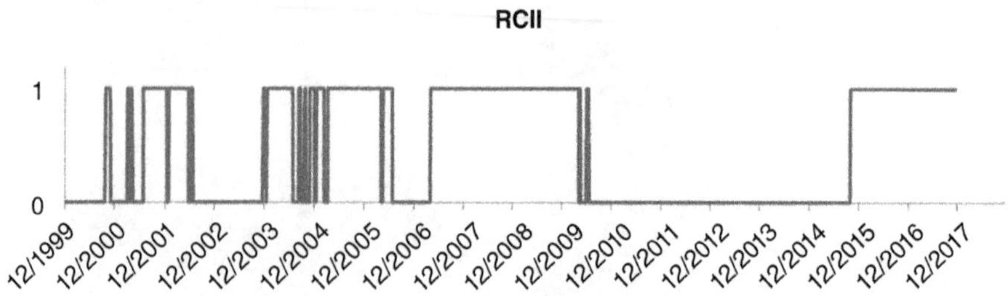

Figure 10.4 LBO TOP 100 Buyout Predictions over 19Y (% of Buyouts).

enough to capture the buyout premium in June 2018, the model would have still monetized about 178% arithmetic (as the dot product of the binary in/out of the model × weekly RCII return). This particular example is even more interesting because the approximately 42% buyout premium (to its 20-day moving average closing price) would usually have expelled the name from the model (provided it was no longer undervalued on relative basis) but on 12/18/18 the deal fell apart (−9.8% that day), which would allow the model to once again speculate on the stock's LBO prospects. Note that RCII more than doubled into early May 2019 from 12/18/18.

Active risk decomposition in Figure 10.5 of a sample (09/06/18) portfolio of the long LBO Top 100 versus R2000V index (courtesy of Bloomberg's Equity Risk model) shows 16.08% total risk but only 6.07% tracking error (TE) to the R2000V index with 5.42% attributable to common factor risks, that is, 79.8% contribution to the TE with the remaining 20.2% contribution due to idiosyncratic risks. For obvious reasons (United States only), there is no country or currency risk, while the TE is dominated chiefly by industry and then style components. The raw SPX Index (S&P 500) beta of 1.24 is understandably higher reflecting the exclusively small-cap value composition of the LBO Top 100. The Bloomberg adjusted beta (based on a two-year weekly

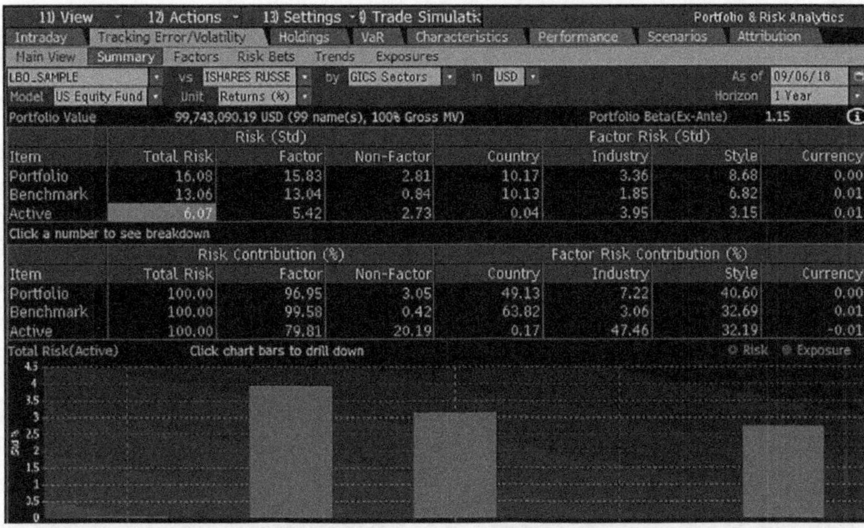

Figure 10.5 LBO 100 Moderate Active Risk Versus R2000 Value.
Source: Bloomberg

estimate) of 1.16 simply reflects the one-third shrinkage toward the SPX beta of 1.

Returns-based style analysis (Figure 10.6) performed via Bloomberg against the Dow Jones market-neutral style factor indices shows the obvious dominance of market beta followed by size. In this case the overwhelming dominance of market beta drowns out the significance of the value tilt which would be more apparent were the style analysis rerun on a hedged market-neutral basis. Regardless, there is ample pure alpha left beyond just that attributable to the Fama-French factors.

The 19-year [2000–2018] R-squared to various hedge fund research (HFR) hedge fund indices (in Figure 10.7) shows only 8.4% to HFRMA, the risk arbitrage index, given that LBO Top 100 only speculates on anticipated buyouts, while the latter strategy largely plays the deal convergence

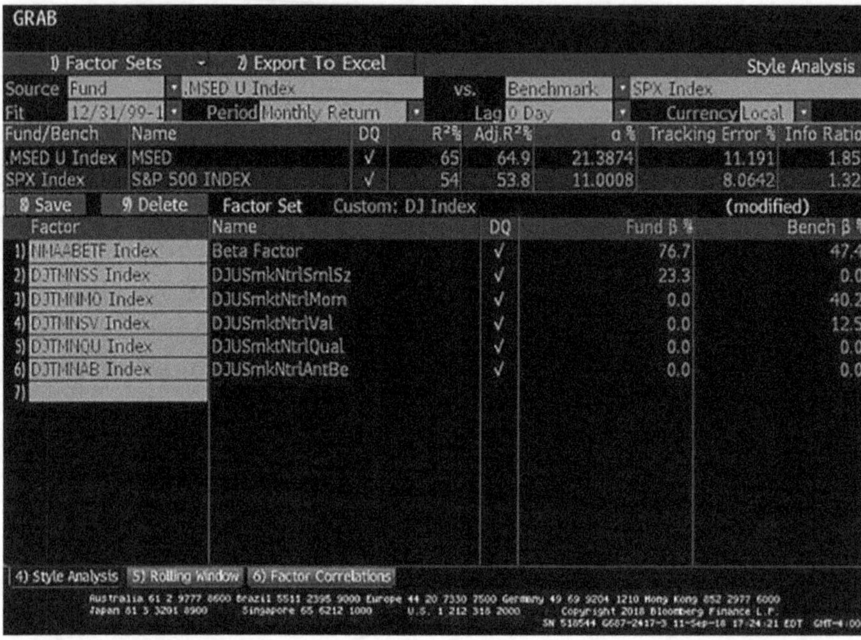

Figure 10.6 LBO TOP 100 Style Analysis.

post-announcement. The 13.2% R-squared to HFRED (event driven) is not surprising although the 24.4% R-squared to HFRFI is and that maybe an artifact of the financing spread. More interestingly though, one should note the *extremely low correlation to HFR indices for equity long-short and market-neutral funds*, thereby hinting at the merits of deploying such a strategy in their mix.

For completeness we present the view in Figure 10.8 showing the LBO Top 100 style analysis relative to Russell 2000 Value index exposures and remind the reader that these (aggregate single-stock-based) factor exposures are rather distinct from the top-down returns-based style analysis shown in Figure 10.6 or our extension of Sharpe (1992) in Chapter 6.

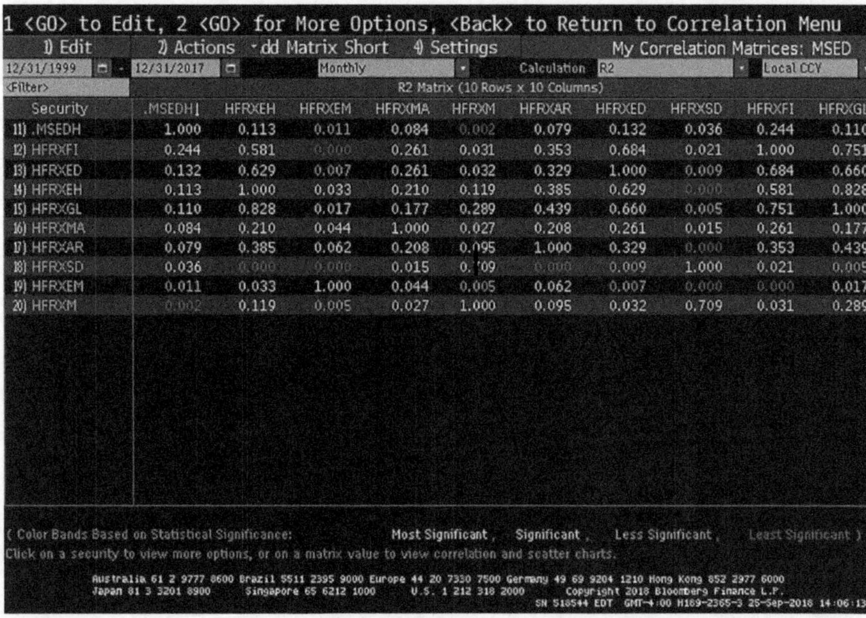

Security	.MSEDH	HFRXEH	HFRXEM	HFRXMA	HFRXM	HFRXAR	HFRXED	HFRXSD	HFRXFI	HFRXGL
11) .MSEDH	1.000	0.113	0.011	0.084	0.002	0.079	0.132	0.036	0.244	0.110
12) HFRXFI	0.244	0.581	0.000	0.261	0.031	0.353	0.684	0.021	1.000	0.751
13) HFRXED	0.132	0.629	0.007	0.261	0.032	0.329	1.000	0.009	0.684	0.660
14) HFRXEH	0.113	1.000	0.033	0.210	0.119	0.385	0.629	0.000	0.581	0.828
15) HFRXGL	0.110	0.828	0.017	0.177	0.289	0.439	0.660	0.005	0.751	1.000
16) HFRXMA	0.084	0.210	0.044	1.000	0.027	0.208	0.261	0.015	0.261	0.177
17) HFRXAR	0.079	0.385	0.062	0.208	0.095	1.000	0.329	0.000	0.353	0.439
18) HFRXSD	0.036	0.000	0.000	0.015	0.[illegible]09	0.000	0.009	1.000	0.021	0.005
19) HFRXEM	0.011	0.033	1.000	0.044	0.005	0.062	0.007	0.000	0.000	0.017
20) HFRXM	0.002	0.119	0.005	0.027	1.000	0.095	0.032	0.709	0.031	0.289

Figure 10.7 **18Y R-Squared to HFR Hedge Fund Indices [2000–2017].**

10.3. OPTIMAL HEDGE RATIOS FOR QMIT's LBO MODELS

Gordon Gekko and Bud Fox sure could have benefited from QMIT's LBO strategies to stay out of jail. Indeed, in the age of AI, Gekko could have profitably deployed our quantamental ML-enhanced trading signals to almost quadruple $ in 6Y LIVE with our Sizzling LBOs model for a gain of about +298.4% (gross). Or Gekko could have obtained equivalent exposure via structured notes/swaps (with bespoke features such as principal protection offered by bank QIS desks in conjunction with QMIT). QMIT's Sizzling LBOs strategy index (Table 10.4) has annualized 25.9% or 18.43% on a hedged basis over 6Y of publication with a 1.5 Sharpe and 2.43 Sortino ratios net of commissions, and short rebates but not including fees or market

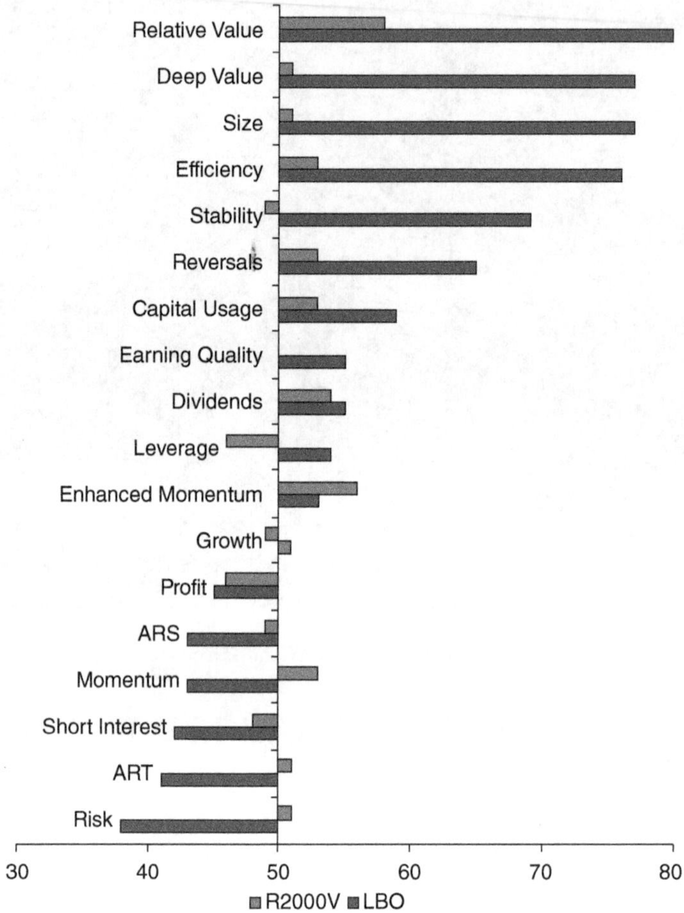

Figure 10.8 LBO TOP 100 Factor Exposures – QMIT ESBs.

impact. The 2023 robust performance of the Top 100 Longs, with a rise of 40.8% and a hedged gain of 28.75% YTD, is noteworthy. The lackluster 2024 aside at 1.47%, the model notched up 14.44% hedged in 2022, marking its 24th year of outshining the index. All performance numbers herein are subject to the disclaimers: https://www.quantzqmit.com/disclaimers.

Table 10.4 Sizzling LBOs Index Over 6 Years.

2019–YTD	**Sizzling LBOs Hedged**	**Benchmark**	**Sizzling LBOs**	**S&P 500**
Annualized Return	18.43	9.44	25.91	17.09
Annualized Volatility	12.38	26.78	31.59	17.39
Sharpe	1.49	0.35	0.82	0.98
Sortino	2.43	0.50	1.22	1.60
Max Drawdown	16.83	44.56	53.05	23.92

**Sizzling LBO Hedged is Sizzling LBO portfolio hedged with the Benchmark (Russell 2000 Value Index)*

Over the past 6+ years of LIVE publication, our QMIT LBO Top 100 model has been harnessing this strategy within the public markets. The model has also significantly outperformed the Russell 2000 Value Index (R2000V) over 25 years since January 2000. But it's in the Sizzling LBOs model where we see even more promising results as per above. As a signal based on liquid US stocks ripe for LBO speculation it can be used both for managing event risk on the short side as well as for speculation on the long side. Interestingly, the returns come from anticipating the activist catalysts that we've data-mined the history for. In other words, the strategy is not solely dependent on the buyout premium and can outperform regardless of the actual number of candidates that get bought out, even though we've seen about 41% of cumulative predictions result in acquisition offers at some future point. In fact, when we last looked at it in 2019, the buyout names (usually about a 20% premium) drive only (1/3) of the total gains LTD with the remaining (2/3) coming from rumors, buybacks, dividend hikes, or other favorable catalysts which propel the stock. This feature, along with the cash flow support, is why the LBO – IWN signal delivers in bear markets like the Nasdaq crash and 2008. Post-crash, it acts like a coiled spring, which is why we saw the extraordinary outperformance in September 2002–2003, 2009, and post-COVID in 2020.

The Sizzling LBOs model is where we turn up the heat by refining the Top 100 to an elite Top 35 to 50 names, with more stringent criteria to filter out only those stocks that not only have LBO potential but also pass our Sizzling Seven checks – averting the so-called falling knives and earnings torpedoes. These stocks are further vetted for their feasibility in LBO financing from a broad universe of about 2,500 major US stocks. The result is a model that's ripe for idea generation, long-side speculation, or event risk hedging, all while maintaining the flexibility to be used in a hedged format against the Russell 2000 Value ETF for sharper risk-adjusted returns.

Interestingly after major financial upheavals, like the global financial crisis in 2008 and the COVID downturn, these models have snapped back dramatically. The Sizzling LBO longs, for instance, more than tripled from the COVID lows. While these deep value small-cap longs get trashed in the initial stages of a market crash, they then find cash flow support and start trading like call options, which benefit substantially coming out of the crisis.

Figure 10.9 shows the value-added monthly index (VAMI), which measures the performance of an investment over six years, starting with a base value (typically 100) at a starting date. The Sizzling LBOs, which represent a more aggressive strategy by selecting the top-performing stocks from the LBO predictions, have shown the highest growth from 2019 onwards. The strategy has seen significant upward

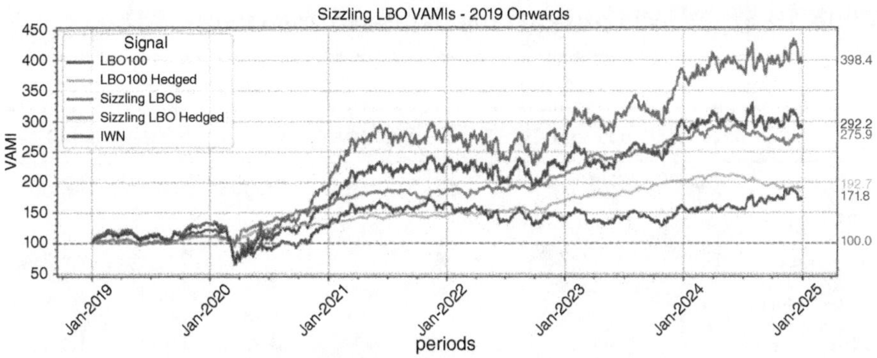

Figure 10.9 LBO Top 100 Versus Sizzling LBOs – 6Y (as of 2025-01-01).

trends and has the highest VAMI, exceeding 400%. Both the LBO 100 and Sizzling LBO strategies have hedged (HR 100) and unhedged (HR 0) versions. The hedged versions underperform compared to their unhedged counterparts, which is expected since hedging typically reduces volatility and potential maximum returns in exchange for lower risk. Both the Sizzling LBO strategy and its hedged version are outperforming the IWN (Russell 2000 Value ETF), which is used as a benchmark. This suggests that the Sizzling LBO strategies provide pure idiosyncratic alpha even after hedging out the Fama-French size and style factors as per the IWN hedge (Table 10.5 offers a performance summary for the related QUMN TMX index), which is based on the same signal that intersects with the LBO Top 100 to narrow it down to the Sizzling LBOs.

In Figure 10.10, we present the cumulative returns of LBO 100 and Sizzling LBO portfolios against the benchmark index IWN (Russell 2000 Value). These are adjusted by hedge ratios of 100%, 85%, and 70%. A hedge ratio of 0% indicates the total return, without any hedging influence, that is, long only, whereas a hedge ratio of 100% means fully dollar neutral.

Table 10.5 QUMN Index (Weekly) Performance on TMX.

					Annualized		
	3 Month	**6 Month**	**YTD**	**1 Year**	**3 Year**	**5 Year**	**ITD**
Total Return	1.6%	8.2%	27.3%	27.3%	28.0%	26.9%	22.4%
Excess Return	0.4%	5.7%	21.3%	21.3%	23.4%	24.2%	19.8%
Volatility					11.8%	14.0%	13.2%
Sharpe Ratio					2.38	1.92	1.69

$$\text{Return Hedged} = (\text{Long} - \text{HR} \times \text{Benchmark})$$

The Sizzling LBO variant, unadjusted for hedging, concluded the period with the highest cumulative return. However, it's also with higher volatility when compared to the hedged variants. As demonstrated in the corresponding statistics table, the annualized returns for both the LBO 100 and Sizzling LBOs significantly outperform their hedged counterparts. However, they do incur greater volatility – 31.32% for LBO 100 and 33.20% for Sizzling LBO compared to the more modest volatility seen in the hedged strategies (9.88% for LBO 100 (HR 100) and 12.82% for Sizzling LBO (HR 100)).

As shown in Table 10.6, the Sharpe ratio favors the hedged returns over the non-hedged LBO 100 or Sizzling LBOs. Within the five-year dataset, a hedge ratio of 100% was optimal in terms of maximizing the Sharpe ratio for both LBO 100 and Sizzling LBOs. This conclusion is similar to the Sortino ratio, which also supports a 100% hedge ratio, with values of 2.63 for LBO 100 and 2.85 for Sizzling LBOs. Max

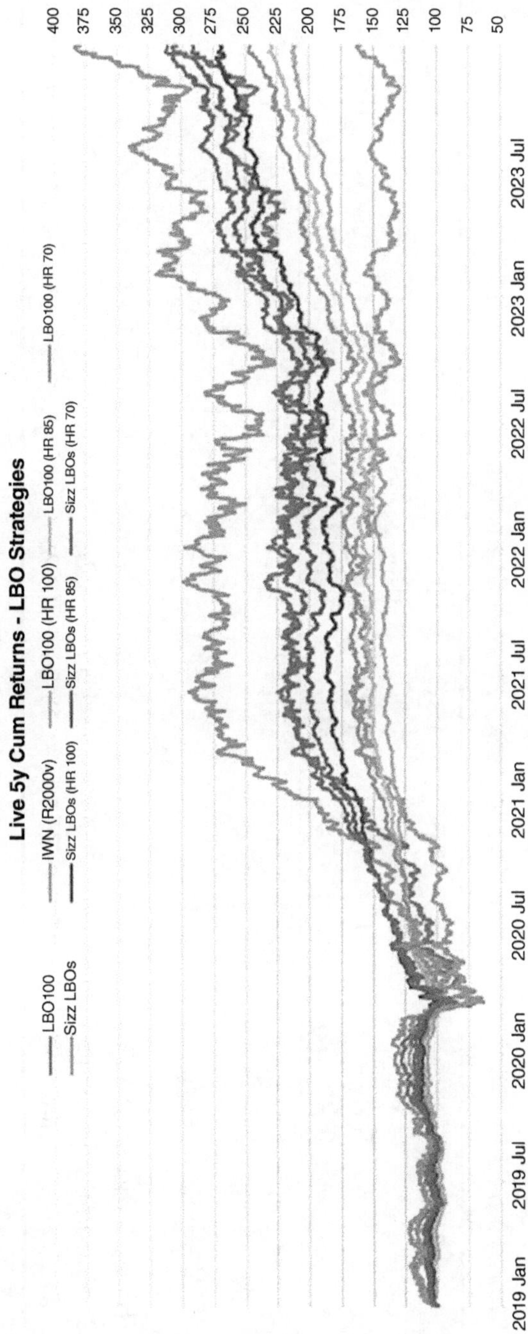

Figure 10.10 Optimal Hedge Ratios for QMIT LBOs: Five-Year Cum Returns.

Table 10.6 LBO Top 100 Versus Sizzling LBO Flavors Statistics.

	IWN (R2000v)	LBO 100 (HR 0)	LBO 100 (HR 70)	LBO 100 (HR 85)	LBO 100 (HR 100)	Sizz LBOs (HR 0)	Sizz LBOs (HR 70)	Sizz LBOs (HR 85)	Sizz LBOs (HR 100)
Annualized Return	9.82	24.88	19.77	18.12	16.28	30.56	25.52	23.84	21.97
Annualized Vol	27.83	31.32	14.14	11.46	9.88	33.20	16.82	14.36	12.82
Sharpe Ratio	0.35	0.79	1.40	1.58	1.65	0.92	1.52	1.66	1.71
Sortino Ratio	0.50	1.17	2.20	2.55	2.63	1.37	2.45	2.74	2.85
Max DD	44.56	50.66	26.10	19.86	13.24	53.05	29.11	23.15	16.83

drawdown is quite high for unhedged long-only flavors but in the same ballpark as that of the IWN index ETF. These are significantly higher risk than the hedged drawdowns, which for obvious reasons decline from 50% down to 13.24% for HR100 in the LBO 100.

The Sizzling LBOs strategy, with its higher-risk, higher-return profile, has demonstrated the ability to significantly outperform both the LBO 100 strategy and traditional market indices. The hedged versions of the strategies have provided more stability and have shielded against downside risks, as seen in the negative market year of 2022. These results suggest that investors who are willing to accept higher volatility for the chance of higher returns would have been well-served by the Sizzling LBOs strategy. Meanwhile, those looking for more stable returns, possibly as part of a diversified portfolio, might find the hedged LBO strategies more appealing.

In conclusion, the data from both graphs indicate that QMIT's LBO strategy indices have been reasonably successful at delivering robust returns over the observed period, outperforming traditional market benchmarks. The Sizzling LBOs, despite their higher volatility, have offered substantial growth potential, while the hedged LBO strategies have provided a more consistent return profile.

10.4. LBO TOP 100 – HEDGE RATIO PROFILES OVER 24Y

For the 24-year dataset, we observe a pattern similar to the five years. The LBO 100 strategy, without hedging, achieves remarkable cumulative returns of 11,918%, and the hedged returns stand at 4,218% and 3,088% for HRs of 100% and 85%, respectively (as shown in Figure 10.11).

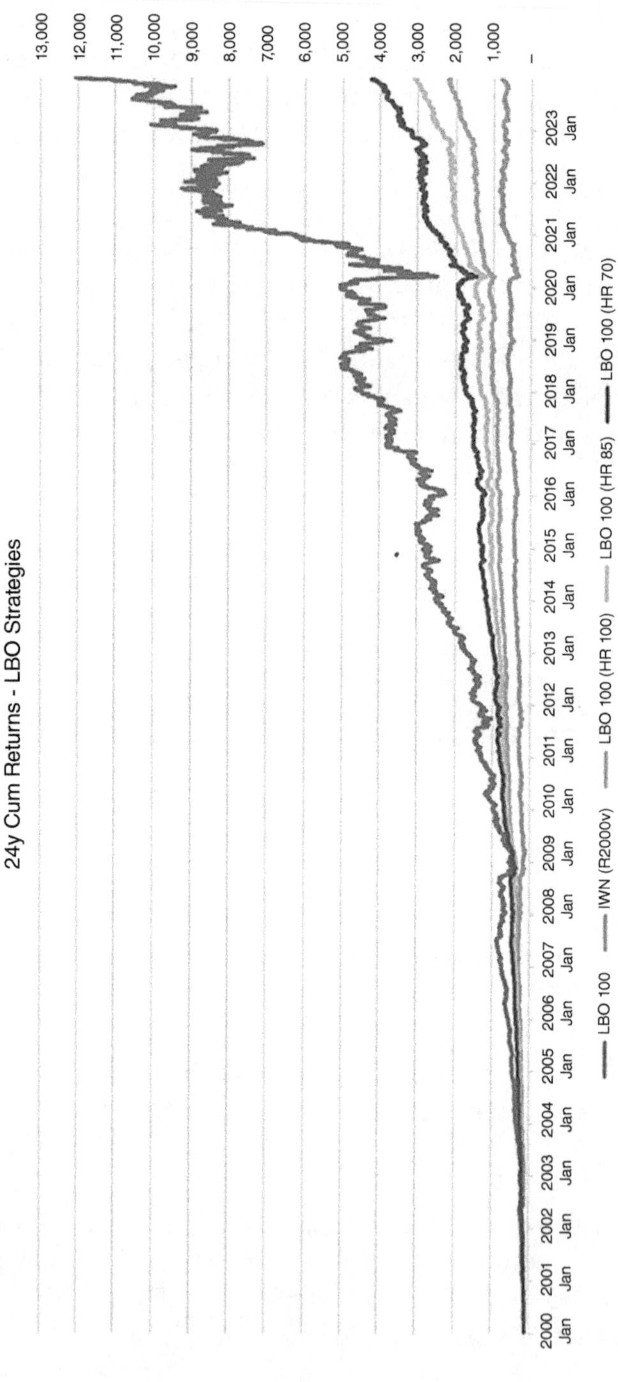

Figure 10.11 LBO VAMI with Different Hedge Ratio.

Although the LBO 100 gets higher cumulative returns, it's much lower in risk-adjusted terms, hence the desire to find the Optimal hedge ratio toward maximizing the risk-adjusted outcome. The 24-year statistics reveal an annualized volatility of 25.58% for LBO 100, which is considerably higher than the hedged alternatives. The Sharpe ratios further elucidate this point, with the highest Sharpe ratio of 1.7 occurring at a hedge ratio of 85%, surpassing even the 100% hedge ratio.

In order to solve for the optimal hedge ratio, which maximizes the Sharpe ratio of the hedged strategy let's consider the objective function:

$$argmax_{HR} \frac{mean(LBO100 - HR \times IWN)}{std(LBO100 - HR \times IWN)}$$

The resulting optimal HR* = 91% for 24y which includes the LIVE 5Y. If we were to only consider the LIVE 5Y trailing ex post one can see that the optimal HR would have been 100% as per the previous example. It's clear from this analysis that if one were to look at the in-sample 19Y versus the LIVE 5Y trailing ex post the HR* is quite consistent and about 90%. This is also evident by the Sortino ratios, which peak at 2.69 for LBO 100 (HR = 85). However, maximum drawdowns are somewhat more pronounced for LBO 100 (HR = 85) than for LBO 100 (HR = 100), though both are significantly lower than the unadjusted LBO 100 and the benchmark IWN (R2000 Value). It's noteworthy that even without any portfolio construction or risk optimization, merely hedging out the Fama-French size and style factors results in volatility reduction by 2/3 from 25.6% down to 8.26%. There's enough idiosyncratic alpha in the signal to power a 2.6 Sortino after the Russell 2000 Value hedge as shown in Table 10.7.

Table 10.7 LBO Top 100 Hedge Ratios.

	IWN (R2000v)	LBO 100 (HR 0)	LBO 100 (HR 70)	LBO 100 (HR 85)	LBO 100 (HR 100)
Annualized Return	8.96	22.04	16.87	15.36	13.72
Annualized Vol	24.13	25.58	11.30	9.05	8.26
Sharpe Ratio	0.37	0.86	1.53	1.70	1.66
Sortino Ratio	0.53	1.26	2.38	2.69	2.60
Max DD	61.75	57.48	28.48	22.12	16.05

The analysis of both 5-year and 24-year periods suggests that while higher cumulative returns are dominant, they come with an increase in risk, as indicated by higher volatility and maximum drawdowns. An optimized hedge ratio can potentially offer a more balanced risk-return profile, enhancing the Sharpe and Sortino ratios, and thereby suggesting a more reliable investment strategy over the long term.

Chapter 11

QMIT's LBO model with NLP Sentiment

11.1. HISTORY OF FINANCIAL SENTIMENT ANALYSIS

11.1.1. Lexicon Method

The lexicon method relies on predefined sentiment dictionaries to assign scores to words based on sentiment polarity. Early general purpose sentiment dictionaries, such as the Stanford Sentiment Treebank, provided a foundation by labeling words and phrases with fine-grained sentiment scores across a variety of contexts (Socher et al., 2013).

However, in the financial sector, specialized lexicons are essential to capture domain-specific terminology accurately.

Henry's financial dictionary, a small finance-specific lexicon, was developed for earnings reports but has limited word coverage, restricting its utility in broad financial sentiment analysis (E. Henry, 2008a). The Loughran-McDonald (LM) dictionary expanded this by including words from annual reports, introducing categories like uncertainty and litigation, widely recognized for its adaptability in corporate finance contexts (Loughran & McDonald, 2011).

More recent developments in finance-specific lexicons include the Stock Market Sentiment Lexicon, designed for social media sentiment, particularly on platforms like StockTwits (Oliveira et al., 2016), and SentiEcon, a multi-word lexicon for economic news and commentary (Moreno-Ortiz et al., 2020). Additionally, Senti-DD addresses sentiment contextually with direction-dependent terms, while FinSenticNet provides concept-level financial sentiment analysis, supporting the understanding of complex financial expressions (Cambria et al., 2020; Park et al., 2020).

11.1.2. Word Embedding

Word embedding techniques offer a more nuanced way to represent text than traditional lexicons. Initial embedding methods, like bag of words and Word2vec, capture basic relationships between words, with Word2vec generating vectorized word representations that position semantically similar words close in vector space (Mikolov et al., 2013). GloVe builds on this by using global co-occurrence information, effectively capturing broader contextual relationships ideal for comprehensive sentiment detection (Pennington et al., 2014). FastText goes further by incorporating subword information, making it especially useful in finance, where domain-specific terms and abbreviations abound (Bojanowski et al., 2017).

To capture complex, context-dependent meanings, recent models like Context2Vec, CoVe, ELMo, and ULMFiT provide contextual embeddings, with each advancing the ability to understand sentiment in dynamic financial environments by capturing multi-word expressions and nuanced dependencies (Howard & Ruder, 2018; McCann et al., 2017; Melamud et al., 2016; Peters et al., 2018).

11.1.3. Algorithms

Machine learning approaches leverage classifiers such as support vector machine, random forest, and XGBoost, combined with feature engineering, to improve sentiment classification accuracy over lexicon-based methods. While these techniques offer improvements, they require substantial labeled data and manual feature extraction (Du et al., 2024).

Deep learning methods, particularly convolutional neural networks (CNNs) and Long Short-Term Memory models (LSTMs), enable more advanced sequence modeling and context capture, which is critical in finance. For instance, LSTMs are effective in handling long-form financial reports, while attention-enhanced architectures enable models to focus on sentiment-heavy parts of the text. Hybrid methods combine lexicon resources with machine and deep learning models, such as integrating LM lexicon-based features with CNN architectures to capture domain-specific terms (Du et al., 2024).

Most recently, the large language model (LLM) revolution has completely disrupted the field of natural language processing (NLP)-based sentiment rendering many startups based on prior models (as mentioned) obsolete overnight. In particular, in Chapter 13, Section 13.8, we show an application of agentic AI that can harness LLMs to deliver portfolio-level news sentiment via simple prompting and application programming interface calls that until recently required expensive licensing of third-party NLP models.

Encoder-only models, such as BERT (bidirectional encoder representations from transformers), provide powerful bidirectional context representation. These models are particularly effective for sentiment classification, as they capture both preceding and following context, which is essential for understanding financial documents accurately (Devlin et al., 2019). This architecture has been adapted for specific fields, as with FinBERT, which is pretrained on financial data to improve performance on domain-specific terminology. Other powerful general purpose variations, like RoBERTa, were developed with improved pretraining methodologies on massive general datasets, offering robust performance across a wide range of tasks (Liu et al., 2019).

Decoder-only models, such as the GPT series, including recent developments like BloombergGPT, are decoder-only architectures that excel in text generation and summarization. In financial contexts, GPT models are used for generating sentiment analysis summaries and extracting relevant sentiment data. These models typically require larger datasets for training but perform well in zero-shot or few-shot scenarios due to their generative capabilities (Radford et al., 2018; Wu et al., 2023).

11.1.3.1. Existing Products on the Market

Several startups had sprouted up in the nascent arena of financial sentiment analysis in recent years only to be upstaged by the dramatic disruption caused by LLMs. One of them focused on central bank communications, providing investors with insights into potential policy shifts based on sentiment cues while the other used rule-based models suited for structured data, like earnings call transcripts, offering reliable industry-specific sentiment insights but perhaps underperformed in real time and unstructured data (Li et al., 2021). RavenPack, however, delivered real-time sentiment, relevance, and novelty data for a wide range of listed stocks by aggregating scores across thousands of events (Hafez & Lautizi, 2017).

However, the onslaught of frontier LLM model-driven disruption may render pre-GPT approaches largely obsolete. We demonstrate a cutting-edge application of frontier LLMs toward extracting stock-level sentiment from news feeds as an example of the agentic AI future in Chapter 13, Section 13.8.

11.2. HARVESTING NLP SENTIMENT

At the time of writing in 2019, the choice of RavenPack as a data partner for this study was compelling. The recent innovations in transformers as the underlying technology notwithstanding, our findings in this study remain relevant for the purposes of illustrating whether one can benefit from harvesting NLP-based sentiment to capture buyout rumors that a pure quant model may not. While our conclusion was that with various modifications (such as slowing the signal down substantially) it can, the question remains whether sentiment is indeed a new animal worthy of inclusion in the factor zoo (nothing in the literature would suggest that) or if it's simply capturing short-term noise faster, which on smoothing converges to well-known denizens of the factor zoo such as earnings surprise and revisions?

RavenPack provided real-time structured sentiment, relevance, and novelty data for entities and events detected in unstructured text published by reputable sources on over 45,000 listed stocks. We are going to use the SESI (Sum Excess Sentiment Indicator) signal from RavenPack, which incorporates ESS (their event sentiment score). While it does not explicitly include Event Buzz (which incorporates abnormal event volume), it does so indirectly by taking into account event volume through summation over a 24-hour window. By adjusting for the ambient market sentiment, SESI is more discerning in terms of which sentiment signals will have the greatest market impact (Hafez & Lautizi, 2017).

For the purposes of this section, we only obtained SESI scores for the Top 3,000 US stocks (as detailed in Table 11.1). The scores are available on all calendar days (including weekends), with an average of 288 stocks with SESI scores on a daily basis for the 10 years of data supplied. The year-wise distribution of SESI scores is provided in Figure 11.1.

The SESI distribution is fairly consistent across the years until 2015. Evidently, in 2016, RavenPack substantially increased its coverage, as we see the average number of tickers with SESI scores spike to 445 from the long-term average of 288. We also note the higher max and lower min values along with significantly higher negative skewness and positive kurtosis for 2016.

RavenPack has showcased techniques for incorporating SESI scores into trading portfolios. In particular, they demonstrated how a simple strategy using SESI on the Russell 3000 with a one-day holding period resulted in improvements in cumulative returns. This result was consistent across their back-test period (2007–2018) and for both the large/mid-cap, and small-cap portfolios (Hafez, 2018) as per the chart reproduced in Figure 11.2. It is interesting to note that large and mid-caps benefit more than small caps. However, the absolute impact of SESI on small caps does

Table 11.1 Annual Descriptive Statistics of the Sum Excess Sentiment Indicator (SESI) for the Top 3,000 US Stocks (2007–2016).

Year	Mean	Median	Skewness	Kurtosis	Min	Max	Average No. of Tickers Per Day
2007	(0.1)	0.2	(1.5)	19.8	(35.5)	28.6	262
2008	(0.0)	0.3	(1.7)	24.2	(44.5)	43.4	239
2009	(0.1)	0.2	(1.0)	19.4	(43.2)	38.6	230
2010	(0.1)	0.2	(1.6)	20.8	(40.0)	33.6	241
2011	(0.1)	0.2	(1.7)	25.9	(53.7)	30.1	289
2012	(0.1)	0.2	(2.2)	36.7	(89.1)	49.6	303
2013	(0.1)	0.2	(2.2)	33.2	(73.5)	40.1	300
2014	(0.1)	0.2	(2.2)	31.2	(62.9)	36.9	286
2015	(0.1)	0.2	(1.8)	27.9	(67.1)	44.9	288
2016	(0.1)	0.1	(2.7)	86.3	(158.6)	46.1	445

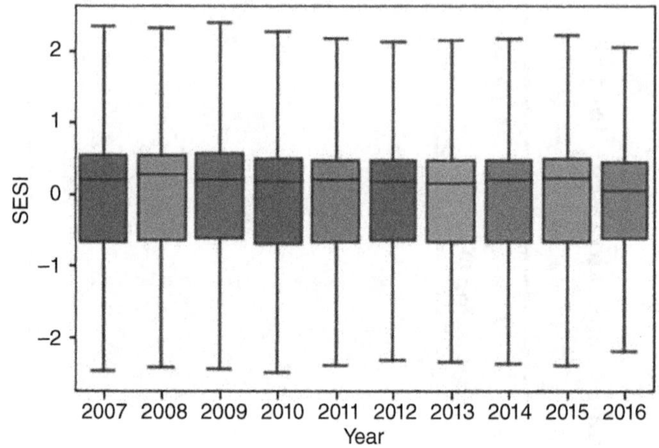

Figure 11.1 Year-Wise Descriptive Statistics of Sum Excess Sentiment Indicator (SESI) Scores for the Top 3,000 US Stocks (2007–2016).

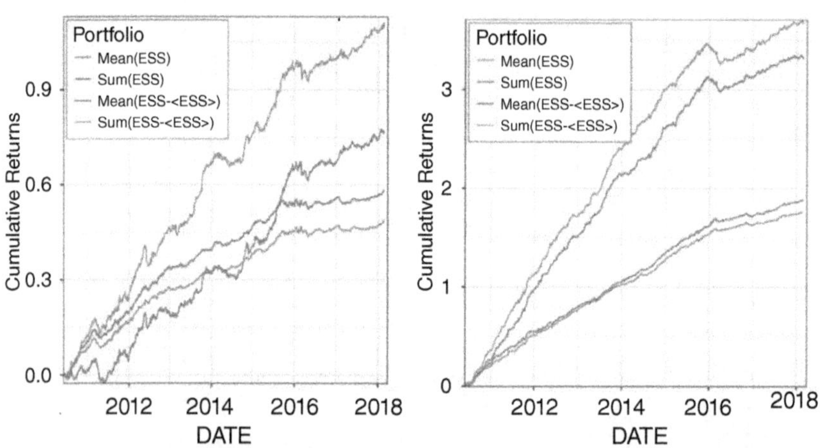

Cumulative returns for United States. Cumulative returns for one-day holding period portfolios of mean and sum sentiment indicators, with and without daily sentiment bias subtraction. Results for large/mid cap (left) and small cap (right).

Figure 11.2 Cumulative Returns for US Portfolios Based on One-Day Holding Period Strategies Using Mean and Sum Event Sentiment Score (ESS) Indicators.

dominate, which is pertinent since our leveraged buyout (LBO) names are by design only small caps. Further details regarding this result can be found in Hafez (2018). Therefore, it seems plausible that SESI scores can be used to enhance the efficacy of traditional factor-based signals such as the LBO 100 model (even though the overlay may be less effective for small caps).

SESI is an excess sentiment measure where the average daily cross-sectional sentiment is removed:

$$\mathrm{SESI}_{I,t} = \mathrm{Sum}\left(\mathrm{ESS} - \langle \mathrm{ESS} \rangle\right) = \sum_{j=1}^{N_{I,t}} \left(\mathrm{ESS}_{i,t,j} - \overline{\mathrm{ESS}_t}\right)$$

where ESS – RavenPack's ESS is a news sentiment index that is useful for capturing the overall sentiment of the market. It is useful for building sentiment signals with the objective of predicting stock returns (Hafez & Lautizi, 2017).

Here, <ESS> is daily sentiment that is used for removing daily sentiment bias:

$$\langle \mathrm{ESS} \rangle = \frac{\sum_i \sum_{j=1}^{N_{i,t}} \mathrm{ESS}_{i,t,j} f\left(\mathrm{ERS}_{\{i,t,j\}}, \mathrm{ESD}_{\{i,t,j\}}\right)}{\sum_i \sum_{j=1}^{N_{i,t}} f\left(\mathrm{ERS}_{\{i,t,j\}}, \mathrm{ESD}_{\{i,t,j\}}\right)}$$

ERS – RavenPack's event relevance score

ESD – RavenPack's event similarity days

Event Buzz is a *z*-score based on mean and standard deviation of a company's daily event volume over a predefined lookback window:

$$\text{Event Buzz}_{i,t} = \frac{\text{Event\_Volume}_{i,t} - \text{Average\_Event\_Volume}_{i,t,\text{lookback}}}{\text{Standard\_Dev\_Event\_Volume}_{i,t,\text{lookback}}}$$

$\text{Event\_Volume}_{i,t}$: Number of events for a company *i* on day *t*,

$\text{Average\_Event\_Volume}_{i,t,\text{ lookback}}$: Average daily event volume for company *i* on day *t* over a lookback period of 365 days,

$\text{Standard\_Dev\_Event\_Volume}_{i,t,\text{ lookback}}$: Standard deviation of daily event volume for company *i* on day *t* over a lookback period of 365 days.

From December 29, 2006, to December 22, 2016, there were a total of 1,048,575 SESI signals, that is, 288 per day on average. However, these only correspond to 5,228 unique companies in the SESI case, as compared to 823 in the LBO history. There are 521 weeks in total from December 29, 2006, to December 22, 2016. The company with the maximum number of SESI signals is Benchmark Electronics, Inc., with 474 scores over 521 weeks.

11.3. COMBINING FACTOR-BASED MFMs (MULTIFACTOR MODELS) WITH ALTERNATIVE DATA SIGNALS

As discussed in Chapter 10, the LBO Top 100 signal is composed of the equally weighted top 100 LBO predictions made on a daily basis but tracked with weekly portfolio rebalancing for performance reporting purposes. The point of the experiment is to under/overweight the Top 100 stocks using SESI scores. The LBO Top 100 is rebalanced weekly since it's derived purely from fundamentals and is by design extremely low turnover. However, since the objective is to overlay the very short-term news sentiment alpha embedded in SESI (24-hour window available every calendar day), it behooves us to rebalance every weekday in order to derive the maximum benefit from sentiment/chatter relating to our putative buyout targets. Given the complexity of tracking daily four-way turnover, transaction costs have not been considered in this part of the experiment although they were included in the LBO results previously shown. Since SESI scores are available in real-time intraday, and because the objective is to investigate the impact of the timely sentiment, we take files cut at 3:30 p.m. EST, which can be traded into the closing auction or via guaranteed close type broker algos in order to ensure execution at the closing price. While this may not be realistic for larger, lower turnover mandates, it is in fact quite typical of hedge funds (from our extensive trading experience), although such a rebalancing routine does imply limited scalability. Distribution of SESI scores for only the intersecting tickers in the LBO Top 100 is shown in Figure 11.3. The detailed year-wise descriptive statistics for these intersecting tickers, including their mean, median, and other measures, are presented in Table 11.2.

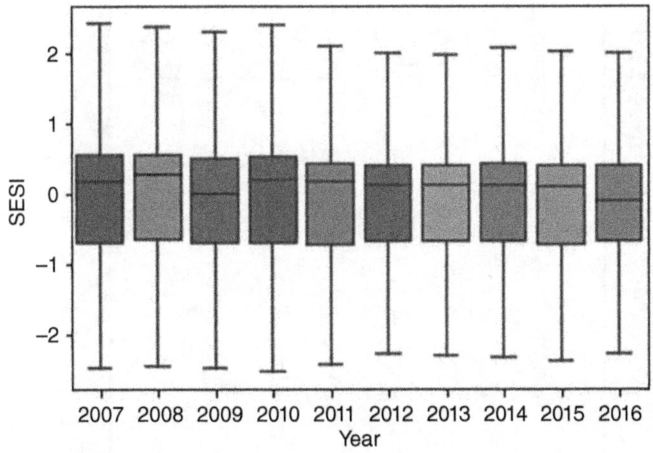

Figure 11.3 Annual Distributions of Sum Excess Sentiment Indicator (SESI) Scores.

Table 11.2 Year-Wise Descriptive Statistics of Sum Excess Sentiment Indicator (SESI) Scores.

Year	Mean	Median	Skewness	Kurtosis	Min	Max	Average No. of Tickers Per Day
2007	(0.2)	0.2	(1.7)	11.4	(17.7)	12.3	7
2008	(0.2)	0.3	(1.7)	13.8	(26.0)	17.3	6
2009	(0.3)	(0.0)	(1.1)	13.1	(22.1)	25.3	7
2010	0.1	0.2	(0.9)	16.5	(31.4)	19.3	7
2011	(0.2)	0.2	(1.8)	25.1	(36.8)	24.0	9
2012	(0.5)	0.1	(3.2)	29.4	(38.2)	25.8	10
2013	(0.4)	0.1	(2.7)	25.1	(36.1)	22.2	9
2014	(0.4)	0.1	(1.9)	17.2	(36.4)	27.9	8
2015	(0.5)	0.1	(1.9)	15.7	(29.9)	30.9	8
2016	(0.6)	(0.1)	(3.4)	26.8	(45.1)	20.8	13

Based on a *t*-test, the mean SESI scores of the stocks in the intersecting LBO Top 100 universe is lower than the mean SESI scores of all the stocks in our universe of about 3,000 names. While we only compare 10 points for the *t*-test (to keep them comparable) each data point is already the aggregate of all scores within that calendar year. Results of the *t*-test are available in Table 11.3. The deep value tilt inherent to the LBO Top 100 names could explain the statistically significant negative sentiment bias as per the summary statistics in Table 11.2. That said, the model profits from subsequent positive catalysts (like buybacks or activists), which propel the stock. This observation merits further study.

The *t*-test of mean annual SESI scores for the SESI universe versus the LBO Top 100 is as follows:

Null Hypothesis – Difference between the means = 0

Table 11.3 Statistical Results of a *t*-Test Comparing the Mean Annual SESI Scores Between the SESI Universe and the LBO 100 Universe.

	SESI Universe	LBO 100 Universe
Mean	(0.0908)	(0.3297)
Variance	0.0005	0.0388
Observations	10	10
Pearson Correlation	0.4470	
Hypothesized Mean Difference	0	
df	9	
t Stat	4.0234	
$P(T<=t)$ one-tail	0.0015	
t Critical one-tail	1.8331	
$P(T<=t)$ two-tail	0.0030	
t Critical two-tail	2.2622	

11.3.1. SESI Aggregation

While RavenPack data has 288 stocks with SESI scores on an average on a daily basis during the 10-year back-test period (2007–2016), only eight stocks on average intersect with the LBO Top 100 on a daily basis. There are 823 unique stocks that appear within the LBO Top 100 universe (during 2007–2016) with 516 stocks having a SESI score at some point of time during the back-test period. While stocks with no SESI score are taken to have a SESI score of zero, we did not consider these stocks while computing the above statistics. This is because stocks with SESI scores of zero are interpreted as not having material positive/negative excess sentiment in the market during the 24-hour window (essentially N/A is equivalent to an offsetting bona fide neutral sentiment). Given that the number of stocks with SESI scores on average on a daily basis within the LBO Top 100 universe is quite small, it behooves us to aggregate SESI scores over the following lookback periods (also to benefit from decaying but still relevant alpha):

{7 days, 30 days and 91 days}

Furthermore, the SESI scores are aggregated using the following methodologies:

{Simple Average (SMA), Exponential Average (EMA)}

Whereas for the ESS it makes sense to compare and contrast (as per Hafez, 2018) the differing outcomes for sum versus average (see Figure 11.3); for SESI they amount to the same (as long we do indeed count the N/As zeros. which is important to be able to compare over time). Hence, we expect to be comparing and contrasting results for six unique aggregate SESI scores (three aggregation windows and two aggregation methodologies).

Aggregation results in a substantially higher number of intersecting stocks with SESI scores within the LBO Top 100 universe, as detailed in Table 11.4. However, note that nearly all of the doubling in count occurs from 1 week to 1 month, after which it plateaus off by the time we get to a quarter.

The aggregate SESI score is then converted into a *z*-score. Since SESI is already an excess sentiment measure, to calculate a *z*-score we simply divide the aggregate SESI score by the cross-sectional standard deviation of the aggregate SESI scores. While the simple moving average (SMA) is self-explanatory, it's worth pointing out that under the standard exponential decay there can be substantial weight allocated beyond our horizon of a week/month/quarter due to the recursive nature of the calculation. This results in the exponential moving average (EMA) scenarios having almost twice as many stocks in the daily count versus SMA at the one-week horizon. To make it pari passu, we enforce a hard cut off at the week/month/quarter horizon then rescale the weights back to 100%. This leads to cleaner and more intuitive results by eliminating the noise introduced by stock counts (and effective horizons) that would otherwise have not been comparable.

Table 11.4. Average Number of Stocks per Day Within the LBO Top 100 Universe That Have Aggregated SESI Scores.

	Sum1w	EMA1w	Sum1m	EMA1m	Sum1q	EMA1q
Avg no. of stocks with SESI scores per day	30	30	57	57	63	63

$$\mathrm{EMA1}w_{i(1\mathrm{to}7)} = \prod_{j=1}^{i} 0.5, \mathrm{EMA1}m_{i(1\mathrm{to}30)} = \prod_{j=1}^{i} 0.75, \mathrm{EMA1}q_{i(1\mathrm{to}91)} = \prod_{j=1}^{i} 0.9$$

We further rescale the weights back to 100%:

$$\mathrm{EMA1}w_{i(1\mathrm{to}7)} = \frac{\mathrm{EMA1}w_i}{\sum \mathrm{EMA1}w}, \mathrm{EMA1}m_{i(1\mathrm{to}30)} = \frac{\mathrm{EMA1}m_i}{\sum \mathrm{EMA1}m} \mathrm{EMA1}q_{i(1\mathrm{to}91)} = \frac{\mathrm{EMA1}q_i}{\sum \mathrm{EMA1}q}$$

11.3.2. Design of Experiment

We have designed multiple experiments for investigating the efficacy of SESI as an overlay by varying the following two levers:

- Varying the *z*-score thresholds for under/overweighting
- Varying the magnitude of under/overweighting

11.3.2.1. Test 1: The Base Case

The decision to overweight/underweight is based on the following logic. Recall that the basic LBO Top 100 portfolio is a long-only portfolio and all stocks are equally weighted at 1%.

- Overweight

  Aggregate SESI *z*-score 1 to 2→2% weight instead of 1% weight

  Aggregate SESI *z*-score >2→3% weight instead of 1% weight
- Underweight

  Aggregate SESI *z*-score −1 to −2→0.5% weight instead of 1% weight

  Aggregate SESI *z*-score <−2→0% weight instead of 1% weight

Weights are then adjusted pro rata to sum to 100% across the overlaid portfolio. Based on the *z*-score thresholds, Table 11.5 summarizes the average number of stocks that would be under/overweighted on a daily basis across the six weighting schemes. As expected, the count grows with the horizon. Further, there are always more candidates available for underweighting, which is consistent with the statistically significant negative sentiment bias among our LBO targets as per Table 11.5.

Table 11.6 shows the back-test results for the six overlaid scenarios along with the basic LBO Top 100 model.

The trajectory of excess cumulative returns for these Test 1 overlay strategies over the 2007–2016 period is visually presented in Figure 11.4.

Summary of Results for Test 1

- All six techniques show improvement in annualized returns by about 88–190 basis points (bps) before *t*-cost.
- Increase in returns combined with a marginal drop in volatility results in a 5–11% improvement in Sharpe ratios.
- EMA does marginally better across all three lookback periods. This could be due to the substantially sharper drop off in lookback weights, which overweights recent

Table 11.5 Average Daily Number of Stocks Within the LBO Top 100 Portfolio.

	SMA1w	EMA1w	SMA1m	EMA1m	SMA1q	EMA1q
Overweight	2	2	4	2	6	3
Underweight	4	3	8	4	14	6

Table 11.6 Performance Metrics of the LBO Top 100 Model Versus Six SESI Overlay Strategies.

	Cumulative Return (%)	Annual Return (%)	Standard Deviation	Sharpe Ratio	Maximum Drawdown (%)
LBO Top 100	412	17.8	27.5	0.65	57
SMA1w	479	19.2	27.5	0.70	57
EMA1w	501	19.7	27.5	0.72	56
SMA1m	452	18.7	27.4	0.68	57
EMA1m	488	19.4	27.5	0.71	57
SMA1q	456	18.8	27.3	0.69	56
EMA1q	482	19.3	27.5	0.70	57

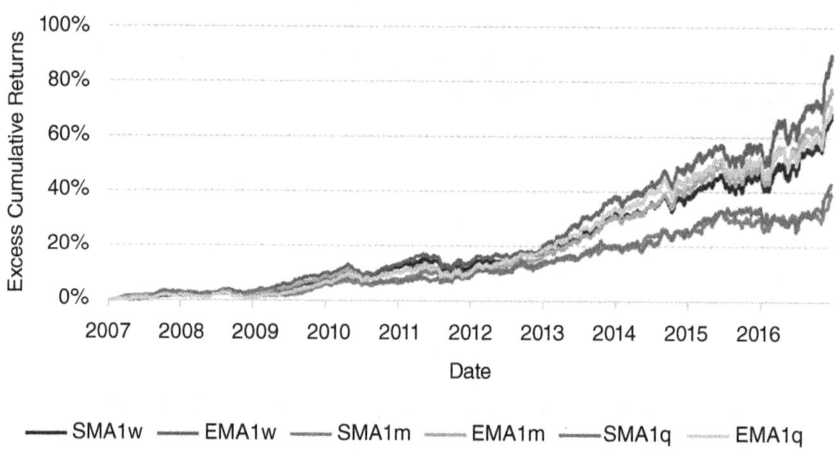

Figure 11.4 Excess Cumulative Returns (2007–2016) of the LBO Top 100 Portfolio When Overlaid with the Six Different Test 1 SESI Aggregation Strategies.

news. Over 90% of the EMA weights are assigned within the past 4, 8, and 22 days for the 7-, 30-, and 91-day windows as opposed to the uniformly distributed nature of the SMA schema.

- One week appears to be the better lookback period but again a *t*-test on the difference of means (EMA one week versus one month versus one quarter) is not surprisingly inconclusive since all horizons are quite similar at least in risk-adjusted terms.
- One of the key issues is that even after aggregation of SESI scores the intersection portfolio at these thresholds is too low. The monthly and quarterly horizons do not multiply the counts substantially, which may explain why the performance does not improve monotonically with longer horizons. We can overcome this by reducing the *z*-score thresholds as per Test 2 for the same magnitude of under/overweighting.
- Worth pointing out that the base case LBO Top 100 Sharpe of 0.65 (and 17.8% annualized return) for the 10-year overlapping period here is substantially lower than the 0.82 Sharpe ratio for the full 25 years shown in Table 10.2. This is due to the three down years (2007/08/15), a flat year (2011), and extremely good years (2010/12/13/16), along with the outlier swings across 2008/2009 resulting in substantially higher volatility during this subperiod.

11.3.2.2 Test 2: Reducing Z-Score Threshold

The decision to overweight/underweight is now based on the following logic:

- Overweight
  - Aggregate SESI *z*-score 0.5 to 1 → 2% weight instead of 1% weight
  - Aggregate SESI *z*-score >1 → 3% weight instead of 1% weight

- Underweight
  - Aggregate SESI *z*-score –0.5 to –1→0.5% weight instead of 1% weight
  - Aggregate SESI *z*-score <–1→0% weight instead of 1% weight

Table 11.7 summarizes the average number of stocks that would be under/overweighted on a daily basis across the six weighting schemes.

Table 11.7 Average Daily Count of LBO Top 100 Stocks Designated for Overweighting or Underweighting Under Test 2.

	SMA1w	EMA1w	SMA1m	EMA1m	SMA1q	EMA1q
Overweight	5	3	9	4	14	6
Underweight	7	4	14	7	23	11

Table 11.8 Performance Metrics for Test 2 (Reduced *Z*-Score Thresholds) SESI Overlay Strategies Compared to the LBO Top 100 Model.

	Cumulative Return (%)	Annual Return (%)	Standard Deviation	Sharpe Ratio	Maximum Drawdown (%)
LBO Top 100	412	17.8	27.5	0.65	57
SMA1w	504	19.7	27.4	0.72	56
EMA1w	518	20.0	27.5	0.73	56
SMA1m	502	19.7	27.3	0.72	55
EMA1m	527	20.2	27.4	0.74	55
SMA1q	503	19.7	27.2	0.73	53
EMA1q	530	20.3	27.2	0.75	54

Table 11.8 shows the back-test results for the six overlaid scenarios along with the basic LBO Top 100 model:

The corresponding excess cumulative returns generated by these Test 2 overlay strategies throughout the 2007–2016 period are illustrated in Figure 11.5.

Summary of Results for Test 2

- All six techniques show improvement in annualized returns by about 192–257 bps.
- Increase in returns combined with a marginal drop in volatility results in an 11–15% improvement in Sharpe ratios.
- EMA does marginally better across all three lookback periods likely due to overweighting of recent news.
- All three lookback periods once again turn out to be surprisingly similar with the SMA being practically identical across all three despite increasing counts.
- The issue of too small an intersection portfolio still plagues us even at the lowered *z*-score threshold. To overcome this, we remove the *z*-score threshold altogether in Test 3 while maintaining the same magnitude of under/overweighting.

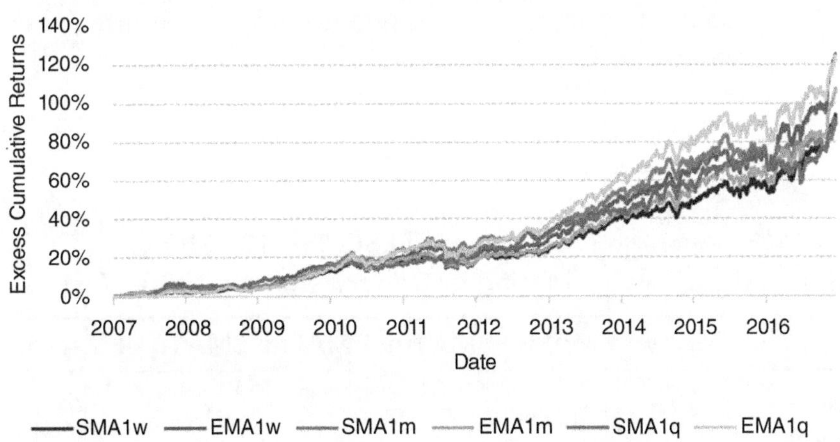

Figure 11.5 Excess Cumulative Returns of the LBO Top 100 Portfolio When Applying Test 2 SESI Overlay Strategies.

11.3.2.3. Test 3: Dropping the Z-Score Threshold

The decision to underweight/overweight is now based on the following logic:

- Overweight
  - Aggregate SESI *z*-score 0 to 1 → 2% weight instead of 1% weight
  - Aggregate SESI *z*-score >1 → 3% weight instead of 1% weight
- Underweight
  - Aggregate SESI *z*-score –0 to –1 → 0.5% weight instead of 1% weight
  - Aggregate SESI *z*-score <–1 → 0% weight instead of 1% weight

Table 11.9 summarizes the average number of stocks that would be under/overweighted on a daily basis across the six weighting schemes. Clearly, dropping the *z*-score thresholds all the way down to zero enables us to capture all of the intersecting stocks. For example, EMA1q here has a total of [28 + 35] stocks being under/overweighted, which corresponds to the total of 63 intersecting stocks previously reported in Table 11.4.

Table 11.10 shows the back-test results for the six overlaid scenarios along with the basic LBO Top 100 model.

Table 11.9 Average Daily Count of LBO Top 100 Stocks Designated for Overweighting or Underweighting Under Test 3.

	SMA1w	EMA1w	SMA1m	EMA1m	SMA1q	EMA1q
Overweight	15	15	26	28	27	28
Underweight	15	15	31	29	36	35

Table 11.10. Performance Metrics for Test 3 (Z-Score Thresholds Dropped to Zero) SESI Overlay Strategies Compared to the LBO Top 100.

	Cumulative Return (%)	Annual Return (%)	Standard Deviation	Sharpe Ratio	Maximum Drawdown (%)
LBO Top 100	412	17.8	27.5	0.65	57
SMA1w	503	19.7	27.4	0.72	57
EMA1w	511	19.9	27.4	0.73	56
SMA1m	543	20.5	27.4	0.75	53
EMA1m	529	20.2	27.4	0.74	54
SMA1q	562	20.9	27.2	0.77	53
EMA1q	573	21.1	27.3	0.77	54

The corresponding visual performance, illustrated by the excess cumulative returns for these Test 3 strategies from 2007 to 2016, is presented in Figure 11.6.

Summary of Results for Test 3

- All six techniques show substantial improvement in annualized returns by about 193–306 bps. With the maximum of intersecting stocks being captured in the count, we do see correspondingly better performance.
- Longer aggregation windows do witness monotonically (albeit still only) marginally better performance.
- Increase in returns coupled with a reduction in volatility results in an 11–19% improvement in Sharpe ratios.
- Maximum drawdown also reduces by 91–434 bps with the number of days to recovery dropping from 299 to 256–274 days.

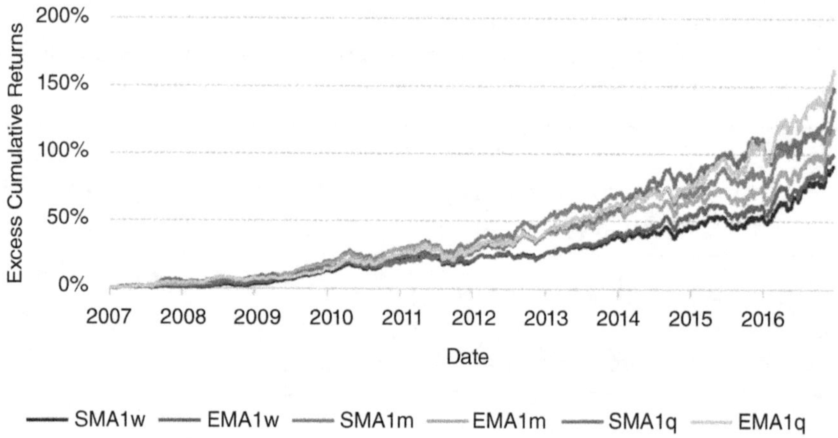

Figure 11.6 Excess Cumulative Returns (2007–2016) of the LBO Top 100 Portfolio When Applying Test 3 SESI Overlay Strategies.

We have stayed away from shorting stocks within the LBO Top 100 portfolio thus far since it is by construction a long-only portfolio and in general it may not be advisable to short LBO targets – at least over *longer* horizons. We now relax this constraint given the single-day holding period over which SESI scores may capture meaningful short-term opportunities. Analyzing the average daily underperformance of stocks that we underweight based on SESI scores gives us another reason to short these stocks as per Table 11.11.

Table 11.11 Average Daily Returns of LBO Top 100 Stocks Designated as "Overweight" Versus Those Designated as "Underweight" Based on Test 3's Zero *Z*-Score Threshold SESI Criteria.

SMA1w	EMA1w	SMA1m	EMA1m	SMA1q	EMA1q
	Average daily returns of overweight stocks				
0.11%	0.10%	0.10%	0.09%	0.11%	0.10%
	Average daily returns of underweight stocks				
0.07%	0.07%	0.06%	0.07%	0.06%	0.07%

11.3.2.4. Test 4: Relaxing Short Constraints

Overweights are now based on the following logic which includes symmetric shorting while keeping the *z*-score thresholds the same as in Test 3:

- Overweight
  - Aggregate SESI *z*-score 0 to 1 → 2% weight instead of 1% weight
  - Aggregate SESI *z*-score >1 → 3% weight instead of 1% weight
- Underweight
  - Aggregate SESI *z*-score 0 to −1 → 0% weight instead of 1% weight
  - Aggregate SESI *z*-score <−1 → −1% weight instead of 1% weight

Since we have not changed our thresholds, the number of stocks that would be under/overweighting remains the same as in Test 3. Table 11.12 show the back-test results for the six overlaid scenarios along with the basic LBO Top 100 model.

Table 11.12 Performance Metrics for Test 4 (Relaxing Short Constraints, Allowing Symmetric Shorting) SESI Overlay Strategies Compared to the LBO Top 100.

	Cumulative Return (%)	Annual Return (%)	Standard Deviation	Sharpe Ratio	Maximum Drawdown (%)
LBO Top 100	412	17.8	27.5	0.65	57
SMA1w	529	20.2	27.4	0.74	57
EMA1w	551	20.7	27.5	0.75	55

(Continued)

Table 11.12 *(Continued)*

	Cumulative Return (%)	Annual Return (%)	Standard Deviation	Sharpe Ratio	Maximum Drawdown (%)
SMA1m	646	22.3	27.5	0.81	52
EMA1m	592	21.4	27.4	0.78	53
SMA1q	726	23.6	27.3	0.86	50
EMA1q	678	22.8	27.3	0.84	53

The corresponding visual performance, showing the excess cumulative returns for these Test 4 strategies from 2007 to 2016, is presented in Figure 11.7.

Summary of Results of Test 4

- All six techniques show substantial improvement in annualized returns, by about 244–577 bps due to the removal of the short constraint, which now enables us to symmetrically monetize the negative sentiment afflicting our LBO names.

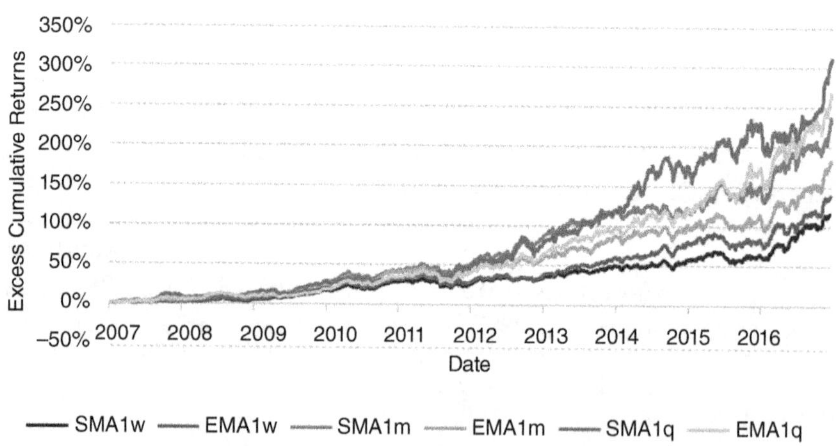

Figure 11.7 Excess Cumulative Returns (2007–2016) of the LBO Top 100 Portfolio When Applying Test 4 SESI Overlay Strategies.

- Longer aggregation windows do witness monotonically better performance as expected. Interestingly, SMA now does slightly better over one month and one quarter. Significant increase in returns and reduction in volatility resulting in a 14–33% improvement in Sharpe ratios.
- Maximum drawdown also dropped by 79–731 bps with the number of days to recovery dropping from 299 days to 252–274 days.

While relaxing the short constraint has significantly improved performance, we must still contend with the limited intersection set of SESI scores overlapping with our LBO longs on any given day. Hence, the final scenario seeks to *exacerbate the under/overweighting schema* in order to show a demonstrably pronounced result that might do justice to the signal blending initiative at the portfolio level (implicitly accounting for the limited intersection).

11.3.2.5 Test 5: Relaxing Short Constraints with Higher Weighting Logic

Under/overweights are now based on the following logic:

- Overweight.
  - Aggregate SESI z-score >0 → +3% weight instead of 1% weight
- Underweight
  - Aggregate SESI z-score <0 → −1% weight instead of 1% weight

Since we have not changed our thresholds, the number of stocks that would be under/overweighting remains the same as in Test 3. Table 11.13 shows the back-test results for the six overlaid scenarios along with the basic LBO Top 100 model.

Table 11.13 Performance Metrics for Test 5 (Relaxed Short Constraints with Higher Weighting Logic) SESI Overlay Strategies, Benchmarked Against the LBO Top 100.

	Cumulative Return (%)	Annual Return (%)	Standard Deviation	Sharpe Ratio	Maximum Drawdown (%)
LBO Top 100	412	17.8	27.5	0.65	57
SMA1w	566	20.9	27.4	0.76	56
EMA1w	535	20.4	27.5	0.74	56
SMA1m	824	25.0	28.0	0.89	51
EMA1m	664	22.6	27.6	0.82	52
SMA1q	938	26.4	27.9	0.95	48
EMA1q	857	25.4	27.6	0.92	51

The resulting excess cumulative returns for these highly effective Test 5 strategies over the 2007–2016 period are visually depicted in Figure 11.8.

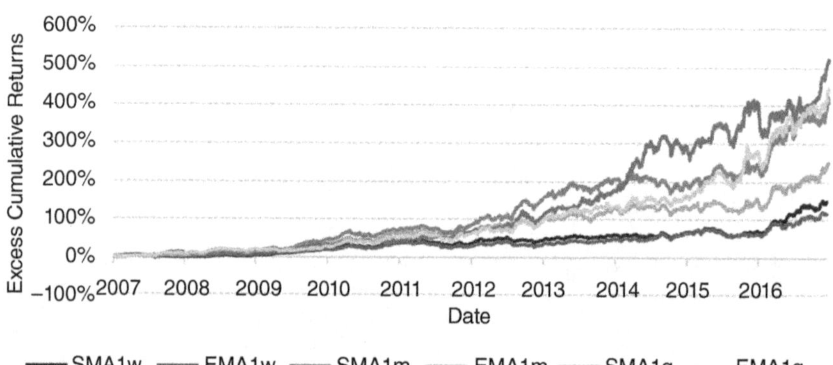

Figure 11.8 Excess Cumulative Returns (2007–2016) of the LBO Top 100 Portfolio When Applying Test 5 SESI Overlay Strategies.

Table 11.14 Average LMV, SMV, and GMV as Percentages for the Test 5 SESI Overlay Strategies.

	SMA1w	EMA1w	SMA1m	EMA1m	SMA1q	EMA1q
GMV	132%	130%	175%	165%	199%	185%
LMV	116%	115%	138%	133%	150%	143%
SMV	16%	15%	38%	33%	50%	43%

The average long market value (LMV), short market value (SMV), and gross market value (GMV) associated with these Test 5 strategies are detailed in Table 11.14.

Summary of Results for Test 5

- All six techniques show improvement in annualized returns ranging from about 257 to 864 bps, which is truly phenomenal on the high end. This is due to the removal of the short constraint, which now enables us to symmetrically monetize the negative sentiment afflicting our LBO names.
- Longer aggregation windows do witness monotonically better performance as expected. Interestingly, SMA now does better than EMA over all horizons.
- Significant increase in returns and reduction in volatility results in a 15–46% improvement in Sharpe ratio with a max Sharpe ratio of 0.95.
- Maximum drawdown also declines by 97–899 bps with the number of days to recovery declining from 299 days to 251–260 days.
- Table 11.14 shows that the net market value is maintained at 100% in all cases, hence these six scenarios are in the spirit of 130/30 type portfolios where the shorting results in gross leverage for the same level of delta-one exposure.

- Analysis of calendar returns for Test 5 shows us that there is performance improvement across both bull and bear markets as per Table 11.15, which shows the annualized excess alpha added to the LBO Top 100 via an overlay.

Note that the cumulative excess alpha will not be same as the geometric cumulative return of the annual excess alpha since it does not take into consideration the compounding effect on the LBO Top 100 returns.

11.4. CONCLUSION

- The QMIT LBO Top 100 model's 41% long-term hit rate speaks to the efficacy of this approach in anticipating buyouts that should be of interest to activists, risk arbitrageurs, and speculators on the long side as well as market participants (typically quants) looking to eliminate event risk on the short side.
- The QMIT LBO Top 100 can also be traded profitably as an equal-weighted long portfolio while a Russell 2000 Value index hedge increases the Sortino ratio to about 2.5 over the 19-year history.
- Results across all five SESI overlays tested (for the 10-year period 2007–2016) demonstrate improvements in performance as well as Sharpe, Sortino, and Max drawdowns versus the baseline LBO Top 100 model.
- Aggregating SESI scores over certain lookback periods make sense in situations where the intersection set is small and the investment horizon is longer than just a day. Longer lookbacks, especially quarterly aggregation, should in general provide better results (consistent with the conclusions in the academic literature), which could simply be because there are more stocks in the intersection set for longer lookback periods.

Table 11.15 Annual Excess Alpha (2007–2016) Generated by Test 5 SESI Overlay Strategies Relative to the LBO Top 100 Model.

	SMA1w	EMA1w	SMA1m	EMA1m	SMA1q	EMA1q	Russell 2000
2007	–0.1%	0.1%	9.3%	3.1%	10.8%	8.1%	–9.8%
2008	5.7%	5.6%	11.3%	13.4%	8.9%	14.3%	–29.0%
2009	17.4%	12.3%	12.1%	8.0%	0.6%	–12.7%	20.5%
2010	6.3%	6.4%	6.0%	8.7%	0.0%	9.7%	24.5%
2011	–2.2%	–3.7%	4.5%	0.2%	9.1%	4.2%	–5.5%
2012	0.0%	–1.1%	18.7%	6.0%	11.0%	7.1%	18.1%
2013	–3.0%	–0.4%	–6.5%	–4.3%	4.8%	–2.1%	34.5%
2014	–0.6%	2.5%	–7.1%	–2.4%	17.0%	1.5%	4.2%
2015	1.8%	0.3%	9.5%	4.9%	18.4%	22.6%	–7.5%
2016	13.6%	9.3%	13.1%	8.1%	–3.9%	9.8%	31.7%
Cumulative Excess Alpha	**153%**	**123%**	**411%**	**252%**	**526%**	**444%**	

- Valuable information is available across the entire distribution of aggregated SESI scores. Therefore, overlaying LBO names with SESI scores, especially without any threshold (which helps to maximize the counts), significantly improves performance.
- The best overlay scenario (Test case 5 for SMA1q) results in a Sharpe of 0.95 with an 8.6% absolute improvement to annualized returns, which is indicative of meaningful value added from the SESI overlay across bull and bear markets.
- As promising as these results appear to be, it should be enunciated that practitioners will want to model realistic *t*-costs germane to their rebalancing routine and consider a full-risk optimization with sector and factor constraints appropriate to their mandate.

In closing, we believe that the future of active management lies in the ability of portfolio managers to act more like orchestra conductors (in terms of being able to time and tilt uncorrelated alpha signals) as opposed to the obsolete Bill Miller/Bill Ackman stereotype. We hope that the quantamental use cases highlighted in this chapter – as motivated by our live trading experience – serve as a road map towards that paradigm.

Chapter 12

The Causal Critique

12.1. INTRODUCTION

The goal of causal models is to move from correlation to cause-effect such that these models can reason about interventions (what happens if we change *X*?) rather than only forecast status quo trends. The foundations covered in this chapter include structural causal models (SCMs), directed acyclic graphs (DAGs), confounders, colliders, counterfactual reasoning, and so on. We contrast the econometric notion of Granger causality with that of Judea Pearl's before providing an exposition of the causal critique as it applies to factor investing. We then bring it home with an application of the Peter Clark (PC) and linear non-Gaussian acyclic models (LiNGAM) algorithms to QMIT enhanced smart betas (ESBs) and the QUMN index. Finally, to balance out the unresolved debate we offer a rebuttal to the "causal necessity" literature, which suggests that for most practitioners, the causal critique may seem like a tempest in a teapot but leaves it to the reader to decide.

Investors ought to care because noncausal predictive machine learning (ML) can fail under regime shifts while causal models are designed to better generalize out of sample. Use cases in asset management may include (1) macro research framed with causal graphs to separate drivers from coincident indicators, (2) portfolio optimization via causal risk channels rather than covariance alone, (3) discovery of non-overlapping factors guided by causal structure, and (4) causal risk assessment to stress-test strategies under hypothetical interventions and so on.

12.2. GRANGER VERSUS PEARL'S CAUSALITY

Granger causality and Pearl's structural causality represent two fundamentally different frameworks for causal inference, distinguished by their underlying assumptions and the types of causal questions they are designed to answer.

Granger causality, originating in econometrics, is a statistical method for determining whether one time series is useful in forecasting another. A time series X is said to Granger-cause a time series Y if including lags of X in a predictive regression of Y significantly improves the forecast of Y, compared to a model with lags of Y alone. In other words, past values of X contain predictive information for future values of Y not already in the history of Y.

The framework is thus based on temporal precedence and predictive accuracy. However, as Granger causality does not explicitly model the underlying data-generating mechanism, it cannot distinguish between genuine causation and spurious correlations that may arise from unobserved confounding variables or indirect pathways.

However, in Pearl's causal framework, X is a direct cause of Y if X appears in the structural equation that determines Y. More generally, X is a cause of Y if interventions on X (holding other variables fixed) change the distribution of Y. The formal method to rigorously define causal assumptions and modeling how nature assigns values to variables and how they interact is the SCM. Every SCM is linked to a graphical causal model (often a DAG), where nodes represent variables and directed edges represent functional dependencies.

12.3. THE CAUSAL CRITIQUE

The framework developed by Rebonato and Denev (2014) marks a shift from the traditional mean variance framework (with its flawed reliance on unstable historical correlations) toward a more robust approach grounded in causality.

The cornerstone of their methodology is the use of Bayesian networks as causal tools. In this framework, economic variables are represented as nodes, while directed edges between them signify causal dependencies. This enables the model to capture not just association but also the actual transmission mechanisms of financial shocks. Instead of treating extreme events like a sovereign default as unexplained outliers, the framework models them as root causes whose effects propagate logically through these defined causal pathways. This makes the entire system ideal for rigorous stress testing and scenario analysis.

A key feature of this approach is its ability to synthesize quantitative data with qualitative insights. Expert judgment is systematically incorporated alongside historical data to estimate the conditional probabilities that govern how a cause influences its effects. This disciplined process makes all underlying assumptions explicit. Furthermore, by structuring relationships causally, the model inherently helps to control for confounding variables and bias, thereby reducing the risk of making decisions based on spurious patterns in raw data.

The ultimate practical implication is the construction of more resilient portfolios. By moving beyond simple statistical diversification, a portfolio designed with causal awareness is better aligned with the complex reality of how shocks propagate through the financial system. This leads to significantly improved resilience in the stressed regimes where traditional models fail most spectacularly.

More recently, Marcos López de Prado presented a comprehensive critique of the current state of factor investing – published by *Cambridge Quant Finance* in October 2023 – titled "Causal Factor Investing: Can Factor Investing Become Scientific?" He argues that it largely operates in a phenomenological stage (where empirical anomalies are documented and characterized without positing a structural or causal explanation) rather than as a truly scientific discipline. His primary criticism is that the denial or ignorance of the causal content inherent in factor models, leading to findings that are likely false due to various methodological errors. Following are the key points of his critique.

12.3.1. Conflation of Association and Causation

The following outlines common ways in which association is mistakenly interpreted as causation within the factor investing literature:

- **Associational claims versus causal content.** Factor investing literature predominantly makes associational claims, focusing on correlations, rather than identifying the underlying causal mechanisms. However, de Prado claims that factor models inherently possess causal content, as their specifications and estimation methods imply directed relationships (e.g., *X* causes *Y*) rather than just co-dependence.
- **Misunderstanding of econometric models.** Many econometric textbooks and practitioners, including factor researchers, mistake association for causality and misunderstand the meaning of regression coefficients.
- **Misuse of Granger causality.** While Granger causality is a widely cited concept in econometrics for investigating causal relations in time series, it relies on a prediction error reduction approach. However, López de Prado notes that it's often misused as a definitive causal statement when it's primarily a tool for directional dependence between unconfounded variables, and more sophisticated causal discovery methods exist.

12.3.2. Absence of Causal Theory and Falsifiable Mechanisms

The following points highlight the lack of explicit causal reasoning and falsifiable mechanisms that putatively undermine the scientific validity of much of the extant factor investing literature:

- **Lack of why.** Authors typically do not identify the causal graph consistent with observed phenomena, justify model specifications based on correlations, or propose experiments to falsify causal mechanisms. This means factor investing studies fail to explain *why* observed phenomena occur, leaving investors without a scientific basis for understanding performance. While most factor investing studies rely on correlations and lack causal justification, several notable exceptions challenge this critique. For example, Lettau and Ludvigson (2001) link factor returns to macroeconomic risk through the consumption–wealth ratio, offering a structural explanation for time-varying risk-premia. Behavioral models by Barberis et al. (1998) and Daniel et al. (1998) propose testable psychological mechanisms behind momentum and reversal effects. More recently, Gu et al. (2020) apply ML in ways that can support causal interpretation when combined with economic theory.

- **Unfalsifiable explanations.** Proposed economic rationales for factors often lack the rigor of scientific theories because they don't declare causal relationships, elucidate ideal interventional studies, or propose methods to estimate causal effects from observational data, rendering them experimentally unfalsifiable. Finance isn't an exact science, and markets are influenced by complex, adaptive behavior, examples stated in the previous list item show that it is still possible to build theories that go beyond descriptive correlations, offering clear predictions that can be evaluated, and potentially refuted through observation.

12.3.3. Proliferation of Spurious Claims (False Discoveries)

López de Prado categorizes spurious claims into two types, which prevent factor investing from advancing scientifically.

- Type-A spuriosity (false association/noise mistaken for signal):
  - **P-hacking.** Researchers make numerous subjective decisions when building models (e.g., data cleaning, variable choice, dates) and often run multiple regressions, reporting minimal *p*-values without adjusting for selection bias. This practice is compounded by publication bias, leading to many claimed findings being likely false and the results not being replicable out of sample.
  - **Back-test overfitting.** Historical simulations (backtests) are presented as evidence of causal effects but are neither controlled experiments nor natural experiments. It is trivial to overfit a back-test through selection bias, making it hard to distinguish signal from noise.
- Type-B spuriosity (true but noncausal associations due to specification errors):
  - **Undercontrolling (missing confounders).** Omitting relevant confounding variables biases factor estimates, leading to incorrect performance attribution, poor risk management, and the appearance of time-varying risk-premia, misleading investors.
  - **Overcontrolling (controlling for mediators or colliders).** Including variables that should *not* be controlled for (like mediators or colliders) that distort total effects and open noncausal paths of association, biasing estimates and leading to time-varying risk-premia. This is the deadliest sin in causal inference.
  - **Specification searching.** Choosing model specifications based on explanatory power (e.g., higher R-squared – an associational concept) rather than on a predefined causal graph or specified causal graph that leads to factor mirages.

12.3.4. Poor Performance and Lack of Transparency

The following points examine the empirical shortcomings and transparency challenges often raised against factor investing strategies, while also acknowledging notable counterexamples:

- **Disappointing out-of-sample performance.** Despite academic claims, broad multifactor indices have shown statistically insignificant Sharpe ratios over long periods, especially when considering transaction costs and fees. The QUMN index published by TMX is a counterexample to this claim. It has delivered strong performance (gross of fees), finishing at over three times the initial value in under seven years, while benefiting from interest earned on the short proceeds and after commissions. Further broad, rules-based multifactor indexes (e.g., MSCI Diversified Multiple-Factor, S&P Quality, Value & Momentum) have delivered positive long-run Sharpe ratios in multiple regions. It is therefore too strong to state that such indexes have "statistically insignificant Sharpe ratios over long periods."
- **Black box nature.** The lack of declared causal graphs and mechanisms makes factor investing strategies black boxes. This contradicts scientific principles and fiduciary duties. A direct counterexample would be vanilla Multifactor models (MFMs), like QMIT's Val+Mom (GARP). These are clearly not black boxes since the ingredients are transparent and the performance rather easy to explain based on the underperformance of specific factors like Value. One straightforward explanation is that the zero-interest rate policy and subsequent aggressive fiscal stimulus during the COVID period encouraged investors to seek higher yields thereby fueling speculative behavior and risk-taking in markets. Indeed, vanilla MFMs (e.g., value + momentum + quality) implemented

by index providers that publish transparent rules and weights are interpretable even without explicit causal graphs. Further, US fiduciary standards require advisors to act in clients' best interest and provide full and fair disclosure. They do not mandate causal diagrams per se.

Two recurring risks in associational workflows are confounding and collider bias, which can distort effect estimates and lead to false discoveries even when back-tests look strong. This critique is central to López de Prado's "factor mirage" argument. One can go a step further to be prescriptive since in this fledging field there are no clear answers yet. Given the paucity of established protocols, López de Prado and Zoonekynd (2025) advance a seven-step causal protocol for factor investing in their recent working paper: (1) data-driven variable selection via non-parametric/ML tools, (2) causal-graph construction guided by discovery algorithms and economic logic, (3) identification via valid adjustment sets (backdoor criteria), (4) testing causal *and* predictive power (e.g., double ML), (5) portfolio construction aligned with estimated causal effects, (6) walk-forward and Monte-Carlo back-tests to gauge robustness, and (7) multiple-testing corrections (e.g., DSR/Holm) to control false discoveries. The aim is to reduce misspecification and improve interpretability and OOS resilience.

Overall, although interesting perspectives have been presented in favor of a causal framework, there is limited practical value and insufficient justification for requiring factor investing to adopt a strictly causal approach. Given the probabilistic, adaptive nature of financial markets, predictive usefulness and economic intuition often carry more weight than formal causal identification. For many investors, the ability to generate robust, repeatable signals is more important than establishing cause-and-effect relationships.

12.3.5. End-to-End Causal Factor Pipeline

The criticisms surrounding the lack of a systematic and scalable method for causal discovery have spurred innovation in automated protocols. For instance, the integration of LLMs into the DAG discovery process was recently explored (Sokolov et al., 2025). Historically, identifying true causal relationships – as opposed to mere correlation – has required intensive, subjective expert judgment to build the DAGs that guide factor models. This new framework effectively automates that expertise by leveraging the vast, implicit "world knowledge" of LLMs. The process breaks down the traditionally complex, data-driven challenge into a series of LLM-assisted steps: first, the LLM clusters large sets of financial features into smaller, manageable groups; second, it iteratively generates and validates causal edges within and between these groups, using techniques like chain-of-thought prompting to ensure logical coherence. This innovation significantly scales the applicability of causal discovery, making it feasible for the high-dimensional, nonlinear environment of financial markets.

Furthermore, these automated causal models are not merely theoretical constructs but empirically validated using sophisticated quantitative techniques that mirror the rigorous protocols advocated in the literature. The initial LLM-derived DAGs, which represent the hypothesized relationships among factors, are refined through a statistical lens. Specifically, the framework applies Do-calculus[1] to observational data to assign a significance value to each proposed causal link, pruning those that lack statistical

[1] Do-calculus, introduced by Judea Pearl, is a set of mathematical rules for reasoning about cause-and-effect relationships in probabilistic models. It enables researchers to distinguish between mere correlations and true causal effects by analyzing interventions. These rules enable converting observational data into causal conclusions when certain graphical conditions are met.

support. This is followed by a robust feature selection and validation step using Lasso regression, which dynamically reinforces the identified causal structure within a back-testing environment. Professor Luis Seco of the University of Toronto and the Fields Institute has been a proponent of such an end-to-end framework that moves beyond simple correlation-based models, offering a systematic path toward building more robust and explainable investment strategies based on actual cause and effect.

12.4. CAUSALITY WITH QMIT ESBs AND COMBO SIGNALS[2]

In this research, we focus on causal discovery on different ESB used by QMIT based on six years of daily data from 2019 to 2024. Causal discovery, also referred to as causal learning or structure learning, is the process of inferring causal structures from observational data.

To explore causal relations among the 18 ESB variables, we used DAGitty (Textor et al., 2016) to specify and analyze DAGs. In each specification we designated exposures and an outcome and used DAGitty to derive minimal valid adjustment sets for identification; numerical effect estimation was then performed outside DAGitty using the suggested covariate sets. For structure learning we applied the PC algorithm in dedicated discovery software and treated the learned graph as hypothesis-generating, pending domain review.

A confounder causes both the treatment and the outcome. In the DAG underlying Figure 12.1, variables such as [ART/MOM/RV]* were identified (by the learned/specified graph) as potential confounders of the Value Momentum composite

[2] Thanks to our interns Lorena Rodriguez Pineda and Shih-hung Wang for their key contributions to this section.

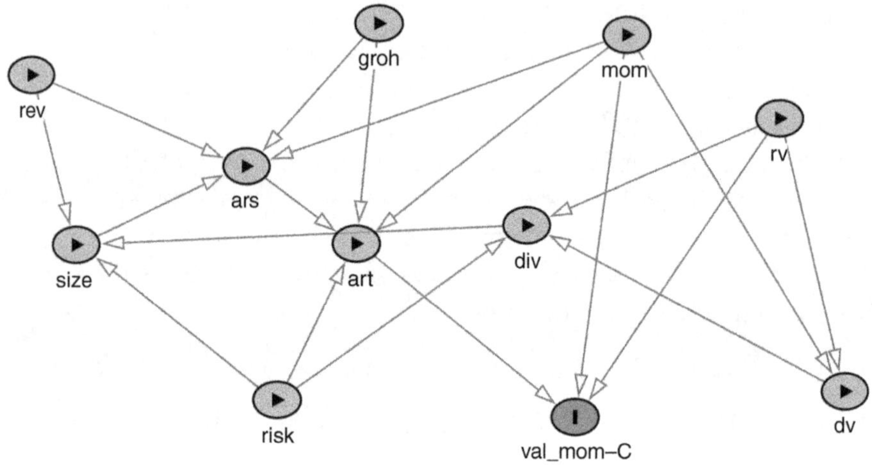

Figure 12.1 Estimating Causal Graph with PC Algorithm; Ten Covariates and Outcome Value Momentum Composite (val_mom_C).

(val_mom_C) and, per the graph, also had direct arrows into the outcome. Confounding bias occurs when unblocked backdoor paths link treatment and outcome; DAGitty's adjustment set analysis is designed to block such paths if the DAG is correct. This bias tends to "confound our reading" and distort the estimate of the effect being studied. In our case the paths are correctly accounted for, so there are no spurious associations or backdoor paths between covariates and the value momentum composite index.

A collider is a node with two arrows pointing into it (e.g., $X \rightarrow Z \leftarrow Y$). Conditioning on a collider or its descendants opens a noncausal path and induces bias. In our graph, nodes such as [ARS/ART/SIZE/DIV/DV] were flagged as colliders; avoiding adjustment for these nodes (and their descendants) prevents collider bias. Note that collider parents are independent only absent other open paths – a property that must be verified in the full DAG. None of these is downstream of the dependent value momentum composite variable (since val_mom_C, which has no descendants), so there are no spurious paths or collider bias in our example.

We can also identify different mediators in our example as per Figure 12.1. A variable Z is a mediator when it lies on the causal path between X and Y, meaning X causes Z, and Z causes Y ($X \rightarrow Z \rightarrow Y$). For example, ART is a mediator in the causal path from Historical Growth (GROH) → ART → val_mom_C and RISK → ART → Value Momentum composite (val_mom_C).

Additionally, there are common causes in the system. For instance, MOM is a confounder for DV, ART, ARS, and the Value Momentum composite (val_mom_C). Identifying and adjusting for such common causes is crucial toward avoiding bias in causal estimates.

While effective, the standard PC algorithm can fail in the presence of hidden (unobserved) variables, such as SIRF and QUAL. In light of the multicollinearity documented in Chapter 3, Section 3.8, we choose to omit the six ESBs components of QUAL, which may well and likely be confounders in this picture, but we did so deliberately in order to get a cleaner DAG. In Section 12.5, we provide a technical description of both the PC and LiNGAM algorithms.

12.5. PC AND LiNGAM ALGORITHMS[3]

We consider two widely used algorithms for causal discovery, PC, which is an independence-based method and LiNGAM, which is a more recent approach to exploit information about the joint distribution beyond conditional independencies. The functionality of these methods rests on key assumptions about the relationship between graphical structures and probability distributions.

[3] Thanks to our interns Lorena Rodriguez Pineda and Shih-hung Wang for their key contributions to this section.

The most foundational of these is the causal Markov condition. This condition provides the crucial link between the graph's structure in Figure 12.1 and the data's statistical properties, asserting that any variable is conditionally independent of its non-descendants given its direct causes (or "parents"). In essence, it enables us to read causal assumptions from a graph and translate them into statements about statistical independence. This principle is what empowers algorithms like PC to infer the causal graph from observational data. A complementary assumption is faithfulness, which posits the reverse: that all conditional independencies in the data correspond to graphical separations (*d*-separation), ensuring that the statistical relationships are a true reflection of the underlying causal structure.

The primary goal of the PC algorithm is to estimate the correct Markov equivalence class of the underlying DAG, which is partially directed graph compatible with the observed conditional independences. This means it aims to identify graphical structures that represent the same set of conditional independences.

Assumptions for the PC algorithm. It assumes that the observed data distribution is Markovian and faithful with respect to the underlying DAG.

- The Markov condition relates conditional independence in the distribution to graphical separation statements (*d*-separation) in the graph.
- Faithfulness implies a one-to-one correspondence between *d*-separation statements in the graph and conditional independence statements in the distribution.

PC algorithm mechanism:

1. Start with a fully connected undirected graph (Figure 12.2).
2. Step-by-step removes edges by checking for conditional independence between pairs of variables. For each pair of nodes (X, Y), it searches for a set of other variables (A) that *d*-separates them (i.e., renders them conditionally independent given A). If such a set is found, the edge between X and Y is removed. The size of the conditioning set A is incrementally increased, starting from zero (order-0). By applying the Fisher *z*-test we get:

Order-0 (Marginal independence):

a. mom_C and val_C – *p*-value = 0.131 → Fail to reject H_0 → likely independent, edge removal. Even though mom_C and val_mom_C are positively correlated with Pearson and Spearman correlation coefficients of 0.59 and 0.55, respectively, the *p*-value is not statistically significant to reject the null hypothesis.
b. QUMN and val_C – *p*-value ≈ 1e-118 → Reject H_0 → dependent
c. QUMN and mom_C – *p*-value ≈ 1e-49 → Reject H_0 → dependent

Order-1 (Conditional independence):

a. val_C ⊥ mom_C | QUMN – *p*-value ≈ 1e-31 → Reject H_0 → dependent
b. QUMN ⊥ mom_C | val_C – *p*-value ≈ 1e-78 → Reject H_0 → dependent
c. QUMN ⊥ val_C | mom_C – *p*-value ≈ 1e-148 → Reject H_0 → dependent

3. After identifying adjacencies based on conditional independencies, it orients edges where possible to form a

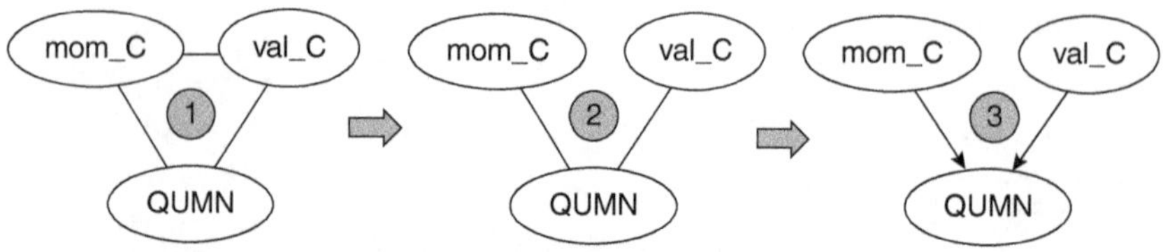

Figure 12.2 A Simple Example Using the PC Algorithm.

partially directed graph as per Figure 12.2. PC looks at the triplet {mom_C, QUMN, val_C}, finding that mom_C and val_C are not adjacent. Then, the PC checks whether the middle node was in the separating set used to remove the edge from mom_C to val_C. Since mom_C and val_C were found to be independent without conditioning (empty set), the separator did not include QUMN. This means we can orient it as a collider.

LiNGAM is a model class and an associated algorithm for causal discovery that specifically exploits the non-Gaussian characteristics of the noise terms. Importantly, LiNGAM always outputs directed edges, identifying the direction of causality between variables.

Purpose. LiNGAM aims to distinguish between cause and effect (causal directionality) directly from observational data, even in the bivariate case where traditional conditional independence tests are not useful.

Assumptions. The algorithm is built on three core assumptions:

- **Linearity.** Each variable is a linear function of its direct causes. While usually not true in real life, it is also an assumption of linear MFMs in factor investing.
- **Non-Gaussian, independent noise.** The error terms are mutually independent and follow a non-Gaussian

distribution. This assumption is critical for identifying the true causal direction.

- **Causal sufficiency.** All common causes of the observed variables are included in the dataset (i.e., no hidden confounders).

Additionally, these core assumptions imply the following:

- Causal Markov condition is automatically satisfied under the assumption of independent noise, which implies that each variable is conditionally independent of its non-descendants given its direct causes. This condition is fundamental for applying Do-calculus, as it enables us to factorize the joint distribution into local causal mechanisms. In the context of our LiNGAM model, satisfying the Markov condition means that causal relationships among the selected variables can be represented and manipulated algebraically, providing the foundation for interventional reasoning.
- Faithfulness assumption is automatically satisfied in LiNGAM because non-Gaussian noise prevents path cancellations, avoiding coincidental independence and ensuring that observed statistical dependencies reflect true causal relationships.

These properties make LiNGAM identifiable from the joint distribution and robust in distinguishing $X \rightarrow Y$ from $Y \rightarrow X$.

Here's how it works:

1. **Core principle – exploiting non-Gaussian noise for identifiability.** Consider a simple linear causal model $X \rightarrow Y$ with an additive noise term: $Y = aX + e_Y$, where e_Y is an independent noise term. If e_Y follows a non-Gaussian distribution and is independent of X, then the model is

identifiable – meaning we can determine the correct causal direction from observational data alone. By contrast, with Gaussian noise, $X \to Y$ and $Y \to X$ produce identical statistical dependencies, making the direction unidentifiable without further assumptions.

2. **Independent component analysis (ICA) decomposition.** For multivariate data, LiNGAM assumes: $x = Bx + e$ where B encodes the causal structure and e are independent non-Gaussian noise terms. By rearranging: $x = (I - B)^{-1}e$. This is a linear ICA model, where the goal is to recover both the mixing matrix $(I - B)^{-1}$ and the independent components e. ICA finds a decomposition such that the recovered components are statistically independent – crucial for identifying the order of variables and causal edges.

3. **Testing residual independence for causal direction.** In the bivariate case, LiNGAM compares two regression models:
(1) regress Y on X, obtain residuals e_Y, and check if $e_Y \perp X$
(2) regress X on Y, obtain residuals e_X, and check if $e_X \perp Y$
The correct causal direction is the one where the residuals are independent of the predictor. In the multivariate setting, LiNGAM finds an ordering of variables that satisfies the independence condition for all regressions, producing a fully DAG.

4. **Why it works.** The key is that non-Gaussian independent errors break the symmetry of linear regression, enabling one direction to produce independent residuals while the reverse does not. This property holds even with small samples or just two variables, making LiNGAM effective in domains like factor investing, where datasets may have high correlations and limited sample sizes.

Identifiability. Under the assumptions of linearity and non-Gaussian additive noise, the causal graph structure is identifiable from the joint distribution.

Randomness. While LiNGAM provides a principled framework for causal discovery, its output may vary across runs due to the randomness introduced by ICA. ICA algorithms typically involve iterative optimization methods that rely on random initializations and can converge to different local optima, especially when the data is high-dimensional or weakly non-Gaussian. Consequently, the inferred causal ordering or edge directions may differ across runs, even on the same dataset. To address this, it is common practice to use multiple random seeds, bootstrapping (resampling with replacement), or ensemble methods to evaluate the robustness of the estimated causal structure and identify consistently appearing edges.

We first applied the LiNGAM model to the 18 ESBs along with the QUMN EMN hedge fund index as the outcome, as shown in Figure 12.3. The resulting causal graph looks plausible, suggesting that QUMN was the outcome of a series of causal influences from those ESBs. However, this result was based on a single run and is sensitive to the randomness inherent in ICA. Moreover, the presence of highly collinear variables (as documented in Chapter 3, Section 3.8) – such as EnMom and MOM – violates the model's assumptions and may compromise the reliability of the inferred causal structure.

To address the issues of randomness and collinearity, we applied a bootstrap approach and narrowed our analysis to QUMN and a subset of eight variables (as per Chapter 3, Section 3.8) – SIRF, rev, size, mom_c, div, val_c, risk, qual_c – for which collinearity was reasonably under control.

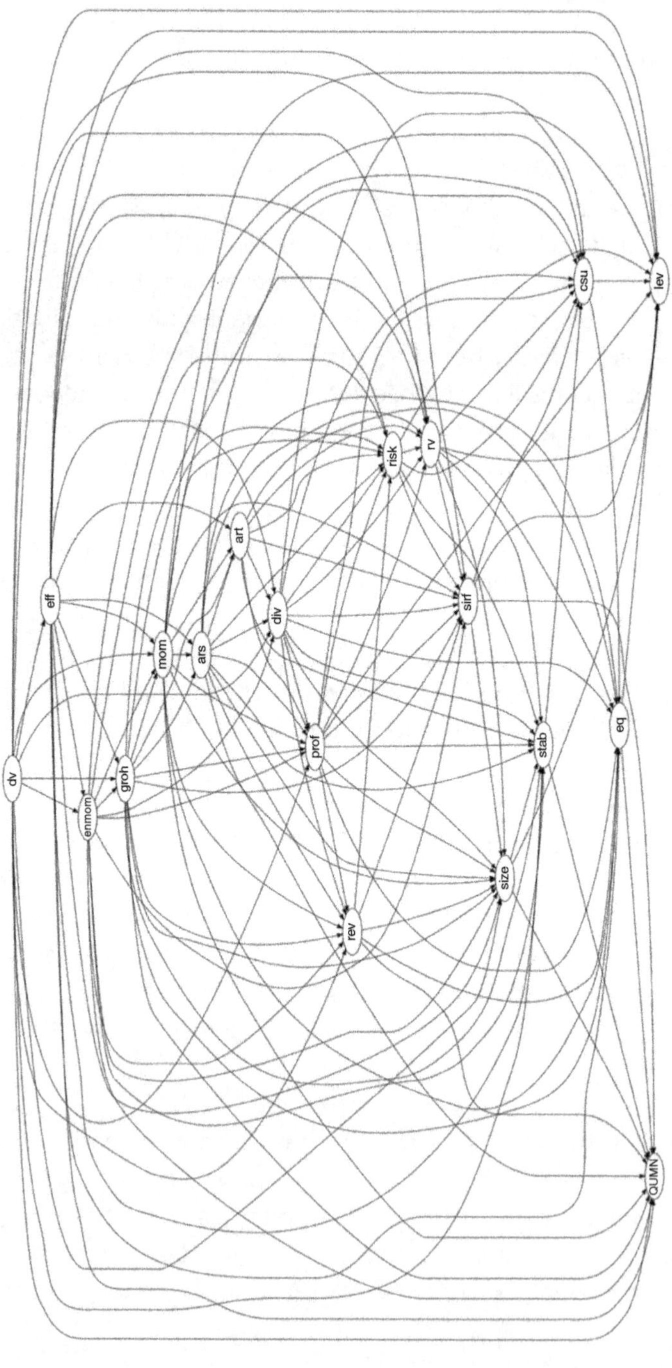

Figure 12.3 Example of a LiNGAM Causal Graph from a Single Run with 18 ESBs.

We performed 1,000 bootstrap trials, generating 1,000 causal graphs using the LiNGAM model. To ensure robustness, we retained only those edges that appeared in more than 70% of the runs, forming the final causal graph.

Figure 12.4 presents four representative causal graphs generated during the bootstrap procedure, illustrating the randomness introduced by the ICA method. Notably, some trials produced opposite causal directions for the same pair of variables – for example, edges between size and risk appeared in both directions. This highlights the importance

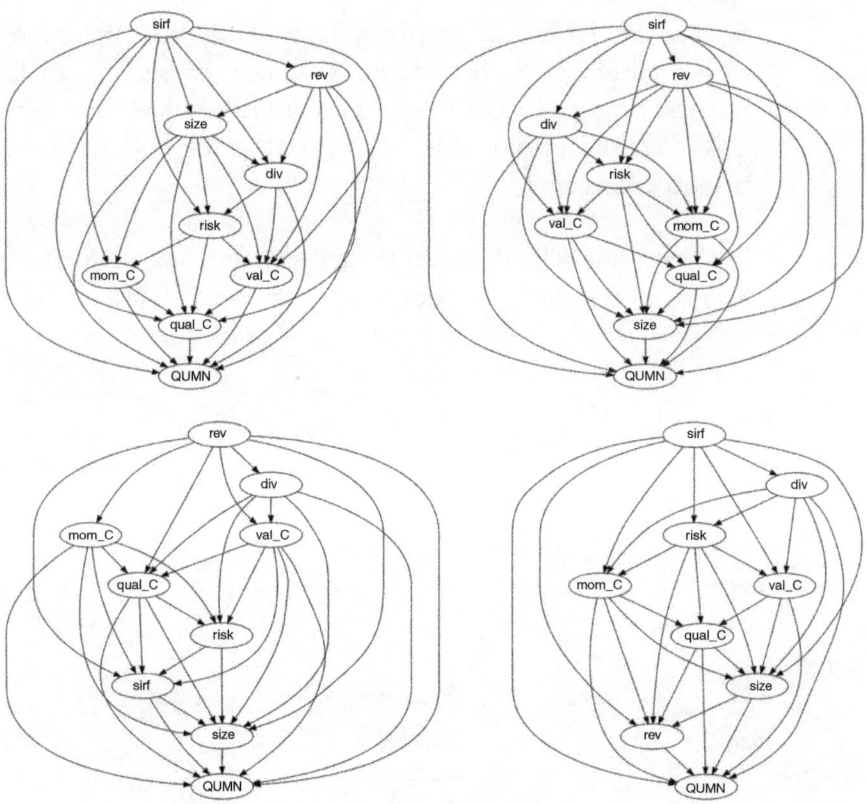

Figure 12.4 Representative LiNGAM Causal Graphs with Eight Explanatory Variables.

of using the bootstrap approach to filter out unstable edges and retain only statistically robust causal relationships.

Figure 12.5 summarizes the 1,000 bootstrap trials, retaining only edges that appeared with a frequency greater than 70%. The graph suggests that QUMN is directly influenced by rev, mom_c, val_c, and qual_c, while val_c itself is a common effect (collider) of div and risk. Additionally, qual_c is directly influenced by risk, indicating that risk-related factors may have both direct and indirect effects on QUMN through multiple pathways. In this structure, rev may act as a potential confounder for the relationship between size and QUMN, as it causally affects both. Notably, SIRF does not appear in the final graph, indicating that its connections were either weak or unstable across bootstrap trials. Recognizing such colliders and confounders is essential for correctly interpreting the causal pathways and avoiding biased inferences.

In summary, unlike PC algorithms that infer causal structures from conditional independence patterns, LiNGAM exploits

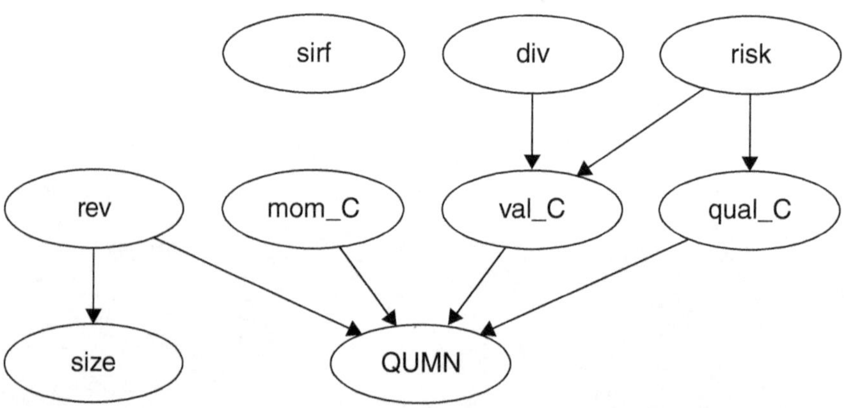

Figure 12.5 LiNGAM Causal Graph Retaining Edges with >70% Bootstrap Frequency.

the non-Gaussian nature of noise in linear models to directly identify causal directions. This property makes it especially powerful for determining cause-effect relationships, even in settings with only two variables or relatively small sample sizes, as demonstrated in Figure 12.5.

In the context of factor investing, such capability is particularly valuable for uncovering directional relationships among factors, helping distinguish true predictive signals from spurious correlations. Interestingly, Figure 12.5 supports the demotion of size as espoused by Douglas Martin and others of late. SIRF is an island to itself, relevant largely for risk and hedging purposes but not central to the causal alpha picture as it pertains to our archetypal EMN construct as embodied by the QUMN index. Risk (low volatility) turns out to have both direct and indirect effects on QUMN through multiple pathways for which the causality goes through the value and quality composite mediators as is the case for dividends (DIV) through value. The key ingredients of QUMN EMN returns (by construction) such as the Value, Momentum, and Quality composites with a dash of mean reversion (REV) in the mix, completes a clean and concise causal picture (Figure 12.5), which reinforces the author's intuition behind the construction of the flagship composite MFM as the alpha underlying QUMN.

12.6. CRITIQUE OF THE CRITIQUE

In this section, we offer a rebuttal to the causal necessity literature as described in Section 12.3. Recall, that López de Prado argues that factor investing must be rebuilt on explicitly causal foundations to avoid factor mirages arising from collider/confounder bias, advocating protocols for causal discovery in lieu of traditional associational approaches (e.g., López de Prado, 2023, 2024). The counter-position offered next maintains that while establishing causality is valuable where feasible, strict causal linkage is not a necessary condition for successful factor investing and alpha generation, as demonstrated throughout this book. Prediction-first workflows – properly validated and transparently risk managed – remain defensible and often lead to superior outcomes in live trading given non-stationarity, low signal to noise, and behavioral feedback loops in markets.

- **Practical predictive success of associational models.** Many traditional factor models, though associational and not rigorously causal, still do have a demonstrated history of live out-of-sample utility as per the QMIT live alphas presented in this book as well as the live performance of the Merrill Lynch Large Cap series funds,[4] which won many accolades from Morningstar, Lipper, and the *Wall Street Journal* due to double digit outperformance against benchmarks through the first five years from inception. Prominent quant firms have generally delivered risk-adjusted returns in excess of their fundamental brethren as opposed to the cherry-picked example of mediocrity in the paper. Indeed, practitioners would argue that prediction not perfect causal identification is paramount for investment returns. If a given factor (e.g., Value or Momentum) provides live outperformance (despite regime-based cyclicality), its predictive and practical utility can be more important than establishing a mechanistic causal link. Besides, for the quantamental portfolio manager this is still an academic debate as no feasible solutions exist based on the causal framework.

[4] Based on the author's experience as the quant for these funds under Bob Doll's stewardship (who was the senior portfolio manager) up until the author's departure from the firm in mid-2004, roughly corresponding to the first five years.

Normative critiques without prescriptive remedies are of little use to practitioners who do not have the luxury of indulging ivory tower debates.

- **Empirical finance's epistemic limits.** In real-world finance, perfect causal discovery may often be infeasible due to unobservable confounders, complexity of market dynamics, and nonstationary regimes not to mention the paucity of long-term factor history in most markets for testing purposes. Even sophisticated causal inference techniques may not fully overcome these empirical limitations, raising the question as to whether the imposition of contrived scientific standards from the physical sciences are appropriate in a social science driven by behavioral anomalies.
- **Natural experiments and interventions are rare.** Unlike in laboratory sciences, one cannot easily conduct controlled experiments in finance; interventions are often hypothetical or untestable. Critics question whether causal graphical models and do-calculus deliver meaningfully actionable improvement over well-calibrated statistical (associational) approaches under real-world constraints.
- **Economic theory and plausible explanations.** The existing body of factor literature posits that economic plausibility (risk-based or behavioral and other justifications for factor efficacy) and robustness across subsamples, instruments, and geographies should suffice, in practice, over strict formal causality.
- **Complexity risks with causal models.** Be careful what you wish for. The complexity associated with causal models could lead the practitioner from the frying pan into the fire in an empirical field already plagued by small sample issues, nonstationarity, p-hacking and a rapidly proliferating factor zoo.

- **Scientific progress without full causality.** Other scientific domains (e.g., astronomy) have advanced with careful empirical modeling and prediction, despite the inability to manipulate variables directly and establish strict causality. After all astronomers cannot even directly observe a contemporaneous cross-section of the universe but only a temporal slice visible from galaxies that existed billions of years in the past. Arguably finance, too, can make meaningful advances without a strict causal framework provided there is transparency about the methodological limitations.
- **Black box.** Arguably factor investing (especially as typified by the DAG in Figure 12.5) is anything but a black box. It's a fairly translucent box that can be fully transparent (certainly in the case of simpler models like Fama-French [FF]3 or FF4 or FF5) given adequate descriptors of the raw factors underlying our ESB ensembles as provided in this book. This is quite the antithesis of the fundamental portfolio manager's psyche, which is a complete black box despite their ability to spin an attributional yarn for every outcome which is strangely palliative to investors in a drawdown. Historically, non-quants often dismissed quantamental as being a black box. In the age of artificial intelligence (with trillions of parameters), that excuse may wear thin.

The application of causality in finance has sparked much debate but specifically applying causal discovery to factor investing is still a fledgling field with few refereed publications . A central counterargument in this discussion is that demonstrating the failure of simple linear factor models is insufficient. Factor investing is no longer limited to linear models, particularly given the applications of ML. For a more balanced perspective we note (not as an endorsement of this yet to be published working paper) the more recent rebuttal by Alejandro Rodríguez Domínguez (2025); in such a fledgling field both sides have yet to be robustly debated:

Directional informativeness. This is the paper's central, proposed criterion. It posits that for a predictive signal to be useful in portfolio construction it doesn't need to come from a causally perfect model. Instead, it primarily needs to be "directionally aligned" with the true expected returns, meaning it correctly identifies whether an asset's expected return is positive or negative.

Signal calibration and sizing. Beyond directionality, the paper acknowledges that the magnitude (or "sizing") of the signal matters. A directionally correct signal that is poorly calibrated (i.e., its magnitude doesn't accurately reflect the magnitude of the expected return) will lead to a suboptimal, though still potentially viable, portfolio as the outcome.

Valid and convex efficient frontiers. The paper demonstrates, both theoretically and empirically, that even signals from mis-specified models can produce smooth, convex, and non-degenerate mean variance efficient frontiers, contradicting claims that such frontiers would "collapse." To summarize the key findings which have yet to be published with wide acceptance by the quant finance community:

- Causal identifiability is *sufficient* but *not necessary*: mis-specified predictive models often remain usable when their signals are directionally aligned.
- Calibration is essential, even with correct signs, wrong magnitudes lower efficiency.
- Sharpe ratio and frontier quality deteriorate *gradually* as alignment weakens; no catastrophic "signal inversion" is observed.

- Quant managers can continue to rely on well-validated predictive signals without proving causality, provided they monitor alignment and calibration.

To synopsize, while López de Prado and others highlight the dangers of mis-attributing causality and the risk of spurious factors due to confounding/collider bias, skeptics contend that (1) association-based models may have greater practical validity, (2) financial markets pose unique challenges for strict causal reasoning, and (3) live predictive efficacy should ultimately be the arbiter by which factor models ought to be judged.

Finally, for what it's worth, the LiNGAM output in Figure 12.5 confirms that our EMN hedge fund construct (QUMN index) does indeed have causal antecedents[5] in the key pillars of factor investing – for example, QMIT's Value, Growth-Momentum, Quality, and mean reversion composite alphas. Indeed, I have been delivering on live alphas in the factor investing realm for decades without having had the luxury of a DAG to provide any such reassurance. Nice to know but in the rough-and-tumble world of ever-changing markets – money managers may not have the luxury of enough data to engage in ivory tower debates about causality before pressing their bets. For most practitioners, the nascent causal critique and unproven rebuttal may seem like a tempest in a teapot. But it'd be best to reserve judgment till robust debate leads to a broader consensus in the quantitative finance community, which clearly does not exist as of yet.

Existential crisis or a tempest in a teapot: you be the judge.

---

[5] Subject to the model assumptions of linearity, acyclicity, non-Gaussian shocks, no hidden confounders, and so on.

Chapter 13

Singularity and the Agentic Future

13.1. AGENTIC AI AND THE AGE OF ABUNDANCE

With the release of GPT-5 (which scored a gold on the IMO (International Mathematical Olympiad) not to mention saturating most other benchmarks except for Humanity's Last Exam[1]) and other frontier models we are now clearly on the precipice of AGI (artificial general intelligence). Based on

[1] Humanity's Last Exam is a comprehensive, expert-curated evaluation designed to measure advanced reasoning and problem-solving capabilities across multiple academic disciplines. It aims to assess the depth, generality, and transferability of an AI system's knowledge beyond conventional benchmark tasks.

any notion of AGI (pre-2022) we have already blown past it and are well on our way to ASI (artificial superintelligence).

AGI entails a level of intelligence that matches or surpasses human capabilities across virtually all cognitive tasks. Unlike narrow AI, which is designed for specific tasks (think DeepMind's AlphaFold for protein folding), AGI can generalize knowledge, transfer skills between different domains, and solve novel problems without needing task-specific programming. AGI systems are expected to be able to reason, learn, plan, use strategy, communicate in natural language, and integrate these skills to complete any given goal, similar to human intelligence. While the latest large language models (LLMs) do check many of these boxes as early forms of emerging AGI, true AGI with full human-level breadth and proficiency has not yet been realized of this writing in August 2025.

It would be rather disingenuous for one not to acknowledge the elephant in the room, meaning that the AI juggernaut remains unstoppable (acing Math Olympiads from scratch in just a couple of months and even proving "new mathematics") with gargantuan implications for humanity while the naysayers fixate on silly errors ("jagged intelligence") relating to counting the number of *r*s in strawberry. The pace of innovation has gone truly exponential. Futurists like Peter Diamandis and Ray Kurzweil (not to mention the Magnificent Seven cognoscenti) speak of the age of abundance resulting from AGI within three to five years and Singularity[2] soon thereafter. The coming onslaught of AI will likely wipe out most of knowledge work as we know it today once the explicit cost of intelligence asymptotes to zero. Indeed, soon access to intelligence will be bounded only by

---

[2] The Singularity refers to a hypothetical point in the future when AI surpasses human intelligence so dramatically that technological progress accelerates beyond human comprehension or control.

the cost of energy and not hardware, software, or human capital as machines learn to self-improve and multiple scaling laws kick in. The societal implications of widescale disruption of white-collar work and resulting unemployment are staggering in a country with over 400 million guns in private hands for obvious reasons given the level of polarization and since there are no societal shock absorbers to deal with potentially high levels of unemployment and psychological distress. The philosophical ramifications are dramatic and disconcerting not just in the United States but also in the world at large, which is rife with inequality. AGI will disintermediate the vast majority of workers (both white and blue collar) while minting a handful of trillionaires. The optimists are gleeful about "winner takes all" scenarios, which will incinerate the social fabric and the social contract. Unequal access will create a two-tier society with a much greater dispersion of outcomes for those off the grid than what we saw in the internet age. This much was quite clear to me at the ChatGPT moment in 2022 when I couldn't sleep for a week as I feverishly tried to work through the far-reaching ramifications of the inevitable race toward AGI. Having worked on old school AI (expert systems) in the 1990s, the political and cybersecurity implications of this new AI race were quite clear although I had not being paying close attention even after the AlexNet moment of 2012.[3] While the AlexNet moment is credited with triggering the modern deep-learning boom in computer vision, the world had to wait until the seminal concoction of the "transformers" architecture at Google with its unique attention mechanism, which when run at massive scale enables "stochastic next word parrots" to become intelligent machines. Such

[3]That was when the SuperVision team (Alex Krizhevsky, Ilya Sutskever, Geoffrey Hinton) submitted AlexNet to the ImageNet Large Scale Visual Recognition Challenge (ILSVRC-2012) and achieved a top-five error of 15.3 %, more than 10 percentage points better than the next best entry.

were the double descent benefits to the loss function that resulted in the vaunted "emergent" properties that no one had really anticipated or predicted.

Ray Kurzweil defines the Singularity as the point (which he dates to around 2045) when machine intelligence surpasses the sum of all human intelligence and then *merges* with it, triggering a "profound and disruptive transformation in human capability." Kurzweil's timeline includes achieving human-level AI about 2029, leading up to the full Singularity by 2045 at which point, the speed of technological change will appear "virtually infinite" to unenhanced humans, making life beyond that "event horizon" impossible to model or predict (by definition). This dire prognosis continues to be borne out by a rudderless, leaderless world unable to frame policies to comprehend or keep up with radical disruption. Yes, this time is indeed different and it's not akin to the industrial revolution or the advent of electricity, which disrupted some jobs but created others in its wake. By definition, once this race culminates in some company and country attaining ASI then the human race will have lost control of its own destiny, and we better hope that our exponentially smarter AI overlords choose to be nice to us. But they don't have to and there is no reason to believe that they will be because "alignment" is not in the objective function.

We are talking about intelligence far superior to that of humankind, which renders knowledge work by humans largely pointless. In such a dramatically disruptive future it's difficult to game out what if any parts of our current linear path from fundamental to quantamental will remain relevant. Will all of traditional education be moot in short order? Will universities survive? Will there be any point to knowledge acquisition once AI can cure all diseases, solve all of mathematics and physics, and find abundant sources of energy? AI certainly has the potential to cure many ills plaguing humanity if it doesn't wipe out humanity first. Such sweeping philosophical ruminations are well beyond the scope of this modest endeavor but let me hazard a guess as to what the current implications for investing are. Clearly, another killer app like quantum supremacy could come along and result in a winner-takes-all scenario where certain incumbents (think Citadel or Renaissance) could harness technological supremacy wiping out other market participants barring regulation to level the playing field. The quantum threat to cryptography could result in bitcoin and cryptos going to zero. It would also pose significant cybersecurity risks to "TradFi" banking. Further, it could unleash an extreme version of the high-frequency trading hardware arms race that has led to the dominance of a few market makers like Citadel and Jane Street.

Let's stick to AI for now and worry about quantum once there are enough qubits to pose an immediate threat. In many ways, the agentic future replete with AI agents does not look terribly different – at least from an investing standpoint. It is true that derivatives pricing, hedging, intraday algorithms, and so on are being rewritten to harness advancements in AI. No doubt, even middle, back-office, legal, human resources, and other firmwide efficiencies will result from applications of AI. *But would Charlie Munger care?* Long-term owners (shareholders) of a business may harness AI to maximize profit margins but are unlikely to act any differently. And not just due to real-world frictions like taxes and transactions costs. Over time we have seen bank execution desks shrink to a shadow of their former selves driven by the commoditization of execution algorithms. Indeed, such operational efficiencies will continue unabated as AI dramatically multiplies the productivity of each investment professional and automates much of the research done by analysts today. As of this writing Claude can produce an automated stock DCF (discounted cash flow) model in a matter of minutes thereby replacing junior investment bankers. It can also produce pitch decks in a flash. Arguably, agentic workflows can automate every part of the buy side and sell side that is amenable to process-driven automation. But, if we step back to reexamine this claim carefully in the context of asset management, the shocking revelation to the casual observer would be that this is *exactly what quantamental investing has been doing all along for the past three decades.* As someone who has been a huge proponent of riding that wave of automation, it's clear to me that we've always been inserting the quintessential "human in the loop" intentional road bumps while automating every subroutine along the way. In the realm of mid- to low-frequency factor investing, where one is severely limited by the paucity of data, it remains to be seen whether AI can bring earth-shattering insights to bear. Skepticism is warranted. Much of the benefit that can be leveraged from AI come from higher-frequency data in the context of natural language processing (NLP)-based sentiment, instantaneous Fed and earnings call sentiment, and so on. But such applications already predated transformers and are discussed in Chapter 11 along with QMIT-specific applications. Such forecasts based on GPT are arguably superior today as the much simpler bag-of-words type of technology (or even FinBERT [finance-specialized BERT classifier]) is now obsolete. We describe the new LLM-age superseding agentic solution in this chapter (Section 13.8). That said, most real money accounts are unlikely to flip their positions and investment theses based on sentiment that typically has a 24- to 48-hour half-life. As I have argued for the past decade, if such AI-based sentiment and related factors did matter for low-frequency long-term investors then they ought to be inducted into the factor zoo. That remains unclear. Chances are the near-term sentiment converges to well-known factors such as earnings momentum and analyst revisions over intermediate horizons. But these factors are already bona fide denizens of the factor zoo. Another key caveat is that as of now there is no way to run point-in-time back-tests with LLMs because there is no obvious mechanism for preventing look-ahead bias.

There are better ways to model the nonlinearity inherent in markets that go well beyond ordinary least squares regression. But most of the successful methods such as random forests fall squarely within the realm of supervised learning on structured data. And that's exactly the conclusion I came to circa 2016, which resulted in QuantZ embarking on the machine learning (ML)-based revamp of our factor framework. All the marketing blather aside, for the most part one does not even need alternative data for low frequency investing. It all comes back to what your explanatory variables are and the forecasting horizon. Even in the most developed markets like the United States, granular factor data courtesy of vendors like Compustat only goes back to 1988. In most countries one would be lucky to find any level of point-in-time factor granularity going back even 25 years. While one can always try to fit the distribution and find fancier techniques for resampling or even generating synthetic data – there are no shortcuts if we are to remain tethered to empirical reality. At the end of the day, paucity of live trading (not synthetic) data is a key stumbling block for deep learning in finance. Generative AI or any neural-net-based technique that requires millions of datapoints is only feasible at the tick level. The benefits to Ilya Sutskever's "double descent" do not accrue without billions or trillions of parameters. Further, unlike GPS-aided autonomous vehicles in the DARPA races, when it comes to markets no one rings a bell at the top or bottom. There are no clear stop signs or speeding limits. One has to guess the regime and the state of the world probabilistically. And once one formulates and enacts an investment thesis, the human feedback loop moves the goalpost somewhat akin to the observer participatory universe of quantum mechanics. At the quantum scale, one can never observe both the position and velocity of a particle with certainty. There must be an intuitive analog to Heisenberg's uncertainty principle for "phynance," which gives us hope yet for the criticality of humans in the loop – at least in the lower-frequency realm of factor investing where factor cyclicality plays out over many years. Value investors will still continue to snap up bargains hoping for a catalyst. Growth investors will still chase the hottest hyped-up stories of the day. The "laws" of financial gravity are the by-product of human biases (which drive positioning and flows), which in turn determine market clearing prices and are unlikely to be disintermediated by machines turning the crank ever faster. Fear and greed on the part of market participants makes phynance inherently distinct from the object of its envy: physics.

While every part of the retail financial advisory business can be streamlined including the asset allocation, chances are that most humans may still prefer to deal with a human (even if most quants do not). Relationships will remain paramount in a world of far greater automation. There is still hope for humans – if only due to contrived human preferences. Even if mathematicians prefer infinitely rich AI-generated art – chances are humans will erect barriers to value human art differently. I was present at the first such auction of artificial intelligence (AI GAN)-generated art in Manhattan, which took place at Christie's on October 25, 2018. The print, titled "Portrait of Edmond Belamy," sold for $432,500, far above its initial estimate due to the novelty factor. However, AI does not appear to have disrupted the art world yet even though the media capabilities offered by frontier models are truly mindboggling and should soon disrupt advertising and media. *But will our eventual AI overlords eventually care?*

Advances in AI are ushering in an era where agentic AI systems – capable of autonomous, goal-directed behavior – become ubiquitous in the financial industry. Unlike earlier AI that simply responded to prompts, agentic AI can *plan and act* independently: it perceives its environment, learns from data, and takes actions with minimal human input based on predefined goals. In a future of *abundant intelligence* limited only by computing costs, these autonomous systems could profoundly reshape white-collar work. The finance sector, with its data-intensive and analytical workflows, is particularly primed for transformation.

13.2. SYSTEMIC DISRUPTION: FROM THE BUY SIDE TO THE SELL SIDE

Agentic AI is poised to revolutionize core functions across finance, from investment and commercial banking to asset management, as well as wealth management. In investment banking, traditionally reliant on large teams for financial modeling and due diligence, autonomous AI "deal bots" can now handle end-to-end processes like raising capital. A prototype system automating equity fundraising demonstrated a 50% reduction in analyst hours with no loss of quality. AI can also create DCF models and pitchbooks in an instant thereby disintermediating junior bankers who were always glorified secretaries. The human element will remain essential to client relationship management and judgment in complex deal advisory until we hit the Singularity. It may come down to 6% for literally a handshake – after all it's the human relationships that are sticky, whether in banking or in real estate.

In trading and asset management, agentic AI may extend beyond existing algorithmic trading by deploying self-directed agents that continually monitor data and execute strategies in real time. This could democratize sophisticated trading capabilities, allowing a retail investor to employ an autonomous portfolio manager to adjust holdings and hedge risks 24/7 but also risk the "algos gone wild" scenarios that led to the abrupt demise of Knight Capital. However, this is a double-edged sword. If many AI agents react to the same inputs simultaneously, this herding behavior could amplify volatility and trigger destabilizing events like flash crashes, thereby increasing systemic risk.

Similarly, wealth management workflows are amenable to being transformed. AI agents can autonomously gather and interpret massive datasets, highlight key trends, and generate draft reports with empirical data, acting as a powerful force multiplier for human analysts. They can even automate asset allocation and rebalancing (both retail and institutional). Across these domains, the current consensus is that AI will complement rather than fully replace human judgment, with experts remaining "above the loop" for oversight and accountability in high-stakes decisions. This will likely be the case in all highly regulated industries where liability cannot be off-loaded on the AI. That could be the sweet spot until we hit the Singularity and cross the event horizon.

13.3. SYSTEMIC DISRUPTION: FROM THE MIDDLE OFFICE TO THE BACK OFFICE

The deployment of agentic AI should herald a profound shift in the operational backbone of finance given that many compliance and back-office jobs are amenable to near full automation. AI systems can continuously monitor transactions and provide regulatory updates in real time. Instead of manually sampling transactions, an AI auditor can autonomously scan entire ledgers, flag anomalies, and reduce human error, streamlining roles in compliance and operational risk. While risk measurement can easily be automated via rules-based systems, the risk management aspect will still require a human in the loop particularly from a liability standpoint. However, this introduces new challenges, as autonomous systems could inadvertently perpetuate biases if trained on flawed historical data, necessitating rigorous human governance. This operational shift directly affects the workforce, but the current narrative is more about augmentation than simple displacement. It remains to be seen whether human roles will evolve to leverage armies of bots or simply disappear resulting in headcount shrinkage, as we saw with the full automation of equity trade execution via volume-weighted average price (VWAP), time-weighted average price, and so on.

13.4. THE MACRO PICTURE

AI is expected to dramatically boost productivity, reduce operational costs, and lower the price of services for consumers. Macroeconomic analyses project that AI could raise global gross domestic product by as much as 7% (nearly $7 trillion) over the next decade. Consumers stand to benefit from hyper-personalized financial advice delivered at scale, and greater financial inclusion may follow as AI makes it profitable to serve previously uneconomical client segments. However, these gains may be unevenly distributed, with early adopters gaining outsized market share and labor displacement imposing adjustment costs on workers and economies.

In the intermediate term, such a major transition will require a significant redesign of workflows and entail major reskilling and upskilling of finance professionals. Institutions will need to invest in training for advanced analytics and AI oversight. New roles such as head of agentic AI will emerge while a plethora of routine jobs will get eliminated. If every back-office job and every call center job gets automated by AI (with your accent and language of choice to boot) then there is no geographical arbitrage left to outsourcing. That could be catastrophic for low-cost countries like the Philippines. There could be massive efficiencies driving enormous cost savings but how much of it will get passed on to consumers? Shareholders and the *owners of capital will continue to extract disproportionate return on investment while labor could find itself left with little if any bargaining chips.*

13.5. REINVENTING CAPITALISM

The rise of autonomous AI in finance presents both substantial economic opportunities and considerable regulatory challenges. These transformative changes will create an urgent need for an adaptive regulatory and governance framework. Regulators care about accountability and fiduciary duties: if an AI agent executes a rogue trade, institutions must have fail-safe mechanisms and clear lines of responsibility. Can one prove that the AI agent acted in a fiduciary capacity with requisite prudence? Policymakers are responding with new legislation, such as the EU's proposed AI Act, which will enforce requirements for transparency, risk mitigation, and human oversight of high-risk systems. Financial institutions will not be able to adopt black box AI agents in a highly regulated industry without providing the requisite audit trail and explainable logic, especially in sensitive areas like credit where the AI may discriminate due to its training data.

Furthermore, regulators must address systemic risks, such as AI-induced volatility, by updating safeguards like circuit breaker rules and mandating stress-testing for AI strategies. As AI's role expands, wider socioeconomic policies may also be necessary. If job displacement becomes significant, governments might consider measures like large-scale retraining programs or even "automation taxes" to fund social safety nets. AI will also lead to exponential increases in cybercrime. Soon we will need "good AIs" to preempt the malicious AIs. Ultimately, though the challenges confronting democratic, civil societies will be far greater than that which can be dealt with through simplistic measures like universal basic income. Such radical disruption and abundance will require a complete reinvention of capitalism. *Traditional economic theory will not suffice in the age of abundance once the cost of labor asymptotes to zero*, once the obvious budget constraints do not apply, and once people are no longer rewarded in direct proportion to their effort. Faced with skyrocketing unemployment, the Fed will find itself impotent – the blunt instruments of cutting rates and helicopter money may not suffice. People will have no way to find meaning in life through their work and capitalism will be faced with an existential crisis. Such turbulent times will create opportunities for the divisive demagoguery of the far-right populists. It's important to note that policymakers were never even able to adequately respond to the threats to democracy posed by social media (Facebook/Cambridge Analytica) and the internet, so this is indeed a tall order. For democracy and open societies to survive, *capitalism will have to be reinvented* for the age of abundance. Meanwhile, oblivious white collar workers continue frolicking on the metaphorical beach even as the "supersonic tsunami" of disruption closes in.

13.6. ROAD MAP TO A FULLY AUTOMATED AGENT-DRIVEN QUANT EQUITY HEDGE FUND

Agentic AI represents a paradigm shift for equity hedge funds, moving beyond current algorithmic tools to fully autonomous systems. These agents are designed for continuous, adaptive decision-making with minimal human intervention, capable of interpreting investment objectives, identifying opportunities, executing trades, and iteratively refining strategies in real time.

Current AI applications in finance, such as AI-powered stock-picking platforms, exchange-traded funds (ETFs), and automated research assistants, still require significant human guidance. Agentic AI advances these capabilities by acting with true agency – setting and executing multistep investment goals independently. This enables concepts like synthetic investment teams, where human managers oversee AI agents that autonomously conduct research, construct orders, and rebalance portfolios.

The primary benefit of this approach is the potential for higher efficiency and superior risk-adjusted returns by reducing emotional biases and processing data at a scale impossible for human teams. However, this shift introduces new challenges in transparency, model risk, and regulatory compliance. Consequently, the human role evolves from direct security selection to supervising goals, risk parameters, and compliance frameworks.

13.6.1. An Agent-Driven Quantitative Equity Hedge Fund

This document outlines a technical workflow for a hypothetical quantitative equity hedge fund run entirely by AI agents (Figure 13.1). The scenario assumes the following:

- **Fund profile.** $100 million in assets under management (AUM) with a weekly trading frequency
- **Team.** AI agents only, with zero human portfolio managers or analysts in day-to-day operations; a human overseer sets initial goals and risk limits

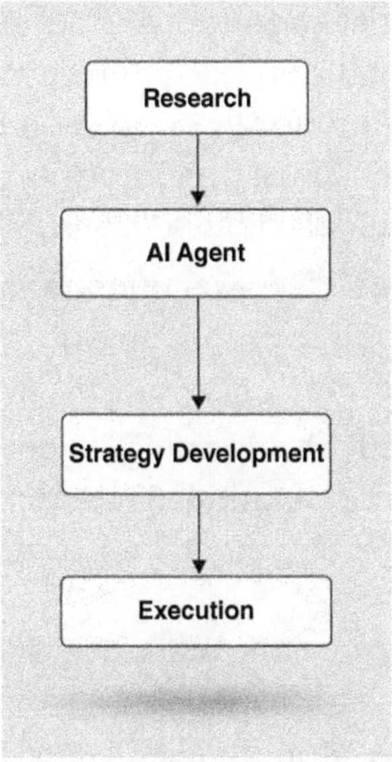

Figure 13.1 Agentic AI–Driven Quant Equity Hedge Fund.

- **Automation scope.** End-to-end automation of research, strategy, execution, risk management, and reporting
- **Infrastructure.** Uses advanced AI agent frameworks and has access to extensive public and proprietary data

The following steps detail the fully automated workflow for such a fund.

13.6.2. Define the Agentic Architecture and Roles

- **Data agents.** A data collector ingests and cleans market data feeds while ensuring quality, and a feature engineering agent derives predictive signals from this raw data.
- **Research and strategy agents.** A strategy generator proposes trading models, and a model trainer trains and validates these models on historical data.

- **Portfolio and risk agents.** A portfolio optimizer constructs the optimal portfolio from strategy outputs while enforcing diversification and position limits. A risk manager agent continuously monitors exposures to ensure they remain within predefined bounds.
- **Execution agent.** An execution agent handles order placement and logistics, minimizing market impact and transaction costs.
- **Reporting agent.** A reporting agent compiles performance, risk, and operational reports, including natural language commentary for stakeholders.

An orchestration framework, managed by a controller agent, coordinates these specialists. This supervisor calls other agents in sequence or in parallel as required by the fund's weekly cycle, ensuring a modular and reliable system where each agent can be improved or replaced independently.

13.6.3. Set Up Infrastructure and Data Pipelines

A robust technical infrastructure is required to support the agent ecosystem.

- **Computing environment.** This requires a high-performance cloud or on-premises environment with sufficient CPU/GPU capacity for model training and inference. The environment should be containerized to ensure each agent runs reliably and can scale.
- **Data pipelines.** An automated data pipeline feeds agents with historical and real-time data from various sources, including market data, financial statements, and alternative datasets. Automated extract, transform, load (ETL) processes continuously clean and update this information.

- **Market access.** The execution agent requires application programming interface (API) connectivity to brokers or execution management systems to place orders. This includes trading APIs, Financial Information eXchange connections, and reconciliation systems to verify executed trades.
- **Monitoring and observability.** This requires extensive logging to track every agent's actions and decisions, providing a complete audit trail from research to execution. Dashboards display system health and performance metrics, with alerts configured to flag anomalies (e.g., data feed failure, excessive risk exposure) that may require human intervention. Emergency stop controls are integrated as a final safeguard.

13.6.4. Data Acquisition and Processing by AI Agents

With the infrastructure in place, the data agents begin their work.

- **Data ingestion.** The data collector connects to APIs to gather historical and current market data, company financials, news articles, social media sentiment, and analyst reports. LLM-powered agents excel at parsing unstructured text from sources like 10-K filings and earnings call transcripts to extract structured metrics and sentiment scores.
- **Data cleaning and feature engineering.** Agents clean and normalize raw data, handling missing values and adjusting for corporate actions. The feature engineer then creates derived features, such as technical indicators, fundamental ratios, and NLP-based sentiment scores, which are stored in a feature store for other agents to access.

- **Quality control.** Data agents perform continuous quality checks for anomalies and inconsistencies. Since all subsequent decisions depend on data quality, this stage is critical for the fund's integrity.

13.6.5. AI-Driven Research and Strategy Development

Autonomous research agents handle idea generation, backtesting, and strategy formulation.

- **Generate trading ideas.** The strategy generator agent hypothesizes potential trading signals. It can use ML techniques like genetic algorithms or reinforcement learning to discover patterns or use an LLM to parse financial literature for new alpha factors. This enables the AI to rapidly explore a vast number of hypotheses.
- **Back-test and evaluate.** For each candidate strategy, a performance analyzer agent conducts a rigorous backtest against historical data. It calculates key performance metrics like compound annual growth rate (CAGR), Sharpe ratio, and drawdowns, while employing disciplined research practices such as cross-validation to avoid overfitting.
- **Refine or reject strategies.** The agents apply performance thresholds to select promising strategies. Poorly performing ideas are discarded or refined in an iterative loop. A macroeconomic analyzer agent may also filter strategies based on the prevailing macroeconomic environment.
- **Select weekly strategy.** Each week, the research agents repeat this process with the latest data to generate or update a validated strategy for deployment. The output is a clear model or set of signals, such as a stock ranking system based on a composite score of fundamental, technical, and sentiment factors.

13.6.6. Portfolio Construction and Optimization Agent

The portfolio optimizer agent translates the selected strategy into a concrete portfolio, determining position sizes and allocations subject to the fund's risk constraints.

- **Position sizing.** The agent uses optimization techniques (e.g., mean variance optimization) to allocate the $100 million AUM across selected assets, maximizing expected return for a given level of risk.
- **Constraints and diversification.** The agent enforces all risk rules, including maximum position sizes, sector exposure limits, and leverage constraints, to ensure a well-diversified portfolio.
- **Scenario analysis.** Before finalizing the portfolio, the agent may run stress tests using generative AI to simulate what-if market scenarios (e.g., a sudden inflation spike). If a vulnerability is detected, the agent adjusts positions to mitigate the identified risk.
- **Final orders.** The process concludes with a target portfolio and a precise list of trades required to achieve it. This list is passed to the execution agent.

13.6.7. Trade Execution via Autonomous Agents

The execution agent is responsible for implementing the trades efficiently to minimize transaction costs.

- **Order scheduling and routing.** The agent receives the trade list and intelligently schedules the orders, often breaking large trades into smaller chunks to be executed over time using algorithms like VWAP.
- **Smart execution decisions.** The AI can then use short-term prediction models to time trades, avoiding periods of low liquidity or high volatility. Over time, it learns which

execution tactics are most effective for different types of trades and market conditions.

- **Execution and confirmation.** The agent sends orders to the market via broker APIs and tracks fills until the target positions are achieved. It handles any unfilled orders by carrying them over or reporting back to the portfolio agent for reconsideration.
- **Cost monitoring.** The agent logs execution prices against benchmarks to measure implementation shortfall (slippage). If costs exceed expected levels, it can slow or pause execution.

13.6.8. Continuous Risk Monitoring and Management

Once the portfolio is live, the risk manager agent provides constant surveillance.

- **Real-time surveillance.** The agent continuously tracks key risk metrics such as profit and loss (P&L), value at risk (VaR), and factor exposures. If any metric breaches a predefined limit, the agent can automatically trim positions or execute hedges to bring risk back in line.
- **News and event monitoring.** An LLM-based subagent scans news feeds, regulatory filings, and other unstructured data for events relevant to portfolio holdings. On detecting a significant development (e.g., a profit warning or CEO resignation), the agent can flag it and automatically reduce or exit the position.
- **Anomaly detection.** The agent uses ML to detect unusual market conditions, such as a breakdown in asset correlations. In such black swan scenarios, it can be programmed to de-risk the entire portfolio by reducing overall exposure.
- **Intra-week adjustments.** The AI can make minor portfolio adjustments between weekly rebalances in response to market events or positions hitting stop-loss levels.

13.6.9. Performance Reporting and Audit Trail

The reporting agent compiles results and activities into comprehensive reports for human stakeholders.

- **Performance summary.** The agent generates reports detailing the fund's return, benchmark comparisons, and performance attribution, identifying the key drivers of P&L.
- **Risk and exposure report.** This report documents the risk profile over the period, including average leverage, VaR, and end-of-week exposures. Any risk limit breaches and corrective actions are detailed.
- **Audit trail.** A complete log of every trade is maintained with timestamps, sizes, prices, and the rationale behind the decision. This ensures full transparency and auditability.
- **Narrative commentary.** A key feature is the LLM's ability to generate natural language commentary explaining performance drivers and summarizing the actions taken by the AI system, enhancing trust and clarity. These AI-generated reports can be automatically distributed or updated on a stakeholder dashboard.

13.6.10. Continuous Learning and System Improvement

The final, ongoing step is to ensure the AI system adapts and improves over time.

- **Model retraining.** The model trainer agent periodically retrains all ML models with the latest market data to prevent strategy decay and adapt to changing market dynamics.
- **Multi-agent collaboration.** The agents are designed to provide feedback to one another. For instance, high transaction costs reported by the execution agent could

prompt the strategy agent to incorporate liquidity as a factor in its models. This collaborative correction improves overall system accuracy.

- **Reinforcement learning.** The entire workflow can be framed as a reinforcement learning problem where the reward is the fund's risk-adjusted return. This feedback loop enables a high-level agent to refine the strategy generation and risk management policies over time.
- **Periodic human review.** Although the fund operates autonomously, periodic human oversight is prudent. Quarterly reviews of the AI's performance and decision-making logic can be used to tune parameters and safeguards, ensuring the system remains aligned with its overarching goals.

13.7. AGENTIC AI MEETS REAL-WORLD DEPLOYMENT

Financial firms are racing to embrace AI toward harnessing productivity gains whether that be in the front or back office. Automating the drudgery of middle and back-office tasks is appealing.

A rather simple but tedious task that lends itself to such automation would be the penning of market updates that take up a lot of the portfolio managers' time and attention. QuantZ has used AI agents to automate the task of writing monthly investor letters and market commentary by modularizing each component and letting the agent fetch the market data for different asset classes before populating the corresponding commentary. The template then allows for more customized insertions of our signature heatmaps through the latest month end (Figure 13.2).

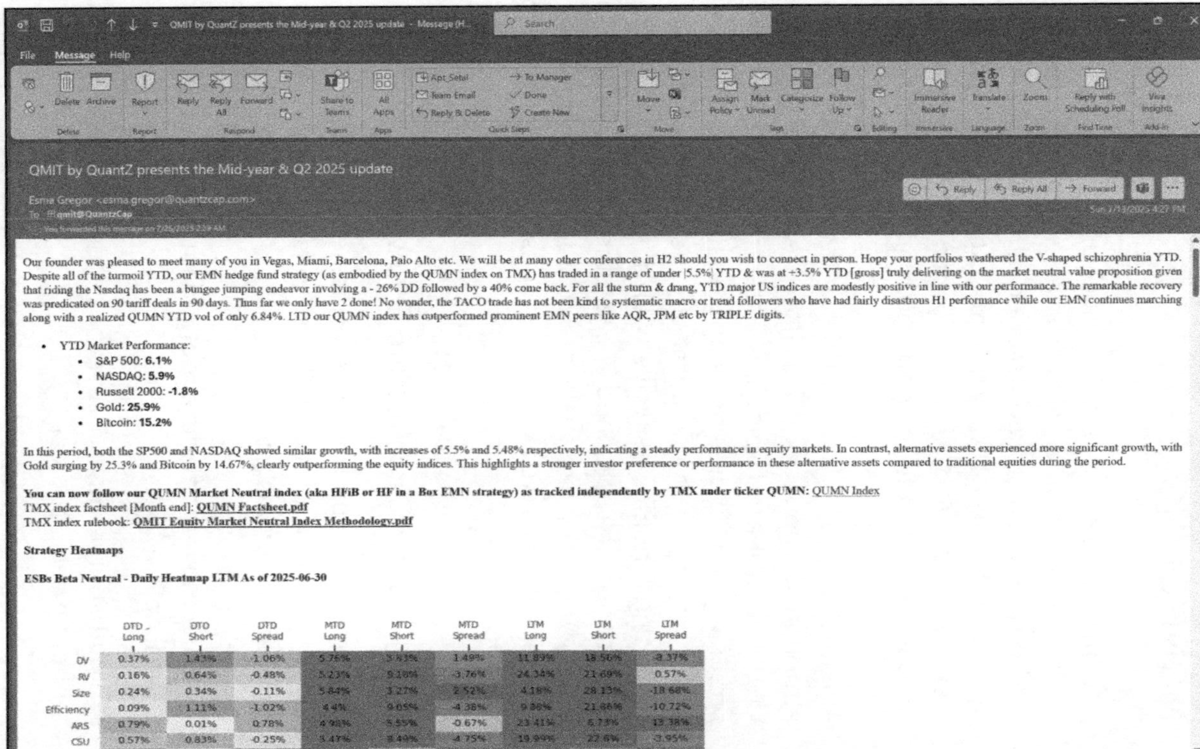

Figure 13.2. The Template with Our Signature Heatmaps Through the Latest Month End Date.

13.8. AGENTIC AI AND NLP-BASED SENTIMENT FOR PORTFOLIO MONITORING

A far more powerful example of such an agentic deployment would be that toward fully automated news monitoring via LLM-based sentiment as described in this section.[4] The ability to have agents not only monitor but also synopsize sentiment of relevance to live portfolios can provide an enormous productivity boost to the portfolio management team.

This section presents a scalable, end-to-end framework for attributing large stock price movements using agentic AI. Our Python-based pipeline integrates real-time price screening, multisource news aggregation, LLM-driven relevance scoring and summarization, and sentiment classification using FinBERT, as well as LLMs. Designed to emulate the intuition of a seasoned analyst, the system delivers precise, low-latency explanations for stock price movements. This pipeline was created using modest resources as a proof of concept.

13.8.1. System Architecture Overview

The pipeline is composed of six main stages, each of which replicates a part of the analyst's workflow when investigating large price swings:

1. **Price movement detection.** Identify stocks with abnormal daily returns.
2. **Multisource news retrieval.** Aggregate relevant news from diverse sources.

---

[4] Thanks to QMIT interns Brian MacSweeney and Quang Viet Tran for their key contributions to this section.

3. **Relevance scoring with Gemini.** Filter articles for company-specific relevance.
4. **Article summarization and key point extraction.** Condense news into actionable insights.
5. **Sentiment classification.** Quantify the sentiment of news summaries.
6. **Structured output generation and reporting.** Produce interpretable reports.

13.8.2. Price Signal Detection: Identifying Abnormal Returns

The pipeline begins with the set of stocks from QMIT's QUMN index (EMN hedge fund): https://www.vettafi.com/indexing/family/qmit.

Using the Yahoo Finance library, we retrieve daily adjusted closing prices and returns for the past three days. Stocks with returns exceeding ±5% are flagged as significant. This threshold balances sensitivity to meaningful events (e.g., earnings, mergers and acquisitions [M&A] rumors) with the need to filter out routine volatility. On average, three to seven stocks are flagged daily, ensuring a manageable yet diverse set of candidates for analysis.

13.8.3. Multisource News Retrieval

Once the abnormal moves are flagged, the pipeline collects relevant news for each ticker-date combination. We use three major sources to maximize coverage and redundancy:

- **NewsAPI.** Provides premium content from sources like Reuters, Bloomberg, the *Wall Street Journal*, CNBC, and *Financial Times*. We query using the company name or ticker, targeting articles within a one-day window of the price move (for relevance).

- **Google News RSS.** Uses structured queries (e.g., "TICKER stock after: YYYY-MM-DD before: YYYY-MM-DD") to capture additional headlines, enhancing recall.
- **Yahoo Finance RSS.** Supplies company-specific headlines, often with high relevance to stock movements.

In all three sources, article headlines, URLs, and (where publicly accessible) full text are retrieved. Full article content is scraped using BeautifulSoup, with URLs normalized to remove query strings that may cause 404 errors. Headlines and URLs are deduplicated based on normalized text and domain paths to eliminate redundant or syndicated content, ensuring a clean dataset for analysis.

It's critical to rely only on credible, reputable mainstream news sources to prevent contamination of the feed by rampant disinformation on the internet.

13.8.4. Relevance Scoring with Gemini

Raw news feeds often include irrelevant content: industry-wide trends, broad market commentary, or passing mentions of a company with no material bearing on its stock price. To isolate genuinely explanatory articles, we employ Google's Gemini-2.5-Pro LLM to score the relevance of each article with appropriate prompts. A relevance score is extracted from Gemini's output. Articles scoring below a default threshold of 0.70 are discarded. If no articles meet that cutoff, the system lowers the threshold successively to 0.50 and 0.25. If no article crosses even the lowest bar, the system outputs: "No news articles found meeting relevancy score criteria." This multitiered fallback ensures resilience while avoiding spurious attribution.

13.8.5. Structured Summarization of Key News

For the subset of high-relevance articles, we re-engage Gemini with a summarization task. The prompt instructs the model to extract up to three sentences that summarize the key drivers of the move, followed by a single narrative explanation of the likely cause and sentiment (positive, negative, or mixed). The key is to enumerate the list of 20 catalysts/news categories that we care about:

- Earnings report
- Guidance/forecast
- Mergers and acquisitions (M&A)
- Share buyback
- Analyst upgrade/downgrade
- Dividend changes
- FDA/clinical-trial news
- CEO/CFO change
- Stock split announcement
- Index rebalancing
- Activist investor news
- Short squeeze/meme hype (Wall Street bets)
- Insider transactions
- Litigation/regulatory action
- Secondary offering (equity issuance)
- Cybersecurity breach/data leak
- Trade/tariff news
- Economic data/Fed announcements
- Major contract wins or product launches
- Patent/licensing news

This stage of the process transforms a large corpus of unstructured text into a compact, human-readable summary suitable for internal notes, dashboards, or research briefings.

13.8.6. Sentiment Classification with FinBERT

Each of the Gemini-generated sentences is then passed to FinBERT, a pretrained transformer model fine-tuned for sentiment analysis in financial text. FinBERT outputs probabilities for three classes:

- Positive
- Negative
- Neutral

We compute a sentiment score for the single paragraph synopsis of all stories as the difference between positive and negative probabilities for each stock-date pair. It provides a normalized, interpretable measure of sentiment intensity. In most cases, the sentiment aligns with the direction of the stock move (e.g., highly positive scores on strong up days), providing additional signal validation. Here is the formula for sentiment score:

$$\text{Sentiment Score} = \frac{1}{N}\sum_{i=1}^{N}\left(P(\text{positive})_i - P(\text{negative})_i\right)$$

13.8.7. Final Report Generation

All results are consolidated into a structured output table that includes the following fields for each stock and date:

- **Date.** Date of the price movement
- **Ticker.** Stock ticker symbol

- **Percent change.** One-day percentage return
- **Number of relevant articles.** Count of articles meeting the relevance threshold
- **Sentiment score.** Sentiment score for the single paragraph synopsis
- **Overall sentiment label.** Classified as positive (>0.2), negative (<–0.2), or neutral
- **Summary paragraph.** List of key news summaries
- **Full LLM explanation.** Gemini's narrative explanation

The final output is suitable for internal reporting, post-trade review, or alerting systems. It is both interpretable and extensible – supporting applications in quant signal development, trader commentary, and risk diagnostics.

13.8.8. Preliminary Results and Observations

Testing on a sample of US small- and mid-cap stocks from August 7, 2025, demonstrates the pipeline's effectiveness:

- **Coverage.** The system identified relevant articles for about 95% of large-move days as per our ± 5% threshold, with Yahoo Finance and Google RSS providing robust coverage when premium sources were limited by paywalls.
- **Accuracy.** LLM-generated summaries accurately pinpointed catalysts in cases with clear drivers (e.g., earnings announcements), validated by sentiment scores aligning with price direction (positive scores > 0.2 for up days, negative scores <–0.2 for down days). FinBERT sentiment is generally reliable based on the paragraph synopsis approach, but the far more parsimonious FinBERT model has clearly been superseded by GPT-5 and Gemini 2.5 Pro.
- **Null Cases.** When no relevant news was found, the system correctly flagged ambiguous or technical price movements, mirroring a human analyst's judgment.

- **Limitations.** Paywalled articles reduced full-text availability, forcing reliance on headlines and descriptions. This occasionally limited Gemini's summarization depth but did not significantly impair relevance scoring. Clearly this is not a realistic issue for any commercial production system with the appropriate licensing of news feeds.

13.8.9. Case Study: ARIS +19.32% on August 7, 2025

- Number of relevant articles used: 5
- Date: 2025-08-07
- Ticker: ARIS (Aris Water Solutions)
- Percent change: +19.32%
- Overall sentiment score: 0.9500 (Positive)
- Top headlines summary:
    - Aris Water Solutions surged after Western Midstream Partners announced a definitive agreement to acquire the company. The $1.5 billion transaction was the key driver of the price increase. Acquisition news created a decisive positive sentiment, reflected in the immediate market reaction.

Analysis of output: A major M&A announcement with clear, unambiguous implications drove strong positive sentiment and a near 20% gain – an excellent example of event-driven price action captured accurately by the LLM.

13.8.10. Case Study: CROX −29.24% on August 7, 2025

- Number of relevant articles used: 14
- Date: 2025-08-07

- Ticker: CROX (Crocs)
- Percent change: –29.24%
- Overall sentiment score: –0.9000 (Negative)
- Top headlines summary:
  - Crocs beat Q2 earnings and revenue estimates but issued weak forward guidance. The company forecasted a sales decline for the upcoming quarter and withheld its full-year outlook. Concerns about consumer demand and potential tariffs amplified the negative market reaction.

Analysis of output: Despite an earnings beat, the sharp downward guidance shift generated a strong negative sentiment, fully aligned with the steep sell-off. This is a textbook "guidance-over-earnings" market reaction.

13.8.11. Case Study: UDMY –5.43% on August 7, 2025

- Number of relevant articles used: 0
- Date: 2025-08-07
- Ticker: UDMY (Udemy)
- Percent change: –5.43%
- Overall sentiment score: 0.0000 (Neutral)
- Top headlines summary:
  - No articles met the relevancy cutoff for this ticker.

Analysis of output: The absence of relevant news articles explains the neutral sentiment score despite the stock decline. This demonstrates the LLM's ability to avoid manufacturing sentiment where no substantive news context exists.

13.8.12. Discussion

The pipeline replicates an analyst's workflow with the ability to identify and explain notable movers both during market hours and immediately after close with significant advantages:

- **Scalability.** Processes hundreds of stocks daily, far exceeding manual capabilities
- **Speed.** Delivers insights within seconds, supporting real-time decision-making
- **Precision.** Combines LLM reasoning with transformer-based sentiment analysis for high-fidelity attributions

Challenges include the following:

- **Ambiguity.** In cases of no relevant news, price moves may stem from technical factors (e.g., short squeezes, rebalancing) not captured by news feeds.
- **Technological vulnerability.** This shows the exposure to both reliability of cloud provider, ISP, and API.

We present a tabular comparison of GPT versus FinBERT in Table 13.1 to demonstrate that in order to accurately capture the nuances of earnings calls and FOMC (Federal Open Market Committee) statements it's important to ingest the full text via an LLM instead of the far smaller FinBERT. The attention mechanism of the LLM transformer architecture enables it to pick up on seemingly conflicting sentiment when dealing with earnings versus revenue beats/misses and forward guidance with much greater accuracy and richer nuance, but at materially higher cost.

Table 13.1 Financial Sentiment Engines: Open-Source FinBERT Versus Proprietary LLMs.

Dimension	FinBERT	LLM-Based Sentiment (e.g., GPT-4/ChatGPT)
Model family and size	BERT-base encoder (≈110 M params, 12 layers). Built for classification, no generative head.	Decoder-only or mixture-of-experts LLMs with 7 B-1 T+ params; full-text generation plus instruction tuning.
Training corpus	Continues BERT pretraining on financial news (Reuters TRC2) and fine-tunes on Financial PhraseBank sentences.	Trained first on massive general web corpora; sentiment queries rely on zero/few-shot prompting or light domain fine-tuning. Domain knowledge is incidental unless an extra financial adaptor is added.

(Continued)

Table 13.1 *(Continued)*

Dimension	FinBERT	LLM-Based Sentiment (e.g., GPT-4/ChatGPT)
Task formulation	Supervised three-way classifier (positive, negative, neutral) with a soft-max head; outputs probabilities directly.	Sentiment expressed via generated text (e.g., "POSITIVE, score = 0.87"). Requires prompt design or post-processing to map prose into numeric scores.
Compute and latency	Runs on a single CPU/GPU and accepts ≤512 tokens; deterministic inference.	High VRAM/TPU demand, longer context windows, higher latency and cost.
Adaptability	Must be retrained to add classes or new jargon; architecture fixed.	New labels or dimensions (tone, policy stance, sarcasm) can be added with prompt engineering; no weight update needed.

Table 13.1 *(Continued)*

Dimension	FinBERT	LLM-Based Sentiment (e.g., GPT-4/ChatGPT)
Empirical accuracy	Long-standing baseline for finance – beats generic BERT on news and 10-K sentiment.	Recent studies show GPT-3.5/4 zero-shot beats FinBERT by about 35% F1 on forex-news sentiment, given carefully designed prompts.
Explainability	Attention heatmaps; limited to 512-token window.	Can return chain-of-thought justifications (if enabled), aiding auditability but also raising privacy risk.
Licensing/ cost	Apache-2.0, free to deploy on-premises.	Mostly proprietary API access billed per token; open-weight LLMs exist but still heavier than FinBERT.

13.8.13. Conclusion

This system provides a practical and scalable proof of concept for a common workflow bottleneck in institutional asset management: determining the reason behind a stock's large move. By combining structured data filtering, LLM-based reasoning, and sentiment modeling, it produces high-precision, low-latency attributions nicely leveraging the benefits of the transformer's attention mechanism in ways that should align with PMs (portfolio managers) (the HITL [human-in-the-loop] here).

Implementation considerations may include the following:

- Using web search APIs like Perplexity for broader news discovery.
- Incorporating Securities and Exchange Commission filings or earnings call transcripts for better attribution and coverage.
- Real-time deployment via cloud functions or trading dashboards.
- Integrating explainability metrics (e.g., Gemini confidence) for auditability.
- Expanding the coverage to international stocks and ETFs.

As markets become increasingly data-driven, such tools will be essential for bridging human expertise with computational scale, enabling faster and more informed financial decisions. This highlights the power of the agentic AI framework and the promise of deploying multi-agent systems to handle the described multifaceted issues. Of course, given the exponential pace of innovation in this arena, our futuristic musings may well seem banal by the time this book is actually in print.

13.9. AGENTIC AI IN FACTOR INVESTING

To bring it back to factor investing, in conclusion we consider the obvious question as to how agentic AI might reshape the field of our study. We consider the obvious workflow which comes to mind (Figure 13.3).

Step 1. Create a factor universe, exactly as described in Appendix A.1.

Step 2. Use LLMs to study the potential addition/deletion of new factors from the universe including possibly combining them.

Step 3. Test factor inclusion criterion. Each new factor is back-tested and must meet certain thresholds for efficacy prior to inclusion.

Step 4. Periodically stress-test factors to justify continued inclusion on an ongoing basis for live trading purposes.

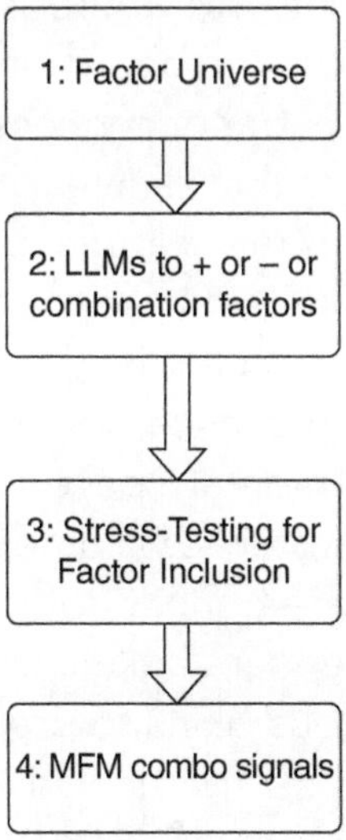

Figure 13.3. Agentic AI Workflow in Factor Investing.

> Desirable factors that meet requisite thresholds, and their sufficiently fit progeny, are to be retained while others get filtered out in this Darwinian process to continuously improve the factor pool makeup.

If this sounds revolutionary, it is. But it is not new because this is exactly what we in the quantamental factor investing world have now been doing for decades. The more dynamic and evolutionary aspect of "ensemble learning" was pioneered in the mid-2010s by QMIT's ML-driven ESBs, which were specifically designed to continuously evolve in precisely this manner. Similarly, QuantZ was also early in espousing the regime-based approach to factor investing shortly after the GFC in 2009 as described in Chapter 7, Section 7.1. While our current implementation is deterministic and based on largely supervised ML techniques applied to mostly structured data, there is no reason one could not plug in LLMs to substitute for certain modules in the process described provided that one can obtain deterministic outputs if desired. That said, there is also no compelling rationale to do so across the board since most elements of the quantamental investment process benefit from deterministic expert systems that deliver predictable outcomes as opposed to the more capricious and hallucinatory LLMs, which fail the key test of reproducibility. The lack of reproducibility is a fatal flaw in the investment context, particularly from a compliance standpoint. In the mid- to low-frequency quantamental space, quants have already fully automated their existence via deterministic (rules-based) expert systems, and the benefits of deploying "stochastic parrots" with their attendant hallucinations is unclear given that there are no obvious gains to productivity or precision therein – only downside, particularly from a compliance standpoint in a highly regulated industry. That brings us full circle to the raison d'etre for QMIT's ML-enhanced approach to factor investing, which would be the perfect place to end this journey.

I sit here in the shadows of the Roman Colosseum as I conclude my musings. Humanity's race with AGI hurtles toward its inevitable gladiatorial tryst with an untimely demise – the existential implications of which will render quantamental factor investing inconsequential. But it doesn't have to end that way. Ciao from Roma.

Appendices

APPENDIX A.1 COVERAGE UNIVERSE

1. About 4,000 US names domiciled in the United States and listed on major exchanges like NYSE, NASDAQ, and PHLX based on the following constraints:
   a. Minimum market capitalization: USD 250 million based on unsplit prices from prior close.
   b. Minimum $ price criterion: USD 3.00 based on unsplit prices from prior close.
   c. Certain industries are excluded due to event risk or because a generic quant model is not appropriate for those industries (such as biotechs, biopharma, bioscience, biomedical, and real estate investment trusts [REITs]). However, we do include the mega-cap biotechs like Amgen, Celgene, Gilead, which do not have such event risk.
   d. Liquidity screen: Top 3,000 based on average daily trading volume for history up until March 2021 at which point this requirement was relaxed to include Top 4,000 however the final universe subject to all criteria comes down to under 3000 names.

e. Only common stocks excluding non-primary share classes and ETFs, mutual funds, closed-end funds, pooled vehicles, and so on.
f. Canadian stocks (dual listings) and ADRs (hence all GAAP-compliant reporting) have been added to the live history since March 2021 but were not included in the estimation universe historically.

APPENDIX A.2 TABLE OF QMIT'S ENHANCED SMART BETAS (ESBs)

Table A.1 QMIT ESBs and Signals.

No.	QMIT Combo Signals	Constituent ESBs
1	Value composite	• Deep value (DV) • Relative value (RV)
2	Growth + momentum composite	• Analyst revisions (ARS) • Analyst ratings (ART) • Enhanced momentum (EnMom) • Growth (GroH)
3	Quality composite	• Quality – leverage (LEV) • Quality – profitability (PROF) • Quality – capital structure/usage (CSU) • Quality – stability (STAB) • Quality – efficiency (EFF) • Quality – earnings quality (EQ)

No.	QMIT Combo Signals	Constituent ESBs
4	Fabulous 14	• Growth + momentum composite ◆ Analyst revisions (ARS) ◆ Analyst ratings (ART) ◆ Enhanced momentum (EnMom) ◆ Growth (GroH) • Quality composite ◆ Quality – leverage (LEV) ◆ Quality – profitability (PROF) ◆ Quality – capital structure/ usage (CSU) ◆ Quality – stability (STAB) ◆ Quality – efficiency (EFF) ◆ Quality – earnings quality (EQ) • Reversal (REV) • Risk (RISK) • Size (SIZE) • Deep value (DV)
5	Enterprise 18	• All 18 ESBs
6	Value momentum composite	• Value composite • Growth + momentum composite
7	Quality value composite	• Quality composite • Value composite
8	Quality momentum composite	• Quality composite • Growth + momentum composite
9	Famous five	• Quality composite • Value composite • Growth + momentum composite • Risk (RISK) • Size (SIZE)

(Continued)

Table A.1 *(Continued)*

No.	QMIT Combo Signals	Constituent ESBs
10	Sizzling seven	• Quality composite • Value composite • Growth + momentum composite • Risk (RISK) • Size (SIZE) • Reversal (REV) • Short interest (SIRF)

APPENDIX A.3 PERFORMANCE MEASURES

In this section, we provide definitions of various performance measures.

Cumulative return. A cumulative return is calculated by geometrically linking daily ESB returns over the estimation period:

$$\text{Cumulative Return}_i = \prod_{t=1}^{n}(1+D_{ti})-1$$

where i is a particular ESB, $t = 1,..,n$ days, and D_{ti} is return of ESB i on day t.

Annualized return. The annualized return is calculated as a geometric average of the full period cumulative return based on the number of years taken to achieve the cumulative return:

$$\text{Annualized Return}, \mu_p = (1+\text{Cumulative Return})^{\frac{1}{n}}$$

where n is the number of years.

Volatility. Volatility is defined as the standard deviation of factor returns. Monthly standard deviations are annualized using the following formulas:

$$\text{Annualized Volatility} = \text{Monthly Volatility} * \sqrt{12}$$

Sharpe ratio. Measure of risk-adjusted return as defined:

$$\text{Sharpe Ratio} = \frac{\mu_p - r_f}{\sigma_p}$$

where μ_p is the portfolio's annualized return; r_f is the risk-free rate, which is assumed to be zero; and σ_p is the portfolio's annualized standard deviation.

Sortino ratio. An alternate measure of risk-adjusted return, wherein risk is defined as standard deviation of downside risk:

$$\text{Sortino Ratio} = \frac{\mu_p - r_f}{\sigma_d}$$

where μ_p is the portfolio's annualized return, r_f is the risk-free rate that is assumed to be zero, and σ_d is the portfolio's annualized standard deviation of the downside risk.

Maximum drawdown. The maximum observed loss from a peak to a trough of a portfolio. Maximum drawdown is an indicator of downside risk over a specified time period:

$$\text{Maximum Drawdown,MDD} = \frac{\text{Trough Value} - \text{Peak Value}}{\text{Peak Value}}$$

Information coefficient (IC). Full period Pearson correlation between ESB rank by ticker at time t and return by ticker at time $t+1$ (one-month forward return)

Rank information coefficient (rank IC). Full period Spearman correlation between ESB rank by ticker at time t and the return rank by ticker at time $t+1$ (one-month forward return)

Hit rate. Percentage of months that the portfolio delivers positive returns

Turnover. Turnover is measured on a two-way monthly basis before being annualized as per:

$$\text{Turnover} = 12 * \frac{\text{Turnover}\,L + \text{Turnover}\,SS}{\text{Long}\,\$MV + \text{Short}\,\$MV}$$

$$\text{Turnover}\,L = \text{Average value of all buy and sell transactions on the long side}$$

$$\text{Turnover}\,SS = \text{Average value of all buy and sell transactions on the short side}$$

This can also be computed in terms of the number of names being flipped in each fractile instead of the % weight.

Spread return computation. Month to date (MTD)/year to date (YTD) spread returns are geometrically chain-linked DTD spread returns where both are based on ESB portfolios formed at the prior month end close in the case of monthly heatmaps and formed at the prior trading day's close in the case of daily heatmaps. For this reason, the MTD/YTD spread returns will not exactly match the long return–short return for that period.

Further, we provide relevant explanatory notes regarding tables/figures in this section:

- Daily rebalance implies position rebalancing into the close (based on fundamentals as of T-2) with 100×100 exposure each day. Weekly rebalance entails position rebalancing into the close on Fridays but with daily chain-linked returns intra-week that assume 100×100 exposure each day. Monthly rebalance entails position rebalancing into the end of month close but with daily chain-linked returns intra-month that assume 100×100 exposure each day.
- Geometric compounding of spread returns can yield rather counterintuitive results that do not align with a simple difference of the longs versus shorts as seen in the heatmaps. This is due to the effect of correlations and volatility between the two legs of the spread return being compounded.
- LTM, 3Y, and 5Y numbers are 11 months + current MTD, 35 months + current MTD and 59 months + current MTD correspondingly while the rest are on an expanding not trailing window.
- Annualization factors for 3Y and 5Y are based on 35 and 59 months, respectively (not taking into account current partial month).
- LTD is defined as the out-of-sample expanding window starting January 2002 because the first two years (2000–2001) on the LTD were in-sample equal weighted. Those two in-sample years of the Nasdaq crash had to be excluded even though the returns were extraordinarily high due to the favorable confluence of factors surrounding the implosion of the tech bubble at the time.
- Annualization factor for LTD is based on number of calendar days between as of date and 2002-01-01.
- Factor portfolios are not sector neutral.

- Generated weekly as of last night's close this report shows the DTD, MTD, YTD, and LTD returns for our smart beta composite spreads.
- Factors within the cohort spreads are long-short based on top versus bottom 5%-tile (about 150×150) of the largest liquid US traded stocks (usually about 3,000 depending on market capitalization and minimum $ price criterion for stocks listed on NYSE and Nasdaq).
- Certain industries like biotechs and REITS are excluded due to event risk or because a generic quant model is not appropriate for those industries.
- Individual composites are top and bottom 5%-tile portfolios based on equally weighted ESB BFOM scores mentioned previously.
- Daily versus monthly rebalancing: Our monthly heatmaps are based on a T-1 month end optimization to solve for the optimal factor weights. While we use optimal factor weights based on month end optimization, in daily heatmaps, we refresh individual factor ranks on a daily basis therefore resulting in an intra-month varying long/short portfolio. The optimal factor weights and selection of the "best flavor of the month" is still static intra-month in order to prevent excessive turnover and unnecessarily noisy ESBs.
- Dollar neutral versus beta neutral: Beta neutrality implies daily de-levering of the higher beta side of the long/short factor portfolio. Indeed, the beta neutrality has to be enforced via daily rebalance since the factor ranks (and top/bottom portfolios) are being refreshed daily.
- MTD returns/spreads are geometrically chain-linked DTD returns/spreads where both are based on factor portfolios formed at the prior month end close.

- YTD and LTD returns are based on geometric chain-linking of monthlies.
- Multi-period spread returns are not the difference of cumulative top versus bottom returns. Instead, they represent the daily geometrically compounded and rebalancing of the market-neutral "active return" differential of the top versus bottom portfolios.
- Since liquid equity commissions are now de minimis for both the institutional and even the retail world and market impact is really a function of the investor's assets under management we simply leave out the impact of *t*-costs as is customary in factor research.

APPENDIX A.4 CHART BOOK

QMIT's chart book is meant to be a pictorial appendix that illustrates the evolution of our smart betas and signals. This first chart ($ neutral as of 2024-12-31) shows the evolution of our flagship Sizzling Seven composite and its constituents over the LIVE 6Y[1] period of publication. Analogously, Figures A.2 through A.12 show the evolution and hit rate of QMIT's signals.

[1] LIVE 7Y as of publication.

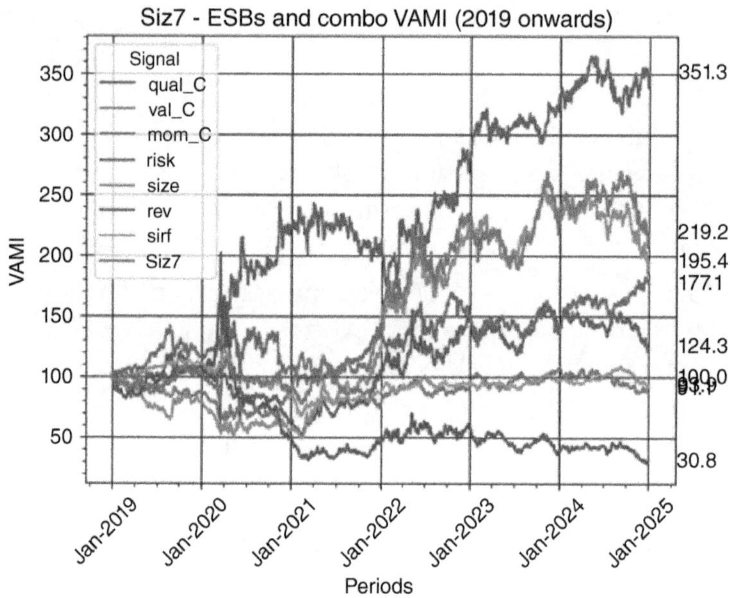

Figure A.1 LIVE Dollar-Neutral VAMIs for QMIT's Sizzling Seven Signal + Component ESBs – as of 2024-12-31.

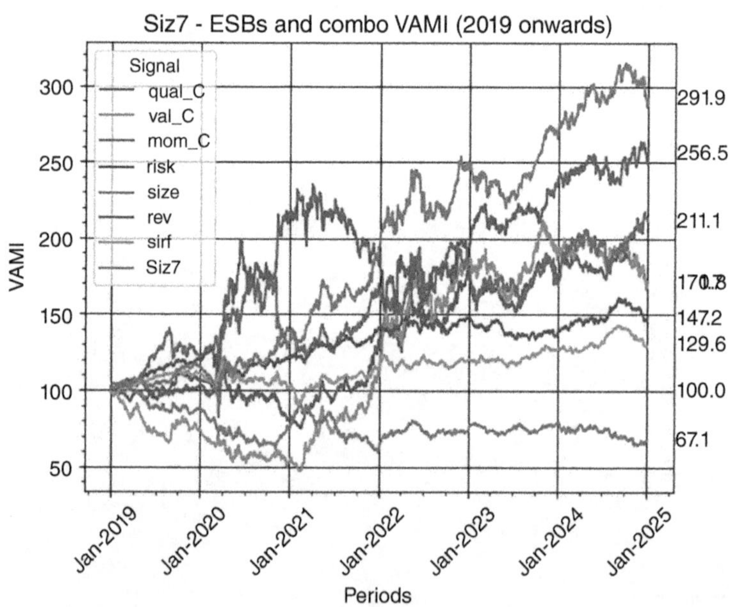

Figure A.2 Beta-Neutral VAMIs for QMIT's Sizzling Seven Signal + Component ESBs – LIVE as of 2024-12-31.

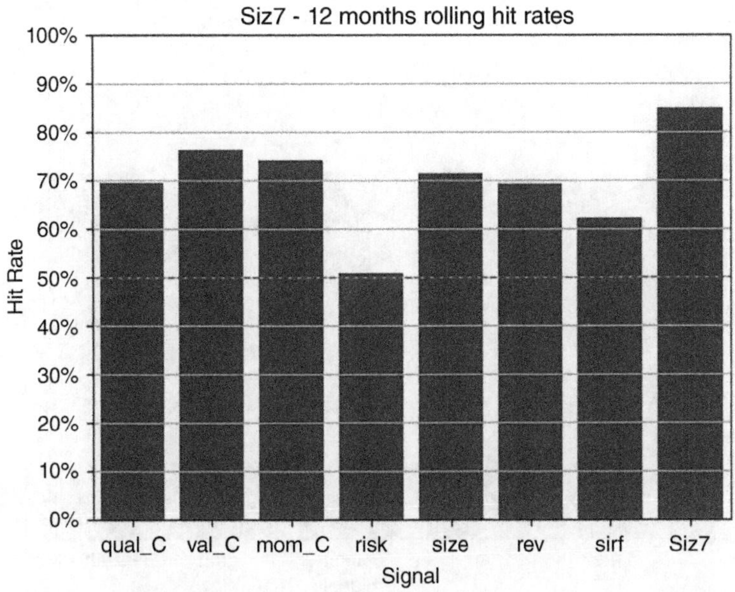

Figure A.3 Hit Rate (% of Positive Months) for $-neutral ESBs in the Sizzling Seven Composite – LIVE as of 2024-12-31.

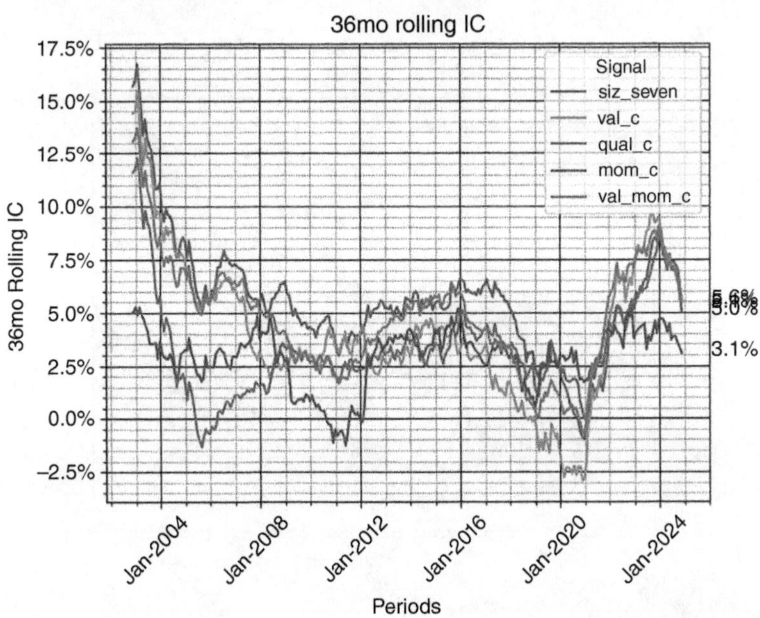

Figure A.4 QMIT 36-Month Rolling Signal ICs – LIVE as of 2024-12-31.

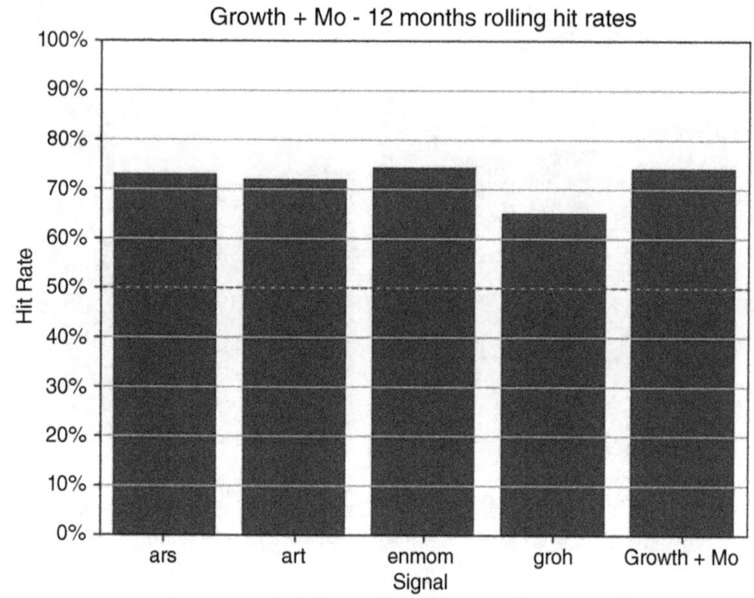

Figure A.5 12-Month Rolling Hit Rates (% of Positive Months) for ESBs in the GrowthMo Composite – LIVE as of 2024-12-31.

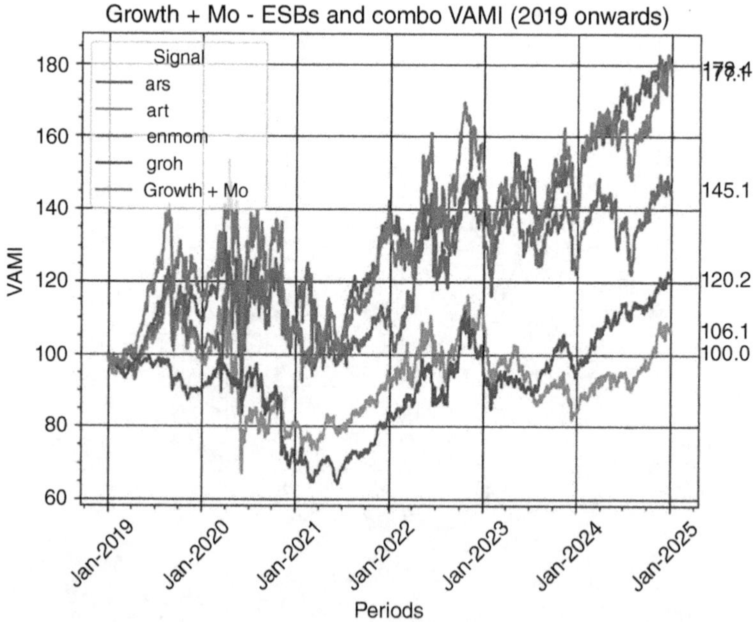

Figure A.6 GrowthMo Composite + Constituent VAMIs Show Clear Benefit from Combining ESBs – Dollar-Neutral LIVE Period Since 2019 – as of 2024-12-31.

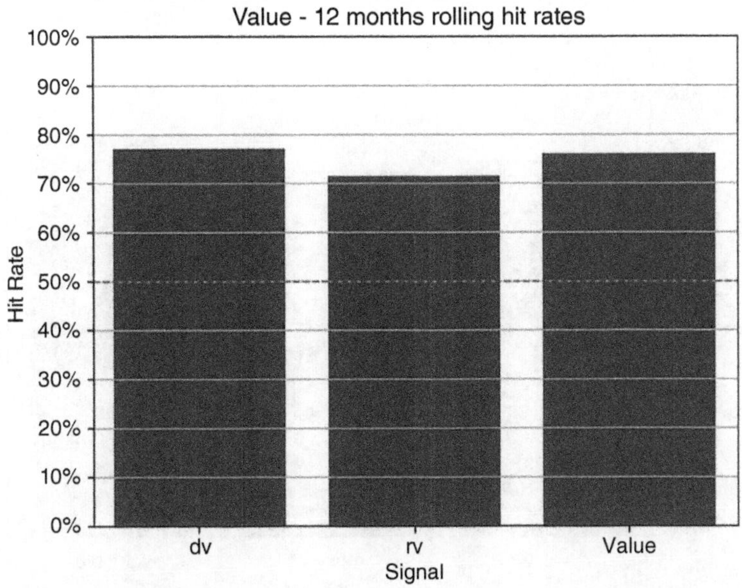

Figure A.7 Rolling 12-Month Hit Rates (% of Positive Months) for ESBs in the Value Composite – LIVE as of 2024-12-31.

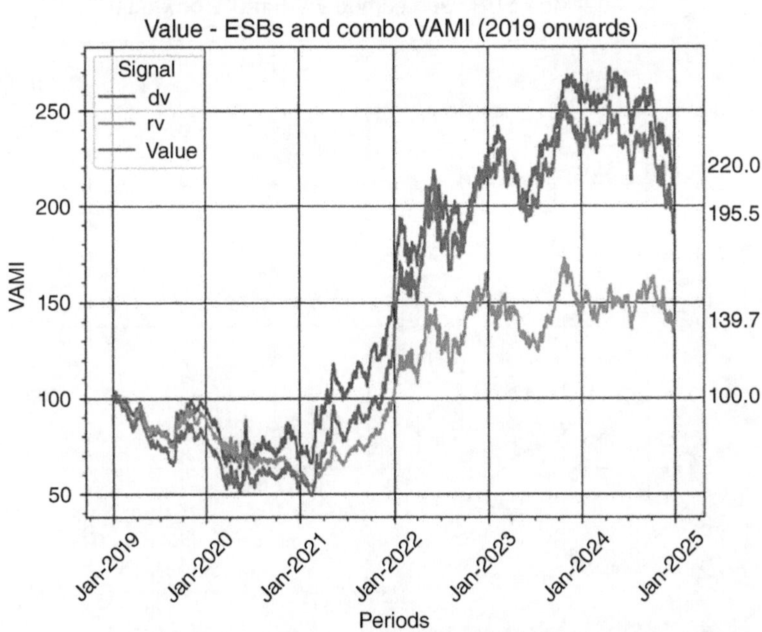

Figure A.8 Value Composite and Constituent VAMIs ($-Neutral) – LIVE as of 2024-12-31.

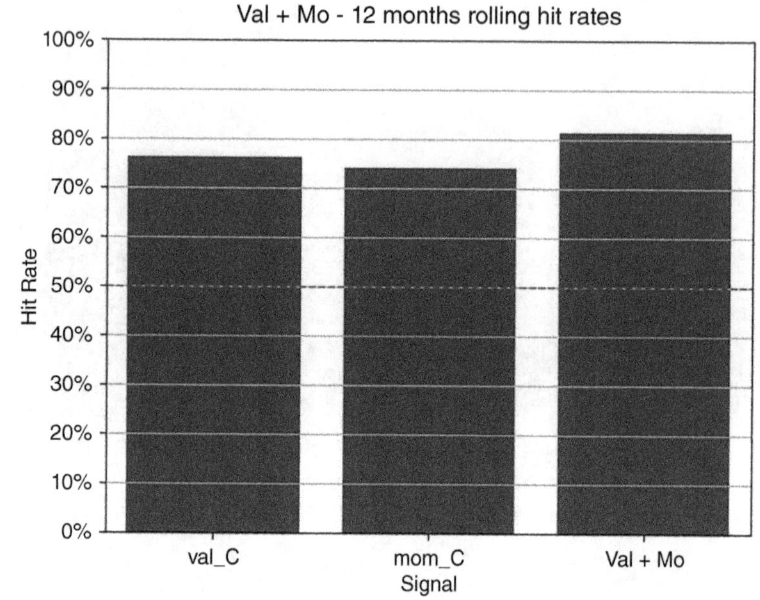

Figure A.9 12-Month Rolling Hit Rates (% of Positive Months) Across ESBs in the Value + Mom (GARP) Composite – LIVE as of 2024-12-31.

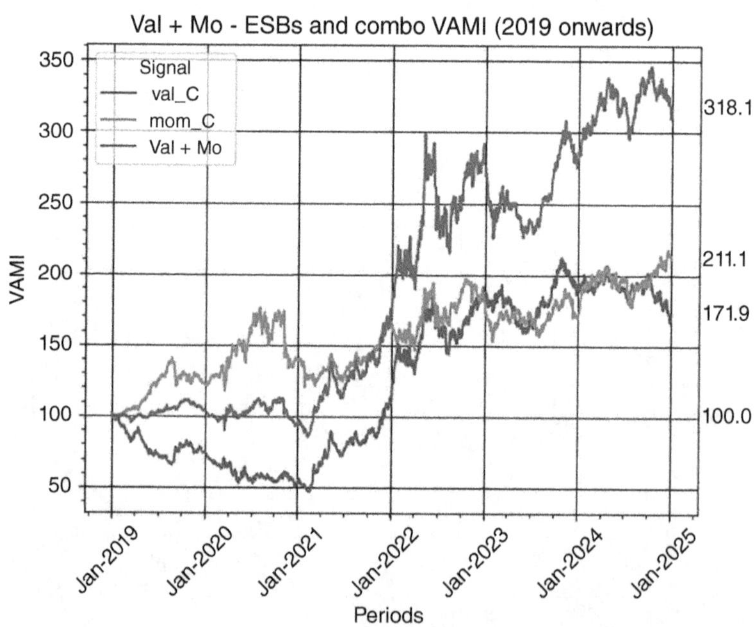

Figure A.10 GARP (Value + Momentum) Composite VAMI (Beta-neutral) with Constituents – LIVE as of 2024-12-31.

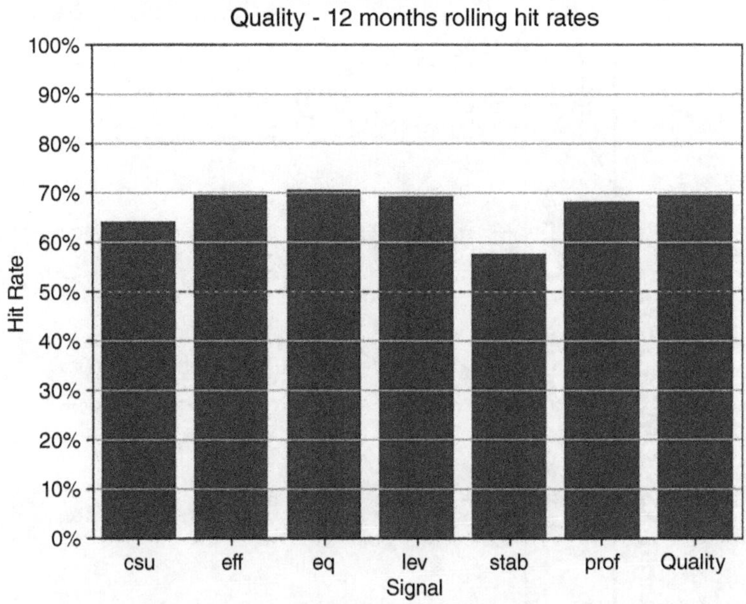

Figure A.11 12-Month Rolling Hit Rates (% of Positive Months) for ESBs in the Quality Composite – LIVE as of 2024-12-31.

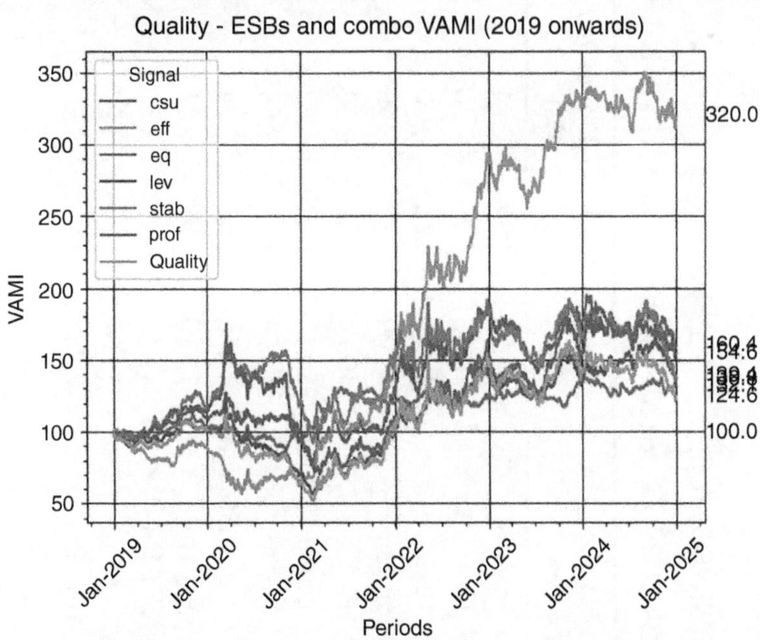

Figure A.12 Quality Composite VAMI ($-neutral) – with Constituents – LIVE as of 2024-12-31.

APPENDIX A.5 FACTOR MOMENTUM RESULTS

APPENDIX A.5.1: 24.75Y Results

Table A.2 Factor Momentum Results: Beta Neutral Without XSMOM 24.75Y

Strategy	Mean (%)	Std (%)	DownDev (%)	MDD (%)	Sharpe	Sortino	Calmar	CumRet (%)
LW, 6m/1m	13.56	7.89	2.74	7.92	1.72	4.94	1.71	2208.66
LW, 12m/1m	12.13	7.08	2.86	9.08	1.71	4.25	1.34	1587.97
LW, 12m/3m	12.19	7.20	3.00	9.96	1.69	4.07	1.22	1611.06
LW, 6m/3m	12.39	7.39	2.98	9.44	1.68	4.15	1.31	1685.23
EW18	10.74	6.52	2.58	7.85	1.65	4.16	1.37	1139.05
Enterprise 18	24.17	14.80	6.62	16.10	1.63	3.65	1.50	20,831.24
LW, 1m/3m	13.04	8.27	3.54	12.45	1.58	3.68	1.05	1960.29
EW16 ex-XSMOM	11.16	7.30	2.94	8.46	1.53	3.80	1.32	1261.73
LW, 1m/1m	12.20	8.56	3.51	9.99	1.43	3.48	1.22	1615.55
LW, 3m/1m	12.66	8.97	3.57	10.68	1.41	3.55	1.19	1795.36
LW, 3m/3m	11.37	8.33	3.53	11.69	1.36	3.22	0.97	1325.32
LL, 1m/3m	7.74	8.91	4.55	18.60	0.87	1.70	0.42	529.83

LL, 3m/3m	7.20	8.40	4.77	18.60	0.86	1.51	0.39	456.63
LS, 6m/1m	8.93	11.05	5.79	19.42	0.81	1.54	0.46	725.21
LL, 1m/1m	6.45	8.51	4.47	12.09	0.76	1.45	0.53	368.03
LL, 12m/1m	6.33	8.78	4.72	27.05	0.72	1.34	0.23	354.68
LS, 6m/3m	7.74	10.86	5.93	23.23	0.71	1.30	0.33	530.13
LL, 12m/3m	6.12	8.60	4.52	21.80	0.71	1.35	0.28	333.41
LS, 12m/3m	7.49	10.53	6.47	23.11	0.71	1.16	0.32	495.10
LL, 3m/1m	5.84	8.68	5.06	17.98	0.67	1.15	0.32	305.64
LS, 12m/1m	6.96	10.73	6.45	23.77	0.65	1.08	0.29	426.61
LL, 6m/1m	4.34	7.93	4.67	23.10	0.55	0.93	0.19	185.26
LL, 6m/3m	4.26	8.19	5.01	17.22	0.52	0.85	0.25	180.16
LS, 3m/1m	5.66	12.17	7.45	22.58	0.47	0.76	0.25	289.56
LS, 1m/1m	4.74	12.08	7.63	24.37	0.39	0.62	0.19	213.29
LS, 1m/3m	4.17	10.98	7.39	43.59	0.38	0.56	0.10	174.20
LS, 3m/3m	3.27	11.66	7.33	31.42	0.28	0.45	0.10	121.32

Table A.3 Factor Momentum Results: Dollar Neutral Without XSMOM 24.75Y

Strategy	Mean (%)	Std (%)	DownDev (%)	MDD (%)	Sharpe	Sortino	Calmar	CumRet (%)
LW, 6m/1m	15.57	12.79	5.86	17.34	1.22	2.65	0.90	3456.52
LW, 6m/3m	14.87	12.64	5.82	17.34	1.18	2.55	0.86	2959.62
LW, 12m/1m	13.98	12.35	5.81	18.41	1.13	2.41	0.76	2424.71
LW, 12m/3m	12.96	12.68	6.32	29.81	1.02	2.05	0.43	1924.69
LW, 1m/3m	13.63	13.36	7.08	18.40	1.02	1.93	0.74	2241.97
Enterprise 18	28.88	28.35	13.80	43.82	1.02	2.09	0.66	52,336.32
EW18	11.88	11.81	5.77	19.73	1.01	2.06	0.60	1497.56
LW, 3m/3m	13.69	13.74	6.97	23.99	1.00	1.96	0.57	2271.22
EW16 ex-XSMOM	12.33	12.39	5.88	20.09	0.99	2.10	0.61	1664.76
LW, 3m/1m	13.93	14.06	7.29	21.11	0.99	1.91	0.66	2397.57
LW, 1m/1m	13.31	13.51	6.84	20.79	0.99	1.95	0.64	2086.77
LL, 1m/3m	9.64	14.24	7.45	34.53	0.68	1.29	0.28	868.64
LL, 6m/3m	8.57	13.43	7.24	27.44	0.64	1.18	0.31	660.41

LL, 3m/3m	8.28	13.20	6.90	29.40	0.63	1.20	0.28	612.54
LL, 6m/1m	7.88	13.07	7.46	26.54	0.60	1.06	0.30	549.91
LL, 12m/1m	8.17	13.63	7.64	29.81	0.60	1.07	0.27	595.07
LL, 1m/1m	8.43	14.35	8.01	26.38	0.59	1.05	0.32	637.00
LL, 12m/3m	7.83	14.10	8.24	24.40	0.56	0.95	0.32	542.70
LL, 3m/1m	7.55	14.15	7.62	27.98	0.53	0.99	0.27	503.10
LS, 12m/1m	7.33	16.42	10.47	35.11	0.45	0.70	0.21	473.72
LS, 12m/3m	6.82	17.20	11.06	57.43	0.40	0.62	0.12	410.15
LS, 6m/1m	5.69	17.15	11.06	33.31	0.33	0.51	0.17	292.10
LS, 6m/3m	4.82	16.54	11.02	31.44	0.29	0.44	0.15	219.93
LS, 3m/3m	3.47	17.63	11.64	47.91	0.20	0.30	0.07	132.22
LS, 3m/1m	3.32	20.01	14.14	43.36	0.17	0.23	0.08	123.96
LS, 1m/1m	3.03	20.31	13.32	39.21	0.15	0.23	0.08	108.85
LS, 1m/3m	1.98	18.06	13.07	58.55	0.11	0.15	0.03	62.43

Table A.4 Factor Momentum Results: Beta Neutral with XSMOM 24.75Y

Strategy	Mean (%)	Std (%)	DownDev (%)	MDD (%)	Sharpe	Sortino	Calmar	CumRet (%)
LW, 6m/1m	13.28	8.04	3.08	8.27	1.65	4.31	1.61	2072.20
EW18	10.74	6.52	2.58	7.85	1.65	4.16	1.37	1139.05
Enterprise 18	24.17	14.80	6.62	16.10	1.63	3.65	1.50	20,831.24
LW, 6m/3m	12.01	7.61	3.37	10.81	1.58	3.56	1.11	1542.93
LW, 12m/1m	11.93	7.59	3.26	10.00	1.57	3.65	1.19	1515.53
LW, 12m/3m	11.79	7.66	3.36	10.91	1.54	3.51	1.08	1464.60
LW, 1m/3m	12.46	8.73	4.03	21.56	1.43	3.09	0.58	1715.17
LW, 3m/1m	12.36	8.95	3.88	10.68	1.38	3.19	1.16	1675.94
LW, 3m/3m	10.83	8.32	3.96	11.35	1.30	2.73	0.95	1166.50
LW, 1m/1m	11.47	9.14	4.11	11.44	1.25	2.79	1.00	1358.60
LL, 3m/3m	7.57	8.59	4.51	17.22	0.88	1.68	0.44	506.09
LL, 1m/3m	7.64	9.45	4.82	19.63	0.81	1.58	0.39	515.07

LS, 6m/1m	8.78	11.04	6.16	20.83	0.80	1.43	0.42	698.11
LL, 12m/3m	6.59	8.59	4.62	21.80	0.77	1.43	0.30	383.45
LL, 12m/1m	5.92	8.60	4.77	27.05	0.69	1.24	0.22	313.19
LL, 1m/1m	6.43	9.98	5.81	21.40	0.64	1.11	0.30	365.26
LS, 12m/1m	7.14	11.16	6.80	27.02	0.64	1.05	0.26	448.87
LS, 6m/3m	6.75	11.17	6.60	22.97	0.60	1.02	0.29	401.33
LS, 12m/3m	6.53	10.95	6.91	31.29	0.60	0.94	0.21	376.06
LL, 6m/3m	4.85	8.26	4.98	14.99	0.59	0.97	0.32	221.90
LL, 3m/1m	5.09	9.21	5.61	16.94	0.55	0.91	0.30	240.33
LL, 6m/1m	4.23	7.99	4.69	16.59	0.53	0.90	0.25	177.71
LS, 3m/1m	5.90	13.14	8.56	28.72	0.45	0.69	0.21	311.34
LS, 1m/3m	3.41	13.23	9.77	60.22	0.26	0.35	0.06	128.62
LS, 1m/1m	3.57	15.02	9.70	35.56	0.24	0.37	0.10	137.52
LS, 3m/3m	2.29	12.51	8.68	38.15	0.18	0.26	0.06	74.67

Table A.5 Factor Momentum Results: Dollar Neutral with XSMOM 24.75Y

Strategy	Mean (%)	Std (%)	DownDev (%)	MDD (%)	Sharpe	Sortino	Calmar	CumRet (%)
LW, 6m/1m	14.30	13.20	6.71	19.62	1.08	2.13	0.73	2606.71
LW, 6m/3m	13.97	13.02	6.49	19.62	1.07	2.15	0.71	2423.45
LW, 12m/1m	13.31	12.88	6.40	18.10	1.03	2.08	0.74	2083.83
Enterprise 18	28.88	28.35	13.80	43.82	1.02	2.09	0.66	52,336.32
EW18	11.88	11.81	5.77	19.73	1.01	2.06	0.60	1497.56
LW, 12m/3m	12.47	13.22	6.89	26.81	0.94	1.81	0.46	1716.60
LW, 1m/1m	12.53	13.74	7.26	21.86	0.91	1.72	0.57	1742.14
LW, 1m/3m	12.42	13.90	7.91	30.02	0.89	1.57	0.41	1697.17
LW, 3m/1m	12.57	14.27	7.87	24.13	0.88	1.60	0.52	1760.42
LW, 3m/3m	12.20	14.19	7.84	23.12	0.86	1.56	0.53	1615.18
LL, 6m/1m	9.28	12.65	7.31	24.44	0.73	1.27	0.38	793.18
LL, 3m/3m	9.29	12.70	6.59	26.92	0.73	1.41	0.35	795.07

LL, 1m/3m	10.12	14.20	7.33	30.05	0.71	1.38	0.34	979.36
LL, 12m/3m	9.71	13.98	8.04	24.54	0.69	1.21	0.40	884.42
LL, 12m/1m	8.79	13.82	7.91	32.41	0.64	1.11	0.27	699.59
LL, 6m/3m	8.25	13.32	7.94	34.88	0.62	1.04	0.24	607.25
LL, 3m/1m	8.28	14.18	7.61	26.32	0.58	1.09	0.31	612.26
LL, 1m/1m	8.19	15.40	9.14	29.88	0.53	0.90	0.27	597.68
LS, 12m/1m	6.06	16.18	10.53	35.85	0.37	0.57	0.17	326.90
LS, 6m/3m	4.50	15.72	10.46	33.32	0.29	0.43	0.14	196.61
LS, 12m/3m	4.61	17.19	11.64	53.79	0.27	0.40	0.09	203.94
LS, 6m/1m	3.39	16.55	11.13	35.54	0.20	0.30	0.10	127.70
LS, 1m/1m	1.82	22.88	15.07	47.10	0.08	0.12	0.04	56.12
LS, 3m/1m	1.38	19.95	14.83	46.04	0.07	0.09	0.03	40.26
LS, 3m/3m	1.22	17.92	12.68	56.42	0.07	0.10	0.02	35.04
LS, 1m/3m	0.11	19.87	15.09	73.84	0.01	0.01	0.00	2.81

APPENDIX A.5.2: 22.75Y Results

Table A.6 Factor Momentum Results: Beta Neutral Without XSMOM 22.75Y

Strategy	Mean (%)	Std (%)	DownDev (%)	MDD (%)	Sharpe	Sortino	Calmar	CumRet (%)
Enterprise 18	19.52	12.45	6.01	16.10	1.57	3.25	1.21	5524.69
LW, 6m/1m	10.59	6.84	2.72	7.92	1.55	3.89	1.34	873.25
EW16 ex-XSMOM	8.45	5.48	2.42	8.46	1.54	3.49	1.00	525.04
LW, 12m/1m	9.50	6.23	2.85	9.08	1.52	3.34	1.05	677.29
LW, 1m/3m	10.77	7.08	2.96	12.45	1.52	3.64	0.87	909.90
LW, 6m/3m	9.27	6.12	2.99	9.44	1.51	3.10	0.98	641.02
LW, 12m/3m	9.57	6.38	3.00	9.96	1.50	3.19	0.96	688.58
EW18	8.23	5.57	2.54	7.85	1.48	3.24	1.05	497.89
LW, 1m/1m	9.35	6.63	2.91	9.91	1.41	3.21	0.94	654.70
LW, 3m/1m	9.77	7.10	2.85	8.63	1.37	3.43	1.13	722.03
LW, 3m/3m	8.27	6.53	3.24	11.69	1.27	2.55	0.71	502.35
LL, 3m/3m	5.75	7.76	4.78	18.60	0.74	1.20	0.31	253.49
LL, 1m/3m	4.97	7.01	4.32	18.60	0.71	1.15	0.27	199.11
LL, 1m/1m	4.78	7.07	4.10	12.09	0.68	1.17	0.40	187.07

LS, 1m/3m	5.16	8.70	4.75	19.83	0.59	1.09	0.26	211.88
LS, 6m/1m	5.95	10.17	5.95	19.42	0.58	1.00	0.31	268.88
LL, 3m/1m	4.36	7.71	4.99	17.98	0.57	0.87	0.24	162.63
LS, 12m/3m	5.35	9.64	6.02	23.11	0.55	0.89	0.23	224.70
LL, 12m/1m	4.11	7.77	4.82	27.05	0.53	0.85	0.15	148.35
LL, 6m/3m	4.04	7.68	4.79	17.22	0.53	0.84	0.23	144.91
LL, 12m/3m	3.94	7.56	4.61	21.80	0.52	0.85	0.18	139.51
LL, 6m/1m	3.91	7.59	4.69	23.10	0.52	0.83	0.17	137.94
LS, 12m/1m	4.83	9.88	5.99	23.77	0.49	0.81	0.20	190.51
LS, 1m/1m	4.12	8.73	5.46	16.23	0.47	0.76	0.25	149.16
LS, 6m/3m	4.43	9.70	6.09	23.23	0.46	0.73	0.19	166.66
LS, 3m/1m	4.50	9.92	5.81	17.20	0.45	0.78	0.26	170.67
LS, 3m/3m	1.74	10.55	7.05	31.42	0.16	0.25	0.06	47.65

Table A.7 Factor Momentum Results: Dollar Neutral Without XSMOM 22.75Y

Strategy	Mean (%)	Std (%)	DownDev (%)	MDD (%)	Sharpe	Sortino	Calmar	CumRet (%)
LW, 6m/1m	11.60	9.68	5.32	17.34	1.20	2.18	0.67	1096.11
LW, 1m/3m	11.21	9.71	5.27	16.97	1.16	2.13	0.66	1004.90
LW, 6m/3m	10.83	9.46	5.31	17.34	1.14	2.04	0.62	922.64
LW, 1m/1m	10.08	9.44	4.96	20.79	1.07	2.03	0.48	776.56
LW, 12m/1m	10.09	9.55	5.32	18.41	1.06	1.90	0.55	778.95
LW, 3m/1m	11.07	10.64	5.86	21.11	1.04	1.89	0.52	974.08
EW16 ex-XSMOM	8.72	8.50	4.39	20.09	1.03	1.98	0.43	561.36
EW18	8.43	8.82	4.97	19.73	0.96	1.70	0.43	522.51
LW, 3m/3m	10.09	10.67	6.24	23.99	0.95	1.62	0.42	778.15
Enterprise 18	19.71	21.05	11.94	43.82	0.94	1.65	0.45	5736.87
LW, 12m/3m	8.94	9.95	5.95	29.81	0.90	1.50	0.30	592.95
LL, 6m/3m	7.04	12.36	6.81	27.44	0.57	1.03	0.26	365.64
LL, 3m/3m	6.36	11.19	6.50	29.40	0.57	0.98	0.22	302.67
LL, 6m/1m	6.83	12.23	7.09	26.54	0.56	0.96	0.26	344.80

LL, 12m/1m	6.61	12.08	6.79	29.81	0.55	0.97	0.22	324.66
LL, 12m/3m	6.39	12.59	7.39	24.40	0.51	0.87	0.26	305.44
LL, 1m/1m	5.51	11.61	7.30	26.38	0.47	0.75	0.21	235.97
LL, 1m/3m	4.40	10.98	6.85	34.53	0.40	0.64	0.13	164.47
LS, 1m/3m	5.29	14.62	9.05	44.57	0.36	0.58	0.12	220.70
LS, 3m/1m	5.44	15.59	10.13	39.01	0.35	0.54	0.14	230.80
LL, 3m/1m	3.77	11.52	7.45	27.98	0.33	0.51	0.13	130.74
LS, 1m/1m	3.32	15.63	9.69	39.21	0.21	0.34	0.08	109.16
LS, 6m/1m	3.10	16.08	11.10	33.31	0.19	0.28	0.09	99.16
LS, 12m/1m	2.83	15.18	10.72	35.11	0.19	0.26	0.08	87.71
LS, 3m/3m	2.22	15.51	10.95	47.91	0.14	0.20	0.05	64.30
LS, 6m/3m	2.10	15.51	11.19	31.44	0.14	0.19	0.07	60.12
LS, 12m/3m	2.07	16.11	11.35	57.43	0.13	0.18	0.04	58.97

Table A.8 Factor Momentum Results: Beta Neutral with XSMOM 22.75Y

Strategy	Mean (%)	Std (%)	DownDev (%)	MDD (%)	Sharpe	Sortino	Calmar	CumRet (%)
Enterprise 18	19.52	12.45	6.01	16.10	1.57	3.25	1.21	5524.69
EW18	8.23	5.57	2.54	7.85	1.48	3.24	1.05	497.89
LW, 1m/3m	11.12	7.53	3.09	11.94	1.48	3.60	0.93	983.02
LW, 6m/1m	10.57	7.24	3.09	8.27	1.46	3.43	1.28	868.99
LW, 6m/3m	9.10	6.62	3.41	10.81	1.37	2.67	0.84	615.39
LW, 12m/1m	9.37	6.86	3.28	10.00	1.37	2.85	0.94	657.31
LW, 12m/3m	9.21	6.93	3.39	10.91	1.33	2.72	0.84	632.91
LW, 3m/1m	9.78	7.56	3.25	9.13	1.29	3.00	1.07	723.56
LW, 1m/1m	8.90	7.08	3.39	10.00	1.26	2.63	0.89	586.97
LW, 3m/3m	8.06	7.02	3.74	11.35	1.15	2.15	0.71	476.08
LL, 3m/3m	6.21	7.49	4.16	17.22	0.83	1.49	0.36	290.26
LL, 1m/1m	4.95	7.61	4.51	15.23	0.65	1.10	0.33	198.32
LS, 6m/1m	6.71	10.46	6.31	20.83	0.64	1.06	0.32	334.45

LS, 1m/3m	5.90	9.21	4.92	18.27	0.64	1.20	0.32	265.58
LL, 1m/3m	4.53	7.18	4.63	19.63	0.63	0.98	0.23	172.10
LL, 12m/3m	4.63	8.07	4.73	21.80	0.57	0.98	0.21	177.95
LL, 6m/3m	4.33	7.79	4.78	14.99	0.56	0.91	0.29	160.88
LL, 3m/1m	4.04	7.99	5.29	16.94	0.51	0.76	0.24	144.66
LL, 12m/1m	3.72	8.04	4.89	27.05	0.46	0.76	0.14	128.35
LS, 12m/1m	4.96	10.87	6.97	27.02	0.46	0.71	0.18	198.54
LS, 3m/1m	4.75	10.44	6.39	21.20	0.46	0.74	0.22	185.63
LL, 6m/1m	3.14	7.54	4.73	16.59	0.42	0.66	0.19	100.97
LS, 12m/3m	4.11	10.60	7.09	31.29	0.39	0.58	0.13	148.73
LS, 6m/3m	3.93	10.44	6.77	22.97	0.38	0.58	0.17	138.81
LS, 1m/1m	3.42	9.64	6.21	23.47	0.35	0.55	0.15	113.63
LS, 3m/3m	1.14	10.60	7.60	38.15	0.11	0.15	0.03	29.08

Table A.9 Factor Momentum Results: Dollar Neutral with XSMOM 22.75Y

Strategy	Mean (%)	Std (%)	DownDev (%)	MDD (%)	Sharpe	Sortino	Calmar	CumRet (%)
LW, 6m/1m	10.73	10.24	6.04	19.62	1.05	1.78	0.55	900.94
LW, 6m/3m	10.30	9.96	5.81	19.62	1.03	1.77	0.52	816.34
LW, 1m/3m	10.75	10.42	6.04	21.08	1.03	1.78	0.51	905.05
LW, 1m/1m	9.36	9.74	5.35	21.86	0.96	1.75	0.43	655.91
LW, 12m/1m	9.67	10.09	5.78	18.10	0.96	1.67	0.53	705.93
EW18	8.43	8.82	4.97	19.73	0.96	1.70	0.43	522.51
Enterprise 18	19.71	21.05	11.94	43.82	0.94	1.65	0.45	5736.87
LW, 3m/1m	10.12	11.07	6.37	24.13	0.91	1.59	0.42	783.16
LW, 12m/3m	8.68	10.51	6.40	26.81	0.83	1.36	0.32	555.79
LW, 3m/3m	9.13	11.38	7.06	23.12	0.80	1.29	0.39	620.93
LL, 12m/3m	7.98	12.09	7.05	24.54	0.66	1.13	0.33	467.11
LL, 3m/3m	6.91	10.60	6.27	26.92	0.65	1.10	0.26	353.14
LL, 6m/1m	7.29	11.56	6.94	24.44	0.63	1.05	0.30	390.68

LL, 12m/1m	6.81	11.85	6.98	32.41	0.57	0.98	0.21	343.33
LL, 6m/3m	6.11	12.23	7.63	34.88	0.50	0.80	0.18	282.00
LL, 1m/1m	5.69	11.99	7.83	29.88	0.47	0.73	0.19	249.02
LL, 1m/3m	4.63	10.54	6.70	30.05	0.44	0.69	0.15	178.37
LL, 3m/1m	4.40	11.24	7.33	26.32	0.39	0.60	0.17	164.65
LS, 1m/3m	4.74	14.57	9.24	48.43	0.33	0.51	0.10	185.02
LS, 3m/1m	4.01	15.37	10.01	39.56	0.26	0.40	0.10	143.36
LS, 6m/3m	2.64	15.04	10.52	33.32	0.18	0.25	0.08	80.12
LS, 1m/1m	2.36	16.20	10.02	44.45	0.15	0.24	0.05	69.39
LS, 12m/1m	2.17	15.28	10.76	35.85	0.14	0.20	0.06	62.40
LS, 6m/1m	2.01	15.87	11.03	35.54	0.13	0.18	0.06	56.87
LS, 3m/3m	0.94	15.56	11.08	56.42	0.06	0.08	0.02	23.56
LS, 12m/3m	0.38	16.38	11.94	53.79	0.02	0.03	0.01	8.87

APPENDIX A.5.3: LIVE 5.75Y Results

Table A.10 Factor Momentum Results: Beta Neutral Without XSMOM 5.75Y

Strategy	Mean (%)	Std (%)	DownDev (%)	MDD (%)	Sharpe	Sortino	Calmar	CumRet (%)
LW, 6m/1m	16.15	10.96	4.02	7.92	1.47	4.02	2.04	131.03
LW, 1m/3m	17.06	11.73	4.73	12.45	1.45	3.61	1.37	141.28
LW, 3m/1m	14.78	11.52	3.83	8.63	1.28	3.85	1.71	116.13
LW, 12m/1m	11.73	9.34	4.38	9.08	1.26	2.68	1.29	85.93
Enterprise 18	23.03	18.63	9.67	16.10	1.24	2.38	1.43	218.65
EW16 ex-XSMOM	10.43	8.63	3.89	8.46	1.21	2.68	1.23	74.14
LW, 12m/3m	11.58	9.61	4.80	9.96	1.21	2.41	1.16	84.58
EW18	10.49	8.77	4.06	7.85	1.20	2.58	1.34	74.66
LW, 6m/3m	9.87	9.28	4.74	9.44	1.06	2.08	1.05	69.28
LW, 1m/1m	11.50	10.98	4.81	9.91	1.05	2.39	1.16	83.76
LW, 3m/3m	9.07	9.87	4.45	11.69	0.92	2.04	0.78	62.45
LS, 1m/3m	11.56	12.66	6.10	15.75	0.91	1.89	0.73	84.32
LS, 6m/1m	12.41	14.57	6.87	19.42	0.85	1.81	0.64	92.37

LS, 3m/1m	10.37	13.74	6.41	17.20	0.75	1.62	0.60	73.59
LL, 1m/1m	6.37	9.50	4.76	8.01	0.67	1.34	0.80	41.24
LL, 12m/3m	5.96	11.18	6.91	18.79	0.53	0.86	0.32	38.21
LL, 12m/1m	5.32	11.28	7.35	22.85	0.47	0.72	0.23	33.61
LL, 1m/3m	4.34	9.92	6.44	18.47	0.44	0.67	0.24	26.84
LL, 3m/3m	4.92	11.26	7.73	18.60	0.44	0.64	0.26	30.83
LS, 6m/3m	5.71	13.93	8.34	23.23	0.41	0.68	0.25	36.43
LS, 12m/1m	5.02	13.86	7.93	23.77	0.36	0.63	0.21	31.51
LS, 1m/1m	4.22	12.23	7.71	16.23	0.35	0.55	0.26	26.01
LS, 12m/3m	4.00	13.77	8.92	23.11	0.29	0.45	0.17	24.53
LL, 6m/1m	2.63	10.45	6.91	20.12	0.25	0.38	0.13	15.64
LL, 6m/3m	2.77	11.07	7.43	14.29	0.25	0.37	0.19	16.53
LL, 3m/1m	2.45	10.93	7.58	17.08	0.22	0.32	0.14	14.48
LS, 3m/3m	2.70	14.81	8.16	31.42	0.18	0.33	0.09	16.07

Table A.11 Factor Momentum Results: Dollar Neutral Without XSMOM 5.75Y

Strategy	Mean (%)	Std (%)	DownDev (%)	MDD (%)	Sharpe	Sortino	Calmar	CumRet (%)
LW, 1m/3m	16.59	12.34	5.70	12.16	1.34	2.91	1.36	135.87
LW, 6m/1m	14.75	12.52	6.22	10.20	1.18	2.37	1.45	115.84
LW, 6m/3m	10.15	12.18	6.78	15.54	0.83	1.50	0.65	71.69
LW, 12m/1m	10.55	12.71	7.18	18.41	0.83	1.47	0.57	75.25
EW16 ex-XSMOM	9.62	11.67	6.18	20.09	0.82	1.56	0.48	67.13
LL, 3m/3m	10.67	13.19	7.43	18.41	0.81	1.44	0.58	76.31
EW18	9.10	11.50	6.45	19.73	0.79	1.41	0.46	62.77
LS, 1m/3m	13.74	18.07	8.98	13.71	0.76	1.53	1.00	105.43
LL, 1m/1m	10.68	14.33	7.47	18.84	0.75	1.43	0.57	76.36
LW, 3m/1m	10.56	14.84	7.78	14.76	0.71	1.36	0.72	75.32
LL, 6m/1m	9.46	14.11	8.31	26.54	0.67	1.14	0.36	65.78
Enterprise 18	16.97	26.96	16.03	43.82	0.63	1.06	0.39	140.20
LW, 1m/1m	7.05	13.24	8.01	20.79	0.53	0.88	0.34	46.36

LW, 3m/3m	7.02	14.33	8.08	23.99	0.49	0.87	0.29	46.15
LL, 12m/3m	7.30	16.93	10.29	21.71	0.43	0.71	0.34	48.29
LL, 6m/3m	5.71	13.75	8.23	23.56	0.42	0.69	0.24	36.43
LL, 12m/1m	6.42	15.57	9.12	27.78	0.41	0.70	0.23	41.61
LW, 12m/3m	5.38	13.78	9.03	29.81	0.39	0.60	0.18	34.05
LL, 3m/1m	5.73	15.36	10.30	26.87	0.37	0.56	0.21	36.57
LS, 6m/1m	4.05	17.50	11.39	33.31	0.23	0.36	0.12	24.85
LS, 6m/3m	3.06	16.43	11.33	31.44	0.19	0.27	0.10	18.37
LS, 3m/1m	1.57	19.75	12.71	39.01	0.08	0.12	0.04	9.12
LS, 12m/1m	0.98	18.53	12.13	35.11	0.05	0.08	0.03	5.62
LL, 1m/3m	0.47	15.38	10.85	34.53	0.03	0.04	0.01	2.66
LS, 12m/3m	–4.43	21.07	14.88	57.43	–0.21	–0.30	–0.08	–22.36
LS, 3m/3m	–4.53	16.62	12.50	47.91	–0.27	–0.36	–0.09	–22.82
LS, 1m/1m	–5.14	18.85	13.56	36.11	–0.27	–0.38	–0.14	–25.57

Table A.12 Factor Momentum Results: Beta Neutral with XSMOM 5.75Y

Strategy	Mean (%)	Std (%)	DownDev (%)	MDD (%)	Sharpe	Sortino	Calmar	CumRet (%)
LW, 1m/3m	17.90	12.30	4.77	11.94	1.46	3.75	1.50	151.17
LW, 6m/1m	15.38	11.36	4.42	8.27	1.35	3.48	1.86	122.54
LW, 3m/1m	15.02	11.78	4.01	9.13	1.28	3.74	1.64	118.67
Enterprise 18	23.03	18.63	9.67	16.10	1.24	2.38	1.43	218.65
EW18	10.49	8.77	4.06	7.85	1.20	2.58	1.34	74.66
LW, 12m/1m	11.26	10.04	4.74	10.00	1.12	2.38	1.13	81.58
LW, 12m/3m	10.78	10.26	5.11	10.91	1.05	2.11	0.99	77.31
LW, 1m/1m	11.35	11.32	4.96	10.00	1.00	2.29	1.13	82.40
LS, 1m/3m	12.81	13.14	6.42	15.08	0.97	1.99	0.85	96.20
LW, 6m/3m	9.39	9.82	5.19	10.81	0.96	1.81	0.87	65.22
LL, 3m/3m	8.81	9.60	5.24	9.23	0.92	1.68	0.95	60.38
LW, 3m/3m	8.42	10.22	5.03	11.35	0.82	1.67	0.74	57.15
LS, 6m/1m	10.90	14.26	7.34	20.83	0.76	1.49	0.52	78.31

LS, 3m/1m	9.83	13.42	6.88	21.20	0.73	1.43	0.46	68.90
LL, 12m/3m	7.77	11.32	6.74	18.79	0.69	1.15	0.41	51.97
LL, 1m/1m	6.34	9.94	5.28	10.37	0.64	1.20	0.61	41.05
LL, 12m/1m	5.33	10.99	6.97	22.85	0.48	0.76	0.23	33.67
LL, 6m/3m	4.28	10.95	7.10	9.44	0.39	0.60	0.45	26.38
LL, 1m/3m	3.91	10.06	6.62	19.63	0.39	0.59	0.20	23.94
LL, 6m/1m	3.45	10.15	6.65	14.44	0.34	0.52	0.24	20.90
LS, 1m/1m	4.05	12.64	7.87	17.92	0.32	0.51	0.23	24.85
LS, 12m/1m	4.53	14.40	8.77	27.02	0.31	0.52	0.17	28.10
LL, 3m/1m	3.21	11.12	7.83	16.94	0.29	0.41	0.19	19.31
LS, 6m/3m	3.76	14.19	8:83	22.97	0.27	0.43	0.16	22.95
LS, 12m/3m	1.48	14.25	9.87	31.29	0.10	0.15	0.05	8.56
LS, 3m/3m	–1.13	12.87	8.67	38.15	–0.09	–0.13	–0.03	–6.15

Table A.13 Factor Momentum Results: Dollar Neutral with XSMOM 5.75Y

Strategy	Mean (%)	Std (%)	DownDev (%)	MDD (%)	Sharpe	Sortino	Calmar	CumRet (%)
LW, 1m/3m	15.30	12.55	6.06	11.90	1.22	2.52	1.29	121.64
LL, 3m/3m	12.79	12.33	6.99	17.86	1.04	1.83	0.72	96.03
LW, 6m/1m	12.79	12.54	6.63	10.33	1.02	1.93	1.24	96.04
EW18	9.10	11.50	6.45	19.73	0.79	1.41	0.46	62.77
LL, 6m/1m	10.60	13.55	8.06	24.44	0.78	1.32	0.43	75.63
LW, 6m/3m	9.39	12.23	6.86	15.21	0.77	1.37	0.62	65.19
LW, 12m/1m	9.60	12.72	7.20	18.10	0.76	1.33	0.53	67.00
LL, 1m/1m	10.12	14.19	7.40	16.70	0.71	1.37	0.61	71.42
LS, 1m/3m	12.12	17.22	9.16	12.98	0.70	1.32	0.93	89.63
Enterprise 18	16.97	26.96	16.03	43.82	0.63	1.06	0.39	140.20
LW, 3m/1m	8.72	14.60	7.84	17.59	0.60	1.11	0.50	59.60
LL, 12m/3m	9.27	15.70	9.63	21.96	0.59	0.96	0.42	64.15
LL, 3m/1m	7.51	14.74	9.59	22.99	0.51	0.78	0.33	49.92

LL, 12m/1m	7.14	14.69	8.65	27.18	0.49	0.83	0.26	47.03
LL, 6m/3m	6.03	13.27	8.11	22.51	0.45	0.74	0.27	38.71
LW, 1m/1m	5.35	13.15	8.27	21.86	0.41	0.65	0.24	33.86
LW, 3m/3m	5.85	14.43	8.32	23.12	0.41	0.70	0.25	37.40
LW, 12m/3m	5.40	13.66	8.68	26.81	0.40	0.62	0.20	34.17
LS, 6m/3m	2.29	15.39	10.38	27.12	0.15	0.22	0.08	13.48
LS, 6m/1m	1.38	16.86	11.50	28.90	0.08	0.12	0.05	7.97
LL, 1m/3m	1.07	14.59	10.30	30.05	0.07	0.10	0.04	6.15
LS, 12m/1m	−0.55	17.96	12.07	35.48	−0.03	−0.05	−0.02	−3.02
LS, 3m/1m	−1.64	19.17	13.20	39.56	−0.09	−0.12	−0.04	−8.83
LS, 12m/3m	−5.75	19.79	14.45	53.79	−0.29	−0.40	−0.11	−28.18
LS, 1m/1m	−6.06	18.18	13.37	32.25	−0.33	−0.45	−0.19	−29.48
LS, 3m/3m	−7.17	15.91	12.51	50.84	−0.45	−0.57	−0.14	−34.02

APPENDIX A.5.4: Q-Q Plots of Strategy Returns

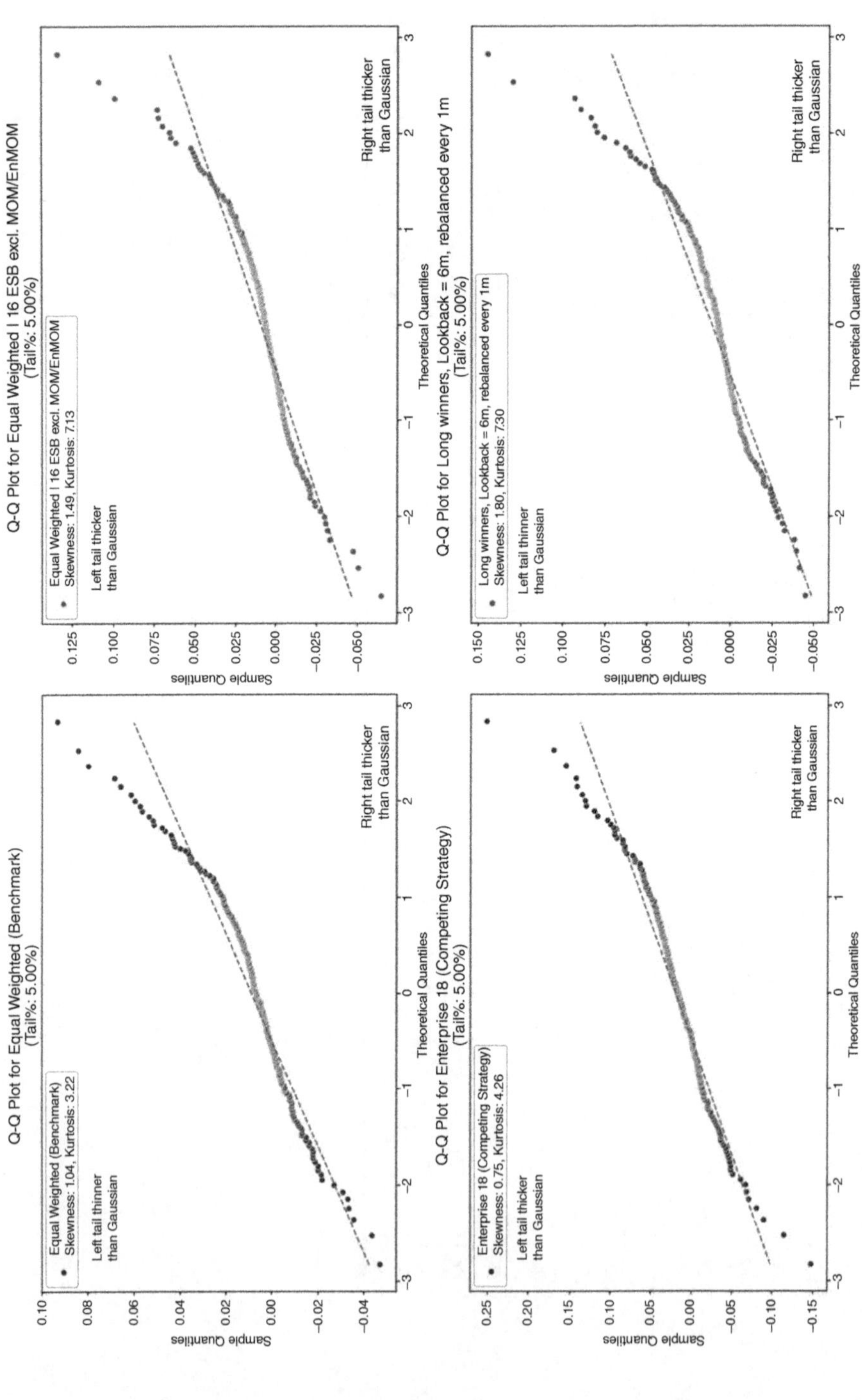

Figure A.13 Visualizing Positive Skew and Asymmetric Tails in Strategy Returns.

Long-only factor portfolios exhibit diversification benefits that truncate the left tail of the return distribution – reducing extreme negative returns – while amplifying the right tail, enhancing extreme positive returns. This pattern provides evidence of factor momentum combined with downside protection when compared to the Ent18 signal. Notably, the Ent18 signal represents a single equity market-neutral combined signal, whereas the EW18, EW16, and LW portfolios are all long-only portfolios of individual ESBs, offering diversification across different ESBs.

APPENDIX A.5.5: Kernel Density Estimate of Strategy Returns

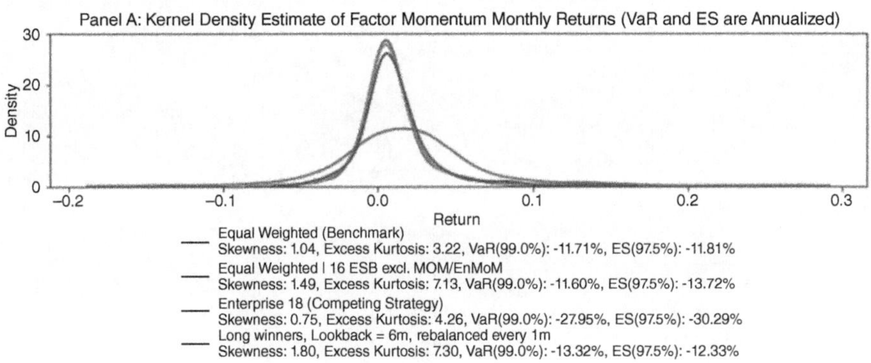

Figure A.14 Kernel Density Estimates of Positively Skewed Strategy Returns.

Disclaimers

- All content herein is owned by QuantZ Machine Intelligence Technologies ("QMIT") and/or its affiliates and protected by United States and international copyright laws. QMIT content may not be reproduced, transmitted, or distributed without the prior written consent of QMIT.
- QMIT is a provider of market research, signals, analytics, and QIS indices for synthetic hedge fund swaps/structured products. It is neither a broker-dealer nor an investment advisor.
- QMIT makes no representation regarding the advisability of investing in any investment fund, other investment vehicle, security or other financial product regardless of whether or not it is based on, derived from, or included as a constituent of any QMIT research. QMIT bears no responsibility or liability for any business decision, input, recommendation, or action taken based on QMIT research or any products based on, derived from, or included as a constituent of any such research. This content is not intended as an offer to sell or a solicitation of any investment product or service to any person in any jurisdiction in which such offer or solicitation is not authorized or to any person to whom it would be unlawful to make such offer or solicitation.

- This information has been prepared by QMIT for informational and educational purposes only. This information should not be construed as investment, legal, and/or tax advice. This information was produced by and the opinions expressed are those of QMIT as of the date of writing and are subject to change. Any research is based on QMIT proprietary research and analysis of global markets and investing, including opinions that are expressed based on statistical forecasting from historical data. The information and/or analysis presented have been compiled or arrived at from sources believed to be reliable; however, QMIT does not make any representation as their accuracy or completeness and does not accept liability for any loss arising from the use hereof. There is no assurance that such events or targets will be achieved. They may turn out to be significantly different than that shown here. The information presented, including statements concerning financial market trends, is based on current market conditions, which will fluctuate and may be superseded by subsequent market events or for other reasons. Neither QMIT nor its third-party content providers shall be liable for any errors, inaccuracies, or delays in content, or for any actions taken in reliance thereon.
- QMIT EXPRESSLY DISCLAIMS ALL WARRANTIES, EXPRESSED OR IMPLIED, AS TO THE ACCURACY OF ANY OF THE CONTENT PROVIDED, OR AS TO THE FITNESS OF THE INFORMATION FOR ANY PURPOSE.
- Broad-based securities indices may be included in this report as benchmarks to provide context reflecting general market results during the period. QMIT may propose certain securities that are not represented by such indices. Accordingly, no representations are made that the performance or volatility of securities mentioned in the research will track or reflect any particular index. Broad-based securities indices are unmanaged and are not subject to fees and expenses typically associated with

managed accounts or investment funds. The number and types of securities found in the index can differ greatly from that of current or past QMIT research. Investments cannot be made directly in an index.

- Any securities or allocations referenced by QMIT may or may not be represented in portfolios of clients of QuantZ and do not represent all of the securities purchased, sold, or recommended for the managed private fund(s). In addition, QuantZ may have concentrations in a number of securities and in asset classes that differ from the QMIT research. Due to differences in actual account allocations, account opening date, timing of cash flow in or out of the account, rebalancing frequency, transaction costs, fees, and various other transaction-based or market factors, a client's actual return may be materially different than those derived from the research. The performance results for individuals following the strategy could also differ based on differences in treatment of dividends received, including the amount received and whether and when such dividends were reinvested.
- The information contained herein is provided for informational and educational purposes only and should not be construed as investment advice or a recommendation with respect to any security, strategy, or investment product. Nothing herein constitutes an offer to sell or a solicitation of an offer to buy any securities or other financial instruments. Any such offering will be made only pursuant to a confidential offering memorandum, subscription agreement, and other definitive documentation, which should be carefully reviewed in their entirety.
- Past performance is not necessarily indicative of, nor a guarantee of, future results. The value of investments and the income derived from them can decrease as well as increase, and investors may lose some or all of their capital. Future performance may vary materially from historical performance due to changes in market conditions,

economic factors, interest rates, political and geopolitical developments, and other risks and uncertainties. Certain performance results presented may be based on back-tested or simulated data, which are hypothetical in nature and subject to inherent limitations, including the fact that they do not reflect actual trading, liquidity constraints, or the impact of material economic and market factors on decision-making.

- Forward-looking statements, forecasts, or projections are based on assumptions, expectations, and information available at the time of writing and are subject to change without notice. Actual results may differ materially from those expressed or implied. No representation or warranty, express or implied, is made as to the accuracy, completeness, or reliability of the information contained herein, and all such information is subject to revision, verification, and completion. Neither the author(s), nor their affiliates, shall have any liability whatsoever for any direct, indirect, or consequential losses arising from the use of this material or reliance on the information contained herein.
- Investors should perform their own due diligence and consult with their independent financial, legal, tax, or other professional advisors before making any investment decision.
- All data used in this book should be assumed to be taken from public sources such as Yahoo Finance or Google Finance or Perplexity, else through paid subscriptions such as FactSet Data Systems, Inc.
- The Chapter 9 study of transaction costs is based on data from the BEAST model provided by FactSet Data Systems, Inc. courtesy of Christopher Sparrow and Melinda Bui.
- The Chapter 11 study was based on data and collaborative input provided by RavenPack and initially presented at their conferences in 2019.

Bibliography

Aghassi, M., Asness, C. S., Ilmanen, A., & Liew, J. (2023). Finding and exploiting orthogonal factors. *The Journal of Portfolio Management, 49*(3), 113–133.

Aharoni, G., Grundy, B., & Zeng, Q. (2013). Stock returns and the Miller Modigliani valuation formula: Revisiting the Fama French analysis. *Journal of Financial Economics, 110*(2), 347–365.

Almeida, H., Fos, V., & Kronlund, M. (2016). The real effects of share repurchases. *Journal of Financial Economics, 119*(1), 168–185.

Almgren, R., & Chriss, N. (2001). Optimal execution of portfolio transactions. *Journal of Risk, 3*(2), 5–39.

Ang, A., Chen, J., & Xing, Y. (2006). Downside risk. *The Review of Financial Studies, 19*(4), 1191–1239. https://doi.org/10.1093/rfs/hhj035

Angrist, J. D., & Pischke, J.-S. (2009). *Mostly harmless econometrics: An empiricist's companion*. Princeton University Press.

Araci, D. (2019). *FinBERT: Financial sentiment analysis with pre-trained language models*. arXiv preprint1908.10063.

Arnott, R. D., Clements, M., Kalesnik, V., & Linnainmaa, J. T. (2021). Factor momentum. *The Journal of Portfolio Management, 47*(4), 84–101.

Artzner, P., Delbaen, F., Eber, J.-M., & Heath, D. (1999). Coherent measures of risk. *Mathematical Finance, 9*(3), 203–228.

Asness, C. S. (2014). Fact, fiction, and value investing. *The Journal of Portfolio Management, 40*(4), 15–33.

Asness, C. S., & Frazzini, A. (2013). The devil in HML's details. *The Journal of Portfolio Management, 39*(4), 49–68.

Asness, C. S., Frazzini, A., Israel, R., Moskowitz, T. J., & Pedersen, L. H. (2018). Size matters, if you control your junk. *Journal of Financial Economics, 129*(3), 479–509.

Asness, C. S., Frazzini, A., & Pedersen, L. H. (2019). Quality minus junk. *Review of Accounting Studies, 24*(1), 34–112.

Asness, C. S., Moskowitz, T. J., & Pedersen, L. H. (2013). Value and momentum everywhere. *Journal of Finance, 68*(3), 929–985.

Athey, S., & Imbens, G. (2019). Machine learning methods that economists should know about. *Annual Review of Economics, 11*, 685–725.

Avellaneda, M., & Lee, J.-H. (2010). Statistical arbitrage in the U.S. equity market. *Quantitative Finance, 10*(7), 761–782.

Aydınhan, A. O., Kolm, P. N., Mulvey, J. M., & Shu, Y. (2024). Identifying patterns in financial markets: Extending the statistical jump model for regime identification. *Annals of Operations Research*, 1–37.

Baker, M., Bradley, B., & Wurgler, J. (2011). Benchmarks as limits to arbitrage: Understanding the low-volatility anomaly. *Financial Analysts Journal, 67*(1), 40–54.

Bali, T. G., Brown, S. J., Murray, S., & Tang, Y. (2017). A lottery demand-based explanation of the betting against beta anomaly. *Journal of Financial and Quantitative Analysis, 52*(6), 2369–2397.

Bali, T. G., Cakici, N., & Whitelaw, R. F. (2011). Maxing out: Stocks as lotteries and the cross-section of expected returns. *Journal of Financial Economics, 99*(2), 427–450.

Banz, R. W. (1981). The relationship between return and market value of common stocks. *Journal of Financial Economics, 9*(1), 3–18.

Barberis, N., Shleifer, A., & Vishny, R. (1998). A model of investor sentiment. *Journal of Financial Economics, 49*(3), 307–343.

Basu, S. (1977). Investment performance of common stocks in relation to their price-earnings ratios. *Journal of Finance, 32*(3), 663–682.

Bauman, W. S., & Dowen, R. (1988). Growth projections and common stock returns. *Financial Analysts Journal, 44*(4), 79–80.

Berk, J. B. (2023). Discussion of "The Virtue of Complexity in Return Prediction". *The Review of Asset Pricing Studies, 13*(2), 296–301.

Berkin, A. L., & Swedroe, L. E. (2015). *Your complete guide to factor-based investing: The way smart money invests today*. Buckingham.

Black, F. (1972). Capital market equilibrium with restricted borrowing. *The Journal of Business, 45*(3), 444–455.

Black, F., Jensen, M. C., & Scholes, M. (1972). The capital asset pricing model: Some empirical tests. In M. C. Jensen (Ed.), *Studies in the theory of capital markets* (pp. 79–121). Praeger.

Blitz, D., & van Vliet, P. (2007). The volatility effect: Lower risk without lower return. *The Journal of Portfolio Management, 34*(1), 102–113.

Boehmer, E., Huszar, Z., & Jordan, B. (2010). The good news in short interest. *Journal of Financial Economics, 96*(1), 80–97.

Bojanowski, P., Grave, E., Joulin, A., & Mikolov, T. (2017). Enriching word vectors with subword information. *Transactions of the Association for Computational Linguistics, 5*, 135–146. https://doi.org/10.1162/tacl_a_00051

Breiman, L. (2001). Statistical modeling: The two cultures. *Statistical Science, 16*(3), 199–231.

Brown, L. D., & Rozeff, M. S. (1978). The superiority of analyst forecasts as measures of expectations: Evidence from earnings. *Journal of Finance, 33*(1), 1–16.

Buncic, D. (2025). Simplified: A closer look at the virtue of complexity in return prediction. Available at SSRN.

Carhart, M. M. (1997). On persistence in mutual fund performance. *The Journal of Finance, 52*(1), 57–82.

Cambria, E., Li, Y., Xing, F. Z., & Poria, S. (2020). SenticNet 6: Ensemble application of symbolic and subsymbolic AI for sentiment analysis. In *Proceedings of the 29th ACM International Conference on Information & Knowledge Management (CIKM '20)* (pp. 2597–2604). Association for Computing Machinery. https://doi.org/10.1145/3340531.3412001

Capponi, A., Du, C., & Stiglitz, J. E. (2024). *Are supply networks efficiently resilient?* (No. w32221). National Bureau of Economic Research.

Cassel, A., Edwards, D., Harshfield, A., Rhodes, K., Brimicombe, J., Payne, R., & Griffin, S. (2018). The epidemiology of multimorbidity in primary care: A retrospective cohort study. *British Journal of General Practice, 68*(669), e245–e251. https://doi.org/10.3399/bjgp18X695465

Causal AI. (2022, October 18). *An introduction to Causal AI for institutional investment managers* [Video]. YouTube.

Chan, K., & Chen, N. (1991). Structural and return characteristics of small and large firms. *Journal of Finance, 46*(4), 1467–1484.

Chan, L. K. C., Jegadeesh, N., & Lakonishok, J. (1996). Momentum strategies. *Journal of Finance, 51*(5), 1681–1713.

Chen, A. Y., Lopez-Lira, A., & Zimmermann, T. (2023). Datamining, selection bias, and the cross-section of stock returns. SSRN Working Paper.

Chen, A. Y., & Zimmermann, T. (2022). Open source cross-sectional asset pricing. *Critical Finance Review, 11*(2), 207–264.

Chen, N., & Zhang, F. (1998). Risk and return of value stocks. *Journal of Business, 71*(4), 501–535.

Chernozhukov, V., Chetverikov, D., Demirer, M., Duflo, E., Hansen, C., Newey, W., & Robins, J. (2018). Double/debiased machine learning for treatment and structural parameters. *The Econometrics Journal, 21*(1), C1–C68.

Chordia, T., & Shivakumar, L. (2006). Earnings and price momentum. *Journal of Financial Economics, 80*(3), 627–656.

Cochrane, J. H. (1996). A cross-sectional test of an investment-based asset pricing model. *Journal of Political Economy, 104*(3), 572–621.

Cochrane, J. H. (2011). Presidential address: Discount rates. *Journal of Finance, 66*(4), 1047–1108.

Connor, G. (1995). The three types of factor models: A comparison of their explanatory power. *Financial Analysts Journal, 51*(3), 42–46.

Cortese, F. P., Kolm, P. N., & Lindström, E. (2023). What drives cryptocurrency returns? A sparse statistical jump model approach. SSRN Electronic Journal.

Cortese, F. P., Kolm, P. N., & Lindström, E. (2024). Generalized information criteria for high-dimensional sparse statistical jump models. SSRN Electronic Journal.

Daniel, K., Hirshleifer, D., & Subrahmanyam, A. (1998). Investor psychology and security market under- and overreactions. *The Journal of Finance, 53*(6), 1839–1885.

Daniel, K., Hirshleifer, D., & Sun, L. (2020). Short- and long-horizon behavioral factors. *The Review of Financial Studies, 33*(4), 1673–1736.

De Bondt, W. F., & Thaler, R. (1985). Does the stock market overreact? *The Journal of Finance, 40*(3), 793–805. https://doi.org/10.1111/j.1540-6261.1985.tb05004.x

Devlin, J., Chang, M.-W., Lee, K., & Toutanova, K. (2019). BERT: Pre-training of deep bidirectional transformers for language understanding. In *Proceedings of the 2019 Conference of the North American Chapter of the Association for Computational Linguistics: Human Language Technologies,* Volume 1 (Long and Short Papers) (pp. 4171–4186). Association for Computational Linguistics. https://doi.org/10.18653/v1/N19-1423

Diamandis, P. H., & Kotler, S. (2012). *Abundance: The future is better than you think.* Free Press.

Diether, K., Malloy, C., & Scherbina, A. (2002). Differences of opinion and the cross-section of stock returns. *Journal of Finance, 57*(5), 2113–2141.

Du, W., Ju, T., Ren, G., Li, G., & Liu, G. (2024). Backdoor NLP models via AI-generated text. In *Proceedings of the 2024 Joint International Conference on Computational Linguistics, Language Resources and Evaluation (LREC-COLING 2024)* (pp. 2067–2079). ELRA and ICCL.

Ehsani, S., & Linnainmaa, J. T. (2022). Factor momentum and the momentum factor. *Journal of Finance, 77*(3), 1675–1716.

Elgers, P. T., Lo, M. H., & Pfeiffer, R. J. (2001). Delayed security price adjustments to financial analysts' forecasts of annual earnings. *Accounting Review, 76*(4), 613–632.

Ezekiel, M. (1930). The sampling variances of correlation coefficients. *Journal of the American Statistical Association, 25*(171), 52–59.

Fabozzi, F. J., Focardi, S. M., & Kolm, P. N. (2002). The legacy of modern portfolio theory. *Journal of Investing, 11*(3), 7–22.

Fama, E. F., & French, K. R. (1988). Dividend yields and expected stock returns. *Journal of Financial Economics, 22*(1), 3–25.

Fama, E. F., & French, K. R. (1992). The cross-section of expected stock returns. *Journal of Finance, 47*(2), 427–465.

Fama, E. F., & French, K. R. (1993). Common risk factors in the returns on stocks and bonds. *Journal of Financial Economics, 33*(1), 3–56.

Fama, E. F., & French, K. R. (1996). Multifactor explanations of asset-pricing anomalies. *Journal of Finance, 51*(1), 55–84.

Fama, E. F., & French, K. R. (1997). Industry costs of equity. *Journal of Financial Economics, 43*(2), 153–193.

Fama, E. F., & French, K. R. (2006). Profitability, investment, and average returns. *Journal of Financial Economics, 82*(3), 491–518.

Fama, E. F., & French, K. R. (2015). A five-factor asset pricing model. *Journal of Financial Economics, 116*(1), 1–22.

Fama, E. F., & French, K. R. (2016). Dissecting anomalies with a five-factor model. *The Review of Financial Studies, 29*(1), 69–103.

Feng, G., Giglio, S., & Xiu, D. (2020). Taming the factor zoo: A test of new factors. *The Journal of Finance, 75*(3), 1327–1370.

Foucault, T., Kadan, O., & Kandel, E. (2013). Liquidity cycles and make/take fees in electronic markets. *Journal of Finance, 68*(1), 299–341.

Frazzini, A., Israel, R., & Moskowitz, T. J. (2015). Trading costs of asset pricing anomalies (Working Paper). AQR Capital Management.

Frazzini, A., & Pedersen, L. H. (2014). Betting against beta. *Journal of Financial Economics, 111*(1), 1–25.

Frijns, B., Margaritis, D., & Psillaki, M. (2012). Firm efficiency and stock returns. *Journal of Productivity Analysis, 37*(3), 295–306.

Fung, W., & Hsieh, D. A. (2001). The risk in hedge fund strategies: Theory and evidence from trend followers. *The Review of Financial Studies, 14*(2), 313–341. https://doi.org/10.1093/rfs/14.2.313

Gara, M. A., Minsky, S., Silverstein, S. M., Miskimen, T., & Strakowski, S. M. (2019). A naturalistic study of racial disparities in diagnoses at an outpatient behavioral health clinic. *Psychiatric Services, 70*(2), 130–134. https://doi.org/10.1176/appi.ps.201800223

Gaughan, P. A. (2015). *Mergers, acquisitions, and corporate restructurings* (6th ed.). John Wiley & Sons.

Gödel, K. (1992). *On formally undecidable propositions of principia mathematica and related systems*. Dover Publications. (Originally published in German in 1962).

Graham, B., & Dodd, D. L. (1934). *Security analysis*. McGraw-Hill.

Graham, J. R., Grennan, J., Harvey, C. R., & Rajgopal, S. (2022). Corporate culture: Evidence from the field. *Journal of Financial Economics, 146*(2), 552–593. https://doi.org/10.1016/j.jfineco.2022.07.008

Green, J., Hand, J. R. M., & Zhang, F. (2017). The characteristics that provide independent information about average U.S. monthly stock returns. *Review of Financial Studies, 30*(12), 4389–4436.

Gu, J., & Mulvey, J. M. (2021a). Factor momentum and regime-switching overlay strategy. *Journal of Financial Data Science, 3*(4), 101–129.

Gu, J., & Mulvey, J. M. (2021b). Regime-switching methods in portfolio management. *Journal of Investment Management, 19*(4), 23–40.

Gu, S., Kelly, B., & Xiu, D. (2020). Empirical asset pricing via machine learning. *The Review of Financial Studies, 33*(5), 2223–2273.

Gupta, T., & Kelly, B. T. (2019). Factor momentum everywhere. *The Journal of Portfolio Management, 45*(4), 13–36.

Hafez, M. (2018). Measuring the impact of corporate social responsibility practices on brand equity in the banking industry in Bangladesh: The mediating effect of corporate image and brand awareness. *International Journal of Bank Marketing, 36*(5), 806–822. https://doi.org/10.1108/IJBM-04-2017-0079

Hafez, P., & Lautizi, F. (2017). *Abnormal media attention impacts stock returns.* RavenPack. https://www.ravenpack.com/research/abnormal-media-attention-impacts-stock-returns

Harvey, C. R. (2017). Presidential address: The scientific outlook in financial economics. *The Journal of Finance, 72*(4), 1399–1440.

Harvey, C. R. (2022). The Pitfalls of Asset Management Research. Available at SSRN 4078138.

Harvey, C. R., Liu, Y., & Zhu, H. (2016). . . .and the cross-section of expected returns. *The Review of Financial Studies, 29*(1), 5–68.

Haugen, R. A., & Heins, A. J. (1975). Risk and the rate of return on financial assets: Some old wine in new bottles. *Journal of Financial and Quantitative Analysis, 10*(5), 775–784.

Henry, A. (2008a). *Understanding strategic management.* Oxford University Press.

Henry, E. (2008b). Are investors influenced by how earnings press releases are written? *Journal of Business Communication, 45*(4), 363–407.

Hirschey, M. (2001). Cisco and the kids. *Financial Analysts Journal, 57*(4), 48–59.

Hou, K., Xue, C., & Zhang, L. (2015). Digesting anomalies: An investment approach. *The Review of Financial Studies, 28*(3), 650–705.

Hou, K., Xue, C., & Zhang, L. (2020). Replicating anomalies. *The Review of Financial Studies, 33*(5), 2019–2133.

Howard, J., & Ruder, S. (2018). Universal language model fine-tuning for text classification. In *Proceedings of the 56th Annual Meeting* of the *Association for Computational Linguistics* (Volume 1: Long Papers; pp. 328–339). Association for Computational Linguistics. https://doi.org/10.18653/v1/P18-1031

Jacobs, B. I., & Levy, K. N. (1988). Disentangling equity return regularities: New insights and investment opportunities. *Financial Analysts Journal*, *44*(3) (May/June 1988), 18–43.

Jegadeesh, N. (1990). Evidence of predictable behavior of security returns. *The Journal of Finance, 45*(3), 881–898. https://doi.org/10.1111/j.1540-6261.1990.tb05110.x

Jegadeesh, N., & Titman, S. (1993). Returns to buying winners and selling losers: Implications for stock-market efficiency. *Journal of Finance, 48*(1), 65–91.

Jensen, M. C. (1968). The performance of mutual funds in the period 1945–1964. *Journal of Finance, 23*(2), 389–416.

Jensen, T. I., Kelly, B. T., & Pedersen, L. H. (2023). Is there a replication crisis in finance? *Journal of Finance*, *78*(5), 2465–2518. https://doi.org/10.1111/jofi.13249

Kelly, B., Malamud, S., & Zhou, K. (2024). The virtue of complexity in return prediction. *The Review of Asset Pricing Studies, 14*(1), 1–52.

Kelly, B., & Xiu, D. (2023). Financial machine learning. *Foundations and Trends® in Finance, 13*(3–4), 205–363. https://doi.org/10.1561/0500000064

Kindleberger, C. P., & Aliber, R.(2005). *Manias, panics, and crashes: A history of financial crises* (5th ed.). Wiley.

Knez, P. J., & Ready, M. J. (1997). On the robustness of size and book-to-market in cross-sectional regressions. *The Journal of Finance, 52*(4), 1355–1382.

Kozak, S., Nagel, S., & Santosh, S. (2020). Shrinking the cross-section. *Journal of Financial Economics, 135*(2), 271–292.

Kraus, A., & Litzenberger, R. H. (1976). Skewness preference and the valuation of risk assets. *The Journal of Finance, 31*(4), 1085–1100.

Krizhevsky, A., Sutskever, I., & Hinton, G. E. (2012). ImageNet classification with deep convolutional neural networks. *Advances in Neural Information Processing Systems, 25*, 1–9.

Kurzweil, R. (2005). *The Singularity is near: When humans transcend biology*. Viking.

Kyle, A. S. (1985). Continuous auctions and insider trading. *Econometrica, 53*(6), 1315–1335.

Lehalle, C.-A., & Laruelle, S. (2018). *Market microstructure in practice* (2nd ed.). World Scientific.

Lehmann, B. N. (1990). Fads, martingales, and market efficiency. *The Quarterly Journal of Economics, 105*(1), 1–28. https://doi.org/10.2307/2937810

Lettau, M., & Ludvigson, S. (2001). Consumption, aggregate wealth, and expected stock returns. *The Journal of Finance, 56*(3), 815–849.

Lewis, M. (1989). *Liar's poker: Rising through the wreckage of Wall Street.* Norton.

Li, Y., Li, X., Chen, H., Zhang, N., & Li, X. (2021). Financial sentiment analysis: Techniques and applications. *ACM Computing Surveys (CSUR), 54*(1), 1–37. https://doi.org/10.1145/3430971

Linnainmaa, J. T., & Roberts, M. R. (2018). The history of the cross-section of stock returns. *The Review of Financial Studies, 31*(7), 2606–2649.

Lintner, J. (1965). Portfolios and capital budgets. *Review of Economics and Statistics, 47*(1), 13–37.

Liu, Y., Ott, M., Goyal, N., Du, J., Joshi, M., Chen, D., Levy, O., Lewis, M., Zettlemoyer, L., & Stoyanov, V. (2019). *RoBERTa: A robustly optimized BERT pretraining approach.* arXiv. https://doi.org/10.48550/arXiv.1907.11692

Lo, A. W. (2004). The adaptive markets hypothesis. *Journal of Portfolio Management, 30*(5), 15–29.

Loughran, T., & McDonald, B. (2011, When is a liability not a liability? Textual analysis, dictionaries, and 10-Ks, *Journal of Finance, 66*(1), 35–65. https://doi.org/10.1111/j.1540-6261.2010.01625.x

López de Prado, M. (2023). Causal factor investing: Can factor investing become scientific? SSRN Working Paper.

López de Prado, M. (2024). The case for causal factor investing. SSRN Working Paper.

López de Prado, M., & Zoonekynd, V. (2025). Causality and factor investing: A primer. SSRN Working Paper.

Malkiel, B. (2023). *A random walk down Wall Street* (13th ed.). Norton.

Martin, R. D., & Xia, D. Z. (2022). A Hausman type test for differences between least squares and robust time series factor model betas. *Journal of Mathematical Finance, 12*(2), 414–434. https://doi.org/10.4236/jmf.2022.122023

McCann, B., Bradbury, J., Xiong, C., & Socher, R. (2017). Learned in translation: Contextualized word vectors. In *Advances in Neural Information Processing Systems 30 (NIPS 2017)* (pp. 6294–6305). NIPS.

McLean, R. D., & Pontiff, J. (2016). Does academic research destroy stock return predictability? *Journal of Finance, 71*(1), 5–32.

Melamud, O., Goldberger, J., & Dagan, I. (2016). context2vec: Learning generic context embedding with bidirectional LSTM. In *Proceedings of The 20th SIGNLL Conference on Computational Natural Language Learning (CoNLL)* (pp. 51–61). Association for Computational Linguistics. https://doi.org/10.18653/v1/K16-1006

Meucci, A., Santangelo, A., & Deguest, R. (2015). Risk budgeting and diversification based on optimized uncorrelated factors. SSRN Working Paper 2276632.

Mezrich, B. (2004). *Ugly Americans: The true story of the Ivy League cowboys who raided the Asian Markets for millions.* William Morrow.

Mikolov, T., Chen, K., Corrado, G., & Dean, J. (2013). *Efficient estimation of word representations in vector space.* arXiv. https://doi.org/10.48550/arXiv.1301.3781

Miller, G. (2006). Needles, haystacks, and hidden factors. *Journal of Portfolio Management, 32*(2), 25–32.

Mitchell, M., & Pulvino, T. (2001). Characteristics of risk and return in risk arbitrage. *The Journal of Finance, 56*(6), 2135–2175. https://doi.org/10.1111/0022-1082.00401

Moreno-Ortiz, A., Fernández-Cruz, J., & Pérez-Hernández, M. C. (2020). Design and evaluation of SentiEcon: A fine-grained economic/financial sentiment lexicon from a corpus of business news. In *Proceedings of the 12th Language Resources and Evaluation Conference (LREC)* (pp. 1362–1369). European Language Resources Association.

Moskowitz, T. J., & Grinblatt, M. (1999). Do industries explain momentum? *Journal of Finance, 54*(4), 1249–1290.

Moskowitz, T. J., Ooi, Y. H., & Pedersen, L. H. (2012). Time series momentum. *Journal of Financial Economics, 104*(2), 228–250. https://doi.org/10.1016/j.jfineco.2011.11.003

Mossin, J. (1966). Equilibrium in a capital asset market. *Econometrica, 34*(4), 768–783.

Nagel, S. (2025). Seemingly virtuous complexity in return prediction. *Chicago Booth Research Paper*, (25-10).

Nevmyvaka, Y., Feng, Y., & Kearns, M. (2006). Reinforcement learning for optimized trade execution. *Proceedings of the 23rd International Conference on Machine Learning*, 673–680.

Nissim, D., & Ziv, A. (2001). Dividend changes and future profitability. *Journal of Finance, 56*(6), 2019–2065.

Novy-Marx, R. (2013). The other side of value: The gross profitability premium. *Journal of Financial Economics, 108*(1), 1–28.

Novy-Marx, R. (2015). Fundamentally, momentum is fundamental momentum. NBER Working Paper No. 20984.

Nystrup, P., Kolm, P. N., & Lindström, E. (2020). Greedy online classification of persistent market states using realized intraday volatility features. *Journal of Financial Data Science, 2*(3), 25–39.

Nystrup, P., Kolm, P. N., & Lindström, E. (2021). Feature selection in jump models. *Expert Systems with Applications, 184*, 115558.

Oliveira, T., Thomas, M., Baptista, G., & Campos, F. (2016). Mobile payment: Understanding the determinants of customer adoption and intention to recommend the technology. *Computers in Human Behavior, 61*, 404–414. https://doi.org/10.1016/j.chb.2016.03.030

Park, J., Lee, H., & Cho, S. (2020). *Automatic construction of context-aware sentiment lexicon in the financial domain using direction-dependent words*. arXiv. https://doi.org/10.48550/arXiv.2106.05723

Patterson, S. (2010). *The quants: How a new breed of math whizzes conquered Wall Street and nearly destroyed it*. Crown Business.

Pearl, J. (2009). *Causality: Models, reasoning, and inference* (2nd ed.). Cambridge University Press.

Penman, S. H., Richardson, S., & Tuna, A. (2007). The book-to-price effect in stock returns: Accounting for leverage. *Journal of Accounting Research, 45*(2), 427–467.

Pennington, J., Socher, R., & Manning, C. D. (2014). GloVe: Global vectors for word representation. In *Proceedings of the 2014 Conference on Empirical Methods in Natural Language Processing (EMNLP)* (pp. 1532–1543). Association for Computational Linguistics. https://doi.org/10.3115/v1/D14-1162

Perold, A. F. (1988). The implementation shortfall: Paper versus reality. *Journal of Portfolio Management, 14*(3), 4–9.

Peters, M. E., Neumann, M., Iyyer, M., Gardner, M., Clark, C., Lee, K., & Zettlemoyer, L. (2018). Deep contextualized word representations. In *Proceedings of the 2018 Conference of the North American Chapter of the Association for Computational Linguistics: Human Language Technologies* (Volume 1: Long Papers; pp. 2227–2237). Association for Computational Linguistics. https://doi.org/10.18653/v1/N18-1202

Piotroski, J. D. (2000). Value investing: The use of historical financial statement information to separate winners from losers. *Journal of Accounting Research, 38*(Supplement), 1–41.

Radford, A., Narasimhan, K., Salimans, T., & Sutskever, I. (2018). *Improving language understanding by generative pre-training*. OpenAI.

Raju, N. S., Bilgic, R., Edwards, J. E., & Fleer, P. F. (1997). Methodology review: Estimation of population validity and cross-validity, and the use of equal weights in prediction. *Applied Psychological Measurement, 21*(4), 291–305.

Rebonato, R., & Denev, A. (2014). *Portfolio management under stress: A Bayesian-net approach to constructed stress-testing*. Cambridge University Press.

Reinganum, M. R. (1982). A direct test of Roll's conjecture on the firm-size effect. *Journal of Finance, 37*(1), 27–35.

Renneboog, L., & Vansteenkiste, C. (2017). Leveraged buyouts: Motives and sources of value. *Annals of Corporate Governance, 2*(4), 291–389. https://doi.org/10.1561/109.00000017

Rodríguez Domínguez, L. (2025, July 30). *Is causality necessary for efficient portfolios? A computational perspective on predictive validity and model misspecification*. SSRN Working Paper.

Ross, S. A. (1976). The arbitrage theory of capital asset pricing. *Journal of Economic Theory, 13*(3), 341–360.

Sarwar, G. (2021). Earnings momentum and price momentum: International evidence. *The Quarterly Review of Economics and Finance, 80*, 584–601.

Schneider, P., Wagner, C., & Zechner, J. (2020). Low-risk anomalies? *Journal of Finance, 75*(6), 3189–3239.

SEC Division of Economic and Risk Analysis. (2022). *Tick sizes and market quality: Revisiting the Tick Size Pilot*. SEC.

Sharma, M (2004). A.I.R.A.P. – Alternative RAPMs for alternative investments. *Journal of Investment Management, 3*(4).

Sharma, M. (2006). Hedge fund investing. In M. K. Ong (Ed.), *Risk management* (pp. 113–143). Academic Press.

Sharma, M., & Stein, J. (1997). Valuation of cancelable cross currency Bermudan swaps. SSRN Electronic Journal. https://ssrn.com/abstract=498142

Sharpe, W. F. (1964). Capital asset prices: A theory of market equilibrium under conditions of risk. *Journal of Finance, 19*(3), 425–442.

Sharpe, W. F. (1992). Asset allocation: Management style and performance measurement. *Journal of Portfolio Management, 18*(2), 7–19.

Shmueli, G. (2010). To explain or to predict? *Statistical Science, 25*(3), 289–310.

Shu, Y., Yu, C., & Mulvey, J. M. (2025). Dynamic asset allocation with asset-specific regime forecasts. *Annals of Operations Research, 346.1*, 285–318.

Sloan, R. G. (1996). Do stock prices fully reflect information in accruals and cash flows about future earnings? *Accounting Review, 71*(3), 289–315.

Socher, R., Perelygin, A., Wu, J., Chuang, J., Manning, C. D., Ng, A. Y., & Potts, C. (2013). Recursive deep models for semantic compositionality over a sentiment treebank. In *Proceedings of the 2013 Conference on Empirical Methods in Natural Language Processing (EMNLP)* (pp. 1631–1642). Association for Computational Linguistics.

Sokolov, A., Sabelli, F., Faraz, B. A., Li, W., & Seco, L. (2025). Toward automating causal discovery in financial markets and beyond. In H. Simon (Ed.), *Transactions of ADIA Lab: Interdisciplinary Advances in Data and Computational Science* (pp. 359–392). World Scientific.

Stambaugh, R. F., Yu, J., & Yuan, Y. (2015). Arbitrage asymmetry and the idiosyncratic volatility puzzle. *The Journal of Finance, 70*(5), 1903–1948.

Stambaugh, R. F., & Yuan, Y. (2017). Mispricing factors. *The Review of Financial Studies, 30*(4), 1270–1315.

Stattman, D. (1980). Book values and stock returns. *The Chicago MBA: A Journal of Selected Papers, 4*(1), 25–45.

Stefanini, F. (2006). *Investment strategies of hedge funds*. John Wiley & Sons.

Textor, J., van der Zander, B., Gilthorpe, M. S., Liskiewicz, M., & Maclaren, G. P. (2016). Robust causal inference using directed acyclic graphs: The R package 'dagitty.' *International Journal of Epidemiology, 45*(6), 1887–1894.

Titman, S., Wei, K. C. J., & Xie, F. (2004). Capital investments and stock returns. *Journal of Financial and Quantitative Analysis, 39*(4), 677–700.

Treynor, J. L. (1961). Market value, time, and risk [Unpublished manuscript].

Vaswani, A., Shazeer, N., Parmar, N., Uszkoreit, J., Jones, L., Gomez, A. N., Kaiser, Ł., & Polosukhin, I. (2017). Attention is all you need. *Advances in Neural Information Processing Systems, 30.* https://arxiv.org/abs/1706.03762v7

World Economic Forum. (2023). *The future of jobs report 2023.* Author.

Wu, J., Chen, J., Li, Z., Wang, H., & Yang, L. (2023). Federated learning for financial fraud detection: Challenges and opportunities. *IEEE Internet of Things Journal, 10*(8), 6215–6229. https://doi.org/10.1109/JIOT.2023.3235372

Zhang, L. (2005). The value premium. *Journal of Finance, 60*(1), 67–103.

Zhu, H. (2014). Do dark pools harm price discovery? *Review of Financial Studies, 27*(3), 747–789.

About the Author

Milind Sharma's 30 years of market experience span running proprietary trading desks at Deutsche Bank (Saba entity) and RBC Capital Markets (GAT entity) as well as hedge funds (QuantZ) and mutual funds (MLIM). He has been associated with several award-winning funds (including accolades from Morningstar, Lipper, the *Wall Street Journal*, etc.). He was a founding member of Quant Strategies at Merrill Lynch Investment Managers (now BlackRock) and Manager of the Risk Analytics and Research Group at Ernst & Young. His QMIT entity has been a pioneer in applying machine learning to factor investing. QuantZ is also the world's first fully synthetic hedge fund accessible via bank QIS swaps.

He has published with the *Journal of Investment Management*, Risk Books, Wiley, Elsevier, and World Scientific. His educational background includes Oxford, Vassar, Carnegie Mellon, UWC, and Wharton. He has guest-lectured and/or directed Capstone courses at Columbia, Carnegie Mellon, UCLA, UCSD, NYU etc. He is founder and president of New York's premier quant society <QWAFAxNEW>.

Index

B

C

D

G

H

N

P

Q

U

V

W